Investigative
Interviewing

Psychology, Method, and Practice

10/2014
Fredrick —
Best wishes and
much success!

[signature]

Investigative
Interviewing

Psychology, Method, and Practice

Eugene F. Ferraro, CPP, SPHR

CRC Press
Taylor & Francis Group
Boca Raton London New York

CRC Press is an imprint of the
Taylor & Francis Group, an **informa** business

CRC Press
Taylor & Francis Group
6000 Broken Sound Parkway NW, Suite 300
Boca Raton, FL 33487-2742

© 2015 by Taylor & Francis Group, LLC
CRC Press is an imprint of Taylor & Francis Group, an Informa business

No claim to original U.S. Government works

Printed on acid-free paper
Version Date: 20140519

International Standard Book Number-13: 978-1-4665-9086-1 (Hardback)

Visit the Taylor & Francis Web site at
http://www.taylorandfrancis.com

and the CRC Press Web site at
http://www.crcpress.com

For Marine Corps First Lieutenant Rob Brown.

He was 23 years old when he stepped on a landmine in the Republic of South Vietnam. The day was Thursday, January 25, 1968, and Rob was on point and in front of his men. He always wanted to be the first to have contact with the enemy. "The first time my platoon was ambushed, my men hunkered down and simply took the fire. It wasn't that they were afraid. It took me a moment, but then I realized—they were waiting. They were waiting to be led."

Contents

Disclaimer xv

Preface xvii

Acknowledgments xix

About the Author xxi

Introduction xxiii

1 The Process of Investigation 1

  1.1 The Genesis of Process 2

  1.2 Process of Investigation 3

  1.3 Investigation Terminology 5

    1.3.1 Investigation 5

    1.3.2 The Subject 6

    1.3.3 Interview versus Interrogation 7

    1.3.4 The Suspected Wrongdoer 8

    1.3.5 Fact Finders versus Investigators 8

    1.3.6 Decision Maker versus Prosecutor 8

    1.3.7 Misconduct and Malfeasance 9

  1.4 Elements of a Successful Investigation 9

    1.4.1 Management Commitment 9

    1.4.2 Meaningful Objectives 14

    1.4.3 Well-Conceived Strategy 16

    1.4.4 Properly Pooled Resources 17

    1.4.5 Lawful Execution 18

  1.5 The Eight Methods of Investigation 19

    1.5.1 Physical Surveillance 19

    1.5.2 Electronic Surveillance 20

    1.5.3 Research and Internal Audit 20

    1.5.4 Forensic Analysis 22

    1.5.5 Undercover 24

    1.5.6 Interviews 25

1.6 The Seven Phases of Investigation...26
    1.6.1 Assessment...27
    1.6.2 Preparation and Planning..28
    1.6.3 Information Gathering and Fact Finding 28
    1.6.4 Verification and Analysis 30
    1.6.5 Decision Making..31
    1.6.6 Disbursement of Disciplinary and/or Corrective Action 32
    1.6.7 Prevention and Education..33
1.7 Summary...33
1.8 Frequently Asked Questions 34
Endnotes...35

2 The Differences between the Public and Private Sector 37
2.1 An Historical Perspective...38
2.2 Mission..39
2.3 Advantages of the Public Sector..41
    2.3.1 Powers of Arrest...41
    2.3.2 Search and Seizure.. 42
    2.3.3 Grand Jury and Special Inquiries.. 42
    2.3.4 Prosecution and Punishment...43
    2.3.5 Resources.. 44
2.4 Advantages of the Private Sector...45
    2.4.1 Due Process 45
    2.4.2 Entrapment...47
        2.4.2.1 Establish That the Misconduct Was
            Preexistent... 48
        2.4.2.2 Establish the Motive of the Offender.................48
    2.4.3 A Lower Burden of Proof..49
2.5 Significant Trends in the Private Sector 52
    2.5.1 More Sophisticated Crimes and Perpetrators 52
    2.5.2 Greater Use of Technology 52
    2.5.3 More Litigious Workforce..54
    2.5.4 Expanded Rights and Protections of Employees 55
2.6 Summary..56
2.7 Frequently Asked Questions 56
Endnotes...57

3 The Fundamentals of Interviewing..59
3.1 The Role of the Investigative Interviewer 60
3.2 Qualities of a Professional Investigative Interviewer 60
    3.2.1 Skill..61
    3.2.2 Experience 61
    3.2.3 Impartiality 63

3.2.4   Ethical 63
3.2.5   Fair 67
3.2.6   Deliberate 68
3.3   Evidence Collection and Management 69
3.3.1   Documentation 70
3.3.1.1   Organizing Oneself and Materials 70
3.3.1.2   Using Technology 71
3.3.2   Evidence Collection and Preservation 76
3.3.2.1   Definition of Evidence 76
3.3.2.2   Hearsay Evidence 76
3.3.2.3   Admissibility and Materiality 77
3.3.2.4   Spoliation of Evidence 78
3.3.2.5   Evidence Retention 79
3.3.2.6   Chain of Custody 79
3.3.3   Reporting and Communicating Results 80
3.4   Summary 83
3.5   Frequently Asked Questions 84
Endnotes 85

4   The Investigative Interview Method 87
4.1 Differentiating Interviews from Interrogation 88
4.2 Eight Phases of the Investigative Interview 89
4.2.1   Phase I: Preparation 90
4.2.1.1   Determining Who Should Be Interviewed 91
4.2.1.2   Location for the Interview 92
4.2.1.3   Interviewer Selection and Preparation 95
4.2.1.4   Case File Preparation 96
4.2.1.5   Theme and Question Development 97
4.2.1.6   Request for Representation 99
4.2.1.7   Selection and Use of Witnesses 101
4.2.1.8   Timing 103
4.2.2   Phase II: Introduction 104
4.2.3   Phase III: Presentation 105
4.2.4   Phase IV: Admission 109
4.2.5   Phase V: Discussion 112
4.2.6   Phase VI: Written 115
4.2.7   Phase VII: Oral 117
4.2.8   Phase VIII: Conclusion 119
4.3 Summary 120
4.4 Frequently Asked Questions 121
Endnotes 126

5 Administrative Interviews and Communicating Our Results............129
  5.1   Introduction 130
  5.2   Purpose of Administrative Interviews......................................130
  5.3   Administrative Interview Process..131
      5.3.1   Determining Who Should Be Interviewed 131
      5.3.2   Selecting the Interviewer 132
      5.3.3   Location of the Interview 132
      5.3.4   Introduction 133
      5.3.5   Presentation...133
      5.3.6   Discussion 135
      5.3.7   Documentation 135
      5.3.8   Confidentiality 137
  5.4   Communicating Our Results 138
      5.4.1   Bulletized Summary Reports.......................................138
      5.4.2   Findings of Fact..142
      5.4.3   Executive Summaries..142
      5.4.4   Electronic Communications 144
  5.5   Testifying and the Preparation for Testimony...........................145
      5.5.1   Lay Witnesses 145
      5.5.2   Expert Witnesses 146
      5.5.3   Hearsay Rule 146
      5.5.4   Presenting the Evidence...147
              5.5.4.1   Testifying..148
              5.5.4.2   Dempsey's Ten Commandments of
                        Courtroom Testimony....................................148
              5.5.4.3   Impeachment..148
  5.6   Frequently Asked Questions 149
  Endnotes...151

**6 Deception Detection and the Process of Overcoming Objections
  and Denials 153**
  6.1   Introduction 154
  6.2   Why Most People Tell the Truth 155
  6.3   Why Good People Sometimes Do Bad Things 156
      6.3.1   Guiltlessness and the Enemy Within 156
      6.3.2   The Ability to Rationalize...158
      6.3.3   Motive and the Consciencelessness of Greed 159
              6.3.3.1   The Greedy 159
              6.3.3.2   The Needy 159
              6.3.3.3   The Stupid and Foolish..................................159
      6.3.4   Importance and Influence of Opportunity 159
      6.3.5   But for Bad Decisions and Mistakes 160
      6.3.6   Prevention and the Path to Better Guardrails 161

6.4   Why Some People Lie..162
6.5   Confront Objections and Overcome Denials.....................165
6.6   Indications of Deception 169
      6.6.1   Lack of Self-Reference 169
      6.6.2   Verb Tense..170
      6.6.3   Answering Questions with a Question 171
      6.6.4   Equivocation 171
      6.6.5   Oaths...171
      6.6.6   Euphemisms 172
      6.6.7   Lack of Narrative Balance.................................172
6.7   Deception Detection Technology 173
      6.7.1   Employee Polygraph Protection Act......................174
      6.7.2   Voice Stress Analyzer.....................................176
      6.7.3   Kinesics 177
            6.7.3.1   Types of Lies...................................177
            6.7.3.2   Body Language of the Guilty 178
            6.7.3.3   Body Language of the Interviewer.................183
      6.7.4   Statement Analysis..186
6.8   Final Thoughts 188
      6.8.1   Providing the Interviewee a Reason to Be Truthful.........188
      6.8.2   Failure to Assign Guilt....................................189
6.9   Frequently Asked Questions 191
Endnotes..193

7   **Legal Challenges and Litigation Avoidance 195**
7.1   Introduction 196
7.2   Jurisdiction over Workplace Investigations 196
      7.2.1   Origin and History of Law................................196
      7.2.2   Jurisdiction 197
      7.2.3   Evidentiary Burdens and Standards.......................199
      7.2.4   Multiple Agency and Court Review 200
7.3   Preparatory Legal Considerations 202
      7.3.1   Legal Duty to Investigate 202
      7.3.2   Investigator Selection.....................................205
            7.3.2.1   Liability for Employee Fact Finder/
                         Interviewer Misconduct.....................205
            7.3.2.2   Liability for Contract Fact Finder/
                         Interviewer Misconduct.....................205
            7.3.2.3   Contractual Shifting of Liability Risk 206
      7.3.3   Investigative Objectives 207
      7.3.4   Identifying Standards of Proof.............................207
      7.3.5   Documentation Control 208
      7.3.6   Confidentiality 209

7.4 Information Gathering and Fact-Finding Considerations 209
7.5 Constitutional Considerations 210
   7.5.1 Self-Incrimination 210
   7.5.2 Search and Seizure...211
   7.5.3 Joint Action and Public Function Exceptions 212
   7.5.4 State Constitutional Issues.......................................213
7.6 Federal Law and Employee Rights..214
   7.6.1 Unfair Labor Practices..214
   7.6.2 Union Representation..215
   7.6.3 Investigations into Protected Concerted Activities............217
   7.6.4 Federal Preemption and State Tort Actions......................219
   7.6.5 Union Contract Restrictions.....................................220
   7.6.6 Arbitration..221
   7.6.7 Civil Rights Law...221
      7.6.7.1 Duty to Investigate....................................222
      7.6.7.2 Discriminatory Practices...............................223
   7.6.8 Select Federal Statutes 224
      7.6.8.1 Employee Polygraph Protection Act......................224
      7.6.8.2 Fair Credit Reporting Act..............................226
      7.6.8.3 Federal Sentencing Guidelines..........................227
7.7 State Tort Law Issues 227
   7.7.1 Assault and Battery...227
   7.7.2 False Imprisonment and False Arrest 228
   7.7.3 Defamation 229
   7.7.4 Invasion of Privacy 231
      7.7.4.1 State Statutes 232
      7.7.4.2 Common Law Right of Privacy 233
   7.7.5 Emotional Distress or Outrage 239
7.8 Negligent Investigation...242
   7.8.1 A New Tort Action 242
   7.8.2 Implicit and Explicit Duties to Investigate......................244
7.9 Claims Arising from Employee Interviews.....................................245
   7.9.1 Constitutional Warnings 246
   7.9.2 Assault and Battery...247
      7.9.2.1 Sympathetic Touching...................................248
   7.9.3 False Imprisonment 248
      7.9.3.1 Economic and Moral Compulsion..........................249
      7.9.3.2 Precautionary Protocols 249
   7.9.4 Defamation 250
      7.9.4.1 Precautionary Protocols 250
      7.9.4.2 Escorting of Employees 251
   7.9.5 Duty to Investigate an Alibi 252
   7.9.6 Allegations of Discrimination....................................253

       7.9.7   Admissible Admissions 254
   7.10 Claims Arising from Employee Disciplinary Actions....................255
       7.10.1 Defamation 255
            7.10.1.1 Self-Published Defamation 259
       7.10.2 Wrongful Discharge 261
            7.10.2.1 Union and Personal Employment Contracts.....261
            7.10.2.2 Implied Contract of Employment....................262
            7.10.2.3 Whistleblower and Similar Statutes.................262
            7.10.2.4 Public Policy...262
            7.10.2.5 Discriminatory Discharges 263
            7.10.2.6 Covenant of Good Faith and Fair Dealings......263
            7.10.2.7 Additional Cases to Consider 263
       7.10.3 Malicious Prosecution 266
       7.10.4 Emotional Distress or Outrage 269
       7.10.5 Unemployment Claims..270
            7.10.5.1 Off-Duty Misconduct...................................271
       7.10.6 Workers' Compensation 272
   7.11 Prevention and Education...273
       7.11.1 Defamation and False Light Invasion of Privacy..............273
       7.11.2 Emotional Distress 275
   7.12 Litigation Avoidance and Employee Dignity 276
       7.12.1 Awareness and Liability Avoidance 276
       7.12.2 Employee Dignity and Liability Avoidance.....................276
   Endnotes...277

8 The Future of Investigative Interviewing 283
   8.1 Introduction 283
   8.2 Criticality 285
   8.3 Skills..285
   8.4 Protecting the Rights of Others.. 286
   8.5 Privacy.. 286
   8.6 Higher Standards and More Proof....................................287
   8.7 Summary..288
   Endnotes...288

9 Improving Results 289
   9.1 Investment and Cost Management.......................................289
   9.2 Establish Milestones and a Budget.....................................291
   9.3 Importance of Measuring Results.......................................291
       9.3.1 First Collect Information...292
       9.3.2 Analyze the Data 293
       9.3.3 Put the Information to Use..294

9.4   Alternatives..295
Endnote 296

Afterword 297

Appendix 1: Glossary of Common Investigative Terms and Terminology....299

Appendix 2: Investigations Checklist 305

Appendix 3: Interview Guidelines..307

Appendix 4: Interview Guidelines for Management 309

Appendix 5: Employee Information Sheet 311

Appendix 6: Written Statement Checklist....................................313

Appendix 7: Preprinted Statement Form......................................315

Appendix 8: Oral Statement Checklist..317

Appendix 9: Executive Summary 319

**Appendix 10: The Practical Application of Forensic Psychology
as an Investigative Tool**...325

Annotated Bibliography..335

Index 341

Disclaimer

It should surprise no one that my lawyers insist that I must emphatically state that neither this work nor the opinions contained herein should be construed as legal advice or relied upon as such. Should such advice be necessary, it is suggested that competent professional assistance be sought. Furthermore, while many of the practices and methodologies that will be presented are considered industry best-practices, specific circumstances and fact patterns should drive your process and approach. If unsure as to how to properly proceed, stop and seek the advice of a competent professional.

Throughout this work, I have attempted to avoid gender stereotyping or the preference of one gender over another. Any appearance of having done so was the product of my writing style and was not intentional. Hopefully, my use of both genders does not create a distraction.

The case studies that have been used in this work are based on real investigations and interviews conducted by me or those I know. However, in order to protect the reputations of the guilty and the privacy of the innocent, I have substantially altered some facts. Any similarity to real situations or real people is unintentional and purely coincidental.

And, finally, you will note that I have occasionally referenced my organization or a competitor and its methods. My doing so is not intended to sell my services or diminish my competitors or suggest that they are inferior. To the best of my ability I have attempted to be fair and, where possible, impartial regarding any organization, including my own. In the final analysis, it is the responsibility of the reader to choose the methods and processes best suited for his/her needs and objectives.

Preface

Of all of the methods of investigation, interviewing is probably the least understood and most overused. It is logistically simple, inexpensive, and often spectacularly effective. Its ability to reveal previously unknown information and answer the seemingly unanswerable is unmatched. However, its apparent simplicity and fruitfulness disguise its true complexity. This book is an attempt to share my knowledge and experience regarding this fascinating investigative tool and the human psychology that makes it work. My goal with this work is simple. I wish to provide both the novice and experienced fact finder with the most insightful and useful information possible. In the pages that follow, I will briefly revisit many of the topics and strategies covered in my earlier works. However, this time I will dive deeper than ever before into some of the deepest corners of the human mind to explore the origins of malfeasant behavior and the tools the miscreant uses to protect his darkest secrets. I will challenge conventional thinking and methodology. I will defy mainstream thought and wisdom. Most critically, I will reveal a method of interviewing that is unlike anything you have encountered or dreamed of before. I call it the *Investigative Interview Method* or I²M.

In this work, I have arduously resisted ordinary convention and sought new solutions to old problems and challenges. With the encouragement and assistance of my students and those with whom I have worked and studied, I will reveal for you new ideas and some of the most sophisticated approaches and strategies in interviewing known today. I think you will find the result both refreshing and very possibly inspiring.

Whether you are a professional licensed investigator or someone tasked by your employer to conduct an investigative interview, this work will shine new light on your techniques and approach. It also will serve to provide executives, human resource professionals, and the lawyers who represent them with new insights into this powerful investigative tool.

The reader should know that I am more than a writer, I am a practitioner. The knowledge I offer in this book goes far beyond what is available in the current literature or that which is offered on the seminar circuit. I have drawn upon my years of practical experience and that of my colleagues to craft a work that dispels the myths and troublesome theories promulgated by some of my predecessors. My intent is to provide you, the reader, with the backstory behind the methodology, rationale, and subtle practices that have made thousands of fact finders like you successful interviewers. But, most importantly, I want you to become the best interviewer possible. I also want to make your learning both rewarding and fun. To that end I have included stories, humorous experiences, and many simple, but powerful insights. I also have added a host of checklists and visuals to help hold your attention and make the content more useful and actionable.

Inside this book you will find as well that I have provided an exhaustive table of contents, innumerable references, and expansive appendices. Another feature to help capture my salient points and simplify the learning process is my use of *Tips* and *Traps.*

Tip: Read my Tips and Traps to get the most out of this book. If you read nothing else, these little gems will inform as well as inspire.

Acknowledgments

It seems that no endeavor of any importance or value is possible without the help of others. This work is no exception. One such person is my longtime friend and counselor, Bill C. Berger, Esq. Bill is an employment lawyer with the prestigious firm Brownstein Hyatt Farber Schreck, in Denver, Colorado. Bill's practice emphasizes matters including both preventative counseling and litigation. His contribution to Chapter 7, Legal Challenges and Litigation Avoidance, was invaluable.

Of the many who helped form my thoughts, ideas, and methods, the least visible and most influential were the professionals and thought leaders who plowed this space before me. Though I have met few of them, they include Fred E. Inbau, John E. Reid, Joseph P. Buckley, Brian C. Jayne, Frank A. Colaprete, James S. Cawood, D. Glenn Foster, Paul Babiak, Robert Hare, Martha Stout, Nathan J. Gordon, William L. Fleisher, Douglas E. Wicklander, David E. Zulawski, and many, many others. Their willingness to share and memorialize their ideas in writing is a testament to their courage and professionalism. I, as well as every reader of this book, owe them thanks.

I also wish to thank my acquisition editor, Mark Listewnik at CRC Press/ Taylor & Francis Group. Without his persistence and good spirits, your hands at this moment might be empty.

And, finally, I want to thank my loving wife, Shelley. She is my princess.

About the Author

Eugene F. Ferraro, CPP, CFE, PCI, SPHR, is currently the chief ethics officer of Convercent, Inc., Denver, Colorado. He has been involved in the study of organizational culture, workplace misconduct, and compliance for over 32 years. He is a prolific author and frequently speaks and trains on the topics of complex corporate investigations, culture management, and unethical behavior in the workplace. He is board certified in both security management and human resources management (CPP and SPHR designations, respectively). He has been a member of ASIS (American Society for Information Science) International since 1987 and a commissioner on the ASIS Standards and Guidelines Commission. He is also a member of the Association of Certified Fraud Examiners and is a certified fraud examiner (CFE designation) as well as a professional certified investigator (PCI designation).

Ferraro is a former military pilot, intelligence officer, and a graduate of the Naval Justice School. He is a frequent book critic for *Security Management* magazine and is the author of *Investigations in the Workplace,* 2nd ed. (Taylor & Francis Group, 2012), which is a textbook used by universities and other institutions of higher learning in the United States and abroad.

Those wishing to reach him may do so via email: Gene.Ferraro@Convercent.com.

Introduction

Imagine, if you can, not having a conscience—none at all. Imagine a life absent the feelings of guilt and remorse, no limiting sense of concern for others, their safety, or their boundaries. Imagine having no capacity for shame, sorrow, or sense of responsibility; imagine instead a life filled with deceit, deception, and the ability to conceal one's innermost thoughts and desires. Distinctly, you are free of all internal restraints, unhampered by the burdens of spiritual beliefs, cultural morals, or the rule of law. You are carelessly speeding through life with no guardrails, intentionally colliding with unsuspecting victims, leaving behind only the wreckage of sorrow, disappointment, and economic ruin.

Now place our imaginary monster into the turbulent culture that is ours. All around him he is encouraged and liberated by sinking morals and flagging values. Like him, many of those he knows and associates with regard the acceptance of personal responsibility, honest discourse, and respect for the rule of law as a matter of choice. He is in a society where distain for spiritual values, the embrace of political correctness, social justice, and, for some, even narcissism have become compelling ideologies.

Now imagine you are the employer, co-worker, or business partner of such a person. Imagine you are not only his colleague, but you or your organization are his target. How will you recognize this individual, confine his selfishness and greed, and safely extricate yourself before he destroys you and all that is important you?

Confronted by such an individual, to whom would you turn and where would you hide? For the modern investigative interviewer, there can be no such questions, for it is he whom our society often turns to to seek resolution.

Indeed, on the heels of most internal workplace investigations in the private sector the fact finder or his designate must sit and confront the malfeasant. That event is more than a meeting, it is an *investigative interview*. To it the participating parties bring objectives, information, and emotions. They also bring bias, personal experience, survival skills, and sometimes, like our imaginary monster, one of them brings with him his psychopathy. For that reason, among others, this book will take the reader on a fascinating journey into the mind of the malevolent and malfeasant. The readers will learn how to identify and stop those who intend to harm them and/or their organization and obtain from them an admission of guilt. In order to accomplish that feat, a proper investigation must precede it. That investigation must be thorough and complete. For that to happen, the investigation must itself have process. That process is called the *Process of Investigation*™.*

Investigations using the Process of Investigation are complex undertakings. They are time consuming and fraught with enormous potential for legal liability and even danger. When done properly, they combine an intricate mixture of skill, planning, experience, and luck. Those who attempt them without a clear understanding of their fundamentals are recklessly naïve. An improperly conducted workplace investigation can be ruinous and destroy the careers of everyone who touches it. Few workplace activities invoke so much risk and, at the same time, so much opportunity.

An effective and proper investigation is the foundation on which all (regardless of the offender's motive, method, or psychopathy) successful investigative interviews rest. For our purposes, investigative interviews are interviews that are reserved for those we know, or have a strong reason to believe, have committed the offense in question. These interviews are highly structured and carefully choreographed. Generally, they are not fact finding in nature. Instead they rely on the facts generated during the investigation that preceded them. They also are nonaccusatory. Surprisingly, the primary purpose of an investigatory interview is simply to obtain an admission.

> *Tip: Admissions are simple statements of guilt. Admissions are unlike confessions in that they need not contain all of the elements of the crime.*

In the private sector, it is on properly obtained admissions that disciplinary and/or corrective action is most often based. Thus, properly conducted investigative interviews are the most powerful tools available to the modern workplace fact finder and his employer.

> *Trap: Because of their usefulness, the fact finder must not instinctively default to investigative interviewing until the investigation has progressed to the point that his investigation is properly completed and interviews are appropriate.*

---

* The term *Process of Investigation* is a trademark belonging to the author. Its use for any purpose is strictly prohibited without prior written permission.

Investigative interviews are valuable in other ways as well. When done correctly they enable us to:

- fulfill many of our due process obligations
- obtain the other side of the story
- uncover extenuating and mitigating circumstances
- learn who else might be involved and why
- uncover the means by which a reoccurrence of the offense might be prevented

Thus, investigative interviews are useful and powerful tools. However, to appreciate their enormous power and implement them properly and, might I add, consistently, the proper place to begin is with examining the intricacies of the Process of Investigation. Let's get started.

Chapter 1

The Process of Investigation

Key learning points:

1. An investigation is best defined as the logical and intelligent collection of information through inquiry and examination for the purpose of developing evidence so as to solve a problem.
2. Process is the principal driver allowing consistent quality and scalability of one's workplace investigations.
3. Most fact finders have only six methods of investigation available to them when conducting a workplace investigation. Among these the investigative interview is the most powerful.
4. One of the most common mistakes made by fact finders is that they over-investigate. That is, they spend more time and resources than is often necessary.
5. Employers in the private sector generally need only to prove that they conducted a good-faith investigation and, from it, come to a reasonable conclusion in order to sustain the decision to discipline an employee.
6. The foundation for successful investigative interviews is a quality investigation.

"If obtaining an admission of guilt is your destination, your journey must begin with a proper investigation."

E. F. Ferraro

1.1 The Genesis of Process

Large or small, organizations of all types routinely conduct internal workplace investigations. Though the objectives, and certainly the scope of these undertakings, have varied widely, their principal purpose has been that of objective *fact finding*. We call that individual the fact finder. To be effective, he must be fair, impartial, thorough, and certainly purposeful. Then, to fulfill the varied objectives of the assigned investigation, the fact finder must have a process. Remarkably, however, most fact finders, regardless of their level of experience, have little or no process. Their approaches are as varied as their results. Lacking an effective process, fact finders often spend more time and resources than necessary, produce inconsistent results, and create unnecessary liabilities for those they serve. No investigation, regardless of its objectives or scope, can be successful if not properly engineered and driven by process.

This observation became apparent to me almost 30 years ago. Having completed my military obligation, I entered the private sector wide-eyed and naïve. Seeking employment, I happened upon a private investigator. His name was Tracy Schnelker (1918–1992). Los Angeles, California-based, his agency was quaintly named *Hollywood Detectives*. With nothing but my military justice experience, he thrust me into one investigation after another. With no training or supervision, he tasked me with the responsibility of *finding information*. Other than his billing and reporting procedures, his organization was completely devoid of processes. Some years later I joined the prestigious investigative firm of Krout and Schneider, Inc., also headquartered in Los Angeles. In spite of its enormous success, I found it operated much the same.

At Krout and Schneider, I advanced rapidly. In part, my advancement and success was based on having the desire to grow the business. In order to do that, I realized the ability to scale its operations was imperative. However, to do that I needed tools. The tool I chose were processes—carefully engineered activities that had both structure and purpose. Among the many I developed, the most enduring was the Process of Investigation™.

This process holds that, in order for the results of a workplace investigation to be useful, it must have meaningful and well-defined objectives, be properly and lawfully executed, be fair and impartial, and the results accurately documented and communicated. In order for these investigations to be efficient, they must unfold incrementally and progressively in distinct phases. Each progressive phase is engineered to build on the phase that preceded it. Collectively, these phases are called the *Seven Phases of Investigation*. They include:

1. Assessment
2. Preparation and planning
3. Information gathering and fact finding
4. Verification and analysis

5. Decision making
6. Disbursement of disciplinary and/or corrective action
7. Prevention and education

I also determined that due to the lack of resources and experience, most fact finders transfix on the third phase, that of information gathering and fact finding. Unwittingly, they conclude their investigation after amassing an impressive collection of related facts, evidence, and information. Though these elements are obviously important, what was overlooked denied those to whom they reported a complete result and a thorough understanding of the very matter that precipitated the effort. Thus, by imposing process to otherwise disorganized, but seemingly important, activities, the fact finder could create the structure necessary to be uniquely effective. My process allowed the private sector fact finder to transcend the unsophisticated and often tarnished image of corporate gumshoe and elevated him to the professional standing of corporate investigator; better yet, professional investigator. A new way of conducting investigations was born.

1.2 Process of Investigation

Like most effective processes, the Process of Investigation also should produce measurable results. While the output is often measured by the fact finder's customer* in terms of the actionable evidence he accumulates, the first and most immediate, ought to be return on investment (ROI). The properly engineered and executed investigation often should produce tangible, measurable results, such as the recovery of stolen property or money (generally termed as assets), the termination or discipline of dishonest employees or vendors, and, of course, successful prosecution. Also possible are civil recovery, restitution, damage awards, and successful insurance claims.

The process, however, goes beyond this and can even be engineered to allow the employer to recover the actual cost of the investigation from the transgressor. Unique also is the process's suitability to generate statistical results the fact finder can use over time to measure effectiveness and ROI. Without process and structure, the fact finder has no means to measure results or show value to the customer.

The fact finder also must think in terms of process in order to be consistently successful. Long gone are the days when anyone could conduct a workplace investigation. Sloppy techniques, careless fact gathering, and bending the law are no

---

* The reader will note that I will use the word *customer* frequently. When doing so, I am referring to the person or persons to whom the fact finder reports. When the fact finder is in-house, that entity is typically his employer. It also may be a particular individual or group within the organization serving as the decision makers. For fact finders who are not employees of the customer, this entity is then likely to be their paying client.

longer permissible in our litigious society. Neither the public nor our courts will tolerate the practices that just several years ago were considered *industry standards.* Today the fact finder cannot get away with unethical or sloppy investigations, and, if he tries, he will land himself and his customer on the wrong end of a lawsuit.

The last and possibly the least considered benefit of using an investigative process is scalability. Without the means to consistently duplicate processes, one is unable to reliably predict outcomes. This concept of repetitive processes and predictable outcomes is fundamental to scaling every industrial activity. Modern manufacturing, distributing, franchising, and even marketing largely depend on this concept. Any large-scale business activity employs processes that are scalable. In fact, it was the use of scalable processes that allowed these activities to become as large as they are. It is impossible to think of any large enterprise that was not scaled. And, because organizations and the people who run them depend so much on predictable outcomes, it is abundantly obvious that one's investigations should employ replicable processes to achieve them. Take, for example, my organization, Convercent, Inc., of which I am the chief ethics officer. By means of trial and error, we have learned that the most productive investigators we produce are not those that come to us with investigative or law enforcement experience. While these qualifications are required by some organizations, we have found the best investigators are the product of the processes they use, not the amount or type of experience they possess. We have consistently found that intelligent and disciplined professionals of any stripe, when given good processes and proper supervision become good investigators. What's more, they haven't the need to unlearn bad habits or old school methods. Using the modern methods and processes described in this book, my new investigators hit the ground running. As such, we easily scale our business as need demands it.

However, workplace investigations are more than just processes. They typically involve the convergence of many disciplines and an assortment of uncommon skills. More often than not, the investigator must have a comprehensive understanding of criminal, civil, and employment law. They also require a considerable investment of time, money, and patience by the employer. Then, finally, to ensure success, the process must be highly structured and flawlessly executed. Even the most sophisticated organization can find the task consistently challenging. Figure 1.1 illustrates this point.

Therein is the opportunity. Every organization, public or private, eventually finds itself in need of an internal investigation. Be it the suspicious disappearance of tangible or intangible assets, the questionable ethical practices of an employee, or the troubling allegation of sexual harassment. Sooner or later, every organization is confronted with the need to gather evidence, interview suspects, and uncover the truth. With the ability to muster the necessary resources, deploy skilled fact finders, and adhere to a disciplined process, any organization can conduct a successful workplace investigation.

Figure 1.1 **Workplace investigations take place where criminal, civil, and employment law intersect. Note that private sector investigations are performed pursuant to the needs of the organization or person for which it is performed. And, although private sector investigations frequently investigate potential violations of the law, private sector investigators rarely have law enforcement powers.**

In addition to the above factors, workplace investigations are fraught with labiality. Workplace investigations of even the simplest variety are not for the faint hearted. By definition, they involve the investigation of people who have a relationship with the organization. Most often those people are employees. They are insiders. They are people with whom the organization employs or does business. As such, they have special rights, expectations, and very often they carry a sense of entitlement and inflated importance. These considerations significantly add to the complexity of the fact finding process and the manner in which the subject may respond to the investigation's findings and management's corrective actions. Regardless, the path is filled with legal obstacles and challenges. For the unknowledgeable and unprepared employer, it is a virtual legal minefield. On the other hand, the totality of these complexities gives the properly prepared and equipped employer a decisive competitive advantage. The employer that is able to efficiently bring an end to a workplace substance abuse problem, catch thieving employees in the act, or obtain restitution from a dishonest vendor, without litigation or a public relations debacle, has a significant competitive advantage over the employer who cannot.

1.3 Investigation Terminology

1.3.1 Investigation

Etymologically, to *investigate* something is to look for traces, or vestiges, of it. The word can be traced to the Latin word *investigāre*, meaning "search into," a compound verb based on *vestigāre*, meaning "track" or "trace," of which was a derivative from *vestigium,* meaning "footprint." Ergo, the silly and terribly overused human footprint as a component of the business logos used by many private investigators. However, today the noun version of the word, *investigation* is used for many purposes and means different things to different organizations. For our purposes, we might consider the following definitions: *An investigation is the systematic and thorough examination and inquiry into something or someone, and the recording of this examination or inquiry in a report.*[1] Good, but consider instead: *An investigation is the examination, study, searching, tracking, and gathering of factual information that answers questions or solves problems.*[2] Better yet, might be my definition: *An investigation is the logical and intelligent collection of information through inquiry and examination for the purpose of developing evidence so as to solve a problem.*

Notice that the definition does not contain a reference to prosecution or litigation. That is because a workplace investigation is generally undertaken to learn something. The result is then used to prove or disprove an assertion, claim, or allegation. Thus, prosecution and litigation are a byproduct of an investigation, not its purpose. Because of the ability to prove or disprove something, properly employed workplace investigations can provide many dividends for the employer. In addition to uncovering facts and essential information needed to solve problems, a successful investigation helps restore order. It provides the employer the opportunity to analyze process and system failures and reengineer them to prevent future problems.

1.3.2 The Subject

It has only been within the past 40 years that those without law enforcement experience have been openly welcomed to conduct workplace investigations. Historically, most private sector investigators worked first in the public sector. Typically, those with former law enforcement or military investigative experience were the people selected to conduct private sector investigations. For a host of obvious reasons, this choice made sense. These investigators were not only well trained, they were disciplined and knew how to obtain results. With them they brought not only the tools of the trade, but the vernacular that its practitioners used. So, while we have recently seen more workplace investigation conducted by those without law enforcement experience, much of the vernacular used by their predecessors remains in use today. As harmless as this may seem, it has its consequences.

Of the claims made by those who have been the focus of a workplace investigation, one of the most common is that the investigation was too harsh and that the investigators who performed it were heavy-handed and inhumane; that the investigators acted like cops. So, when an investigator conducting a workplace investigation uses the language of cops, the accusation he acted like one seems more credible. In fact, isn't it often possible to identify one's profession by the way he communicates? If you disagree, spend several hours with a lawyer.

Thus, when private sector investigators communicate like public sector investigators, we are conditioned to expect them to behave like it as well. This mistake by the person conducting a workplace investigation may superficially make them appear more professional, but will likely invite challenges otherwise not encountered. Among them might be claims asserting constitutional rights violations, due process violations, the unlawful use of police-like coercion and intimidation, as well as the entire banquet of companion torts associated with these—all because the well-meaning investigator used the vernacular of another profession.

The first such word I recommend you eliminate from your vocabulary is *suspect*. The word is harsh and accusatory. Replace it with *subject*. Throughout the remainder of this book you will see that I only use the word *subject* to describe the investigation's person of interest. Thus, while I may *suspect* someone, I never call them *the* suspect.

> *Tip: Replace police and law enforcement terminology with that which is softer, less harsh. Use the language common to the private sector and be more thoughtful of your customer and how your investigative results will be used.*

1.3.3 Interview versus Interrogation

Few words used by investigators are more misleading and confusing than *interview* and *interrogation*. Without much thought, most people use the words interchangeably. Some workplace investigators think that by using the word *interrogation*, they and their methods sound more sophisticated. Confusing the matter further, organizations, such as the highly regarded firm, John E. Reid and Associates, Inc., which teaches The Reid Technique* and The Reid Technique of Interviewing*, insists that all proper admission-seeking processes involving questioning of a subject include both an interview and interrogation component.[3]

Heaping more confusion onto the matter are reference resources, like USLegal. com, which offer the *legal* definition of interrogation as:

> Interrogation is, in criminal law, the process of questions asked by police to a person arrested or suspected to seek answers to a crime. Such person is entitled to be informed of his rights, including right to have counsel present, and the consequences of his answers. If the police fail or neglect to give these warnings, the questions and answers are not admissible in evidence at the trial or hearing of the arrested person."[4]

Suffice it say, there is little agreement as to what these words mean and how they should be used. What appears to be agreeable to most, however, is that an interview seems less structured, less formal, and maybe even less accusatory than an interrogation. And, it is precisely because of this presumption that I prefer to use the word *interview*. I strongly suggest you use it as well.

1.3.4 The Suspected Wrongdoer

Following the rationale described above, I also find objection with using the word *accused*. Given of the word's root *accuse*, identifying someone as the accused is accusatory. Not only do people find being accused of something objectionable, the misuse of the word has created the impression that to be accused is to be guilty. This connotation is not useful to the furtherance of most workplace investigations. Because those who are accused tend to be defensive and protective, they are generally less cooperative when interviewed. A kinder, gentler substitute is *suspected wrongdoer*. Though I will occasionally use the word *accused* to describe the investigation's person of interest, I prefer the substitute, *suspected wrongdoer*.

1.3.5 Fact Finders versus Investigators

Like the words *suspect, interrogation*, and *accused*, the word *investigator* can be somewhat coarse. Though I use the word frequently, its misuse can connote that not only has the person who has undertaken the investigation engaged in fact finding, he has come to some conclusions as well; conclusions possibly regarding guilt or innocence. Consider the presumptive: "The investigators found no evidence of his guilt." I prefer instead to use the term fact finders.

Fact finder is more descriptive. Its use is more suggestive of what the investigator is actually doing. Therefore, while we may use the word *investigator* (as I just did above) for the purpose of convenience and brevity, in the conduct of workplace investigations, the preferred descriptor is *fact finder*.

1.3.6 Decision Maker versus Prosecutor

Equally disagreeable is the word *prosecutor*. While its use by those routinely involved in workplace investigations is rare, a very descriptive substitute is *decision maker*. I will use this term throughout this book. Should you read enough of it, you will discover as well that I make a strong argument that the fact finder and decision maker should not be one in the same person. Whenever possible, these roles should be held by different persons. Doing so diminishes the appearance (and successful accusation) of bias and preconceived investigatory conclusions. Logically, if the fact finder is not the decision maker, it is very difficult for him to control the decisions of the decision makers and the punishment of the wrongdoer. Make a practice of using the term *decision maker* to describe the customer who the fact finder serves.

1.3.7 Misconduct and Malfeasance

In About the Author in the front matter of the book, you might recall that my experience includes "the investigation of employee dishonesty, substance abuse, and criminal activity in the workplace." This claim is true. However, the reader will note that collectively my experience is in the area of investigating employee misconduct and malfeasance. Some of the things investigated are both employee misconduct (and malfeasance) and, at the same time, crimes. However, as we will discuss later, it is not the criminality that is investigated in these situations, but the misconduct and malfeasance of the wrongdoer. Furthermore, in the context of our discussion, all crimes involve misconduct, but not all misconduct constitutes a crime. Thus, the workplace fact finder is better off consistently describing that which he investigates as misconduct or malfeasance, not crimes.

1.4 Elements of a Successful Investigation

It is common that my customers ask me what is needed for the contemplated investigation to be successful. At the expense of sounding trite, the answer I offer is quite simple. In order to be successful, every workplace investigation requires the following elements:

- Management commitment
- Meaningful objectives
- A well-conceived strategy
- Properly pooled resources and expertise
- Lawful execution

Let's now examine each of these critical elements in detail.

1.4.1 Management Commitment

Because workplace investigations can be extremely complex and often involve potential litigation, a commitment by management is an essential component if success is to be achieved. From the very beginning, management must be prepared to commit the requisite time, patience, and resources in order to achieve its objectives. It is misleading and dishonest for the individual responsible for driving the investigative process (a person from this point forward we shall refer to as the *project manager*) to allow the employer (typically his employer or client) to believe anything less. To obtain quick results with little effort or with few resources is often impossible and even reckless. In accepting the assignment, the project manager must be prepared to accept responsibility and communicate honestly with his customer. Only with the proper information and a thorough understanding of the issues and options can the employer make decisions that are sound and appropriate. Anything less will diminish the return on investment and invite potential litigation.

> *Tip: Complex problems that have evolved over time cannot be solved in an afternoon. Employers and their decision makers must allow the fact finder the time she needs to properly conduct her investigation and bring it to a meaningful conclusion.*

Time is a precious commodity. Each of us is allocated just so much; therefore, how we use it, by and large, will determine what we produce and how much. Because investigations are dynamic, the use of time and the allocation of it to any particular task is a critical aspect of project management. The project manager is responsible, among other things, for the establishment of the project's objectives. In doing so, he will define milestones and deadlines. It is he who will ensure that the investigative team remains on course and the project is accomplished in a timely fashion.

A successful investigation also requires patience, a virtue few practitioners seem to have. The simple truth of the matter is that a proper investigation takes time. They frequently unfold in fascinating and often unexpected ways. Although the experienced project manager can influence the pace in which his or her investigation unfolds, there are aspects of it that may be uncontrollable. Undercover investigations are a perfect example. Undercover investigations are extraordinarily complex. They involve the careful selection and placement of an investigator into an unsuspecting workforce. The investigator must then assimilate into that workforce and gain acceptance. This phase of the investigation is called the *relationship-building* phase. Once assimilated, the investigator moves into the proactive phase. Once there, with the guiding assistance of his project manager, he begins to collect the information necessary to obtain the investigation's objectives. This takes time, and often a lot of it. A four-month undercover investigation is not uncommon. The effort cannot be forced or willed. Despite the anxiousness of the other parties involved (the employer client or law enforcement), the investigation must unfold at its own pace.

In the case of undercover, experience has shown that the relationship building phase is a four-to-six-week endeavor. The proactive phase of the investigation may require an additional 6 to 16 weeks. A whole host of variables will impact the length of the investigation, but in extreme situations, the case may need to be run six months or more. The lack of patience will make an otherwise routine undercover investigation a daunting and painful undertaking.

Additionally, there may be events that impact the pace of the investigation that are beyond the control of anyone. Things like illnesses, weather, holidays, schedules, and the unavailability of the players are all things that sometimes no one can control. In the case of undercover, for example, the winter holiday season often creates challenges. In the aerospace and automotive industry, it is not uncommon for employers to shut their doors for the last two weeks of the year. It is precisely that time of year the undercover investigator can make her best headway. Holiday parties, dinners, and other seasonal events provide excellent opportunities to build relationships and gain confidences. The holiday spirit also increases complacency, making the gathering of otherwise useful information much easier. However, in the aerospace industry, as in several others, no sooner does the holiday spirit set in, then the organization shuts down and operations are not resumed until shortly after the New Year. All the while, the meter continues to run for the employer client. In order to endure such delays, the employer client, as well as the investigators, must have patience.

Another example of the need for patience are those matters involving the management of workplace aggression and potential violence. Often, the employer, upon discovery of the misconduct, wants to immediately discipline or terminate the malfeasant. This, of course, is a common outcome in these types of matters. However, more often than not, the employer has not conducted a thorough investigation and has not met the standard of proof necessary to discipline or discharge anyone. For organizations like mine, which specializes in managing these matters for employers, the rush to judgment and termination of the suspected by our clients is a challenge for us. In haste there is often waste and in these types of cases, haste can produce very dangerous outcomes. Often there is no immediate need to discipline or terminate. What is needed is a proper and thorough investigation. Facts need to be gathered, statements need to be taken, allegations need to be checked, and, most importantly, barring an immediate danger to human life, the alleged aggressor has rights that must be respected and protected. It has been my experience that lack of respect and rush to judgment has been an historical contributor to producing the very behaviors that the organization was attempting to prevent.

In addition to time and patience, a successful investigation requires the dedication of resources—real money. Regardless of the simplicity or complexity of an investigation, some investment of money will be necessary. Like the free enterprise system, money is an essential fuel that in many ways powers the investigation.

My clients sometimes debate this. With all sincerity, they will sometimes contend that they can conduct the investigation under consideration cheaper and faster than me. In rare instances, this may be so. However, most often they have neither the skill nor the experience to conduct the investigation properly, no less materially achieve its specific objectives. The mere availability of manpower, equipment, and other resources does not assure success. The fact that the organization already employs a security director, human resource manager, or house counsel does not mean that they or the organization is capable, qualified, or even has the time to conduct a proper investigation. Even if capable and qualified, it may make more economic sense to outsource the effort. Consider your own organization for a moment. Does it have the human resources, talent, and time necessary to undertake a complex internal investigation? Probably not.

Allow me to put a finer point on it. Regardless of who does the investigation and whose resources and equipment might be used, somebody has to pay for it. Simply because the organization employs one or more of the professionals mentioned above, does not mean that their services are free. The question the organization must ask is: Is it more economical to undertake the project itself or outsource it? In order to answer that question, some cost-benefit analysis should be done.

Cost-benefit analysis in this context is more than just running the numbers. Integral to the process is estimating to the finest degree possible, the return on investment (ROI). ROI should be one of the objectives of almost every investigation. It should be intuitively obvious that the higher the ROI, the smaller the economic risk. What's more, the properly engineered investigation will have established milestones by which those driving the project will be able to periodically measure results, thus enabling them to reassess their plan and modify their objectives dynamically. As such, experienced investigators know cost-benefit analysis is a necessary component of the preparation and preplanning phase of the project. Thus, the more complex the contemplated project, the more critical cost-benefit analysis becomes. Following is a typical example.

Hypothetically, suppose "our" organization suffered what appeared to be a fairly significant loss involving a kickback scheme orchestrated by one of our purchasing agents. Preliminary information suggests that, as a result of the scheme, over a period of a couple of years our organization overpaid several vendors more than $300,000. Our security department is brought to bear and its preinvestigation fact-finding effort reveals the overpayment is closer to $750,000.[5] Based on an organizational pretax net of 5 percent, analysis suggests that, in order to have instead netted the $750,000, the organization would have had to increase sales by approximately $15 million. Depending on the organization and industry, this may or may not even be possible. Our analysis also suggests that the organization's inability to use that money elsewhere increased operating costs in the form of finding replacement capital. Taking other facts into consideration and rounding the numbers, the loss actually exceeds $1.2 million.

Given that such matters lend themselves to recoveries of not only the losses, but, in most instances the cost of the investigation, does it not make sense to look outside the organization for professional assistance?[6] Considering the burden on the organization's internal resources, manpower, and the distraction created by a complex investigation of this sort, the smart move is to engage a qualified external resource. The outcome is likely to be better and the organization can instead dedicate itself to what it does best—running its business. I make this point frequently when testifying as an expert witness in matters involving internal investigations. Even in instances where the organization has employees dedicated to such matters, it often makes sense to outsource the effort. Doing so conserves the scarce resource of personnel, while putting the project in the hands of experienced professionals undistracted by other responsibilities. Additionally, outsourcing enables some of the legal liability to be shared. When things don't go well, the opportunity to blame the vendor who provided the investigative services can be very useful.

The next question, of course, then is what is going to be the cost? The answer is not as simple as it may appear. In the case of undercover, which is typically billed by the week, the organization (the client) and the service provider (the investigative vendor) together can determine the estimated length of the project and do the math. Other types of investigations require a little more analysis in order to determine the investment necessary to assure success. Let's look at this process in a little more detail.

It is estimated that there are approximately 18,000 active private investigation firms in the United States.[7] Although it is nearly impossible to know for sure, it is widely accepted that the private investigation industry in the United States employs something on the order of 40,000 individuals.[8] Of those, only a small fraction is engaged in what has come to be called *corporate investigations*. Corporate investigations are those that specifically involve workplace issues and problems as well as the investigation of crimes and offenses committed against the organization. Of those who claim to offer corporate investigative services, only a handful actually specialize in it. As such, the sample from which I am about to draw the following conclusions is relatively small and, thus, there is some inherent inaccuracy in which I am about to offer. That said, it is fairly safe to say the hourly fees charged by those offering corporate investigative services tend to be on the higher end of the scale for private investigation professionals. And, although fees and pricing practices vary across the country, with some high cost of living areas, such as San Francisco or New York skewing the data, most qualified corporate investigators who offer the service as their specialty, charge something on the order of $250 per hour. Some organizations actually exceed $450 per hour for their top investigators. Associates and field investigator fees begin at about $150 per hour. On the whole, it is my experience that it is difficult, if not impossible to engage a qualified corporate investigator of any sophistication for less than $200 per hour. For those readers interested in pursuing this line of work, that should be very good news. For purchasers of these services, it is equally good news. Here's why.

Because corporate investigations in practice involve an understanding and appreciation of criminal law, civil law, and employment/labor law, few professionals actually have the skills necessary to deliver quality services. Those who do know its value charge accordingly. Conversely, some general practitioners (criminal defense, insurance investigators, and the like) may charge as little as $75 per hour, and some as little as $35 per hour. These professionals find it difficult to even imagine charging $200 per hour for their services, no less someone actually paying it. This gives the consumer of corporate investigative services a decided advantage. Simply by knowing the fee structure of the service offerer, one can generally tell their level of sophistication and experience. This is not to say that by paying more, the client automatically gets more. However, the adage that one gets what one pays for, certainly applies when choosing a corporate investigator.

The sophisticated vendor offers more. Professionals capable of delivering the type of services we are discussing also understand ROI. They have a fine appreciation for business and understand that a mutually beneficial engagement is only possible when the service provider is able to provide a reasonable ROI. Because most crimes against the business are property crimes, recovery is often possible. The professional corporate investigator knows this, and will typically engineer his investigation to facilitate a recovery, to include, if possible, even his fees and expenses. Most private investigators have no appreciation for this opportunity. Many of them, particularly those with law enforcement background, will attempt to drive the process toward prosecution of the perpetrators. Such an effort or even the suggestion of prosecution, as an investigative objective, should be a red flag to the consumer of such services. Unless it can be demonstrated to contribute to the desired ROI, prosecution should not be an objective and should not be pursued.

> *Tip: An organization's decision to prosecute offending employees should be made for business reasons and no other.*

In most instances, the pursuit of prosecution will consume unnecessary resources and contribute little to the outcome of the investigation. For reasons we will discuss later, employee prosecution can be expensive and often very disappointing.

> *Tip: Organizations intending to undertake an internal investigation of any size or complexity are generally better served seeking the services of an external resource to conduct the investigation. From the standpoint of time, money, and the best use of existing internal resources, it is more economical to outsource most internal investigations.*

1.4.2 Meaningful Objectives

No investigation of any complexity can be successful without meaningful objectives. The investigation's objectives define the fact finder's purpose, allow him to benchmark his progress, and provide the framework by which the project manager coordinates the effort to build his case. I am astounded by how many of my colleagues fail to appreciate this critical fundamental and begin their investigations without articulating or even contemplating their objectives. Those that do, often still miss the point. The investigative objectives must be carefully articulated at the beginning of the process, because they establish the investigation's starting point and where it is intended to finish.

I embrace this concept to such a degree that it is my practice and that of my firm to begin every investigation by negotiating the effort's objectives with the client. By negotiating, I mean that together we decide what it is we are going to pursue, what information we are seeking, and under what conditions are we going to obtain that information. Together we talk through that which we are attempting to do, how we intend to do it, and who is responsible for what. The objectives make it clear that the investigation's purpose is proper and lawful. When properly articulated, they demonstrate that both the employer client and the fact finder have pure intentions and that the length they will go to achieve success has been carefully contemplated and is reasonable.

I go so far as to describe the objectives in the investigative proposal I provide my clients. In doing so, I establish that I understand the needs and desires of the client. It also establishes benchmarks by which we can later measure our results. In fact, other than my case intake notes, typically, the first document to be placed in my physical case file is a page on which I have detailed the investigation's objectives.

By articulating and recording the project's objectives early and placing evidence of them in my case file, I also am laying a defensive foundation against claim of bias and discrimination or some other form of investigative misconduct at the conclusion of the project. In the event of subsequent litigation and discovery, I want the plaintiff to be surprised. I want the plaintiff that has claimed bias, discrimination, targeting, and abuse to sustain an early setback when handed documents that demonstrate, from the start of my investigation, that my intentions (and that of my client) were pure, honest, and reasonable. Practical experience also has shown that early setbacks for plaintiffs of this type tend to demoralize them. It tends to take some of the wind out of their sails. At the very least, it demonstrates to them, and, most importantly, the trier-of-fact that the defendant is no amateur and an easy victory is not likely. The objectives of almost all workplace investigations articulate the desire to:

- seek out and identify the true nature and scope of the problem
- identify who is involved and why
- gather any and all information in such a fashion as to allow the proper distribution of disciplinary and/or corrective action when appropriate
- engineer the process in such a fashion that is least disruptive to the organization and its operations
- achieve the best possible return on investment[9]

This is no small order. However, taking the time to negotiate the objectives of the project in advance saves time and money. Moreover, as you have probably already recognized, the objectives stated above are nearly universal. They are so useful that I sometimes call them *the universal objectives*. Reflect back for a moment on the last several workplace investigations you conducted or oversaw. Would these objectives have suited each of them? I suspect so. Imagine also the response of the decision makers and customers to whom you report if you had recited these objectives when your last assignment was handed to you. From a practical standpoint, who could argue with them? Also, note that these objectives, as I have penned them, speak in the language of business. They demonstrate my appreciation of operations, corporate culture, fairness, and return on investment. They tell my client I understand his business and that I too am a businessperson. I don't think the objectives of any workplace investigation could be articulated better.

Several years ago during an arbitration hearing in which a large group of employees were challenging their termination, I was called as a witness. The results of my investigation were used as the basis for the terminations. Following the typical questions regarding my background and experience, the attorney representing the employees began to challenge me. The culmination of his folly was to ask why the investigation of each individual appeared so uniformly similar and the results so consistent. I could hardly wait to answer. But, before I tell you my response, consider the title of this chapter; it's a clue. My answer went something like this: "Because I employed a process. My process not only defined my objectives, it permitted each offense and offender to be investigated properly, uniformly, and fairly. The result precluded the intrusion of bias, mistreatment, and discrimination. It also produced unequivocal admissions of guilt. Without intimidation or coercion, each of the grievants provided his/her employer and me with a written and oral admission. And, that process, by the way, is called the process of investigation." As he was probably reminding himself, *never ask a question of which you do not know the answer,* the now humble attorney's face changed from an expression of arrogance to grief. To my client's delight, all 30 of the terminations were subsequently sustained.

1.4.3 Well-Conceived Strategy

The next key to success is the development and deployment of a sound investigative strategy. There are many different types of issues that may call for a workplace investigation; therefore, I will forego describing strategies for each of them here. However, the topic deserves some brief examination at least.

Effective investigative strategies involve more than mixing and matching investigative methods. The successful project manager needs strategy. That strategy must be sufficiently structured such that it provides efficiencies and the opportunity to measure results. However, the strategy must be sufficiently flexible so that it permits the changing of objectives and strategy as new information is learned. The project manager and her investigators must have the ability to change their objectives and modify their strategy as new information is developed. My clients sometimes make the mistake of being inflexible. On numerous occasions, I have had employer clients tell me that they are interested in only catching the thieves or firing the drug dealers. Although I cannot argue with these goals, upon discovery of other offensive workplace behavior, these same clients chose not to address it. Knowing other egregious and actionable behavior is taking place, they will turn a blind eye to it because the investigation of those offenses was not among our original objectives.

How sad and how wasteful. Investigators make the same mistake. Because one offense or another was not included in their original charter, they ignore them. Their process is so structured; once the train has left the station, there is no changing its destination.

1.4.4 Properly Pooled Resources

Nothing can derail a well-planned investigation more effectively than an organization's failure to support it with the proper resources. The failure to dedicate adequate talent results in a lengthier investigation that will assuredly fail to achieve the desired objectives. Following is an example.

Several years ago, the owner of a regional drug distribution operation called my office seeking my help. The owner claimed that several employees had come forward and alleged that co-workers were stealing. After discussing the particulars, it appeared to me that the allegations were credible and that a proper investigation would likely expose the perpetrators. I suggested the informants be interviewed so that all of the information possible could be extracted from them. As is often the case, the owner— now client— resisted. He said the employees had been promised confidentiality; furthermore, they were said to be unlikely to talk if questioned by an outsider. I told him, in that case, the only solution would be undercover. He resisted again. He said he did not have the time or the money for an undercover. Although he believed his losses were approaching $40,000 a month, he wanted a faster, less-expensive solution. After more discussion and some debate, I acquiesced and agreed to surveillance. To my surprise, the resultant surveillance produced results and several employees were identified engaging in very questionable activity. I suggested they be interviewed. Given what we knew at the time, I proposed that investigatory interviews would likely yield admissions and, based on those admissions, the client could take the necessary disciplinary and/or corrective action. Again anxious to achieve a fast and more convenient result, my client insisted on involving the authorities. Incorrectly, he believed that the police would pick up where we left off and solve his problem. He further professed that "police action" would produce an unqualified deterrent and discourage similar behavior by others in the future. The police agreed, but they insisted in verifying our result and doing additional surveillance themselves. After several weeks of inactivity on the part of the suspect employees, the police became tired of their surveillance and decided to confront them. They did, and even using intimidation and the veiled threat of prosecution, not a single employee offered an admission. Thoroughly frustrated, my client shut the project down and paid our bill. Months later, as I typically do, I followed up and called him. He said his losses had diminished to a trickle, but reluctantly admitted he had no peace of mind. He knew as I did that those responsible for the many months of theft were still in his employ. It was only a matter of time until they gathered the courage and once again resumed their criminal activities.

This scenario is common. Businesses and the people who run them, like most of us, are impatient. Workplace investigations are complex and as I said earlier in this chapter, successful investigations require the investment of time, patience, and resources. If your organization or client isn't prepared to make the requisite investment in each, your investigation will be difficult and probably fail to produce the desired results. In this case, defaulting to law enforcement was a mistake. Instead of using an external resource with the skill and ability to solve his problem, the customer chose a resource that was ill equipped to fulfill his objectives. The outcome was not only disappointing, it was counterproductive. Like many decision makers, he failed to appreciate that the commitment of resources involves the commitment of the *right* resources.

Tip: In matters involving complex issues, it is often necessary to bring to bear resources that have special expertise. Failing to use the right resource often produces disappointing, if not useless, results.

1.4.5 Lawful Execution

Corporate investigators and those who conduct workplace investigations for their employers have enormous responsibility. The outcome of their efforts often impact the organizations they serve and the employees who work for them. The Process of Investigation™ has no rule book (except those like the one in your hand), it is not governed by any oversight body and it is not necessarily bound by criminal law or civil code. It and the people who conduct workplace investigations are governed largely by organizational dictate and ethics. Usually, not until someone complains or sues and the fur begins to fly does anyone ever really scrutinize the typical workplace investigation or the people who performed it. Consider for a moment your own investigations. How many of those were ever really scrutinized and picked apart? Who critiqued you or your team? Certainly there must be exceptions, but by and large very few workplace investigations are looked at carefully. Unless someone challenges the outcome, is dissatisfied with the punishment, or the effort was so glaringly defective, no one cares and no one looks. The case is closed and never looked at again. Not so for criminal investigations. Every aspect is examined.

Regardless of the venue or the likelihood of critical examination, all workplace investigations should be conducted ethically and lawfully. To do otherwise is a disservice to the subject, the customer, and the investigative profession.

Trap: Rules, policies, laws, and codes provide society and the organizations with structure and order. A fact finder's failure to obey them is a disservice to all those that his investigation touches, including his own.

1.5 The Eight Methods of Investigation

Fundamentally, there are eight basic methods of investigation:

1. Physical surveillance
2. Electronic surveillance
3. Research and internal audit
4. Forensic analysis
5. Undercover
6. Interviews
7. Grand jury
8. Search warrants and subpoenas[10]

That's it. There are no others. Every other form of investigation one can identify is a subcategory of one of these. You might have observed, the use of a grand jury and search warrants and subpoenas are not available to most of those who conduct workplace investigations. Typically, workplace investigations have only the first six methods of investigation available to them.

Every workplace investigation uses one or more of these six methods. The challenge for the professional investigator is to select the method or methods most suitable for his particular circumstances and deploy them properly and in the correct sequence. In many instances, the investigator will find that he must combine the methods in some fashion or mix and match them. It is only with knowledge and experience can the investigator know which methods to use and when. It is this unique ability to combine these methods properly and efficiently that separates exceptional investigators from good investigators. Let's look at each of them briefly.

1.5.1 Physical Surveillance

In the context of workplace investigations, physical surveillance is nothing more than watching people, places, things, and activities. Physical surveillance has only two requirements: there is something to watch and someone to watch it. As such, physical surveillance is relatively inexpensive and easy to use. Those who have conducted surveillance know that, as simple as it may seem, to be done properly it requires significant skill and patience. Not everyone is capable of surveillance or doing it well. In some instances, it requires sitting patiently in closed quarters, such as an automobile or van. In other instances, it requires following the subject as he/she drives about. This form of physical surveillance is called *moving surveillance* and requires even greater skill.

Physical surveillance, however, has its limitations. Because it is not interactive, i.e., the observer has no interaction or communication with whom he is observing, the evidence physical surveillance produces is typically only corroborative. That is, it only supports or corroborates other evidence. Here's an example.

If I were to observe an individual remove from the rear door of his workplace a large, sealed corrugated box and suspiciously put it into the trunk of his vehicle under the cover of darkness, what did I actually see? Did I observe a theft? Absent any other evidence, what I observed was likely nothing more than an individual remove from the rear door of his workplace a large, sealed corrugated box and, suspiciously looking over his shoulder, put it into the trunk of his vehicle. You see, absent any other information, I don't know what the box contained, whether he had permission to remove it, or if the box was even his. For this reason, physical surveillance can rarely be used for anything other than developing corroborative evidence.

1.5.2 Electronic Surveillance

Electronic surveillance is similar to physical surveillance in that it, too, is nothing more than watching people, places, things, and activities. However, unlike physical surveillance, electronic surveillance employs the use of electronic technology in order to improve the results. It, too, is relatively inexpensive and easy to use. Electronic surveillance also can be used in places and circumstances where simple physical surveillance cannot. Because electronic surveillance uses technology, such as video, covert cameras, and personal computer monitoring software, it can be used when and where physical surveillance is not possible. For example, if the subject of interest was deep inside a facility, say, inside the employee breakroom, all the possible physical surveillance in the parking lot would never record questionable activity taking place in that breakroom.

However, therein lies the risk. Because electronic surveillance is possible in so many circumstances, users of it must be careful not to deploy it where its use might violate the rights of others. Among them is the right of privacy. The courts have widely held that even in the workplace, employees enjoy a limited right to privacy and the expectation thereof. The limitations of which vary from jurisdiction to jurisdiction. Regardless, a worker's right to a reasonable expectation of privacy is universal, and to violate it may be both criminally and civilly actionable.

Electronic surveillance is not interactive as well. Like physical surveillance, it has no interaction or communication with that which it is observing or monitoring. As such, the evidence it produces is typically only corroborative.

1.5.3 Research and Internal Audit

The third method of investigation is the combination of research and audit. This method involves the collection and examination of information from both public and private sources. Many investigators incorrectly use the terms *research* and *audit* interchangeably. For the purpose of workplace investigations, the activity called *research* defines that work involving the collection and examination of public records or public sources. Such sources include the Department of Motor Vehicles, the county clerk's office where criminal and civil records are stored, and the county recorder's office where all manner of records involving real estate transactions are recorded and kept.

Public records often afford the workplace investigator a huge source of information and depending on the type of matter under investigation, possibly the very clues that may make his case. Take, for example, vendor fraud investigations. These frauds typically involve a dishonest purchasing agent who, without the consent or knowledge of his employer, establishes a business with which he does business. In order to legitimize the business as a viable vendor, by formally organizing it and create a legal entity. In most situations, it must be properly registered as a corporation or a limited liability company (LLC). This permits the business to open business banking accounts and perform other functions customary to a legitimate business. In order to do this, the principal must file certain documents with the Secretary of State in which the business resides. In doing so, public records are created that are available to anyone for the asking. When suspecting vendor fraud, these are precisely the documents the investigator should seek.

On the other hand, *audit* applies to those records and documents internal to the organization—specifically the examination of documents and information that would not normally be available to someone outside the organization. Such records include attendance records, productivity records, financial record, and even prior investigations. Today, the amount of information organizations generate is staggering. Modern enterprises are far beyond merely watching the numbers. Keeping records on customer wants, needs, buying patterns, and consumption; vendor capacity, capability, delivery time and reliability; productivity, up-time, downtime, capacity, and even the amount of waste produced are common. No detail, event, outcome, or result is too small to document. In fact, modern management tools, such as ISO (International Organization of Standardization) business methods standards and Six Sigma require everything to be measured. Assuredly, no organization of any size is short on data.

The use of such data is manifold in many workplace investigations. In fact, I tell my students that every workplace investigation employs the investigative method research and audit at some level. Years ago, I conducted an investigation for an aerospace manufacturer that suspected employee theft. The manufacturer produced a complex component used in jet engine fuel flow regulators. For some time, "per unit" production costs were escalating, yet supply prices and labor costs were stable. The waste stream seemed unchanged and "unit failure" rates were at all-time lows. Buried deep in the mass of information the client kept on its manufacturing process, we discovered that the production of each unit consumed three times the number of screws the unit actually required. Upon inspection of inventories, we found no excesses nor did we discover any undocumented waste or failures. Purchasing records supported the excessive consumption rates of the screws, but where were they going? We decided to dig even deeper. After taking a close look at each screw vendor, we discovered that two of them oddly operated out of the same single-family residence. Further investigation revealed the home was that of one of my client's purchasing agents. In short order, he was interviewed and readily admitted he had committed the crime. He further revealed that it was greed that had motivated him. He explained that after the screws his little firm sold were received and placed into inventory, he would steal them, repackage them, and resell them to his employer again and again. We estimated that some screws had been repurchased as many as twenty times. Had the client not kept the detailed records it had, the case may have never been solved.

1.5.4 Forensic Analysis

Forensic analysis is the fourth method of investigation. It includes all manners of investigation that employ science and/or the scientific method. Included in this category are bodily fluid analysis, chemical and substance analysis, fingerprint examination and comparison, computer forensics, various deception detection methods, and forensic document examination. For the purposes of our study, forensic analysis is the catchall category where science and the investigator meet.

Some of the forensic tools available to investigators are rather interesting. One of the least familiar and more fascinating is Benford's law, a powerful fraud detection tool that predicts the frequency of numbers (digits) in some naturally occurring, unmanipulated groups of numbers. Engineers and mathematicians have long known of a simple but powerful mathematical model that quickly predicts the distribution of numbers for "pointing suspicion at frauds, embezzlers, tax evaders, sloppy accountants, and even computer bugs."[11] Frank Benford, rediscoverer of this phenomenon, was a physicist for General Electric, who in 1938 recognized that certain "nonrandomly behaved numbers in nonnormally distributed data sets" behave in a very predicable fashion. Benford analyzed over 20,000 data sets of various categories and found that all of the seemingly disparate numbers followed the same first-digit probability pattern. Benford's probability distribution (in percent) of the first digit of any database that meets the criteria described above is shown in Figure 1.2.

Thus, if we examined a data set composed of invoice amounts, Benford's law (which is scale invariant) predicts that 30.10 percent of the invoice amounts begin with the digit 1. Those amounts, for example, might be $1.29 or $17,031.81. Regardless, approximately 30% will begin with the digit 1, roughly 18 percent will begin with the digit 2, and so on. The data set that does not conform, therefore, is suspect. My personal investigative use of this powerful forensic tool has consistently provided insight into corrupt data. Note I said *corrupt data*, not fraudulent data. Benford's law only permits us to identify data of interest. It is the job of the fact finder to determine if that data are the result of intentional manipulation and whether that manipulation was the result of a fraud.

Another interesting application of forensics is in the field of psychology. Many consider forensic psychology the intersection where psychology and criminal investigation meet. Forensic psychology for our purposes involves the application of

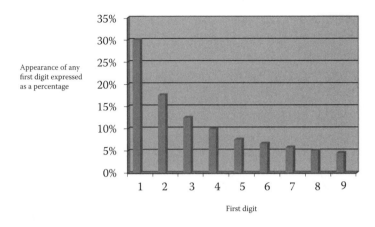

Appearance of any first digit expressed as a percentage

First digit

Figure 1.2   Benford's probability distribution of the first digit in nonnormally distributed data sets.

psychological theory, knowledge, skills, and competencies to the pursuit of civil and criminal justice. Similar to the other forensic methods mentioned above, it, too, is a tool. When properly used, it allows a peek into the mind of the subject and permits the fact finder a fundamental understanding of *why* the subject of his investigation behaved in the manner he did—or may behave in the future. It has applications in a wide array of environments both clinical and corporate. Within the corporate environment, a working knowledge of the subject's mindset is sometimes essential in order to manage and predict the future behaviors of those under investigation. In matters involving threats of violence in the workplace, it is frequently imperative to understand the motivation of the aggressor and their capacity to do harm. Armed with a psychological appreciation for the way environmental stressors and other emotional influences impact behavior, the fact finder and his team can better engineer an intervention strategy. The professionals that provide this type of assistance are specialists. It is a mistake to presume that any attending physician, family psychologist, or EAP (employee assistance program) counselor can provide the forensic assistance necessary for most workplace investigations.

The clinician qualified to provide assistance must be properly trained and have the requisite experience to conduct psychological forensic assessments. The fact finder has a duty to ensure the resources brought to bear are qualified to perform the task assigned. These qualifications might include: credentials in the field of forensic psychology, formal education, and practical experience. Of these, practical experience may be the most important. The clinician without experience in complex workplace investigations will have difficulty balancing the opposing interests of the parties and rendering legally defensible advice. My organization, for example, has employed as many as seven forensic psychologists. As members of our behavioral sciences team, they have the forensic qualifications stated above *and* specific training and experience regarding the process of investigation. Thus, together we are able to engineer investigative solutions that meld their capabilities with a sound investigative strategy.

> *Tip: While forensic psychology does not play a role in every workplace investigation, the fact finder ought to be familiar with this tool and be able to properly use it when appropriate.*

In my firm, our clinicians are most often used to assist our fact finders with violence risk assessments. In matters involving threats of violence, these professionals assess the potential dangerousness of the subject. Even when the act of aggression is nonphysical and only psychological, it can be painful and costly. Employers are expected to have strong policies, effective security protocols, and a well-conceived strategy to confront the potentially violent employee and prevent workplace violence. Our clinicians help make expectations a reality. To see an example of the practical application of this tool, go to Appendix 9.

1.5.5 Undercover

Corporate undercover investigation is one of the most powerful methods of investigation. By definition, it is nothing more than the surreptitious placement of a properly trained and skilled investigator, posing as an employee, into an unsuspecting workforce for the purpose of gathering information.[12] Undercover is one of only two forms of investigations that are interactive. That is, it permits the investigator to interact and communicate with those he is investigating. However, undercover is immensely complex and is fraught with challenges. When conducted improperly, it can create unfathomable liabilities for both the employer client and the fact finder.

Undercover investigations are also time consuming and expensive. The typical investigation might take three to six months and cost as much as $100,000. Because of the cost and liability associated with undercover, I tell my clients it should only be used as the option of last resort. After all other alternatives and solutions have been thoroughly contemplated, only then should undercover be considered. That said, I have personally supervised or managed over 1,000 undercover investigations in my career. I have successfully placed undercover investigators in nearly every working environment imaginable. Over the years, my undercover investigators have harvested trees, planted lettuce, built airplanes, sorted recyclables, emptied bedpans, refined oil, directed traffic, made bath tissue, tended bar, drove trucks, sorted mail, and slaughtered livestock. The only environment where undercover usually is not possible is one in which the employer is not hiring. Even then, undercover is sometimes possible.

However, undercover is not for the fainthearted. It requires a motivated and disciplined investigator and close supervision. It generally cannot be done in-house. Those who wish to use this method of investigation should always use a vendor—and good vendors are hard to find. If you are eager to learn more about undercover and how this fantastic investigative tool can and should be used, obtain a copy of my book, *Undercover Investigations in the Workplace* (Butterworth-Heinemann, 1999). Though out of print, the information it contains is invaluable. Used copies are readily available from book sellers with offering on Amazon.com. For the rest of you, let's move on to interviews and interrogation, indisputably the most powerful tools in the workplace investigator's tool chest.

1.5.6 Interviews

The sixth and final method of investigation is the systematic collection of information via interviews and interrogation. As discussed earlier in this chapter, these terms mean different things to different people. The term *interview* seems less harsh than *interrogation* to most people. It describes a process that is less formal, less structured. But Merriam-Webster® defines these terms similarly, distinguishing interrogation as a process in which one "questions formally and systematically." However, in actuality, the word *interrogation* is rarely used to describe a formal and systematic interview. Instead, when one uses the word *interrogation*, it seems to mean so much more. The thought of interrogation conjures up images of an offensive and coercive interview during which the subject is harshly questioned in a windowless room with hands and feet bound while seated under a bright light. It's stigmatized, carrying with it the inference or suggestion of coercion, intimidation, and thuggery. Some even consider an interrogation to be unlawful. As such, I use the word very cautiously. I don't like the inferences that are associated with it and don't care to offer qualifiers or explain myself every time I use the word. Hence, for the purposes of our study of the subject I will restrict my use of the word.

Interviews conducted during workplace investigations fall into two categories. The less formal of the two is called *administrative* interviews. These include interviews of witnesses, bystanders, process owners, stakeholders, and others not culpable or likely culpable of the offense or matter under investigation. *Investigative* interviews on the other hand, are reserved for those who we have very convincing reason to believe committed the offense or had direct involvement in it. Both forms of interviews are highly structured, but neither is confrontational or accusatory. Largely what distinguishes the two is the intended outcome. During administrative interviews, we are simply looking for information. We are attempting to learn, gain insight, and collect information. During investigative interviews, first and foremost we are seeking an admission.

Another pair of words creating confusion are *admission* and *confession*. They are not the same. A confession is a statement that includes an admission satisfying all of the elements of the crime. In workplace investigations, confessions are not necessary. In order to discipline an offending employee, in most instances the employer needs only to prove the employee in question committed the offense. The employer does not need to prove or demonstrate things like means, motive, and state of mind or intent. Those elements of the offense are inconsequential and have no bearing on the employer's decision to impose discipline. Armed with a properly obtained admission, an employer needs nothing more to take disciplinary or corrective action against the offender. The same is not the case for criminal prosecution.

> *Trap: Employers tend to over-investigate. Many of them believe they must prove their case beyond a reasonable doubt. This extraordinarily high standard (or sometimes referred to as burden) of proof is reserved only for criminal prosecution. In pursuing it, the employer expends more time and resources than necessary.*

Like undercover, interviews are also interactive. They afford the investigator the opportunity to exchange information with the subject. Specifically, interviews afford the investigator the opportunity to determine the who, what, where, when, how, and why from the very person who was there. It also provides the investigator the unique opportunity to peek into the mind of the offender. This benefit, combined with the opportunity to obtain an admission, makes the investigative interview the most powerful form of investigation for those conducting workplace investigations—and the title of this book.

1.6 The Seven Phases of Investigation

Most workplace investigations unfold incrementally. That incremental, yet dynamic, process is called The Process of Investigation. The process includes seven distinct phases. They include:

1. Assessment
2. Planning and preparation
3. Information gathering and fact finding
4. Verification and analysis
5. Decision making
6. Disbursement of disciplinary and/or corrective action
7. Prevention and education

Every proper workplace investigation requires the fact finder to structure his or her investigation such that it systematically contemplates each phase. To do otherwise is insufficient, unprofessional, and, possibly, even negligent. The investigator who imposes process and structure on his investigation obtains better results and does so with more efficiency. What's more, it differentiates him as a professional. It affords him and his employer or client the benefit of ease in assessing and analyzing the result. As in the scientific community, process also permits peer review. In the community of employer–employee relations, others may review the fact finder's efforts and are able to easily and accurately reconstruct that which the fact finder found and how he found it. The ability to reconstruct the process and demonstrate its integrity and propriety lends it credibility. That credibility is the foundation on which all facts rest. An investigative process without credibility is fatally defective. That defect potentially imposes a bar to the admission and ultimate use of otherwise admissible and actionable evidence. It is the implementation and ultimate integrity of this process that is the hallmark of the professional investigator.

1.6.1 Assessment

The Assessment phase of the investigation involves examination and evaluation of the fundamental facts regarding the allegation and some "preinvestigation investigation." Things generally accomplished in this phase include:

- Determining if the parties suspected are, in fact, employees and were working on the date and time in question.
- Determining what policies, practices, and precedents exist that may impact the intended investigation and the manner in which it is to be conducted.
- Who else in the organization should be notified prior to the initiation of the fact finding or before investigative interviews take place?
- Are there any parties external to the organization that should be notified and, if so, who?

Equally useful is the simple mental exercise of determining if the matter is even worthy of an investigation, are the allegations (or suspicions) credible, and what might happen if the matter is simply ignored? Additionally, one also might consider the endgame. For example, what does a successful investigation look like and how might the results be used? Does the result include prosecution, restitution, or discipline? These and other factors will drive one's process and the level of effort he will invest. In order to facilitate this phase of the investigation, see Appendix 2. This easy-to-use tool (called the Investigation Checklist) can be modified to suit your individual needs. In its current form, it covers all of the up-front considerations and actions discussed thus far and can be used to ensure nothing has been overlooked.

> *Tip: Fact finders are well served by properly assessing an allegation and fact pattern before committing themselves and their organization to an investigation. Failing to undertake some simple preinvestigation steps often results in wasted time and resources.*

1.6.2 Preparation and Planning

The next phase of the process has been discussed already in some detail. It involves all of the front-end activities and preparations that normally take place before fact finding begins. It includes such activities as obtaining management's commitment, negotiating objectives, establishing a timeline for the project, deciding a standard of proof, and pooling the necessary resources and expertise to do the job properly.

I take the preparation and planning of my investigations very seriously. I have learned from experience that the time and energy invested up front pays big dividends later. For example, by negotiating and detailing objectives early, I am more easily able to lobby for the resources I need to do the job. By establishing a timeline and communicating it with the client before the project begins, allows both the client and me to better plan and budget our time. It also provides a clearer way to communicate expectations and often reduces confusion later. The old adage, "plan your work, then work your plan," works perfectly here. Without proper preparation and planning, successful workplace investigations are more difficult and less efficient. And sadly, even seasoned investigators overlook this important step. Have you ever intentionally traveled a great distance to a far-off destination without a strategy, itinerary, or map? It's not possible. You would never reach your destination. Why then would you undertake something as complex as an investigation without doing the same preparation and planning? Only a novice would gloss over this important step. Don't be foolish: plan your work, and then work your plan.

1.6.3 Information Gathering and Fact Finding

I have already described in considerable detail the six methods of investigation. This phase of the investigation necessitates the investigator to combine these methods and deploy them in a precise sequence and measure. Tactically, the investigator mixes and matches the methods she determines appropriate at the appropriate time. This mix is largely predetermined during the planning phase. The investigative team, project manager, and client should together determine the investigative tools to be used and when. If you have ever conducted a workplace investigation, you probably did this and gave it very little thought. By front ending the process with sufficient planning and sequencing the investigative tools to be used, the objectives are usually easier to achieve and the investment necessary to achieve them is diminished.

The information-gathering phase of the process, however, is not an end, but a means. The purpose of this important phase is to gather the information necessary to move to the next phase: verification and analysis. This point is missed all too often by many in the industry. Many of my colleagues fail to appreciate that the successful gathering of information does not mark the end of the investigation. The successful gathering of information provides the foundation from which to move forward. Here's a good example:

Hypothetically, suppose our client (external or internal to our organization) suspected an employee was violating his organization's policy regarding the use of the Internet during working hours. Specifically, the organization had credible evidence that the employee in question frequently viewed pornography at his workstation during his scheduled work hours. Suppose also that during the preparation and planning phase, it was decided that, should the suspicions be true, the employee would be terminated. You are asked to conduct the investigation and obtain the proof, should it exist.

Given the objective to obtain the proof, the fact finder also must know the standard of proof. The sophisticated fact finder knows the standard of proof will drive his process and significantly determine the resources necessary to obtain the stated objective. Because only an employment action is sought, the standard of proof should be that of *good faith investigation/reasonable conclusion*.[13]

After some quick preinvestigation investigation and an assessment relative to the size of investment the client is willing to make, the fact finder then begins the information-gathering phase of the investigation. Using elementary computer forensics, he quickly finds temp files, trash bin items, saved images, and bookmarked web pages related to or containing pornography as defined by the organization's policy, on the subject's notebook (he uses a docking station while in the office). Is the investigation sufficient and has the fact finder achieved the standard of proof selected? The answer will surprise you … it is a qualified "yes" to both questions.[14] However, the investigator should not end his process here. He should move his effort to the next phase of investigation, and interview the subject. The reason he should do this is twofold: (1) there may be extenuating and mitigating circumstances unknown to the fact finder, and (2) if the subject is guilty as suspected, an admission should be sought.

In properly interviewing the subject, our investigator fulfills any due process rights the subject might enjoy, and, if he provides an admission, it will be used as proof of his guilt.[15] The decision makers can then effectively discount or discard the evidence developed during the forensic analysis and hang their disciplinary decision on the subject's admission alone. In doing so, the subject is denied the opportunity to attack any aspect of the forensic portion of the process or claim a material defect in the evidence it produced. If he disagrees with the discipline and wishes to fight it, he must first overcome his own admission. In acting upon the admission only, the client has met the good faith investigation/reasonable conclusion standard and has significantly reduced that chance of an evidentiary challenge.

> *Tip: The information gathering and fact finding phase of the investigation is not an end but a means. It affords the investigator the information he needs to interview the subject and successfully obtain an admission.*

1.6.4 Verification and Analysis

As discussed above, the next phase involves the systematic interview of those identified during our information gathering and fact finding. These interviews are called investigative interviews and are reserved for those who we have a very convincing reason to believe committed the offense or offenses in question or had direct involvement in it. Many professional investigators and employers overlook this opportunity. They frequently forego investigative interviews and opt for termination or even arrest. Although termination and arrest might remove the offender from the workplace, it is not a complete solution. Properly conducted investigative interviews often yield information not otherwise attainable by any other means.

A cooperative interviewee can provide information and intelligence spanning the term of his employment. Even a lengthy undercover would only produce direct evidence developed during the course of the investigation. A cooperative interviewee is likely to provide information regarding others as well. It is not unusual for a culpable offender to "give up" or "roll over" on co-conspirators during an interview. This information is corroborative only. However, the accumulation of enough corroboration could justify the interview of an individual not identified during the information-gathering phase of the underlying investigation. In substance abuse investigations, this is very common. The resultant expansion of information and intelligence and ultimate identification of many more additional offenders significantly enhances the ROI. I have had investigations in which my team began interviewing with information involving two employees and when finished had interviewed over 30. In one particularly memorable case, a female employee identified 110 employees whom she alleged sold cocaine at work. Sobbing as she discussed her transgressions, she said she was sure she had sold to additional employees, but could not remember any more names.

As mentioned earlier in the last section, investigative interviews also yield admissions. From an employment law standpoint, properly obtained admissions constitute the best evidence an employer can obtain. Unlike criminal law where admissions and even confessions often only have corroborative value, an employer needs only to proffer an admission to make its case. No other proof is necessary. An admission even trumps other evidence with which it conflicts. From an employer's perspective, there is no better evidence than an admission. Some of the best attorneys I know have failed to leverage this powerful opportunity. Don't make the same mistake. Whenever possible follow your information gathering with investigative interviews.

Tip: Successful investigative interviews are largely predicated on the amount of information the interviewer possesses before the interview. Bypassing the information gathering and fact finding phase and going directly to investigative interviews rarely produces useful results and creates unnecessary liability for both the interviewer and the customer.

1.6.5 Decision Making

Following the third and fourth phases of the investigation, the project manager should assemble the results and present it to the decision makers. This typically involves reducing the findings into a concise report and formally presenting it. To analyze, interpret, and detail one's work is easier than it sounds if the project manager has the proper information management processes in place. I will discuss these and other important subprocesses later. What is important now is to appreciate what has been achieved up to this point and its value to the client. Effectively, the process should have yielded:

- significant factual information regarding the matter under investigation
- information identifying at least some of those involved and some idea of their purpose
- corroborative information from investigative interviews regarding those involved from co-conspirators or witnesses
- admissions from the wrongdoers regarding their transgressions

Demonstrably the investigative team has leveraged the initial information gathered during the fact finding phase into two additional sources of information: that which was provided by the subject and that which others said about him. Armed with this wealth of information, the employer client can then easily and safely determine the equitable disbursement of discipline and/or corrective action if appropriate. Let's look closer.

In the instances in which admissions exist, decision making is simple. Lacking admissions, the employer client might have corroborative statements from those who made admissions as well as other evidence developed during the fact finding phase. Lacking any admissions, the employer client still has the results from the fact finding phase. Even in the face of a denial by any particular subject, armed with sufficient incriminating information, the employer client is afforded the luxury to safely make a tough call if it applies a good faith investigation/reasonable conclusion standard. In other words, the process has engineered defensible fallback options even in the worst case scenario—no admissions from anyone. This may all appear a bit esoteric, but I assure you these intricate machinations will not be missed on a trier-of-fact with any sophistication. At the very least, if challenged, the employer client and its investigators will be able to demonstrate they employed a well-conceived process, one with structure, purpose, and fairness. It is one that epitomizes professionalism and separates it and its principles from the typical bungling incompetents that most judges and juries are accustom. Plaintiffs and the attorneys that represent them, love employers (and investigators) that lack process, fly by the seat of their pants, and make mistakes at every turn.

It should be emphasized that this phase of the investigation is the responsibility of the organization's decision makers. It is often best that the fact finder is not involved in either the decision making or discipline disbursement phase of the investigation. To do otherwise may create the appearance of bias or prejudice. Similarly, those who are not true fact finders should not become part of the fact finding process. Segregating these duties is critical to the protection of the investigation's integrity and those that conducted it.

> *Tip: The fact finder should never play the role of decision maker, or vice versa. In fairness to the subject and the process, separate the duties of the fact finder and decision maker.*

1.6.6 Disbursement of Disciplinary and/or Corrective Action

This phase of the investigation might appear perfunctory, but it is not. Regardless of the quality and sophistication of the process, the decisions regarding discipline and corrective action must be fair and equitable. Good evidence and an admission don't make a minor offense a capital crime. Conversely, punishing all offenders equally is not necessarily equitable. The punishment must first fit the crime, then, like crimes must be punished similarly. The failure to do so, invites discrimination and disparate treatment claims. Successfully defending such claims can be embarrassing and costly.

Once decided, the discipline must be dispensed. How and by whom is the next decision? Here again the fact finder should play no role. These are management (decision maker) decisions and actions. However, some interesting twists exist. As a fact finder, I have often found myself in a consultative role during this phase of the process. Often when confronted by unusual facts or circumstances, my decision makers have turned to me for guidance. While I make it a practice of not recommending one form of discipline or corrective action over another, I have advised my employer clients on such things as the strength of my evidence, the appropriateness of the discipline contemplated and how others in similar circumstances chose to respond. Other options include allowing those selected for termination of employment the opportunity to resign instead or offering those allowed to resign a hold-harmless agreement to sign in exchange for the employer not opposing their application for unemployment insurance. We will discuss these and other interesting options later in the book.

1.6.7 Prevention and Education

Tying the process together is the last phase of prevention and education. During this phase, the employer client and investigative team join together to critique the effort, benchmark, identify best practices, and analyze their performance. Additionally, this employer client/investigative team assesses the damage and attempts to sort out what went wrong in the first place. What was it that allowed the problem to occur and how can it be prevented in the future? This evaluation can be priceless. Clearly, if the organization continues the same practices, it is likely to get the same result again in the future. Such behavior is worse than pointless, it may be negligent as well. Under the legal theory of foreseeability, negligence is compounded when a party should have reasonably foreseen an event that could have been prevented had it taken corrective or preventative action. Organizations make the mistake often and in doing so incur unnecessary additional liability.

Finally, the team should reduce its findings into some sort of recommendations. The recommendations often include altering or modifying policies, changing or imposing new practices, and, finally, training for those who need it. Of all of the phases of investigation, this is the least utilized. In many instances, once the process has reached this phase, no one is interested in doing anything further or expending more resources. However, experience has shown that, if the lessons learned are not leveraged, problems and workplace issues tend to reappear and repeat themselves. As such, passing up the opportunity to learn from past mistakes and record best practices seems to be a heavy price to pay for simply wanting to close a file and move on to the next project.

1.7 Summary

It should now be clear that the foundation on which all successful investigative interviews rest is a quality investigation. All proper and useful investigations are driven by process. That process is called the Process of Investigation. It should be clear as well that without a proper investigation an investigative interview is reduced to merely an interview. Generally, such interviews yield useful information. However, only occasionally will they yield an admission. In the case of workplace investigations, confessions are not necessary, an employer needs only an admission. In order to discipline an offending employee, in most instances, the employer needs only to prove the employee in question committed the alleged offense. The employer does not need to prove or demonstrate things like means, motive, premeditation, and state of mind or intent. Those elements of the offense are inconsequential and have no bearing on the employer's decision to impose discipline. Armed with a properly obtained admission, an employer needs nothing more to take disciplinary or corrective action against the offender when appropriate. For those interested in learning more about the Process of Investigation, obtain a copy of my book, *Investigations in the Workplace,* 2nd ed. (Taylor & Francis, 2012). It can be found through retails online or wherever quality books are sold.

Before moving on and learning how investigative interviews should be conducted, we have one more matter to examine—the differences between the public and private sector. We will take this short diversion because during my trainings many students have demonstrated little understanding of these differences. The failure to appreciate them make both their investigations and investigative interviews more difficult and risky.

1.8 Frequently Asked Questions

1. My organization does not have an established investigative process. Do you recommend it have one?

   Yes. Every organization should have an established investigative process. For larger ones an investigative policy or written protocol is appropriate. A protocol differs from a policy in that it is not as prescriptive, thus more flexible. Regardless, the document should establish how and under what circumstances the organization undertakes an internal investigation.

> *Tip: Every written investigative policy or protocol should stipulate that the subject of an investigation must cooperate and that his failure to do so is a violation of that policy or protocol and may be considered insubordination, an offense that in and of itself may result in disciplinary action, up to and including termination.*

2. My organization has never used the method, undercover. Should we consider it adding to our toolbox?

   No. Undercover investigations are complicated and expensive—and fraught with risk. Undercover should only be used as a method of last resort. If you are interested in learning more about undercover, obtain a copy of my book Undercover Investigations in the Workplace, (Butterworth-Heinemann, Woburn, 2000). Though it is out of print, used copies can still be found on Amazon.com.

3. You have mentioned risk several times. How big are these "risks" and why should the fact finder be concerned?

The risks are enormous, both to one's career and pocketbook. Moreover, the risk of litigation will consume time and money even if the claims are frivolous. The best way to avoid these risks is to use an investigative process to pursue your objectives, obey the law and treat all people with respect and dignity regardless of the circumstances. Bill Berger, Esq. who contributed to Chapter 7, Legal Challenges and Litigation Avoidance, reminds us that happy employees don't sue, only those who are angry sue.

4. What is wrong with choosing employee prosecution as an investigative objective? *First, employee prosecution is expensive and time consuming. Because the standard of proof is so much higher, the organization will have to invest more of both to achieve that objective. Moreover, show me an organization with a mission statement that includes something regarding employee prosecution. I have yet to see one. Why? Because it does little to further the goals of the organization or is it consistent with its purpose. Secondly, organizations don't prosecute lawbreakers, prosecutors prosecute lawbreakers. So, unless a prosecutor decides to take the case, no prosecutions will occur. And, because most asset misappropriations (workplace frauds and thefts) occur as a result of some sort of internal control failure, most prosecutors are not eager to use taxpayer dollars to fix an employer's internal problem, particularly one that was preventable.*

Endnotes

1. John S. Dempsey, *Introduction to Investigations*, 2nd ed. (Farmington Hills, MI: Cengage Learning, 2002), 29.
2. Charles S. Sennewald, *The Process of Investigation*, 2nd ed. (Woburn, MA: Butterworth-Heinemann, 2001), 3.
3. Reid.com. Online at: http://www.reid.com/r_about.html (accessed November 3, 2013).
4. USLegal.com. Online at: http://definitions.uslegal.com/i/interrogation/ (accessed November 3, 2013).
5. Note I did not refer to this amount as the loss. The total loss is actually much greater. In order to calculate it, one must determine the cost of money, transaction and accounting fees, lost interest on the money, as well as the larger economic impact of not having the $750,000 drop to the bottom line. Remember, all economic losses (unless insured) are bottom line deductions.
6. Crimes of this type most often involve legitimate vendors; usually it is only one of its employees that is dishonest. If that employee is an officer, his crime is not only his, but that of his organization as well. He and his organization may be *both* criminally liable. Facing criminal charges, the organization is more likely to pay restitution and, very possibly, the cost of the investigation as well.
7. William C. Cunningham, *The Hallcrest Report II* (Ocean Isle Beach, NC: Hallcrest Systems, Inc., 1990).

8. *The Hallcrest Report II* estimates that the average private investigation firm employs something less than 1.5 individuals. The California Department of Consumer Affairs, which regulates the private investigation industry in California, estimates that the average investigation firm in that state employs 1.4 individuals. Under the department's supervision are approximately 18,000 licensed private investigators and/or agencies.

9. Principally derived from *Undercover Investigations in the Workplace*, 1st ed. (Woburn, MA: Butterworth-Heinemann, 2000), 56, and the author's other works in the field of workplace investigations in which he refers to them as the *universal objectives*.

10. The astute reader will likely note that the rules of civil procedure (in their various forms) provide other methods of investigation as well. For example, in the course of litigation, routine discovery rules allow for mandatory depositions and the production of documents. Because the rules of civil procedure require a plaintiff to have performed an investigation prior to initiation of his suit, I have chosen to exclude the investigative tools available to litigants from my list of investigative methods.

11. M. W. Browne, *The New York Times,* 1998; David Fisher, *Rules of Thumb for Scientists and Engineers* (Cambridge, MA: Elsevier Science & Technology), 1991; and Robert Matthews, *New Scientist,* 1999.

12. Ferraro, E. F., *Undercover Investigations in the Workplace*, 1st ed. (Woburn, MA: Butterworth-Heinemann, 2000), 27.

13. In *Cotran v. Rollins Hudig Hall International, Inc.*, 1998 Cal. LEXIS 1 (January 5, 1998), the California Supreme Court joined the majority of other jurisdictions in holding that good cause existed for terminating an employee for misconduct if an employer had a reasonable and good faith belief that the employee engaged in misconduct. It was ruled that the employer does not have to convince the court or jury that the employee in fact committed the misconduct, only that the employer honestly believed that the employee engaged in misconduct based upon substantial evidence obtained through an adequate investigation that included a fair opportunity for the employee to respond to the charges. The Court further defined the term "good cause" as a "reasoned conclusion ... supported by substantial evidence gathered through an adequate investigation that includes notice of the claimed misconduct *and a chance for the employee to respond.*" So, while the employees of employers in the private sector do not enjoy constitutionally protected due process rights, the California Supreme Court holds that an accused employee indeed has the right to respond.

14. For the purposes of our hypothetical, we will assume that the fact finder has eliminated the possibility that someone else had access to the subject's computer or was able to place files on it.

15. Ibid.

Chapter 2

The Differences between the Public and Private Sector

Key learning points:

1. Public sector law enforcement's principal mission is the enforcement of public law.
2. An employee's refusal to cooperate in her employer's investigation is actionable. Under some circumstances, the termination of uncooperative individuals can be justified merely on their refusal to participate and answer a fact finder's questions. The subject's lack of cooperation is called insubordination.
3. Among other things, due process includes: the right of the accused to know the offense(s) and crime(s) of which one is suspected, the right to view and examine the government's evidence, the right to face one's accusers and examine them as well as any and all witnesses, the right to competent representation, and protection against self-incrimination.
4. Regardless of the nature of the suspected offense, in the private sector employees under investigation by their employer have no due process rights.
5. Entrapment is not a crime, it is a criminal defense. The theory behind the defense suggests that an otherwise law-abiding citizen would not have committed the crime in question had not *the government* or its agent improperly induced him. Thus, only the government or its agents can entrapment.
6. Despite its usefulness for other purposes, an employer needs neither to know motive nor consider it when deciding discipline.

7. When deploying new technology, always attempt to identify exploitable vulnerabilities and address them before they are found by the criminally minded employee.

"Deceptive interviewers usually get deceptive answers."

E .F. Ferraro

2.1 An Historical Perspective

My grandfather was a homicide detective in New York for 30 years. He retired in 1952. During his career, he investigated unimaginable crimes and dealt with many horrible human beings. Like many retired law enforcement officers of his time, he entered the private sector after he left the "job." He quickly found employment at a large racetrack as a security officer and ended up working there for many years. As a small child, I remember him reminiscing and telling stories of police chases and shoot-outs with gangsters. But, of all his work, he loved most working at the track. I have since learned that he and retirees like him were the forefathers of today's industrial security. He and his generation pioneered the private security frontier and were among the first of those we call today *security professionals*. Interestingly, just two years after his first retirement, the American Society of Industrial Security was founded. Today the society has been renamed, ASIS International and boosts almost 44,000 members worldwide. And, like ASIS, the private security industry has come a very long way.

The most significant change in private security is that it has become a true profession. No longer is it a second career option or reserved for just those coming out of law enforcement. It has become a profession in every regard. Secondary schools and universities now offer degrees in security management and even loss prevention. The profession has moved to accrediting and certifying select members who qualify. Designations, such as Board Certified in Security Management (CPP) and Physical Security Professional (PSP), are almost necessities for those in executive security management. Each segment of the profession offers its own designations and publishes its own periodical or journal. The men and women, who make up the profession, write, publish, and subject their work to peer review. These professionals meet, exchange ideas, and offer the results of their research to anyone willing to study it. It has been a marvelous and miraculous transition and its impact on business and society has been significant.

Today nearly every organization, public and private of any measurable size, boasts at least one security management position. Larger organizations have security or loss prevention departments and cutting-edge global enterprises have designated chief security officers to protect their assets and employees. These CSOs typically report directly to the chief executive or chairman and enjoy all of the privileges and responsibilities of their counterparts at the chief executive level. Never in the history of private security has the security professional experienced such recognition and importance.

This evolution, however, has come with a price. No longer can the successful law enforcement professional haplessly migrate from the public to the private sector after retirement as my grandfather did. Like the public sector, the private sector now demands more of its professionals and the men and women who manage them. Even advanced degrees and robust résumés are not enough. In order to transition from the public to private sector successfully, the individual needs an acute appreciation for business; not just budgets, finance, and personnel management, but a deep understanding of business and its purpose. That purpose, of course, is to make money and create wealth. Money is not a dirty word and the creation of wealth is a worthy endeavor. The ability to create and accumulate wealth is the cornerstone of a free-market system. While money is the oil that lubricates the system, it is the accumulation of wealth that provides our capital markets and makes the free enterprise, as we know it, possible. The mechanisms and apparatus that support it are not the same in the public sector.

2.2 Mission

Of the many differences separating the public and private sectors, foremost are their missions. Public sector law enforcement's principal mission is the enforcement of public law. Over the past two decades, this mission has been expanded to include administration of public safety, crime prevention, substance abuse awareness, community service, and even revenue generation. However, job no. 1 is to enforce public law. The principal vehicle used in pursuit of this mission is street enforcement and criminal investigations. Yes, law enforcement both on the local and federal level does other important things. Yes, they make other significant contributions in other ways. But, when one peels back the skin of the onion, one will find at the core street enforcement and criminal investigations. With all due respect to the brave men and women in blue, what cops do best is put lawbreakers in jail. Compare that activity and that which supports it to the purpose of business as I have described for you in the preceding section. Though not diametrically opposed, the principal missions of these important endeavors are vastly different. See for yourself. Look now at your organization's mission statement or that of one of your customers. Does it contain the words public safety, law enforcement, criminal justice, or prosecution? Is it your organization's mission to prosecute its employees to the fullest extent of the law? Is it your customer's mission to produce capital appreciation or enforce public law?

Tip: Although private sector investigations frequently investigate potential violations of the law, private sector investigators rarely have law enforcement powers.

As one drills into the private sector organization and comes upon the security professional, we find that his mission is also vastly different from that of law enforcement. So different are the two that I oppose the use of the term *counterpart* in law enforcement when describing the function of the security professional. The law enforcement officer does not have a counterpart in the private sector. Even security officers are not responsible for the enforcement of public law. Their job, and important it is, is to observe and report. The corporate security professional is not the "company cop." Unfortunately for them and their organizations, many private sector security professionals see themselves as just that. These often very bright and capable people see their position in the private sector as an extension of their former roles in law enforcement. They intentionally retain the demeanor—that somewhat inflated self-confidence and that harsh cop-speak vernacular they cultivated while on the job. Others in their organization call this collective behavior the "cop mentality." Because of it, they don't see the "company cop" as a peer. They perceive him or her as a corporate outsider and necessary nuisance. Tragically, many corporate security professionals relish this image. You know the type. You've met them and so have the executives in your organization—those executives who evaluate your performance and measure your contribution to the organization. If they perceive you as the company cop, that is precisely how they will treat you and, very unfortunately, pay you. It's tragic and it's unnecessary.

Trap: Those who talk and act like a company cop will be treated like one. Instead, talk and act like the people in whose hands your career rests.

By confusing missions, however, the corporate security professional does more than damage his career, he damages his organization. While fixated on enforcing public law and putting workplace transgressors in jail, this type of security professional overlooks his organization's mission and purpose. He tends to forget that prosecuting dishonest employees contributes nothing to the organization's balance sheet and shareholder value. In fact, in some cases, the effect can be quite the opposite. Following is an excellent example.

My client, the corporate director of security for a nationwide auto parts distributor, was a retired FBI agent. A nice enough fellow; he was soft spoken, professional, and principled. He also hated crime and those who committed it. His purpose in life was to put lawbreakers in jail. On numerous occasions, I proposed we pursue restitution in lieu of prosecution. He would hear nothing of it. Then one day, during an undercover investigation my firm was conducting for him, he called and said he had just shut the case down. He said he was at the target facility and that the police were en route and upon their arrival the guilty would be arrested. His plan was defective and I told him so. First, on what grounds might a misdemeanor offender be arrested—or, for that matter, on what grounds might one be arrested for overstaying his break? Second, absent proper investigative interviews, how might admissions be obtained? In other words, on what grounds would discipline be based? He retorted that those prosecuted would be disciplined and that arrest alone was cause for termination. The line went dead.

Sure enough, I later learned that the police showed up, lights flashing, and sirens screaming. Chaos ensued. Panicked employees leapt from windows, hurled themselves over fences, and ran in every direction. The fact that many were undocumented workers didn't help the situation either. The police soon got the upper hand and took away those they had caught. Hours later, an angry police chief released the arrestees and apologized to each as they left his custody. The chief knew very well that his officers had made a terrible mistake. The arrests were unlawful, because probable cause did not exist. There was no proper justification for the arrest and search of these people. But, the security director lost more than face. Shortly after the spectacle, the former arrestees sued their employer. The case was later settled and never went to jury. The settlement remains confidential, but I do know that the former FBI agent and his second-in-command now work elsewhere.

> Trap: Despite popular belief, employee prosecution is neither cost-effective nor a deterrent. In most instances, better results can be achieved by pursuing the organization's mission.

2.3 Advantages of the Public Sector

The second most significant difference separating the public and private sector is the enormous power and authority the public sector possesses. Law enforcement and its companion, the criminal justice system, have at their disposal, mechanisms and tools out of reach of those in the private sector. Let's briefly examine a few.

2.3.1 Powers of Arrest

Designated individuals in law enforcement and the criminal justice system have the incredible power of arrest. Unlike citizens (corporate security professionals among them), the police, district attorneys, and judges can under a host of circumstances arrest people, subject them to custodial interrogations, and even incarcerate them. By fulfilling a few simple requirements and with rather minimal justification, the public sector has the power to detain, forcibly question, and interrogate. In venues such as a properly convened court, the failure to answer a question or cooperate is a crime. The crime is called contempt of court and can be punished with incarceration. There is no equivalent in the private sector. Citizens can, under very special circumstances, make an arrest, but in doing so incur significant liability. To forcibly question or hold another against his will constitutes false imprisonment and is civilly actionable.

2.3.2 Search and Seizure

The public sector also has at its disposal the power to search people and their belongings and seize property. The law permits one's person, property, and papers be searched and/or seized by the government. Although the citizenry enjoys constitutional protections under the Fourth Amendment of the U.S. Constitution and elsewhere against abuse of this power, it is a critical tool in the conduct of criminal investigations and the enforcement of public law. The closest thing to it in the private sector is an employer's search policy. Workplace searches of desks, lockers, and other work areas are permissible only where an employee does not have a reasonable expectation of privacy. The employer can substantially reduce the expectation of privacy by advising employees that such areas are subject to inspection, with or without notice; restricting private use of these areas by issuing its own locks and retaining duplicate keys; and by crafting policies that limit worker's expectation of privacy and permit searches under any circumstances.

Regardless, the powers available to the employer pale compared to those of the government. The ability to search and seize property in the spirit of a criminal investigation or inquiry creates a huge differentiator between the public and private sector.

2.3.3 Grand Jury and Special Inquiries

The ability to convene a grand jury and forcibly extract testimony, absent representation of even the suspect, is unmatched in the private sector.[1] During such proceedings, a citizen's failure to cooperate may be ruled contempt and her failure to tell the truth may be deemed perjury. Although employees have an affirmative duty to cooperate in an organizationally sanctioned investigation, an employee, in fact, may refuse to cooperate (and face possible discipline) and has no obligation (other than an ethical one) to tell the truth.

> *Tip: An employee's refusal to cooperate in her employer's investigation is actionable. Under some circumstances, the termination of uncooperative individuals can be justified merely on their refusal to participate and answer a fact finder's questions. The subject's lack of cooperation is called insubordination.*

	Public Sector	*Private Sector*
Lying	Generally acceptable to the extent the falsehood merely embellishes the quantity or quality of evidence.	Unacceptable and widely considered unethical.
Making promises	Generally acceptable if relied upon by a defendant in making a confession. Some promises, however, are acceptable (see Dempsey, page 191 for several examples).	Unacceptable and widely considered unethical.
Threatening	The use of threats is considered inherently coercive and their use may render a confession as involuntary.	Unacceptable and widely considered unethical—may even be unlawful if threat is used for the purpose of extortion.

Figure 2.1 **Contrasting the lengths to which those in the public and private sector can go to obtain the cooperation of an interviewee.**

However, there are limitations to the length an employer can go to get the cooperation of an interviewee. In the private sector, it is universally accepted that employers may not lie, make undeliverable promises, or threaten an employee to obtain her cooperation. Figure 2.1 illustrates those limitations.

These private sector limitations are construed not from law, but policy and ethical restraints imposed on the employer. Some of these restraints are self-imposed, others are industrially or socially imposed. Regardless, their driver is the commitment to fairness, integrity, and social responsibility. Interestingly, we do not impose these same values on those who conduct custodial interviews (ahem, interrogations) in the public sector.

2.3.4 Prosecution and Punishment

Employers believe they can prosecute lawbreaking employees, but they cannot. Unfortunately, it's a widely held notion even in the private security industry. Only the government can prosecute someone. Even more interesting is the fact that employers cannot even ask the government to prosecute someone. In every jurisdiction of which I am aware, the improper influence of the prosecution is in and of itself a crime.

Furthermore, an employer's threat of prosecution may constitute criminal extortion.[2] Again, contrary to popular belief, the employer can only file a complaint. It is the duty of the government to determine if a law might have been broken and, if so, what charges should be brought based on the evidence available. In property crimes, such as theft, if the employer was the victim, its agent (an owner or manager) could swear out a complaint and ask that the matter be investigated. The authorities would then work the case and hopefully find the suspect and charge him. On the other hand, in matters involving workplace substance abuse, even selling illegal drugs at work, the employer is not the victim. The government is technically the victim and no complaint is necessary. It is the sole discretion of the government to pursue the matter or not. The employer cannot decide who or what offenses shall be prosecuted.

Successful prosecutions also result in punishment. The punishment is designed to fit the crime and ranges from something as passive as a suspended sentence up to and including execution. The private workplace has nothing equivalent. And, employees are not punished, they are disciplined. The notion of workplace punishment does not exist in a free society. However, many liberal-minded triers-of-fact consider employee termination the civil equivalent of capital punishment. As such, termination is frequently considered extreme discipline and only used in extreme circumstances.

Workplace discipline also does not produce a public record. Criminal prosecution, except that of minors, produces a criminal record capable of following the offender his entire life. Not so in the workplace. Employee discipline is a private matter and rarely should co-workers even be told what discipline was dispensed against a co-worker. In the interest of employee privacy and confidentiality, workplace discipline stays in the workplace and any record of it remains under strict employer control. Even prospective employers find it difficult to learn the terms and conditions of an applicant's separation from a prior employer.

The public sector is not bound by such construct. In addition to some of the most powerful investigative tools available only to it, the public sector is largely unconcerned about individual privacy and confidentiality. Of course, its investigations are draped in confidentiality, but the process and results are ultimately disclosed and made available to public scrutiny. In fact, it is this public disclosure that keeps the system sound and its participants honest. The public aspect of a criminal trial is so critical to the fair and proper workings of the process that it is constitutionally protected. The private sector is not bound by such rules and procedures. Only if challenged must the employer make limited disclosures. Even then, special privileges abound ensuring certain communications and evidence remains confidential.

2.3.5 Resources

The question of whether it is the public sector or private sector that has greater resources is debatable. Both sectors have operational and fiscal limitations. Both have manpower and technological limitations. But even today, Microsoft* with a reported $80 billion cash reserve and the U.S. federal government with an annual deficit of something near $1 trillion Microsoft could not outspend the government. Nor could Microsoft° field more people than the government. The total combined capability of all federal, state, and local law enforcement authorities in the United States is unmatched in the world.

On the micro level, I also would argue that the government, at the federal, state, or local level, can probably throw more resources at any particular case than almost any defendant. These same government resources probably can outgun most corporations as well. There are examples, of course, to the contrary. The federal government has waged battle against the likes of Microsoft and IBM° (IBM Corporation, White Plains, New York) in federal court and substantially lost in several cases. In several of these instances, the defendant threw more resources at the case than the federal government and effectively overwhelmed the system. One case in point was the IBM antitrust case that finally ended in the 1970s. During discovery, IBM provided over 100,000,000 documents. Analysts at the time speculated that it would take the presiding authority 3,000 years just to read all of the evidence.

2.4 Advantages of the Private Sector

In spite of the awesome powers of the government and systems that support it, the private sector has some of its own unique privileges and advantages. I have touched upon a few already, but there are more of them and some are remarkably powerful.

2.4.1 Due Process

The Constitution of the United States and its amendments ensure and protect a host of important personal rights. By design, the Constitution protects the citizenry against government oppressions and intrusions. Contrary to the assertions of many advocates and commentators, it does not substantially protect us from each other. More precisely, it restricts the behavior and actions of government, not its citizens. One of the Constitution's more progressive protections is that of due process. Among other things, due process includes the right of the accused to know the offense(s) and crime(s) of which one is suspected, the right to view and examine the government's evidence, the right to face one's accusers and examine them as well as any and all witnesses, the right to competent representation, and protection against self-incrimination. These rights are bolstered by volumes of criminal procedures and case law. Amongst that body of law is Miranda.[3]

The Miranda decision, decided in 1966 by the U.S. Supreme Court, requires those taken into criminal custody and where probable cause exists, which suggests the suspect committed a crime, the suspect be informed of his due process rights before questioned.[4] Remarkably, employees when questioned by their employer or the employer's agent (a hired consultant or private investigator) with regard to possible misconduct have no such rights, even if the suspected

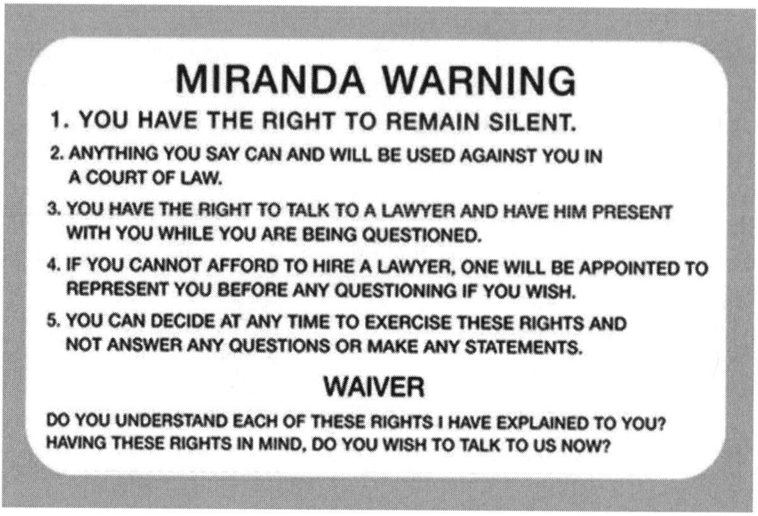

MIRANDA WARNING

1. YOU HAVE THE RIGHT TO REMAIN SILENT.

2. ANYTHING YOU SAY CAN AND WILL BE USED AGAINST YOU IN A COURT OF LAW.

3. YOU HAVE THE RIGHT TO TALK TO A LAWYER AND HAVE HIM PRESENT WITH YOU WHILE YOU ARE BEING QUESTIONED.

4. IF YOU CANNOT AFFORD TO HIRE A LAWYER, ONE WILL BE APPOINTED TO REPRESENT YOU BEFORE ANY QUESTIONING IF YOU WISH.

5. YOU CAN DECIDE AT ANY TIME TO EXERCISE THESE RIGHTS AND NOT ANSWER ANY QUESTIONS OR MAKE ANY STATEMENTS.

WAIVER

DO YOU UNDERSTAND EACH OF THESE RIGHTS I HAVE EXPLAINED TO YOU? HAVING THESE RIGHTS IN MIND, DO YOU WISH TO TALK TO US NOW?

Figure 2.2 The Miranda warnings apply only to "investigative custodial questioning aimed at eliciting evidence of a crime." Miranda has no applicability in the private sector unless the investigative interview is conducted under the color of the law.

misconduct is criminal in nature. Allow me to say it again. Regardless of the nature of the suspected offense, in the private sector employees under investigation by their employer, have no due process rights. The employer has no duty to even tell the employee under suspicion the offense of which he is suspected or what evidence the employer might have against him. Furthermore, the suspected employee does not even have the right to representation or even a witness when questioned by his employer. The right to a lawyer or other representative from outside the organization does not exist.[5] The theory goes that such encumbrances would impinge on the employer's prerogative to run its business as it sees fit and impede the necessary collection of information required to solve internal problems (Figure 2.2).

Employers must be careful, however. Although they have no legal duty to provide the subjects of internal investigations any due process, some triers-of-fact and those who make up juries sometimes think otherwise. The appearance of treating the subject unfairly and the failure to comply with the reasonable requests by the subject may expose the employer to considerable liability. Even absent the rights of due process, it is expected that all people be treated fairly and provided all reasonable accommodations while under suspicion or when accused of misconduct.

Furthermore, the more the employer involves the government in its investigation, the greater these expectations. It is for these reasons that, as a matter of practice, I avoid attaching *agent status* to my investigators whenever possible. The more control and influence law enforcement has over a workplace investigation and its fact finders, the more agent-like the fact finders become. Subsequent to the discipline, should an employee successfully argue the fact finders were agents of law enforcement or that the use of them by law enforcement subjugated rights they might otherwise have enjoyed, portions, if not all of the evidence gathered by the fact finders, could come under attack. A plaintiff (or in the case of criminal trial, defendant) might attempt a motion to exclude the "improperly obtained evidence." If the motion was successful, the entire investigation could be in jeopardy. More easily in an arbitration, where the rules of evidence are more lax, an arbitrator could exclude the grievant's admission or that of others simply on the belief that ample due process was not provided.

> *Tip: Avoid the appearance of being an extension of law enforcement and keep your portion of the investigation separate from that of the government. If prosecution is likely, remand your evidence only after you have received a court order to do so.*

2.4.2 Entrapment

There are employers who are leery of investigative interviews. Among them the most common and unnecessary fear is that of entrapment. Employers and even the lawyers who represent them principally fear entrapment because they don't understand it. Contrary to popular belief, entrapment is not a crime. It is not an offense or something bad employers do to innocent employees. It is not something for which one might be punished or even admonished. Entrapment is nothing more than a criminal defense. The theory behind the defense suggests that an otherwise law-abiding citizen would not have committed the crime in question had not the government or its agent improperly induced him. In order to prevail, the defendant must show the inducement was sufficiently improper and, absent the government's influence, he possessed no predisposition to commit the crime.

Because entrapment is a criminal defense, only the government can entrap someone. An employer cannot entrap an employee and an investigative interviewer cannot entrap an interviewee because a citizen cannot entrap another citizen. Only the government can use entrapment. What's more, the defense of entrapment can only be used *after* a defendant admits to the commission of the crime. That's right; one cannot claim entrapment and also claim innocence. A defendant cannot have it both ways. Let's look at an example of entrapment:

Suppose an undercover police officer posing as a life insurance agent suggests to an otherwise law-abiding prospect that he or she purchase unnecessary life insurance on a spouse and then kill their partner and redeem the policy. To cinch the deal, the undercover agent offers a policy priced well below market and offers to help plan the murder. Acting upon the opportunity, the would-be policyholder is immediately arrested and charged with conspiracy to commit murder or its equivalent. Our hypothetical defendant could easily raise the defense of entrapment and would likely prevail. Unfortunately, his or her marriage would be another matter altogether.

Interestingly, a law enforcement agent's offer to sell an illegal drug to a citizen under most circumstances does not constitute entrapment and the defense is often unavailable to the defendant. Courts will usually insist that the prosecution show some predisposition to the crime, but the offer to sell an illegal substance alone generally does not constitute entrapment. Reverse stings, as these operations are typically called, have increasingly become the weapon of choice in the war against drugs. Simultaneously, civil liberty advocates have increased their opposition to them. Please note, however, that reverse stings are not appropriate in most workplace settings and typically should not be used by the private sector.

Because entrapment is so misunderstood and stigmatized, workplace fact finders should contemplate counters to the claim during the planning phase of their investigations. Of all of the types of investigation subject to this claim, undercover is the most likely. Because undercover is so interactive and the subjects of the investigation are in direct contact with the investigator, claims of entrapment following an undercover investigation are common. Countering the claim is easy, but any counters used must be deployed during the investigation, not after. There are two counters that are particularly effective.

2.4.2.1 Establish That the Misconduct Was Preexistent

The undercover investigator can establish the misconduct was preexistent in numerous ways. The easiest way to accomplish this is for the undercover investigator to simply ask the subject for how long he or she had engaged in the misconduct in question. Here's a simple example:

Suppose our investigator is investigating allegations of employee substance abuse. During a casual conversation during break, the investigator openly expresses interest in purchasing marijuana for the weekend. During the conversation, one of the employee participants off-handedly offers to sell some to the investigator. The employee tells the investigator that she has several bags of marijuana in her possession and wishes to sell one or all for $25 each. To counter the potential claim of entrapment, the investigator should simply ask the seller if she had ever before sold marijuana at work. An affirmative response would demonstrate that the activity had taken place before the investigator had come on the scene. As such, the seller could not later claim she had been induced by the investigator to do something she had already done.

2.4.2.2 Establish the Motive of the Offender

You may recall I mentioned in Chapter 1 that motive is an irrelevant element for an employer who is deciding discipline. Despite its usefulness for other purposes, an employer needs neither to know motive nor consider it when deciding discipline. However, the disciplined employee may attempt to introduce motive when using the defense of entrapment. Because the defense necessitates the offender to show his behavior was adversely influenced by someone else, the argument is bolstered if motive is shown to have been influenced as well. For example, suppose the offender who claims entrapment argues as part of his defense that he was both broke and lonely, and the offer by the investigator included the reward of money and friendship. These claims tend to support the defense and give it the credibility it needs—that is, were it not for the need of money and friendship, and the influence of the investigator, the offender would have never committed the crime. Defeating this argument is easy.

The solution is to deploy the second counter with the first during the fact-finding portion of the investigation. All the investigator needs to do is establish the motive of the potential offender before the offense is committed. For example, in the hypothetical above, had the investigator established that (1) the offender had committed the offense several times prior to the investigator entering the case, and (2) the motive was profit as evidenced by a new vehicle the offender bragged he had just purchased with proceeds, the defense would handily be defeated. What's more, introducing this sort of evidence further incriminates the accused. Our hypothetical offender has not only had to admit he had committed the offense in order to use the defense of entrapment, but now he's stuck with the burden of explaining the purchase of his new pickup truck he had bragged to so many about. He also has the additional burden of recovering his credibility. Remember, he claimed he was broke and needed a friend. The $35,000 red pickup he purchased before he had met the investigator will destroy his credibility and likely his defense.

> *Tip: Entrapment is not a crime, it is a defense. Only the government or its agents can **use** entrapment.*

2.4.3 A Lower Burden of Proof

As mentioned in Chapter 1, the sophisticated fact finder knows the standard of proof selected for his investigation will drive his process and significantly determine the resources necessary to obtain the stated objective. In the private sector, when an employment action is sought, the standard of proof should be that of *good faith investigation/reasonable conclusion*.[6] In the public sector, federal and state judicial and administrative tribunal also have established burdens and standards of proof. Here, burden of proof refers to the duty of a party to present evidence, whereas standard of proof refers to the strength of evidence that must be presented in order to prevail. The elements of proof are the specific facts that must be proved for each cause of action.

In criminal proceedings, for example, the police must show probable cause to obtain a search warrant or make an arrest, and prosecutors must establish guilt of an accused beyond a reasonable doubt. Probable cause means evidence sufficient for a reasonable person to believe a crime has been committed and that the suspect committed it. Guilt beyond a reasonable doubt is the highest standard in the judicial system. It means there is certainty in the minds of jurors and judges. The elements that must be proved are those of the alleged crimes as set forth in the penal codes of the jurisdictions.

In order to prevail in a civil case, the plaintiff must establish fault by only a *preponderance of the evidence.* This means when the competing evidence of the parties is weighed it must tilt in favor of plaintiffs. If the evidence tilts the other way, the defendants prevail. The elements of proof are those of the alleged wrongful acts (e.g., invasion of privacy, malicious prosecution) as set forth in the judicial decisions and statutes of the jurisdictions in which the cases are brought. To illustrate the difference in these standards of proof, see Figure 2.3.

In a discrimination lawsuit, there is a confusing series of *shifting burdens.* First, the employee must establish *prima facie* discrimination, which means he is a member of a protected class and adverse employment action was taken against him. Second, the company has the option to articulate a *legitimate business reason* for the alleged adverse employment action. If it does, the burden shifts back to the employee to show by a preponderance of the evidence the reason set forth by the employer is a *pretext* to hide the alleged discriminatory action. For example, assume an organization fired a female production employee for suspected theft of tools. The employee filed a sex discrimination complaint. She alleged that she was discharged (the adverse employment action) because of her status as a female (membership in a protected group). In response, the company introduced testimonial evidence by co-workers who observed her taking the tools. In response, the employee claimed she borrowed the tools. Further, she introduced evidence that male employees routinely took tools home to work on personal projects and they were never disciplined. Was the firing justified or was it really a pretext by the company to cover up discrimination?

These shifting burdens are especially confusing in discrimination claims because they actually do not shift the *burden of proof.* The burden of proof remains at all times on the plaintiff. These are instead the steps that a judge should go through to decide if the case warrants a trial.

In addition to knowing the burdens and standards of proof necessary when bringing actions, employers and their fact finders need to know what level of evidence will enable them to successfully defend their conduct. For example, in malicious prosecution lawsuits, fact finders may defend their actions by showing they acted upon probable cause. They and their employers may defend against discrimination complaints by showing they acted for legitimate business reasons. Parties may defend against defamation lawsuits by showing their comments were privileged and the communication had a legitimate business purpose.

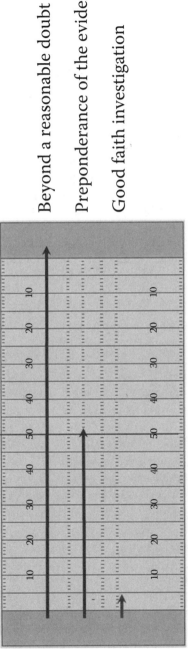

Beyond a reasonable doubt

Preponderance of the evidence

Good faith investigation

Figure 2.3   The standards of proof as illustrated by the relative distances a player must move the ball down the length of a 100-yd playing field.

Though sometimes complicated with burdens shifting and standards seeming to constantly change, one thing is clear: the standard of proof necessary to discipline an employee is lower than that for criminally prosecuting him. This lower standard is a demonstrable advantage of the private sector.

2.5 Significant Trends in the Private Sector

2.5.1 More Sophisticated Crimes and Perpetrators

I began conducting workplace investigations for employers before the advent of fax machines, cell phones, desktop computers, and the Internet. I recall vividly the office of my first corporate employer, Krout and Schneider, Inc. It was a large West Coast investigation firm and I was a cub investigator haphazardly thrust undercover in a large paper distribution facility. The office was set up newsroom-style with rows of metal desks with no partitions. Atop each desk was an in-basket, an out-basket, and an IBM° electric typewriter. The place was inefficient and noisy. But, it was a modern office in its day. Several years later, after I had been promoted into management, I can remember arguing with the senior partner about the proposed purchase of the office's first fax machine. I embraced the technology, but he couldn't reconcile the need for the instantaneous transmission of documents when the organization had successfully used messengers and U.S. mail for nearly 50 years. "Besides," he said, "what could possibly be so important that a client needs it right now?" Can you imagine?

Today's workplaces, of course, are much different. However, it requires no leap in intelligence to appreciate the fact that as the workplace becomes a more sophisticated environment, workplace offenses and offenders will become more sophisticated as well. As employers heap on advanced processes, systems, and technology, the opportunity to exploit them also is advanced. It is for this reason that today's security professional must be more advanced, too. Those who reject the modern workplace and all of its modernity are doomed. The workplace fact finder must embrace the new and ever-changing workplace. For it is impossible to resolve today's modern workplace crimes without a fine understanding or at least appreciation for the environment in which the alleged offenses occurred.

2.5.2 Greater Use of Technology

Technology by definition promises convenience and economy. When technology is properly crafted, the convenience and economy it provides combine and are packaged as solutions. Technological solutions improve efficiency and profitability. Intentionally, they also reduce headcount. Engineers are constantly looking for ways machines can replace humans. Unfortunately, however, from an asset protection and loss prevention perspective, two things happen: (1) the technology provides new opportunity for exploitation, and (2) the quantity of supervision decreases. There is a subtle dichotomy here; as the exposure increases, protections decrease. Look around your own organization. Do employees not have more access to just about everything and is not your organization operating with less supervision?

Furthermore, organizations have been tricked into thinking more can be done with less supervision. Consider for a moment a few of the "revolutionary," often "enterprise-wide," "leadership initiatives" the big name "thought leaders" have sold to America's "bleeding-edge" organizations designed to "empower" employees and create "world-class organizations" that are *Built to Last*.[7] It's sickening. I mean for heaven's sake *Let's Get Real*.[8] It seems that for more than two decades corporate America has been running around looking for *The New New Thing*[9] and has yet to find it. Maybe the chief executive should ask *The Millionaire Next Door*,[10] because she is certainly not going to find it while meandering down *The Road Less Traveled*.[11] With all due respect, what some of these change merchants (see, I cannot help using some of these terms, either) are peddling would not fly even if strapped to a Titan missile if attempted in most organizations. Although, much of this new-era corporate psychobabble and brainwashing nobly embraces employee relations and empowering individual contributors (there I go again), the sad fact of the matter is most people do not care.

Forgive my cynicism, but my experience is that most employees do not want to be empowered, most employees do not want more responsibility and most employees are neither prepared nor willing to make tough organizational decisions. By and large, today's employees could care less about most of the stuff that today's thought leaders think they are interested in. Largely what employees want is a safe, fulfilling job, fair pay for their labor and a work environment in which they are appreciated and treated with respect. Think about it, if the average line employee or staffer wanted more responsibility or to take more risk, they would have started their own company. What has been created in many cases are work environments in which management has involved its employees in the business of running a business to a greater degree than what the typical employee wants. Then, in order to capitalize on the dividend of reduced headcount that the thought leaders and change merchants promised, they slashed the amount of supervision in their organizations; consider the now abandoned concepts of quality circles and self-directed work groups. Do you remember those? (Google the terms, if you don't). Rarely have these initiatives worked as anticipated. Instead they have served as expensive experiments. They often did nothing more than distract management and consume valuable resources. By reducing the quantity of supervision without necessarily improving productivity, many of these well-meaning organizations created nothing more than fertile grounds for employee theft, dishonesty, and misconduct.

Let's not forget the technology component. As management reengineered itself, it often simultaneously embraced advances in technology. The new technologies promised improved efficiency and quality. So is the case in most industries and workplaces. However, as I previously mentioned, new technology also means new vulnerabilities. As fast as the technology is deployed, villains will figure out how to exploit it to some criminal advantage. In some cases, they will even go farther and just steal the technology and the products it produces, as in the illegal practice of ripping off music CDs from the Internet.

> Tip: *When deploying new technology, always attempt to identify exploitable vulnerabilities and address them before they are found by the criminally minded employee. Remind management that bleeding edge is often just that.*

2.5.3 More Litigious Workforce

America is the most litigious industrialized nation in the world. For all its greatness and potential, our society is also one wrapped in rules and regulations. Be it the placement of safety labels on household stepladders (has anyone ever really read them?) to the amount of vacation pay a terminated employee must be paid, we have decided that nearly everything we do, say, or think needs to be regulated. In the post-World War II era of regulation promulgation, we have passed more laws and regulations than were implemented during the 175 years prior. This tangled morass of increasingly contradictory rules, laws, and regulations is rapidly reaching critical mass. Even lawmakers are beginning to recognize the trouble they have created.[12] However, little has been done to solve the problem. Here's an example of one perplexing conflict.

The Americans with Disabilities Act (ADA, 42 U.S.C. 12101, 1990) stipulates employers must reasonably accommodate those with recognized or perceived disabilities. It also imposes an obligation to reassign work, make other accommodations to assist persons with disabilities or those recovering from injuries. This makes sense because early return-to-work policies reduce costs. However, if an employee is injured and an employer in an effort to reduce Workers' Compensation costs attempts to accommodate the employee and return him to an alternative or a light-duty position, the employer may very well violate the Family and Medical Leave Act (FMLA). The Department of Labor has taken the position that if an employee is entitled to leave because of a "serious health condition," which may include a Workers' Compensation injury, the employee is entitled to the same or equivalent position upon return. So, therefore, while the ADA and the employers' Workers' Compensation law may encourage rapid return to a light-duty assignment, the FMLA allows the employee to refuse to do so.

Here's another example. The Equal Employment Opportunity Commission (EEOC) has recently pursued companies that use criminal conviction records for preemployment screening purposes. In two highly visible and controversial cases, the EEOC has alleged the employers in question, BMW and Dollar General, discriminated against black applicants by using criminal conviction records as part of their preemployment screening process. The Commission asserted that while the behavior of the two defendants was not discriminatory, per se, the companies' practices had a disparate impact on blacks. That is, the employers did not actually engage in direct discrimination, but their practices statistically affected more blacks than nonblacks. Thus, they were guilty of discrimination, anyway. In the case of BMW, the Commission's conclusion relied on records that showed that while the workforce was overwhelmingly black and 55 percent of the applicants were black, 80 percent of those rejected were black.[13] Say what you want about an administration that says it wants to create jobs, this sort of government overreach is nothing but a job killer. One must really contort the facts in order to conclude an organization whose workforce is mostly black is practicing discriminatory hiring practices against blacks.

Other government bureaucracies also are confusing employers. Since its creation in 1970, the Occupational Health and Safety Administration (OSHA) has been hard at work creating a safer workplace for everyone. In doing so, the OSHA has published over 4,000 regulations, dictating everything from the height of a railing to the thickness of carpet. The maze of rules and often arcane regulations (how far a plank can stick out from the edge of a temporary scaffold) busy more than 2,000 inspectors and tens of thousands of attorneys that prosecute and defend the litigation that has precipitated. Attempting to toe the line, industry has spent several hundred billion dollars on compliance alone.[14]

Arguably, many of the laws and regulations, such as Title VII of the Civil Rights Act and those mentioned above, have made a safer and fairer workplace for Americans, but the net effect on the employer is more litigation and exposure. People know it, too. In Los Angeles County alone, over 3,000 civil lawsuits are filed each day. Only a mere fraction of these are employment-related, of course; however, the fact remains that Americans like to sue. Most disturbing is that the trend shows no sign of reversing.

2.5.4 Expanded Rights and Protections of Employees

Some, like Philip Howard in his compelling 1994 best seller, *The Death of Common Sense* (Random House), have argued that, to a certain degree, the expansion of rights is a zero sum game. That is, as the rights of one group expand, the rights of another contract. Zero sum theory applies well to aspects of economics, but as we look at the ever-expansion of worker rights it seems to apply perfectly. Legislation, such as Title VII, ADA, FMLA, and, more recently, the Health Insurance Portability and Accountability Act (HIPAA), has certainly provided much good. Few can argue against improving workplace safety or improving the treatment of employees. However, the cost has been the erosion of employer prerogatives and an exponential increase in compliance costs. It is estimated that HIPAA alone will cost employers over $45 billion. The trend has eroded employer doctrines, such as "at-will employment," to the point of meaninglessness. Few employers can terminate at will, no less hire whom they wish without contemplating the litigation potential of perceived inequality or unfairness. We have created a mess.

Sadly, even the employees don't win. Increased employer costs translate into fewer resources for research and development, fewer process and technology improvements, less profit, fewer investments, and ultimately the creation of fewer jobs. It's a sad and pathetic cycle. Even the government loses. With less money in circulation and fewer people working, fewer taxes are collected. The net effect is a less competitive and weaker economy. No one wins when businesses are over-regulated.

2.6 Summary

From the standpoint of the fact finder and the investigative interviewer, there are significant differences between the public and private sector. Those differences include not only the mission of the respective sectors, but the tools available to them. Each of the tools offer their users advantages and disadvantages. What differentiates the public sector from the private sector most significantly is that the public sector is bound by Constitutional restrictions, whereas the private sector largely is not. This seemingly significant advantage is often offset by the rights of workers and the accompanying risk of litigation. To know and respect these differences separates exceptional investigative interviewers from those who are merely useful.

2.7 Frequently Asked Questions

1. Shouldn't an employer want to know the motive before deciding to discipline an employee?

   In the strict sense, no; from a practical perspective, yes. In the first instance, excluding any extenuating or mitigating circumstances, an employer does not need to know or consider motive in order to impose discipline. However from a practical perspective, an employer might want to know motive in order to devise safeguards to prevent the problem from reoccurring.

2. My organization has a practice of providing interviewees a written disclosure that they can either have a union representative or lawyer advise them before they have to agree to participate. Is this a good practice?

   No, nor is it lawfully required. Unless contractually required, such notifications are not necessary. Moreover, did the employee who committed the offense in question tell the organization it should seek the advice of counsel and review its options before he committed the offense? Experience also shows that employees use such offers to delay and obfuscate their employer's investigative process and provide little benefit against frivolous claims by those whose discipline arises from that process.

3. If the word *interrogation* carries such a negative connotation, why do so many fact finders and employers still us it?

Good question. I suppose lack of experience and carelessness are the primary reasons the word remains in the lexicon of many fact finders. To the uninitiated, it sounds professional, even a little important. However, in reality, it only invites trouble. In litigation against my firm many years ago, one of the "facts" offered by the plaintiff was that she was "mercilessly interrogated in a frigid windowless room for more than hour without food, water, or the advice of counsel." If you like that sort of allegation on your résumé, continue to use the term interrogation—in time, someone will add it for you.

Endnotes

1. The statutes and rules that regulate the conduct of grand juries (or their equivalent) vary from state to state. My purpose here is only to demonstrate the power this tool affords the government and the lack of anything equivalent in the private sector.
2. For example, California Penal Code §§153 and 519 make it a crime to threaten criminal action to bargain or obtain the settlement of a civil matter.
3. *Miranda v. Arizona*, 384 U.S. 436 (1966).
4. The author acknowledges the current state of law with regard to when and precisely under what circumstances *Miranda* is required is in flux. As such, this brief treatment is offered for illustrative purposes only and should not be construed as a strict interpretation of the law.
5. There are some exceptions and among them are circumstances involving an employee who is a member of a collective bargaining agreement. See *NLRB v. J. Weingarten, Inc.*, 420 U.S. 251 (1975).
6. In *Cotran v. Rollins Hudig Hall International, Inc.*, 1998 Cal. LEXIS 1 (January 5, 1998), the California Supreme Court joined the majority of other jurisdictions in holding that good cause existed for terminating an employee for misconduct if an employer had a reasonable and good faith belief that the employee engaged in misconduct. It was ruled that the employer does not have to convince the court or jury that the employee in fact committed the misconduct, only that the employer honestly believed that the employee engaged in misconduct based upon substantial evidence obtained through an adequate investigation that included a fair opportunity for the employee to respond to the charges. The Court further defined the term *good cause* as a "reasoned conclusion … supported by substantial evidence gathered through an adequate investigation that includes notice of the claimed misconduct *and a chance for the employee to respond.*" So, while the employees of employers in the private sector do not enjoy constitutionally protected due process rights, the California Supreme Court holds that an accused employee indeed has the right to respond.
7. James C. Collins, *Built to Last* (New York: Harper Business, 2002).
8. Mahan Khalsa, *Let's Get Real* (Salt Lake City, UT: Franklin Quest Co., 1999).
9. Michael Lewis, *The New New Thing* (New York: Penguin USA, 2001).
10. Thomas J. Stanley, *The Millionaire Next Door* (New York: Simon & Schuster, 1999).

11. M. Scott Peck, *The Road Less Traveled* (Carmichael, CA: Touchstone Books, 1998).
12. U.S. House of Representatives Committee on Economic and Educational Opportunities, *Hearing: Conflicts and Inconsistencies in Workplace Regulations*, Washington, D.C., 1995.
13. Scott Thurm, *The Wall Street Journal*, June 11, 2013.
14. Philip K. Howard, *The Death of Common Sense* (New York: Random House, 1994), 12.

Chapter 3

The Fundamentals of Interviewing

Key learning points:

1. Investigative interviewing is a method of investigation. It is typically the cornerstone of the fourth phase of investigation: verification and analysis.
2. The skill of the interviewer should be matched to the type and nature of the project to be undertaken.
3. The fact finder must be impartial and not allow his or her loyalty and self-interests to interfere with the fact finding process or the interviews he conducts.
4. Treat all of your subjects with respect and dignity.
5. Structure your document management process such that it allows your work product to be easily filed and retrieved. Exercising discipline during the early phases of the project can save time and frustration later.
6. Evidence is any type of proof that, when presented, is materially capable of proving or disproving a contention or fact.
7. Spoliation is the intentional or negligent destruction of evidence and constitutes an obstruction of justice. Those who are found guilty of it may be sanctioned.
8. Under the doctrine of the *work product privilege*, all that the fact finder does and produces can be deemed privileged and withheld during discovery. It is a tool that every investigative interviewer should be aware of and use.

"The temptation to lie when questioned is inversely proportional to the professionalism of the one asking the questions."

E. F. Ferraro

3.1 The Role of the Investigative Interviewer

It would not be surprising if the casual reader was slightly confused thus far. Such a reader might wonder if investigative interviewing is a method of investigation or the culmination of an investigation? Succinctly, investigative interviewing is a method of investigation. It is typically the cornerstone of the fourth phase of investigation: *verification and analysis*. Its outcome and success depend on the third phase: *information gathering*. However, it too is an information-gathering tool. It enables the fact finder to verify the findings of the information-gathering effort, which preceded it and assists in the analysis of it. As an investigative method, it is distinctly:

- logistically simple
- interactive
- produces results that are of high evidentiary and corroborative value
- offers some element of due process

Properly conducted investigative interviews also allow the fact finder to obtain the subject's explanation of what took place and why. It also offers him the opportunity to provide any extenuating or mitigating circumstances that may be relevant. If others were involved, the investigative interview also might yield their identity and shed light on motive and intent. Most importantly, the investigative interviews that follow the fact finding should yield admissions of guilt. Singularly, it is the responsibility of the fact finder to identify who should be interviewed and why.[1] He should also decide when and where those interviews take place as well as contemplate all reasonable contingencies. It is not uncommon that the fact finder finds himself investing as much effort into the planning of his interviews as he does his fact finding. However, before we go there, let's first examine the qualities of a professional investigative interviewer.

3.2 Qualities of a Professional Investigative Interviewer

No discussion regarding the qualities of the professional investigative interviewer would be complete without first defining him. The investigative interviewer is a central and critical figure in the fact finding process. Of the assorted members of the investigative team, the investigative interviewer in many regards defines the outcome of the investigation. In less complex investigations, the investigative interviewer may single-handedly fulfill the role of fact finder, counselor, and even decision maker. In small organizations, it is not uncommon for a member of the Human Resources Department to make the decision to undertake an investigation, perform the investigation (including conducting the investigative interviews), and ultimately decide disciplinary and corrective action when appropriate. Although, this is not advised even in the simplest investigations, circumstances sometimes dictate that the *investigative team* be comprised of a single individual. Optimally, the investigative interviewer is one of many individuals who, working together toward common objectives, comprise the team that ultimately drives the investigation from start to successful conclusion.

3.2.1 Skill

The first characteristic the investigative interviewer should have is skill. The skill of the interviewer should be matched to the type and nature of the project to be undertaken. This individual should have the requisite skill necessary to achieve the desired objectives. For example, an interviewer possessing only the training and skills associated with the investigation of sexual harassment would likely be unsuited to undertake the interview of those involved in a complex fraud. Conversely, someone with the training and skills associated with only complex frauds or financial crimes would be equally unsuited to interview those involved in workplace substance abuse. There is, of course, a crossover of skills, and many qualified interviewers may have the skills necessary to conduct all sorts of investigative interviews. Regardless, the outcome of the project will be largely driven by the skill of those involved and their ability to bring to bear that skill and all prior training in an orderly and effective fashion. Just as one would not ask an ophthalmologist to perform heart surgery, one should not expect any particular interviewer to perform every type of interview skillfully. Instead when possible (practicable, if you may), it is best that the skill of the interviewer be matched to the type of investigation to be undertaken.

> *Tip: For best results, whenever possible match the skill of the interviewer to the type of matter in question.*

However, the old maxim, *nothing is as it first appears,* reminds us that even with the best planning there are always surprises. Because few interviewers are skilled in all types of matters, they must be sufficiently flexible in order to deal with those surprises. For those situations, process and experience are one's best allies.

3.2.2 Experience

Some argue that experience trumps skill. However, I believe experience is an integral component of skill. It is experience that allows the properly trained and skilled interviewer to overcome unusual and oftentimes unexpected circumstances that invariably arise during an interview. Here is a good example. As a project lead, I often pinch hit as one of my team's investigative interviewers. In that role, I act as a backup to the core interviewers selected for the project. In one particularly memorable case, I chose to interview the ring leader of a small but very destructive theft ring that had burrowed deep into my client's organization. He was a prominent member of the East Los Angeles street gang White Fence. White Fence was one of L.A.'s oldest and most notorious street gangs with a history that spanned nearly a century. After my introduction and having described to him our methods of investigation, he abruptly said, "I did it; I killed her." Remorsefully, he dropped his head and added, "I am sorry." Mind you, I was interviewing him because of another matter; he thought I was there to discuss something far more serious. I quickly gathered my thoughts and asked for a few details. He told he had stabbed his girlfriend to death in the presence of her father and that the crime had haunted him since. He said he knew the day would come when he would have to take responsibility for the awful things he had done and thought this day was it. I quickly excused myself and ran to my client's office down the hall and shared what I had just learned. Together we called the Los Angeles Police Department (LAPD) and revealed what had happened. The police quickly arrived, questioned the man, and took him into custody. I never saw him again. With his assistance, he was eventually connected to the crime, tried, and found guilty of murder.

Tip: Expect the unexpected and plan for it.

I believe that good judgment comes from experience, and experience comes from bad judgment. However, the experience must be of the proper type. Like skill, experience in sexual harassment investigations may not translate well in complex fraud investigations. Oftentimes, organizations hire individuals with law enforcement experience to run their security or loss prevention functions. Though on its face this seems to make perfect sense, confusing the *experience* of one responsible for the enforcement of public law with that of the needs in the private sector is a serious mistake. Contrary to popular belief, the sad fact of the matter is that there is very little experience crossover between public law enforcement and private sector asset protection and loss prevention. Yet, this mistake is made every day. A whole host of organizations, large and small, intentionally seek out and hire those with prior law enforcement experience for corporate security positions. It is my opinion that the skill and experience of most law enforcement professionals does not match that needed by the private sector. Similarly, human resource professionals are often asked to perform investigative tasks and interviews of which they have no experience, either.

Tip: Whenever possible, use experienced interviewers. Match both the skill and the experience of the individual selected to the specifics of the matter of which he or she will be asking questions. And, remember, having done something many times does not equate to the ability of doing it well.

3.2.3 Impartiality

Impartiality is the innate ability to separate one's self and self-interests from the investigation and its outcome. It is not a common trait, nor is it human nature. Because the human spirit is possessive by nature, we tend to take ownership (and pride) in the things we do. The greater the investment of time and resources, the greater that sense of ownership becomes. Investigators and interviewers are no different. The professional fact finder must divest herself from any interest in the outcome of her investigation or interview. This is not to say one may not be interested in the outcome or take pride in her work. No, the fact finder must instead be impartial and not allow her loyalty and self-interests to interfere with the fact finding process or the interviews she conducts. This unique characteristic is the trademark of a true professional.

There are two effective ways the professional can demonstrate her impartiality. The first is to not decide the investigation's objectives. By removing oneself from deciding objectives, it is reasonable to conclude that the fact finder has little investment in the outcome. By not deciding the objectives of the investigation, the fact finder and interviewer have no vested interest in the effort's results. She risks no investment of pride and has no agenda to prosecute.

The second way the professional can demonstrate her impartiality is by excluding herself from any decision-making process at the conclusion of the investigation. By not being party to the decisions regarding discipline or corrective action, the professional has no say in the outcome. The individual has isolated herself to the solitary role of fact finder and interviewer. Arguably, she is neither judge, jury, nor prosecutor. And without interest in the investigation's objectives or its outcome, it is nearly impossible to accuse her of any bias or prejudice. To claim that she has any partiality is illogical and offends the evidence to the contrary.

3.2.4 Ethical

As my organization's chief ethics officer, this is a subject dear to my heart. It would be fair to argue that impartiality is an ethical characteristic. However, my use of *ethical* in the context of describing the necessary characteristics of the professional investigative interviewer is far more expansive. The American Heritage Dictionary* defines ethical as:

eth–i–cal (ĕth'ĭ-kel) *adj.*
Of or dealing with ethics
Being in accordance with the accepted principles that govern the conduct of a
 group, esp. a profession[2]

As the definition suggests, ethics is a collection of "accepted principles that govern" a particular group or profession. In this case, the operative term is *profession*.

In order to be professional, the interviewer must adhere to an assortment of guiding principles any reasonable person or trier of fact would embrace as proper. Actions, such as truthfulness, honesty, and impartiality, collectively constitute ethical behavior. To be ethical requires the fact finder to behave in such a fashion as to protect the rights of those under investigation, obey the law, and to protect the integrality of the process. The preamble for Private Investigators' Association of British Columbia's Code of Ethics and Professional Conduct elegantly captures this essence with the following:

> Private Investigators have an important role to play in society. In performance of that role, *the investigator's actions have an effect on the welfare of other people*. Because of their social responsibilities, members of a profession are obligated to act in the interest of these other parties, who have a stake in the nature and quality of professional activities. These stakeholders include employers, clients, various identifiable third parties, and the public at large.[3]

To put it another way, ethics for our purposes are the rules of conduct by which members of a profession or group regulate their behavior among themselves and with all other persons with whom they deal.

For example, if the fact finder uncovers exculpatory evidence, exonerating his subject, he brings it forth and reveals it. If the fact finder hasn't the evidence to accuse his subject, he does not conduct an accusatory interview of that subject. If the fact finder knows the employer is likely to discharge an offender who makes an admission, the fact finder does not tell the subject an admission will cleanse his soul, and that his job will be protected if only he makes a "confession."

In this sense, ethics provide us guardrails within which we conduct ourselves, business, and interaction with others. Though many deny it, ethics also provides the construct on which all laws and freedoms are based. A quick look at the U.S. Bill of Rights affirms this assertion, as illustrated in Figure 3.1.

Tip: Treat all of your subjects with respect and dignity. Remember: A reputation of being ethical takes years to develop and moments to destroy.

Professional ethical behavior in this sense is not something we simply possess, it is something we must live. It is something that requires work and constant attention. Even then, the effort to be ethical can pose challenges. For those occasions, I have fashioned for myself this simple ethics test:

- Is it legal?
- Is it fair?

A summary of each right as provided by the U.S. Bill of Rights when adopted in 1791	
I.	Freedom of religion, speech, press, assembly and petition
II.	Right to keep and bear arms
III.	No quartering of soldiers in time of peace
IV.	No unreasonable search and seizure
V.	No unlawful imprisonment; double jeopardy, self-incrimination; taking of private property without just compensation
VI.	Speedy trial, opportunity to confront witnesses
VII.	Trial by jury
VIII.	No excessive bail, no cruel or unusual punishment
IX.	Preservation of states' rights, residual rights to the people
X.	Federal reservation of rights, residual rights to the state or people

Figure 3.1 A summary of each right as provided by the U.S. Bill of Rights when adopted in 1791.

- Is it balanced?
- Is it necessary?
- Is it consistent with our organizational values?

I adopted this test from something I heard discussed at a Rotary International meeting. The members (they called themselves Rotarians) shared with me what they were discussing, something they call The Four-Way Test. According to Rotary International's website (https://www.rotary.org/en/guiding-principles), "The Four-Way Test is a nonpartisan and nonsectarian ethical guide for Rotarians to use for their personal and professional relationships. The test has been translated into more than 100 languages, and Rotarians recite it at club meetings." It goes like this:

Of the things we think, say, or do

1. Is it the TRUTH?
2. Is it FAIR to all concerned?
3. Will it build GOODWILL and BETTER FRIENDSHIPS?
4. Will it be BENEFICIAL to all concerned?

Quaint, but powerful. I was so moved by it I created my own ethics test. Since the creation of my simple little test, it has helped me successfully confront dozens of ethical dilemmas and has yet to fail me or my customers. Here is one example. The matter began with an anonymous tip from a concerned employee. The employee, using his employer's anonymous incident-reporting mechanism (in this case, a toll-free hotline) reported that a small group of co-workers had been co-opted by a foreman and were regularly assisting him divert material from a large jobsite to a relative's home. The concerned individual (CI) also reported that the thieves frequently drank on the job and that on more than one occasion the foreman had nearly wrecked a company vehicle while driving when impaired. The report was quickly passed up the chain of command and soon was on the desk of the CEO. He immediately called my office and requested advice. As the reader might imagine, I suggested that some fact finding was in order. Work orders, timecards, and inventories needed to be examined. First order of business when allegations of this sort are received is to somehow substantiate them. I outlined for the CEO an appropriate plan and he instructed me to coordinate the effort through his director of human resources, a woman with whom I had worked previously. In a short time, together we were able to corroborate some of the allegations and uncover additional irregularities. We quickly packaged the result and recommended that my team interview the suspected transgressors. The CEO balked, however. Concluding that his human resources director better knew the personalities involved and his organization's processes, he directed her to conduct the interviews. Experienced as she was with routine internal investigations, she had never confronted or interviewed anyone suspected of such serious offenses. Reluctantly, she proceeded and resultantly failed miserably. Not a single individual made an admission. Instead, to a person, each accused her and the organization of a witch hunt. Inexperienced in conducting difficult investigatory interviews, she visibly demonstrated her uneasiness and lack of confidence. She was unable to overcome the most meager of denials, and quickly found herself and her employer defending the investigation and all of the evidence it had produced in court. I was ultimately designated as a witness. In preparation for my testimony, the attorney representing my client asked me to testify that I thought the human resources director had the experience and skill necessary to conduct the investigative interviews she had undertaken and that her efforts had met industry standards. It is not hard to see the value of such testimony. However, applying my ethics test, I respectfully declined the request. Instead I offered to tell the truth and testify (I paraphrase) that she was an experienced and highly qualified HR professional, but her effort was less than that of current industry standards. However, because she was not a professional *investigative interviewer,* she ought not to be held to the standard of one. As such, the outcome of the investigation should not be judged on her conduct or result, but on the result of the underlying investigation that had been performed. The matter was soon settled for a small sum and, in exchange for the settlement, the employees involved in the theft agreed to resign.

This example demonstrates that professional ethics is not just the words that comprise an organization's code of ethics but the way the organization behaves. Thrusting a little deeper, ethical behavior is a component of an organization's broader

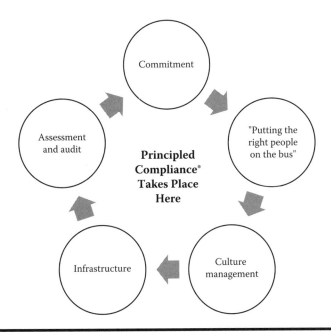

Figure 3.2 Sustaining Principled Compliance™ is a process and involves constant effort on the part of an organization and its members.

goal of something I call *Principled Compliance.™* The state or condition of principled compliance is achieved by properly aligning an organization's culture with effective governance. That governance includes its policies, procedures, practices, and codes, which regulate and prescribe the behaviors of those comprising that culture. To perpetuate principled compliance, the organization and its members must work at it. Figure 3.2 illustrates the relationship of the elements involved in that effort.

Because the examination of ethics and ethical behavior is not the purpose of this book, I will end this discussion here. For more information on the topic of organizational ethics and ethics management visit The Open Compliance and Ethics Group website (OCEG.org). OCEG is a global nonprofit think tank and community. Its mission is to help organizations achieve higher performance by integrating governance, assurance, and management of performance, risk, compliance, and ethics.

3.2.5 Fair

Fairness like beauty is in the eye of the beholder. In workplace investigations, the beholder may be your boss, the director of human resources, the CEO, or a judge. In order to be effective, the fact finder must be fair. But fairness takes many forms. To be honest and ethical, in fact, may be fair, but to be fair to the individuals one investigates is paramount and a trait of a true professional.

Fairness is being truthful to the one we are interviewing. When he asks what evidence we may have against him, it is telling him the truth. It is not embellishing the quantity or quality of that evidence. It is not telling him the evidence is irrefutable when we know it is not. It is not telling him he may not leave when, in fact, he has the right to do so. It is not telling him everyone knows he is guilty and it is only you that thinks so. Being fair is being honest. It is being professional in our actions and with our words. Being fair results in the ability to look oneself in the mirror and not be ashamed of what we see. It is not being ashamed of ourselves, our actions, or our organization. Here is a short list of interviewer behaviors that are typically considered unfair (unlawful in some instances):

- Mistreating the interviewee and inflicting psychological damage
- Making threats
- Making illegal promises
- Using coercion
- Using duress
- Using force or the threat of force
- Employing ruthless or intimidating methods
- Falsely imprisoning the interviewee or holding him against his will
- Failing to treat the interviewee with dignity and respect

3.2.6 Deliberate

Lastly, the fact finder must be deliberate. His actions must be purposeful. He must not prosecute some personal agenda or grievance. The fact finder must act with reason and reason his actions. The fact finder that is deliberate is decisive. He works his plan, and plans his work. His process has purpose and meaning. Each action has a method and function. All actions have meaning and are engineered to fulfill a reasonable and lawful end.

The professional fact finder does not waste time and resources. If his plan is flawed, he confronts and corrects its defects. He rectifies his shortcomings and is always conscious of his objectives. Everything he does is a means toward a fair, honest, and ethical conclusion.

The literature is replete with lists of qualifications good interviewers should possess. While I think the examination above is complete, I would be remiss to not share with you some of the other qualifications my colleagues consider important. In no particular order, list includes:

Observant	Dedicated
Resourceful	Self-starter
Patient	Skeptical
People oriented	Intuitive
Understanding	Energetic

Effective communicator	Intelligent
Receptive	Consistently uses good judgment
Professional	Honest

The list could be expanded, but I suspect you get the idea. So, in the interest of time, let's move to another fundamental aspect of investigative interviewing, that of organizing one's self and the information in our possession or about to come into our possession.

3.3 Evidence Collection and Management

By definition, all fact finders engage in the collection of information. In Chapter 1, we learned that one of the essential elements of a successful investigation is the crafting of meaningful objectives. The objectives of the investigation will drive what facts and evidence are to be gathered. For example, if one of the objectives of the investigation is to determine who was responsible for the disappearance of $1,000 from the office safe, we might start by creating a list of the facts and evidence necessary to meet that objective. Effectively, we can create an *investigative task list*. In no particular order, here is a partial list:

- Determine who had access to the office that contained the safe
- Determine who had access to the safe
- Determine who discovered the loss and when
- Determine who had put the $1,000 into the safe
- Determine who had last seen the $1,000
- Confirm that the $1,000 was actually put into the safe
- Determine the source of the $1,000 and why it was stored in the safe
- Determine cash handling and security procedures
- Determine cash audit procedures and responsibility
- Determine if the procedures were followed (if not, who violated them and why)
- Determine who knew the $1,000 was in the safe
- Determine if those who knew of the $1,000 shared that information with anyone else
- Determine if other similar losses had ever occurred and, if so, obtain the details

This is not an exhaustive list. But, as you can see, the simple exercise of listing tasks and identifying the various pieces of information needed to understand the circumstances surrounding this hypothetical loss has significantly focused our effort. Additionally, if we were able to obtain this information, we would substantially reduce the size of the suspect pool, if not identify the perpetrator. Other pieces of the puzzle also fall into place as well. For example, we may discover process failures, or the lack of adequate controls—information that might be critical to formulating a prevention strategy for the future. In situations in which the subject matter or circumstances are far more complex, the process can be modified where we create subtasks to some of the action items on our task list. Experienced fact finders will find that over a period of time workplace investigations of a similar type take on similar themes. By tracking these recurring themes, the fact finder will eventually create for himself a portfolio of forms, checklists, action items, and processes for each of the assorted investigation types he has conducted.

You probably also realized this list includes many of the questions the interviewer will pose during his interviews, whether administrative or investigatory. Thus, without leaving his desk and with nothing more than what may constitute a simple allegation, the fact finder has already begun determining what is known and unknown about the matter in question. The list also reveals some of the responsibilities of the stakeholders and process owners he will wish to interview. By prioritizing the list and ordering the questions such that the answer of one leads to the next, he has also begun to formulate the line of questioning and fact finding he will employ during his interviews.

3.3.1 Documentation

The fact finder must next document and catalog that which she intends to gather. In some orderly and easy-to-use fashion, she must organize, tag, label, and store the evidence she collects. Concurrently, she must document her efforts, those of her team members (should she be directing the effort of others), and begin thinking about the preparation and form of her final report. In the case of simple matters, this effort is rather straightforward and almost intuitive. However, complex matters require a great deal more organization. I for one have handled matters involving tens of thousands of documents and scores of evidentiary tidbits. Absent a structured process and high degree of organization, the production of a 1,500+-page report would not be possible.

3.3.1.1 Organizing Oneself and Materials

Should the matter under investigation be sufficiently complicated, begin with a three-ring binder. In it place all notes and collateral documents. The items should be placed in the binder in the order in which they are created or developed. Preliminarily Post-it® notes can be used as temporary tabs. Later, as the investigation begins to take shape, tabbed separators can be inserted to help segregate and organize the information. A separate evidence folder or something similar should be used to store all original documents. Only copies should go into the binder. Eventually, additional binders can be created if necessary. Document storage boxes can then be labeled and used to store the binders, evidence folders, and anything else of importance. Evidence labels, rubber stamps, Bates Stamp (a sequential numbering device), and bar code labels can all be used to mark, identify, and further organize the materials.

Many fact finders create a diary or journal detailing their day-to-day efforts. Thus, *journal entries* are made for each activity or event that occurs over the life of the investigation. Incorporating the date and time these activities and events occurred or were accomplished creates a detailed record for future reference. The journal in this sense permits one to figuratively reconstruct the investigation should it be necessary. Most experienced fact finders keep such a record.

3.3.1.2 Using Technology

Using standard office applications, such as word processors and spreadsheets, the fact finder can electronically organize his information and thoughts. The fact finder can create files, folders, and databases to create and organize task lists, records, documents, and reports. Products, such as CaseMap* and TimeMap*, can further help the fact finder organize himself and his investigation. Both of these powerful software applications are available from CaseSoft (www.casesoft.com), now owned by LexisNexis*, one of the nation's largest and most respected providers of litigation support. Though designed for the legal profession, CaseMap can be equally useful to the fact finder managing large investigations. The software allows the user to organize and explore facts, the cast of characters, the issues, and all of the legal aspects of the case. It provides the fact finder the ability to electronically perform link analysis and pull together a cogent expression of his findings. TimeMap is an enhancement that allows the user to create chronology visuals. Because it plugs into CaseMap, the combination of the two makes a powerful investigative tool capable of handling the most complicated of cases. Both of these products are now hosted applications on a Microsoft* SQL Server* platform for centralized and secure remote access to one's data and case files, enabling speedy access to every authorized user within the wide area network.

My firm, Convercent, Inc., also offers a cloud-based case management solution. Over 35,000 customer locations in 150 countries currently use it. You can learn more about it by going to Convercent.com. Figure 3.3 is a screen shot from our case management portal.

Solutions like that of Convercent should at a minimum provide users with:

- web-based access allowing real-time access from anywhere, anytime
- alerts providing notification of overdue tasks and progress updates
- centralized capture of all case details in a secured central repository
- robust task management features
- dashboards that provide real-time information regarding trends, performance, and all relevant investigative activities
- ad-hoc reporting capabilities enabling customized professional looking reports

Figure 3.3   Convergent case management portal.

Another less sophisticated, but useful tool is a product called The Case File. The Case File is a collection of fact finder tools including investigative forms, checklists, and report templates. The product includes an actual sample case file and a CD on which are all of the forms, checklists, and templates in MS Word® and Rich Text Format (.rtf). The documents are professionally formatted and neatly organized. Because they are electronic, they can be easily manipulated and customized. The user license allows unlimited use and duplication of the documents. Both novice and experienced investigators will find The Case File an invaluable tool. It is available from InfoQuest Investigators at www.thecasefile.com. Figure 3.4 summarizes some of the contents of my version of The Case File.

It is easy to see that The Case File contains many useful items. The real value, however, is that, if used properly, it is able to provide enterprise-wide case file and project management standardization. The standardization facilitates easier file review, easy case file sharing or reassignment, and, when used in its electronic form, it permits electronic entry of data and notes.

Because large or complex projects tend to generate a large number of documents, naming one's electronic files also deserves some consideration. The system used may vary depending upon the type of documents being named. For example, the Correspondence folder might contain letters, memorandums, and faxes. Hypothetically, the documents in a multifile folder might be named as follows:

Fredrickson, Robert Letter 01.doc
Fredrickson, Robert Letter 02.doc
Fredrickson, Robert Letter 03.doc
Fredrickson, Robert fax 01.doc
Fredrickson, Robert memo 01.doc
Fredrickson, Robert memo 02.doc
Gross, David Letter 01.doc
Gross, David fax 01.doc
Gross, David memo 01.doc
Gross, David memo 02.doc

This method uses the recipient's name (last name first) as the primary identifier, followed by the type of document, followed by a number representing the sequential order in which the documents were created.

> *Tip: Impose organization and structure on your electronic file folder and file system before you begin your fact finding. Structure your document management process such that it allows your work product to be easily filed and retrieved. Exercising discipline during the early phases of the project can save time and frustration later.*

The necessity of a physical (paper) case file is a matter of opinion. I happen to prefer its use. Others seem to think it is not only unnecessary, but wasteful as well. Because so many of my firm's cases involve matters in litigation or those likely to be involved in litigation, discovery issues are a consideration. An organized case file with all of its contents neatly tabbed and organized under colored covers has eye appeal. It also suggests professionalism and a high degree of sophistication. These

Section/Forms	Notes and Instructions
"Case/Subject"	
Contract of Retainer	This is included since this same file is used as a complete package by private investigators. You may modify this to be a contract you use for outside investigators, or just remove it from your folder.
Subject Data File Table of Contents	Shows category and line number of the main "Subject Data File" and allows you to show which areas of information are provided, needed, and completed.
Subject Data File	A 35-page fill-in-the-blank dossier on the subject of your investigation.
Addendum Sheet	The "Subject Data File" is line numbered. Use the addendum for overflow information or for annotation.
Table of Contents	Shows layout and organization of the Investigative File.
"Theory"	
This section is grouped in the first section with your subject and case. As you start the case with what you already know, you use the "Theory" section to list what you need to know.	
The To-Do List	General list to list necessary activity. Check its completion, and delegate.
Case Activity Gameplan I	A comprehensive checklist of sources to be used in gathering info.
Case Activity Gameplan II	A "to do" list organized by activity rather than source.
Quick-Scan Contact Log	Make a list of people you will talk with on a regular basis or use to match people, phone numbers, e-mail etc. with each other.
Other Contacts – Client	People associated with your client that the investigator may or should contact.
Other Contacts – Subject	People associated with the subject that are friendly to the investigation. OR, people such as the subject's attorney.
Time Line	Use to develop time relationships of factors leading up to an incident, or comparisons of witness testimonies, etc.

Figure 3.4 Case file contents.

impressions are useful to my clients if our files are ever produced in discovery. Your situation might be quite different and, as such, you might decide physical files are entirely unnecessary.

Although all of these aspects of management systems need to be contemplated and decided, case file retention deserves special attention. How long one should retain case files is debatable. Federal law regulates record retention in a variety of areas. For example, aspects of the Occupational Safety & Health Act (OSHA) require some records to be kept the length of the employee's tenure plus *30 years*, and records pertaining to the Employee Polygraph Protection Act, such as why a test was administered and its corresponding results, must be retained only three years. Statutory record keeping under Title VII of the Civil Rights Act of 1964 is less straightforward. The Equal Employment and Opportunities Commission (EEOC), which is responsible for enforcement of Title VII does not require that any record be created, but once created, rules require the record be retained for one year from the date personnel action was taken. In the event a formal charge or lawsuit is filed, all relevant records must be kept until "final disposition." The confusing and often conflicting array of state and federal requirements makes record retention policies complicated and burdensome. Compliance and enforcement of such policies is even more burdensome. As such, many employers keep everything forever. I, for one, think something a little more reasonable is in order.

A nonscientific survey of licensed investigators that specialize in workplace investigations that I recently conducted revealed that most intend to retain their files for somewhere between seven years and indefinitely. Those that stated that they periodically purge their files said they do so only when they thought of it. Only a few of the professional investigators I surveyed said they have systematic record destruction procedures. Fewer still could explain what those procedures were.

My suggestion is to retain case files not less than seven years. Absent a clearly defined policy, in most instances, after seven years, case files tend to be misplaced, lost, or accidentally disposed of in the normal course of business. When someone leaves or changes position, it is very rare they are asked to surrender investigative case files and materials pertaining to past investigations. Usually the stuff just gets misplaced or thrown away. Establishing a policy requiring indefinite retention creates an unnecessary administrative burden and potential liability for the organization. With such policies in place, the organization that cannot produce a file when needed can be accused of a cover-up or worse. Conversely, the systematic destruction of files also can raise questions. However, a reasonable policy that is consistently applied is tough to attack and usually can be defended.

Tip: Case file retention practices deserve thorough consideration before implementation. Retention of case files for seven years from the date of closure is considered the minimum.

3.3.2 Evidence Collection and Preservation

Of equal importance to case file documentation and organization is evidence management, a topic of which entire books have been written. Because evidence is available in so many forms, it is not practical to examine the topic in its entirety here, nor do I intend to do so. However, the subject should be discussed briefly.

3.3.2.1 Definition of Evidence

Evidence is any type of proof that, when presented, is materially capable of proving or disproving a contention or fact.[4] In order to be used or be admissible, the evidence must be:

- competent
- relevant
- material

The competence of the evidence speaks to its credibility and its relevance speaks to its pertinence. That is, one must be able to rely on evidence with some level of certainty and it must pertain to the issue in question. In this sense, materiality speaks to the state or quality of the evidence. Direct evidence is that means of proof that tends to show the existence of a fact without the intervention of proof of any other fact, and is distinguished from circumstantial evidence, which is often called *indirect* evidence.[5] Circumstantial evidence is evidence that is inferential by establishing a condition or premise from which the existence of the principal fact may be concluded by reasoning. By nature, all presumptive evidence is circumstantial. However, all circumstantial evidence is not presumptive, as it leads to necessary conclusions instead of probable ones.

3.3.2.2 Hearsay Evidence

Hearsay evidence is evidence not proceeding from the personal knowledge of the witness, but from the mere repetition of what the witness has heard others say. When the source that had allegedly been heard is not available to testify, hearsay evidence typically is not admissible. One exception is when the defendant's conduct is at issue or is relevant; statements made in his presence by which his conduct can be inferred are admissible when the defendant makes no denial.[6] By their very nature, most statements and declarations (statements taken under oath) are hearsay when the author is unavailable to authenticate the document. Such documents are *double-hearsay* if they include reference to statements made by the accused. However, statements and declarations that include an admission made by the accused (assuming they were properly attained) constitute the highest quality of evidence available in workplace investigations.

Trap: Many fact finders' self-imposed rules of evidence are exceedingly strict. Thus, excluded is evidence that otherwise would be admissible in the typical workplace investigation. Lowering the standard of proof eases the rules of evidence and permits the use of evidence otherwise not possible.

3.3.2.3 Admissibility and Materiality

In many regards, the admissibility, and often the materiality, of evidence are tied directly to the standard of proof. For example, in unemployment insurance benefit eligibility hearings, sometimes called UI hearings, nearly all forms of evidence are admissible. Administrative law judges hearing these cases will usually allow the introduction of any and all evidence. And, in my experience, even evidence of questionable origin (i.e. fabricated). Procedure requires such evidence to be *weighted* (not weighed) and accorded the consideration it deserves. All this makes for rather loose proceedings. However, that is the intent. Because representation is optional in these venues, the rules are relaxed in order to ensure fairness to those who do not have representation. Most arbitration hearings are similar. It is usually the arbitrator that establishes the "rules of evidence" and determines what is admissible and what is not. As such, the outcomes of arbitrations are highly unpredictable. The following is a fine example.

Sometime ago, one of my undercover drug investigations resulted in the termination of over 30 employees. All but one of the employees was a member of a collective bargaining agreement and entitled to grieve their discipline. The grievances ultimately resulted in arbitration. The arbitrator, well known for the liberal application of his authority, allowed the admission of all forms of evidence and claims. Although all of the grievants had provided written admissions during the investigation detailing their transgressions, he allowed them to recant or alter them substantially during the hearing. He allowed the argument that the admissions that were obtained without a union representative present were coerced. He ignored the fact that many of the admissions were corroborative to one another and that several of the grievants admitted that, even had a union representative been present, their statements to our investigative interviewers would not have been substantially different. He also allowed the union to raise the issue of discrimination. Although a full two thirds of the workforce were minorities, less than a third of the grievants were. To cap it off, he allowed several of the grievants to introduce statements written by them asserting their own innocence, which they had penned after the fact. The final travesty of justice was served when the arbitrator rendered his decision and ordered of all of the grievants be returned to work.

The rules of civil and criminal procedure do not allow for such injustices. Both in civil and criminal court, the rules of evidence are codified and, for the most part, adhered to. Uniquely, workplace investigations are subject to the rules of evidence imposed by the employer. Short of legal challenge, the employee enjoys the prerogative of deciding both the standard of proof and the rules of evidence in deciding workplace issues. The challenge is to balance the need for fairness and maintaining workplace order. The employer's decisions regarding discipline must be lawful, fair, impartial, and consistent.

3.3.2.4 Spoliation of Evidence

Spoliation is the intentional or negligent destruction of evidence and constitutes an obstruction of justice. Spoliation is also the destruction, or significant and meaningful alteration, of a document or instrument.[7] The rules of evidence impose an obligation to retain and produce evidence deemed admissible and relevant in criminal and civil matters. The intentional and sometimes even the unintentional destruction of evidence may be unlawful and/or civilly actionable—and for good reason. The destruction of evidence very often provides one party an advantage at the expense of another. Recent cases involving the employees, and, in some instances, the agents (outside accountants and auditors) of public companies intentionally destroying documents and critical records demonstrate the consequences. Litigation and criminal indictments of both the organization and the responsible parties are not uncommon. Worst yet, maybe, is the damage to the organization's reputation and the loss of public confidence in the markets. The destruction these acts can cause can be incalculable. Even the destruction of evidence during a simple workplace investigation can have grave consequences.

During the fact finding process, should items such as emails, notes, and apparently extraneous documents be discarded, claims of spoliation may later arise. In emotionally charged cases, such as those involving the claim of discrimination or sexual harassment, accusations about the destruction of evidence are common. Furthermore, they are difficult to disprove. The mere fact the alleged document (which may have never existed) cannot be produced inferentially suggests that it was destroyed. In most cases, only testimony can be used to prove the document didn't exist (think of one's personal notes and how one would prove they or portions of them didn't exist). If the credibility of the witnesses used to prove the document didn't exist is in question, the charge of spoliation has a good chance of gaining traction. If so, the credibility of these witnesses will suffer further damage.

> *Tip: In the course of your fact finding and investigative interviews, do not destroy anything that may later be considered evidence. The destruction of evidence is considered an obstruction of justice and may be a crime and/or civilly actionable. At the very least, it looks bad.*

3.3.2.5 Evidence Retention

For many of the reasons stated earlier in this chapter, evidence retention and preservation has become a popular topic. The mishandling and misplacing of evidence can be catastrophic. The fact finding process must contemplate this issue from the onset. Reconstruction of evidence is time consuming and expensive. It is best to handle it properly from the onset. The favored tool in workplace investigations to catalog and preserve evidence is the evidence file.

An evidence file may be nothing more than a manila folder in which evidentiary documents are placed for safekeeping. Accordion folders, corrugated boxes, file cabinets, or safes also may be used to store evidence. On the extreme end of the spectrum is the evidence locker or compound. Regardless of its form or construction, the purpose is the safe storage of evidence.

In addition to containing evidence, the evidence folder should contain a document used to identify and track the evidence within it. Variations of this form are largely a matter of preference. Figure 3.5 represents a typical evidence tracking form.

> *Trap: Even the routine and scheduled destruction of documents pursuant to an established document management program is not foolproof. Administrators should routinely conduct inspections to ensure compliance.*

3.3.2.6 Chain of Custody

The transfer of evidence from one party to another should be carefully documented. Each person who handles or takes control of evidence must be recorded, creating what is called the *chain of custody*. The chain of custody, sometimes called the *chain of evidence*, is a document that, at a minimum, identifies each custodian, when they received it, and to whom they transferred it. The chain of custody must not be broken. That is, there cannot be gaps during which the evidence was unaccounted for or out of the control of a custodian of record. A chain of custody that is broken exposes it to challenge and jeopardizes the admissibility of the evidence. Figure 3.6 is a sample evidence custody form.

The sloppy handling of evidence exposes both the fact finder and the evidence to credibility challenges. Claims of evidence tampering, alteration, or contamination are possible when evidence is mishandled. Fact finders should not handle or use originals during their investigation. Whenever possible, copies, photographs, or models should be used in lieu of the actual evidence. Never place an original piece of evidence in the hands of the subject. Knowing the value of the evidence and its implications, the subject may be tempted to not return it or to destroy it.

#	Date Received	Description	Quantity	Received From	Received By	Disposition
1	9-12-11	Hard drive # 74223415099-SH03	1	Jones, L.	Ferraro, E.	Retained
2	9-15-11	CD (marked as # EVID 2314-01)	1	Parker, B.	Ferraro, E.	Retained
3	9-16-11	CD (marked as # EVID 2314-02)	2	Parker, B.	Smith, T.	Retained
4						
5						
6						
7						
8						
9						
10						
11						
12						
13						
14						

Figure 3.5 Evidence tracking form.

Tip: Establish a chain of custody for each piece of evidence. Do not take originals into the field. Use copies, photos, and models instead of the actual evidence.

3.3.3 Reporting and Communicating Results

Because the fact finder should not be a decision maker in the process of deciding discipline, whenever possible the fact finder and decision maker should be two separate people. The fact finder's role should be strictly that of fact finding. His process should be driven by the objectives of the investigation with the intention of providing his result to a party outside of the fact finding project team. As a

---

EVIDENCE CUSTODY FORM

COLLECTION INFORMATION

DATE: _____

TIME: _____

LOCATION: _____

SUBJECT'S NAME: _____

DESCRIPTION OF EVIDENCE: _____

_____

_____

NAMES OF PERSONS HANDLING EVIDENCE

1. _____Time/Date: _____

2. _____Time/Date: _____

3. _____Time/Date: _____

4. _____Time/Date: _____

5. _____Time/Date: _____

6. _____Time/Date: _____

7. _____Time/Date: _____

Figure 3.6   Evidence custody form.

practical matter, the fact finder should report to someone not actively involved in the investigation.

This, of course, is easier said than done. In small organizations, it is nearly impossible. Even in large organizations there may not be the bandwidth to support the hierarchy of separate powers and responsibilities. Similarly, very complex or sensitive investigations involving organizational members at the corporate, or *C level,* may preclude distinctive roles of the participants. In these instances, other safeguards to ensure fairness and impartiality are necessary. One of them is the use of an outside counsel.

Lawyers are expensive and the decision to hire one should be made very carefully. Few organizations engage them without having a very special need or desire. However, in the case of workplace investigations, outside counsel can bring so much to the process that their use should be considered every time an investigation of any substance is contemplated. The properly selected attorney will have the legal knowledge and experience that insiders do not. Competent outside counsel will have resources and time to oversee a complex investigation, and more than likely have handled similar situations and challenges in the past. Outside counsel should be able to provide the counsel and advice needed to make the best decisions when they are needed. Outside counsel also will be viewed as more impartial. Although by definition, outside counsel is an advocate, he or she is still an outsider. They should not be carrying the same baggage as an individual internal to the organization. Nor should they have had the past experiences and interactions with the subject, witnesses, or others involved in the investigation. Usually they lack the *history* that might cloud their judgment and impartiality. Furthermore, outside counsel can be the voice of reason. When temperatures rise and emotions begin to surface, the properly selected attorney can be the voice of reason and the corporate therapist that quiets the waters. He or she also can assuage egos, expose hidden agendas, and mediate differences.

Inside counsel can often do these things as well. But, in many instances, inside counsel lacks some of the specific expertise necessary to do the job properly. Additionally, most staff attorneys are not litigators. They haven't the training or the experience (or the time) to prosecute or defend an action. In other instances, house counsel is already a witness. Their participation began at the onset, before the matter came under investigation. They coached human resources, wrote letters to opposing parties or interviewed participants and witnesses. They are conflicted. They are still able to advise and participate, but, because of their vested interest in the organization, they are subject to the charge of impartiality and self-interest.

Outside counsel offers something else—the ability to protect the investigative work product and result from discovery. If litigation is underway or litigation is anticipated, and the investigation is performed under the direction and supervision of counsel, the work product produced by the fact finders can be protected from discovery and the requirement to be produced. Under the doctrine of the *work product privilege*, all that the fact finder does and produces can be deemed privileged and withheld during discovery. Furthermore, all of the communications between the employer and the attorney are privileged as well. Like the attorney work product privilege, the doctrine of attorney–client privilege protects attorney–client communications from discovery. And for good reason. In order to preserve the integrity of our legal system, it is held that the attorney's effectiveness is significantly impacted by his ability to communicate confidentially with his client. Under the privilege, even the client's admission of guilt is protected. In the case of workplace investigations, all aspects of the matter can be protected. Damaging statements, memos, and other communications created during the investigation can be withheld once the privilege is invoked. Unfortunately, this powerful protective tool is often overlooked and underutilized.

Like many good things, the privilege has its limitations. It is only a tool. It is not a shield. One cannot hide behind it in order to deceive or cover up criminal activity. One cannot use evidence that he holds privileged in the prosecution or defense of his case and not disclose it to the other side. In workplace investigations this can create an unexpected dilemma. If, for example, an employer that possesses information provided by a confidential informant and wishes to use it to discipline an employee, cannot claim that the information is privileged. In order to use the information, it has to disclose it if challenged. The operative term here is *if challenged*. Absent a challenge, the employer is likely to be able to consider and use any evidence it wishes, regardless of its source. The easiest work-around to the confidential informant dilemma is not to use the informant's information directly. Instead, use the information provided by the informant to further the investigation from another direction. That is, the informant's information is only used as intelligence. With it, the project manager can engineer another investigative solution, then produce the results of that effort as the primary evidence for the purpose of deciding discipline.

The reader should not confuse outside counsel's role with that of a decision maker. Outside counsel, like the fact finder plays a functional role that does not include making decisions regarding discipline. If at all possible, the decision maker should have no other role than deciding discipline. Segregating the role of the participants reduces the likelihood of claims of impartiality and unfairness. Because the standard of proof of good faith/reasonable conclusion is so low, appearances of impartiality or unfairness can jeopardize the credibility of the entire process.

For the purpose of clarity, it should be mentioned that the attorney work product and attorney–client privilege can be invoked by either outside or inside counsel. The attorney need not be external to the organization.

3.4 Summary

You might be wondering why I thought it necessary to spend so much time and space on everything leading up to the actual investigative interview when the title of this book is, *The Investigative Interview*. In my two-day training course on investigative interviewing, after the first half day, my students are often wondering the same thing. It is only at the end of the second day do they finally appreciate the answer. However, I provided you the answer in the first chapter. Read it again.

> *Tip: The information gathering and **fact finding** phase of the investigation is not an end but a means. It affords the investigator the information he needs to interview the subject and successfully obtain an admission.*

One cannot be a successful investigative interviewer without first understanding the process of investigation or grasping the assorted fundaments and their many intricacies. Of the many works I read or studied while writing this book, few even mentioned the things and details I have offered you at this point and those that did failed to explain them in the detail I have for you. Do not undervalue the importance of this chapter or the two that preceded it. Your command of the information and technical material I have provided thus far is essential to your success as an investigative interviewer. I hope you study and use every bit of it.

3.5 Frequently Asked Questions

1. My employer refuses to consider hearsay evidence when deciding discipline. Why the resistance and what can I do to change the mindset?

   The resistance to use hearsay evidence for the purpose of deciding discipline is a common error. It is the result of not knowing the law and mistakenly choosing a standard of proof that exceeds that which is necessary. Ask your decision makers to read this chapter or talk to a competent employment law attorney.

2. My organization expects its fact finders to provide recommendations. You make a good case against it, but how do I convince my organization to change that expectation?

   Train your decision makers. Inform them that providing recommendation is not a best practice and doing so diminishes the claim of a fair and impartial investigation. If they still require you to provide recommendations, provide them after the discipline has been dispensed so as to thwart the claim of fact finder bias. For a very detailed examination of this issue, see the FAQs at the end of Chapter 4, specifically no. 4.

3. I always reduce my handwritten notes to some form of a clean electronic document and then destroy the original notes. Why shouldn't I continue that practice if my electronic versions are, in fact, exact copies of those that were handwritten?

   Because the destruction of evidence (and your notes are evidence) may be considered spoliation. Spoliation is actionable and, for it, sanctions can be imposed. It also looks bad. It creates the appearance that the fact finder is attempting to hide something. Moreover, if the electronic version is "identical" to the handwritten version, why did you waste the time and create a new duplicate if all you had to do was photocopy it? By the way, your notes need not be readable by anyone but you. Once during a deposition, a snide attorney exclaimed that he could not read my notes and asked my why. I answered, "Because I wrote them for my use, not yours."

4. I have heard that digital images are often not viewed as reliable evidence because they are so easily manipulated. Is that true?

   No and yes. Digital images are frequently considered reliable evidence. However, because they are easily manipulated, extreme care must be taken in the handling and management of them when they are intended for evidentiary purposes.

Remember also that the credibility and reliability of any evidence (digital included) is only as strong as the credibility and reliability of the individual used to introduce it to the trier-of-fact.

Endnotes

1. For the purpose of readability, from this point forward in this book you will notice I will sometimes use the words *interviewer, investigative interviewer,* and *fact finder* interchangeably. While not all interviewers are investigative interviewers, both are fact finders. When it is necessary to differentiate the activities of these roles, I will clearly indicate such.
2. *The American Heritage Dictionary of the English Language*, 3rd ed. (Boston: Houghton Mifflin Company, 1994).
3. Private Investigators' Association of British Columbia, webpage http://www.piabc.ca/ethics/ (accessed November 7, 2013).
4. J. John Fay, *Encyclopedia of Security Management* (Woburn, MA: Butterworth-Heinemann, 1993), 291.
5. Martin Roth, *The Writer's Complete Crime Reference Book* (Cincinnati, OH: Writer's Digest Books, 1990), 271.
6. Ibid., 277.
7. H. C. Black, *Black's Law Dictionary,* 6th ed. (St. Paul, MN: West Publishing Company, 1997), 1257.

Chapter 4

The Investigative Interview Method

Key learning points:

1. The Investigative Interview Method™ does not employ interrogation.
2. As a matter of general practice, investigatory interviews are reserved for those we know or have a strong reason to believe have committed an offense.
3. Most often the purpose of conducting an investigatory interview is to obtain an admission. An admission is among the most valuable benefits of an investigative interview.
4. Investigative interviews do not use intimidation or coercion; they are highly structured and process-driven.
5. Investigative interviews unfold iteratively and have seven distinct phases.
6. Successful investigative interviewers are professional, ethical, and honest with whom they interview.

"Honesty will be provided to the extent it is expected."

E. F. Ferraro

4.1 Differentiating Interviews from Interrogation

As mentioned in Chapter 1, the terms *interview* and *interrogation* mean different things to different people. Often these terms are used interchangeably, confusing both the user and the public. However, according to some professionals, there are significant distinctions.[1] Readers familiar with The Reid Technique® know this popular method defines an *interview* as nonaccusatory (see www.reid.com). The technique uses the interview to gather information. These interviews are free-flowing and relatively unstructured.[2] Alternatively, the technique proposes that the *interrogation* is accusatory and its purpose is to gain the truth.[3] The Reid method also proposes that an interrogation involves active persuasion to "learn the truth." I respectfully disagree with this distinction and the use of the terminology in this fashion. While I have the utmost respect for the proponents and users of the Reid methodology, I think the technique provides the fact finder limited value in the context of most workplace investigations. Instead of arguing the point or criticizing my professional colleagues, I suggest that the reader research The Reid Technique and decide which method is best suited for his or her purposes. While at it, I also suggest the reader examine other popular methodologies. In fact, there are many. However, the methodology I offer herein has been tried and tested by me and my associates. My investigative interview method is the product of over 30 years of experience and thousands of workplace interviews. It represents that which my associates and I have learned and perfected while working in dozens of industries, investigating all types of misconduct, and dealing with innumerable personalities and cultures. This powerful method has successfully withstood grueling legal challenge time and again.

> *Trap: Remarkably, some fact finders choose not to interview anyone. Based on the results developed using one or more of the other methods of investigation, they conclude that interviewing is unnecessary. Regardless of the quality of information at hand, at least interview your subject. As reasoned by the Court in Cotran,[4] the term* good cause *when for the purpose of deciding discipline is a "reasoned conclusion … supported by substantial evidence gathered through an adequate investigation that* includes *notice of the claimed misconduct and a chance for the employee to respond." [Emphasis added]*

In summary, the advantages of the investigative interview method include:

- A nonaccusatory approach
- It does not use intimidation or coercion
- A process that is highly structured
- Consistent results
- It is easily learned and replicated

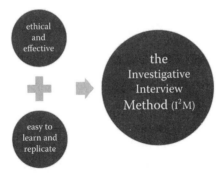

Figure 4.1   The investigative interview method.

Additionally, the method diminishes the likelihood of false admissions (commonly referred to as false confessions), is court admissible, and time-tested and proven. Figure 4.1 illustrates these points.

4.2 Eight Phases of the Investigative Interview

In spite of their many advantages and structured methodology, investigatory interviews are complex undertakings. They are psychologically demanding and require a high level of mental concentration. While investigatory interviews are nonaccusatory, typically the subject is either known to have committed the offense in question or the interviewer has very good reason to believe that he has. Its primary purpose is to obtain an admission. As you will recall, an admission differs from a confession in that a confession typically includes all of the elements of the offense. Those elements might include such things as motive, intent, state of mind, and capacity. An admission is a simple statement of guilt. For disciplinary purposes, most private sector employers need only make a reasonable determination of guilt. The employer need not prove all of the elements of the crime in order to impose corrective action.[5] Therefore, a properly obtained admission from the offender meets the employer's burden of proof. For this reason, it should be no surprise that employers place great value on an admission. Only uninformed or misguided ones attempt to prove all of the elements of a crime and obtain confessions.

Tip: As a matter of general practice, investigatory interviews are reserved for those we know, or have a strong reason to believe, have committed an offense. Most often the purpose of conducting an investigatory interview is to obtain an admission.

Investigative interviews also are valuable because they:

- help fulfill the employer's due process obligations;
- allow the fact finder to obtain another perspective as to what may have occurred; and
- allow the fact finder to learn who else might be involved and why.

Using the investigative interview method, our investigatory interviews will unfold iteratively. What's more, this powerful method can be combined with any other method and used in places other than the workplace. Our methodology has eight distinct phases:

Phase I: Preparation
Phase II: Introduction
Phase III: Presentation
Phase IV: Admission
Phase V: Discussion
Phase VI: Written
Phase VII: Oral
Phase VIII: Conclusion

The Investigative Interview Method, or I2M as my firm calls it, is structured but flexible. When properly employed it can be used to address every type of workplace misconduct the fact finder might confront. Let's begin with the first phase, that of preparation.

4.2.1 Phase I: Preparation

The Preparation Phase involves planning. In this phase, we will consider the following:

- Safety and the need for additional security
- Determining who should be interviewed
- Location for the interview
- Selection and preparation of the interviewer
- Case file preparation
- Theme and question development
- The request for representation
- Selection and use of witnesses
- Timing

Of all of the planning issues to be considered, *safety and the need for additional security* may be one of the most important. This is an over-arching issue that runs through every aspect of the process. Therefore, to improve readability and avoid some redundancies, I will incorporate aspects of this issue throughout this section and not dedicate space to it here. Instead, let's address the other considerations with some specificity.

4.2.1.1 Determining Who Should Be Interviewed

Determining who should be interviewed is sometimes more complex than it might first appear. Employers often suggest everyone be interviewed. Interviewing *everyone* is not a strategy. It consumes time and valuable resources, and it is wasteful. The investigative team should consider the project's objectives, time restraints, and budget before agreeing to interview everyone. A better approach is to first determine what information is needed and then interview those that possess it.

For example, recently, during a complex fraud investigation that I was conducting, my client asked that every one of his employees be interviewed. While it is true my firm is in the business of conducting workplace interviews, to interview everyone was not in my client's best interest, and I told him so. Instead, we selected those who we believed were most involved. Then, very tactically we decided the order in which they should be interviewed. In the final analysis, this approach proved to be very productive and cost effective.

If the investigation is done properly, it is likely that the results clearly indicate who should be interviewed. If the results identified multiple offenders, I generally select those most involved and central to the issue. If there is more than one principal, I will select the one my investigative teams believe will be the most cooperative and likely to be truthful. Interviewing this person first and assuming he will cooperate and be truthful will yield an admission as well as actionable information concerning others. This corroborative evidence will aid the interviewer in the subsequent interviews, but also strengthen the case against his co-offenders. Should one or more of them deny involvement, the combination of the preinterview result and the corroborative evidence provided by those who cooperated should be sufficient to support the corrective action chosen by the decision makers. In situations involving multiple offenders, this strategy tends to compound the amount of information developed. Thus, the interviewer is provided more and more information and detail going into each subsequent interview. The usefulness, if not obvious now, will become abundantly clear when we examine the presentation phase of the interview.

Not all situations permit the use of this strategy. In matters involving allegations of harassment or discrimination, the identity of the most serious offender may not be possible. In classic *"she said, he said"* cases, the accuser is usually interviewed first. Then, armed with that which she provides, combined with the evidence produced from the various fact finding methods used, the accused is interviewed. In situations where even this strategy is not possible, the investigative interviewer must resort to simply selecting the valuable interviewee. In these situations, value is a subjective determination. Some of the factors one might consider include:

- How much useful information the subject might possess
- Years of service (thus, possibly offering an historical perspective)
- Familiarity with the issue and process failures that contributed to it
- Communication and social skills
- Respect for authority and management
- Level of suspected or known involvement
- Work history
- Reputation for honesty and integrity
- Safety

4.2.1.2 Location for the Interview

Assuming we have decided who to interview and who should interview them (see Chapter 5, section 5.31), the next thing to determine is where the interviews should take place. As with administrative interviews, investigatory interviews should not be conducted in the subject's office or work area. A neutral location on or off organizational premises is best. Although I have conducted interviews in hotel lobbies, noisy restaurants, landfills, and in automobiles, the best places are quiet, private, and comfortable to both the interviewer and interviewee. Small conference rooms, meeting rooms, and private offices are best.

Once the location is decided, it should be properly prepared. If possible, the furniture in the room should be arranged so that the interviewee will sit closest to the door. The interviewer should sit so that there is no obstacle between him and his subject. If the room contains a desk, the interviewer might sit behind and configure the remaining furniture so that the subject will sit to the side of the desk instead of in front of it. If a witness is to be present, she should be placed so as to be out of view of the subject yet not sitting behind them or blocking the room's exit.

Knickknacks, heavy objects, unnecessary documents and paperwork, sharp objects, and other distractions should be removed from the desk or table. Any visible clocks, valuables, or other distractions also should be removed from the room. Blinds should be drawn and windows covered in order to provide adequate privacy. The extent to which windows are covered should be considered carefully. The interviewer should balance the quest to provide adequate privacy with the possible appearance of trying to isolate the interviewee. A poorly chosen location can give rise to the annoying allegation of being "interrogated tirelessly in a windowless room." Figure 4.2 illustrates the arrangement of the room.

Notice that the interviewer has chosen not to sit behind the desk and the interviewee sits closest to the door. Both the witness, whose role we will examine later in section 4.2.1.7, and security (if used) or any other nonparticipating witness are out of direct view of the interviewee.

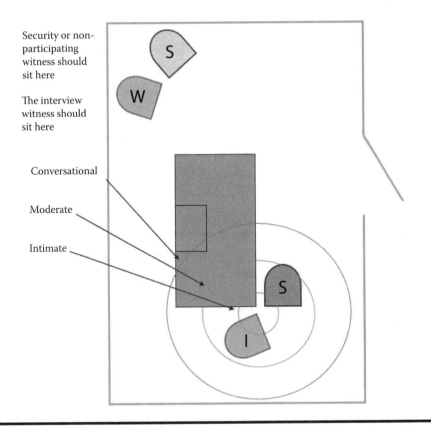

Security or non-participating witness should sit here

The interview witness should sit here

Conversational

Moderate

Intimate

Figure 4.2 **The arrangement of the interview room.**

Tip: If the concern for safety is so great that you do not feel comfortable allowing the subject to sit closest to the door, do not conduct the interview.

This arrangement allows the interviewer to use proxemics and prevents the other participants from distracting the interviewee. Proxemics allows the interviewer to use spatial orientation and the distance between himself and the interviewee during the interview as a form of nonverbal communication with the interviewee. The closer he is to the interviewee, the more intimate or personal his questions and messages will be perceived. The further his distance from the interviewee, the more he will appear to be disengaged and unsatisfied with the interviewee's responses. For example, when posing a question that seeks an admission, I will sometimes move closer to the interviewee as if I am sharing a secret. If he answers with a denial, I might push away, visibly using my hands to distance myself from the subject and the desk. Combining this movement with the slightest turning away of my head, as if disgusted (but much more subtle), the interviewee has no choice but to think I have rejected his answer. Thus, without speaking a word, I have communicated that I think his response was not honest.

Proxemics is a subcategory of the study of nonverbal communication along with haptics (touch), kinesics (body movement), vocalics (paralanguage), and chronemics (structure of time).[6] Proxemics is best described as "the interrelated observations and theories of man's use of space as a specialized elaboration of culture."[7] Edward T. Hall, the cultural anthropologist who coined the term in 1963, emphasized the impact of proxemic behavior (the use of space) on interpersonal communication among humans. Hall believed that the value in studying proxemics comes from its applicability in understanding the way people interact with others in daily life. In his work on proxemics, Hall separated his theory into two overarching categories: personal space and territory. Personal space describes the immediate space surrounding a person, while territory refers to the area that a person may "lay claim to" and defend against others. Figure 4.3 identifies and characterizes this personal space for our purposes.

The location of the interview should be convenient to all parties. The location should be comfortable and private. However, unless absolutely necessary, the interview should not take place in the interviewee's office or immediate work area. Generally, such locations provide too many potential distractions to the interviewee and offer inadequate privacy. A borrowed office, small conference room, or some other place that is mutually agreeable to the parties is often the best.

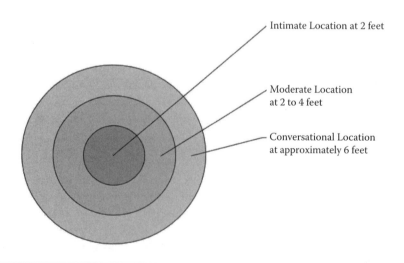

Intimate Location at 2 feet

Moderate Location at 2 to 4 feet

Conversational Location at approximately 6 feet

Figure 4.3 The special orientation and distances between people is called *proxemics*. For the purposes of investigative interviewing, these are the distances between the interviewer and the interviewee.

If at all possible, the subject should not be interviewed in his/her home. Circumstances often make this choice convenient. However, the interviewer should resist the temptation and choose another location. One's home is very private and, for the purpose of conducting an investigative interview, it is usually not suitable. Moreover, in the home of the interviewee, the interviewer is strictly a guest and has no control over the environment. Pets, television, family members, and visitors can be distracting and disruptive. Additionally, the home interview poses privacy and safety issues. Before agreeing to interview someone at their home, carefully consider all alternatives.

We will examine these and other aspects of proxemics in greater detail later in this chapter.

4.2.1.3 Interviewer Selection and Preparation

Good interviewers are conversationalists. They like to talk and, most importantly, they like to listen. Good interviewers are professional and disciplined. They embrace structure and process. Not all fact finders should be considered interviewers. In selecting an interviewer, his skills, training, and experience should be mapped to the intended interviewee or project. Generally, men should be selected to interview men, and women should be selected to interview women. This is not absolutely necessary; however, experience shows that matching the gender of the interviewer and interviewee often eliminates the need for a witness and is often less stressful for the interviewee.

The interviewer should have some knowledge and experience regarding the matter under investigation. Such qualities reduce the steepness of the learning curve and tend to accelerate the investigative process. Moreover, the properly qualified interviewer is less likely to be misled by an interviewee or misunderstand what they are being told. The interviewer also should have empathy. The ability to appreciate and understand the feeling of others is a virtue. Every interviewer should be kind, gentle, and understanding. There is no need to be tough or unsympathetic. The question of interviewer dress frequently arises when discussing workplace interviews. Here is some obvious advice:

- Dress professionally
- Do not wear expensive jewelry or watches
- Practice good personal hygiene
- Do not use perfume or cologne

The interviewer also should:

- be properly rested and fed
- have dealt with all other potential distractions in advance
- have planned his day so that he will have all the time he needs

- place his phone on silent mode
- have proper writing tools and adequate paper

The interviewer also should:

- confirm the name and job title of subject
- acquire full details regarding the type and description of the incident or issue
- confirm the location of the incident or issue
- identify known or suspected witnesses
- acquire all of the details regarding the relationship of the various parties
- determine the subject's whereabouts during the time in question
- determine the existence of any prior discipline or corrective action against any of the parties
- organize his case file, evidence file, and other materials

4.2.1.4 Case File Preparation

The interviewer should carefully prepare a *working* case file to use during the interview. This document is not the same as the original case file created during the fact finding phase of the investigation. That document should be kept in a secure place and not brought to any interview. The working case file is similar to it, but contains no original documents or evidence. It should be tabbed and contain at least the following items:

- Name and job title of subject
- Background of the subject
- Investigative report and notes
- Forensic and/or lab reports
- Witness summaries and statements
- Supporting documents and exhibits
- Images of key pieces of evidence

Tip: Organizing one's materials into a neat working case file with tabs and an index is not only professional, when used it will demonstrate to the subject the seriousness of the matter at hand.

The second item on this list deserves special attention. Because investigative interviews by definition involve those known or strongly suspected of having committed an offense, personal security is an issue. As a matter of practice, a thorough background investigation should be conducted whenever possible before an investigative interview. That investigation should include:

- Identity verification to include name and Social Security Number confirmation.
- Personal history verification. This includes a search for the existence of criminal records, wants, and warrants for arrests. If necessary, retain the services of a preemployment screening and background investigation firm. Thoroughly research the background of each intended interviewee. The background investigation should include at minimum: a seven-year criminal conviction history (examine both felonies and misdemeanors); a driving record history; and a public filing history (notices of default, civil judgments, liens/bankruptcies). Check other states where the applicant lived over the past 7 to 10 years.
- Credentialing. If the subject is known or claims to be licensed or hold professional certifications or other credentials, verify each and document discrepancies if any.

The results of this effort will better equip the interviewer to prepare for his own safety and that of everyone involved. Additionally, discrepancies between that which the subject provided during the employment screening process and that discovered during this research can be the source of additional questions during the interview. What's more, most employers consider providing false or untruthful information during the employment screening process a terminable offense. In such cases, the results of the background can prove invaluable should the employer desire to terminate the employee who's made no admission during his investigative interview.

4.2.1.5 Theme and Question Development

The interviewer also should prepare his theme. A theme is a monologue presented by the interviewer in which he offers a rationale for both the investigation and the known or suspected transgressions of the subject. Some interviewers develop different themes for different circumstances. While some find this helpful, it is not always a good practice. Regardless, your theme should not:

- absolve the subject of any legal consequences for his actions
- reveal everything you know about the offense
- disclose key pieces of evidence
- embellish the strength or amount of evidence

An unsophisticated theme might go like this: "Tommy, last evening someone entered the facility using an access card other than his own. Once inside, the person roamed the executive office area until he found an unlocked office. He entered that office and from it took a notebook computer and several personal items. We suspect you know something about that and either stole the items yourself or helped someone else do it. If you are willing to tell us what happened, maybe we can work something out."

Note how much the interviewer told the subject about the crime and what is known about it. Note also that it is accusatory and immediately puts the interviewee on the offensive. It also provides the subject the false hope that if he comes clean he might be able to keep his job.

A better theme might go like this: "Tommy as you know, this organization has had a long-standing policy regarding individual integrity and improper behavior in the workplace. It recently came to the attention of management here at this facility that that policy possibly had been violated. First, human resources was notified that things had gone missing from some of the executive offices. Then, several employees came forward and made similar complaints. One of these employees went so far as to submit his complaint in writing. As such, management decided to undertake a formal investigation. Today I am going to share with you some of the things we learned during that investigation."

Notice here that the interviewer does not play all of his cards. He carefully lays the foundation for an investigation into suspected misconduct. Without being accusatory, he then vaguely describes what he intends to discuss.

> *Tip: Once a theme is decided, the interviewer should prepare his notes and list the categories of issues he intends to pursue. He also should prepare his line of questioning.*

Preparing one's line of questioning is not the same as preparing a list of interview questions. Think of the line of questioning as a list of question categories. Using the hypothetical situation above, the categories might include:

- Unauthorized building access after hours
- Violation of the organization's policy regarding the use of access control cards
- Misappropriation of organizational property
- Misappropriation of personal property
- Employee ethics or integrity policy violations

Note that these are categories of issues the interviewer intends to discuss with the subject. Instead of questions, they permit flexibility by allowing the interviewer to develop his questions based on the subject's responses. This technique provides for a more fluid question and answer session creating a more dynamic interview. Not using a list also prevents later challenges by a trier-of-fact demanding to know why the interviewer did not ask all of the questions he intended (if, in fact, he did not). The failure of not asking all of one's intended questions tends to support the allegation of interviewer bias and foster the image of unprofessionalism.

4.2.1.6 Request for Representation

Another preparatory consideration is the potential of the interviewee requesting representation. Considerations regarding the request for representation include:

- Organizational policy and/or past practices
- The collective bargaining rights of the interviewee
- Confidentiality
- Practicality
- Location of the interview and availability of the requested representation
- Type of interview (administrative or investigatory)
- Safety

In 1975, the U.S. Supreme Court decided a case that has specific impact on interviews conducted in a unionized workplace. In that case, *NLRB v. Weingarten, Inc.,* the court imposed upon unionized employers the requirement that they allow employees who have requested union representation to have a union representative present at any investigatory interview that the employee reasonably believes may result in disciplinary action against him.[8] Importantly, the court did not impose the requirement that the employer notify the employee of this right. The decision also stipulated that the representative provided could not disrupt the process or otherwise interfere with the interview. However, it also allows the employer the option of declining the request for said representation. Under such a circumstance, the employer must then discontinue the interview. Surprisingly, this last feature has some very useful benefits. For example, suppose in a case involving multiple subjects, the first and most important (the most serious offender) begins his interview with the request for his shop steward (or other recognized union representative). Instead of fulfilling the request, the interviewer might tell the interviewee he has decided to discontinue the interview and does so. Management then places the interviewee on administrative leave with pay (defeating the subsequent claim the employee was disciplined for exercising his right to representation) and sends him home. As a consequence, neither the employee nor his union learn anything about the investigation, its methods, or its results. The interviewer then continues his process of selecting interviewees until one of them does not request a representative. That individual is interviewed and hopefully provides an admission and additional information regarding those who requested representation and were not interviewed. All the while, the union and those who were not interviewed are left in the dark.

It gets better. Suppose several employees don't request representation and cooperate. With no one left to interview, the interviewer then recalls those who had earlier requested representation. Each is provided the requested representation and asked only one question: Did they commit the offense in question? If they deny it, they are now suspended without pay pending a decision regarding discipline by management. Armed with the results of the investigation and the corroborative evidence provided by those who cooperated, the suspended employees are disciplined. If they grieve (a procedure involving the request for a formal hearing reviewing the case and resultant discipline) and an arbitration (the actual hearing) ensues, both the grievant and the union representative will be called to testify. The grievant will likely again deny guilt (claiming innocence) and the representative will be forced to testify that the grievant was provided representation, questioned, and told the interviewer he was innocent. Add to these circumstances an organization that has an ethics or integrity policy. Here's the outcome:

- Those who cooperated are disciplined based on their admissions.
- Those who failed to cooperate are disciplined based on the results of the investigation and the corroborative evidence provided by those who cooperated *and* their violation of the organization's ethics or integrity policy using the union representative as witness to the violation (that of lying to the interviewer).
- The uncooperative grievants are unable to claim they were disciplined for exercising their right to representation (as laid out above).
- The uncooperative grievants are unable to offer any union officials as witnesses who can claim the interviews were coercive or otherwise improper because no representative participated in the interviews in which an employee was cooperative; in other words, none of them witnessed one of the actual investigative interviews.

Another variation of this strategy is to discipline only those who failed to make an admission. This strategy is best employed in situations in which all of the offenders committed similar or like offenses and the evidence against each is roughly identical. Say, for example, we have 10 offenders and only half admit guilt. If the offense in question justified termination, the decision makers might terminate those who failed to make an admission and give those that did a second chance with a final letter of warning. This outcome would send a powerful message to the entire workforce that management honors truthfulness over dishonesty. It is my experience that the strategy also improves employee cooperation in future investigations. Additionally, the fact that those employees who requested representation were fired and that they did not return to work will be not lost on future offenders.

In nonunionized workplaces, employees have no such rights. Lacking the due process rights discussed in Chapter 2, private sector employees have no right to representation during an investigative interview. This, however, does not give license to nonunionized employers to flatly deny the request for representation. Because many triers-of-fact do not understand the law as they should, many think the request is not only reasonable, but that the failure to fulfill it is unlawful. As such, requests should be handled consistent with organizational policies, past practices, and precedent. That said, I am not an advocate of introducing outsiders to the inner workings of an internal investigation. Confidentiality, practicality, and the location of the interview and availability of the requested representation all play a role in the decision to honor the request. Moreover, outsiders, whoever they are, will not likely advise the interviewee to be candid or truthful. They are more likely to advise the subject to make no statement or admission against his interest. I will discuss in detail later how to address these situations tactfully and defensibly.

4.2.1.7 Selection and Use of Witnesses

I advocate the use of witnesses in my investigative interviews. Their use provides the benefit of corroborative testimony to enable the defeat of claims by the interviewee that he was mistreated, subjected to emotional or physical duress, inappropriately touched or contacted, lied to, or was made untrue promises. Similarly, the witness can later testify, if necessary, that the subject freely made an admission. In the event the interviewee later recants his admission and claims innocence, both the interviewer and witness can testify to the contrary. It allows the witness's testimony and notes to corroborate the testimony of the interviewer and strengthen the credibility of an admission. A witness also can diminish the interviewee's credibility if he chooses to attack the interviewer's process.

In my cases, the witness is often an interviewer in training. This benefits both the trainee and the process. By definition, a witness is an observer. My witnesses do not actively participate in the interview. They do not speak unless spoken to by the interviewer. We do not play good cop, bad cop. The witness listens, observes, and quietly takes notes. The witness is instructed not to record everything that is said, instead they capture the interviewee's responses. They do not describe the interviewee's demeanor, tone, or physical expressions. They objectively capture only what he says. Rarely do I allow someone other than one of my team members to be a witness. Occasionally, a customer will insist someone from human resources or a decision maker participate as "their" witness. This is a bad idea. First, experience shows that, in spite of being told not to question the interviewee, they almost always do. Secondly, if the interviewees believe that the witness is a decision maker, they will likely conclude that their attention and responses should be directed to them, not the interviewer. I also have found that in spite of my directions to the contrary, human resource folks and decision makers can say some pretty damaging things. Things such as telling the interviewee that his job is secure, he doesn't have anything to worry about, the police know nothing (when, in fact, the police know everything and plans have been made to file a criminal complaint), tell the truth and everything will be fine.

Tip: If an interview witness is to be used, do not allow it to be another member of the interviewee's organization or a decision maker.

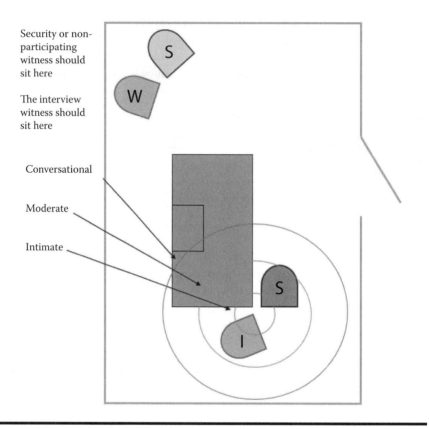

Figure 4.4   The arrangement of the interview room.

In section 4.2.1.2 above, I noted that the interview room should be arranged such that it allowed a place for the witness. In Figure 4.4, the interview room is arranged so that the witness is placed so that he is out of the line of sight of the interviewee. This is done so that the witness does not create a distraction for the interviewee who is focused fully on the interviewer.

However, occasionally, I will remind the interviewee that a witness is present. I do this to diminish the possibility of him offering an untruthful answer to a question if I think he is preparing to give one or to keep his attention. To do this, I simply ask the witness if he has any questions. The pat answer is "no." However, if the witness, in fact, has questions or wishes to bring something to my attention, he is free to do so during a break.

Another consideration is language barriers. I speak only English. If the interviewee's English is poor or nonexistent I will use an interpreter. The preferred interpreter is one that is court certified. Using a co-worker of the interviewee is not advisable for reasons of confidentiality. If using an interpreter during the interview, talk to the interviewee, not the interpreter. Using an interpreter will not affect the usefulness or power of the investigative interview method. It will only make your interview longer in duration.

> *Tip: Use an interpreter whenever there is a question regarding the interviewee's ability to speak and understand the language of the interviewer.*

4.2.1.8 Timing

The timing of one's intended investigative interviews is a critical decision. Subject and management availability, location availability, holidays and vacations, and safety all play obvious roles. Those considerations aside, I have found the best day to interview is the second day of the workweek. Studies show that employees are more likely to be absent the first and last day of their workweek. Choosing the last day of the workweek to interview also poses the potential problem of not being able to continue the momentum generated from the cooperation and information provided by the first interviewees. Similarly, beginning one's interview early in the workday is better than at the end of the workday. The extra hours or days provide the opportunity to conduct additional interviews if appropriate, but also to follow up on any new information developed. The assumption by some that interviewing late in the workweek or workday diminishes the possibility of a violent employee returning to the workplace and finding more targets of opportunity (theoretically, the threat is reduced because fewer employees are available during those off days and hours) neglects much of what we have examined thus far in this chapter. If, in fact, we think an interviewee is that dangerous and capable of an attack, he probably should not be interviewed. An entirely different strategy should be employed than is contained in this book. For those interested in learning more about such a strategy, I suggest you seek out a copy of ASIS International's American National Standard entitled, *Workplace Violence Prevention and Intervention*.[9] I am proud to have been a contributor to that work and highly recommend all investigative interviewers add it to their professional libraries. Another work on the topic is James Cawood's, *Violence Assessment and Intervention: The Practitioner's Handbook*.[10] Co-authored by Michael H. Corcoran, this is an excellent examination of the practical approaches of applying behavioral science to threats of violence in communities, businesses, and schools, and describes how to effectively intervene to preserve the safety of victims.

In moving to the next phase of the interview, now is a good time to look at Appendix 3 entitled Interview Guidelines.

4.2.2 Phase II: Introduction

I recommend that workplace investigatory interviews begin with a proper introduction. In most instances, it is helpful if the interviewee is not told of his intended interview in advance. Therefore, it will be necessary that some form of structured introduction be made. The introduction should be made by someone other than the interviewer. A supervisor, manager, or someone of authority over the interviewee is best. Because the most serious offenders are typically interviewed first, the element of surprise still exists. It should be maintained if possible. The first interviewees are usually the easiest to obtain admissions from and very often the most cooperative. However, a proper introduction is still necessary.

Once a manager has been selected and introduced to the interviewer (if not already familiar with one another), she should be instructed how to introduce the subject to the interviewee. Because few things can derail a well-planned interview more effectively than the failure to properly introduce the interviewee to the interviewer, this effort should be carefully choreographed and rehearsed. The best procedure is for the management representative to contact the interviewee's immediate supervisor (or manager as the case may be) telephonically and tell him or her that the employee (soon to be interviewee) is needed to participate immediately in an internal project underway. Not disclosing that the project is, in fact, an internal investigation or that the employee's participation is that of an interviewee, arrangements should be made for the supervisor to escort the employee to a convenient, less than public place inside the building or site somewhere between where the employee works and the interview will take place. At that location, a handoff will take place and the supervisor will be excused. From that location, the management representative should briskly proceed to the interview room.

Without knocking, the representative and employee should enter the room. The interviewer should be seated and the room properly arranged (see the above section on location (section 4.2.1.2) for more details). The representative should position him/herself such that the employee/interviewee is standing between himself and the interviewer. This should be the only time during the entire interview when the interviewee is not closest to the door. The representative should now make introductions. It is permissible, even desirable for the one making the introduction, to read it to the subject:

> "_____, *this is* _____. (He) *and his team recently assisted us in looking into* (whatever the problem is). *They have completed that effort and today he would like to share with you some of what* (he or she) *and his team learned during that effort. We expect and appreciate your cooperation.*"

This introduction properly introduces the interviewer by name and subtly instructs the interviewee to cooperate. Notice that the party making the introduction does not tell the interviewee that the interviewer has questions for him. Instead the interviewee is told that information will be shared with him. Telling someone he will be questioned puts him on guard and potentially makes the interviewee defensive. It encourages him to anticipate what will be asked and to prepare responses.

> *Tip: Note that the management representative does not use the word* investigation. *It should not be used at this point unless absolutely necessary. The management representative also should not tell the subject "good luck" or inquire if he has any questions. Doing so will increase any concerns the subject already has and invite trouble for which the manager will not be prepared.*

(See Appendix 4, Interview Guidelines for Management, for more details.)

Once a manager has introduced the subject, the interviewer should reintroduce himself and the witness (if present) to the subject. Having done or said nothing more than that which is contained in the introduction script, the management representative should be excused by the interviewer. As he is about to leave, the interviewer should stop him at the door and tell the interviewee that at any time during their "meeting" he may:

■ take a break
■ use the restroom
■ use the telephone
■ discontinue the meeting for any reason

Thus, using the representative as a witness, the interviewee is told he is not going to be held against his will and may leave at any time. From the perspective of the interviewee, his participation is voluntary. However, he has been politely informed that his participation and cooperation is a directive, one made by an individual with the authority to make it. As such, his failure to cooperate could be considered insubordination and resultantly actionable.

4.2.3 Phase III: Presentation

The interviewer should next disclose the following:

■ Context and ground rules (if any)
■ Provide the genesis of the investigation and its methods
■ Disclose the investigation's purpose
■ Reveal some of its findings
■ State his purpose

This monologue is called the theme. The interviewer should know it cold. He should also disclose that he is only a fact finder and not a decision maker. As such, he has no control over the outcome of the investigation or the possibility of discipline arising from it. This portion of the interview should be very structured. Every interviewer should develop a uncomplicated, but credible, theme that can be consistently and efficiently used. The presentation phase reaffirms the investigation's purpose and its genesis. It might begin like this:

> *As you know, this organization has had a long-standing policy addressing sexual harassment and improper behavior in the workplace. Sometime ago, it came to the attention of management here at this facility that that policy possibly had been violated. First, human resources received anonymous reports that something was going on. Then, several employees came forward and made complaints. One of those employees went so far as to submit her complaint in writing. As such, management decided to undertake a formal investigation. Today I am going to share with you some of the things we learned during that investigation.*

It offers the interviewee some rationale as to why an *investigation* was conducted and why the interviewee has been asked to meet the interviewer. The offering must be credible and not misrepresent the truth. If no one actually came forward or put their complaints in writing, it should not be said that they had. Notice also that the interviewer has made no accusations. He has succinctly summarized what the suspected violation under investigation is and some of the evidence already accumulated. It sounds sincere and confident. Also notice how this same script could be used for other purposes. With only a small amount of word substitution, the entire theme is altered:

> *As you know, this organization has had a long-standing policy addressing* substance abuse [emphasis added] *and improper behavior in the workplace. Sometime ago, it came to the attention of management here at this facility that that policy had been possibly violated. First, human resources received anonymous reports that something was going on. Then, several employees came forward and made complaints. One of those employees went so far as to submit his complaint in writing. As such, management decided to undertake a formal investigation. Today I am going to share with you some of the things we learned during that investigation.*

Notice this theme allows its use for any number of issues or workplace problems. With the slightest modification, the theme can be used for almost any circumstance or situation. You are welcome to improvise and create your own theme, but recognize this one is the product of many years of conducting interviews in all sorts of circumstances and situations. It is so effective, I encourage my trainees to read it until it can be memorized. Not once have I observed an interviewee comment or object that the interviewer was reading a script.

> *Tip: Good investigative interviewers know their theme cold.*

Next, the interviewer should disclose his role in the investigative process. He might say something like this:

> *My role in that investigation has been that of an information gatherer. I am not a decision maker. My purpose was to collect information and seek out the truth. The information I have gathered has been packaged in the form of a report and given to those who will make decisions regarding discipline or corrective action. I am only an information gatherer.*

By clearly stating that the interviewer is only an information gatherer and not a decision maker, the interviewer is making it clear that he has no control over the outcome of the investigation and any discipline the interviewee may face. There is no implication that the interviewer has any control over the future employment of the subject. The interviewee's later claim that the interviewer told him he could save his job would not be credible. Thus, the claim that the interviewee was improperly induced to make an admission will not be successful. In fact, such a claim may actually appear contrived or even untruthful.

Next, the interviewer should provide some idea as to how the investigation *could have been* conducted. In doing so, the interviewer should avoid the temptation to exaggerate the quality or quantity of his evidence. The interviewer should generally describe the methods of investigation available to him and explain that, using one or more of them, he learned that the subject had some involvement in the issue under investigation. The interviewer might begin like this:

> *The first method of investigation available to us is something called physical surveillance. Physical surveillance is nothing more than simply watching people, places, or things. All that is needed is something to watch and somebody to watch it. Then to capture what is observed; sometimes that which is seen is photographed or videoed. Early in our investigation, we learned that _____ sometimes was taking place in the parking lot. In some instances, you were actually present.*

This last sentence of this presentation is used only if the interviewee was actually known to have been in the parking lot during the time in question. That being the case, note the difference in what was said and what the interviewee actually heard. He likely heard he was *observed* in the parking lot. However, that was not what was said. Furthermore, if he listened closely, he likely believes his activities there were photographed or videoed. If the organization's culture or policies preclude the use of physical surveillance for this purpose, this presentation should not be used. Instead, the interviewer discloses only the methods of investigations that the organization would use or has used in the past. To reinforce the strength of the presentation used, the interviewer might show the interviewee a preselected page from his field case file. Anticipating its use, the page selected should reveal the name of the subject and details concerning the activity in question. By highlighting the name of the subject and activity in some fashion allows the interviewee to scan and easily see the portions of the document desired without having to read the entire page. The document should not be given to the interviewee, only shown.

Of the methods that workplace investigations have available, the interview method is always used. As such, a presentation like the one above is still possible, absent the use of any other method. Here is how it might be offered:

> *Of the many methods of investigation available to us, interviewing is the most powerful. Used as an investigative tool, interviewing allows us to not only learn what has taken place, but also why. All that is needed is someone willing to cooperate and someone to listen. Then to capture that which is revealed, those who cooperate are asked to provide a written statement. For our purposes, that statement typically contains information regarding _____ and the identity of those involved. Early in our investigation, we learned what was sometimes taking place in the parking lot and, in some instances, you were actually present.*

Again note the difference in what was said and what the interviewee actually heard. He likely heard he was *observed* in the parking lot and those that observed him provided written statements to that effect. But, that was not what was said. It should be mentioned that if the interviewer cannot say this truthfully, it should not be said. If that is the case, maybe the subject should not be interviewed. Remember, investigatory interviews are reserved for those that are either known to have committed an offense or the interviewer has very good reason to believe that he has. The interviewer at this moment is proposing the interviewee is guilty. Without being accusatory or disclosing any of his true evidence, the interviewer is telling the subject he knows he is guilty. Cleverly, he asks the interviewee to justify his misconduct:

> *Using one or more of the methods I just described, we learned you had some role in the problem here at work and on more than one occasion violated our policy involving _____. What is not known at this time is why you behaved the way you did or if you fully recognize why the policy is so important.*

With confidence and conviction, the interviewer is affirming the results of his investigation. He is not asking if the subject is guilty, he is asking *why* he is guilty. Unlike other popular methods of *interrogation*, the interviewee is not asked a string of leading questions or subjected to an obviously contrived conclusion offered up in a transparent interrogation disguised as an *interview*. I have found that most people are not so easily convinced that an interviewer has evidence of their guilt simply because he says he does. Most people, even those who have no intention of lying, want to be convinced that evidence exists. Only by explaining how an investigation might be conducted and offering some detail regarding the methods of investigation can we hope to convince a reluctant interviewee to come clean and make an admission.

4.2.4 Phase IV: Admission

Next, in order to move the interviewee to providing an admission, the interviewer needs to impose some conditions. The conditions create the appearance of an obstacle of which the interviewee must overcome in order for the interview to go forward and he be allowed to explain his actions. Appropriately, those conditions involve honesty. The conditions might be framed like this:

> *In order for us to discuss this matter and for you to have the opportunity to explain what took place, you need to agree to do two things. Both have to do with honesty. The first is to agree to be honest with me and the second is to agree to be honest with management (the decision makers).*

And, here it is, the first question asked during the investigatory interview: Can you promise to be honest with me? Notice that up to this point the interview has been a monologue. The interviewer has asked no questions or prompted the interviewee to respond to his statements. The first question asked is "Can you be honest?"; when delivered properly, it is almost impossible for the interviewee to answer *no*. Moreover, to reply *no*, in and of itself is telling and reveals more about the individual than if he simply answered, *yes*.

By affirming a commitment to be honest with the interviewer and his employer, the interviewee has given the interviewer something to return to if the subject subsequently denies guilt or minimizes his culpability. Should that occur, reminding the subject of his commitment to be honest causes him to make a conscious choice between honesty and the potential commission of two offenses: the matter in question *and lying*. It is permissible for the interviewer to tell the interviewee that lying is the more serious offense, if, in fact, it is. The interviewer also can remind the interviewee that the interview cannot continue unless the interviewee is truthful. The dialogue might go like this:

> *If you cannot be truthful about what took place, this interview cannot continue. The decision makers then will have to make their decisions without your input … and you may not have the chance to explain why you behaved the way you did. You also may lose the opportunity to offer the extenuating or mitigating circumstance that caused you to behave the way you did.*

Again, without being accusatory, the interviewer tells the interviewee that he knows he committed an offense. Experience shows that most interviewees at this point will agree to be truthful. Whether they will is another matter. If the interviewer offered a convincing presentation using a credible theme and communicated a willingness to listen, the interviewee will likely conclude that honesty is now his only choice. If at this point, the interviewee is agreeable and agrees to be truthful, the interviewer can then begin to explore the matter in question. Suggesting the subject start at the "beginning," the interviewer can methodically move from the events leading up to the incident to the actual incident.

The first step involves asking the subject some simple, nonincriminating questions. These questions are called *truth-tellers*. They should be questions of which the interviewer already knows the answers. Asking truth-tellers, the interviewer attempts to build rapport, relax the interviewee, and observe him when responding truthfully. Examples of effective truth-tellers I have used in the past include:

- What is your current position?
- How long have you worked here?
- Where did you work previously?
- Compare for me the style of management there to that here?
- Do you agree that safety, hard work, integrity, loyalty, respect for others, etc. (pick one that is applicable to the case) is important here?

The interviewer should record the responses to each question in his notes. It creates the appearance that the answers to the questions are somehow important and that maybe the decision makers will use them in deciding the interviewee's fate. Instead, the interviewer is carefully making mental (not written) notes of the interviewee's demeanor and behavior when not hiding the truth. The interviewer should be professional and personable.

The interviewer should not:

- Joke or attempt to humor the subject
- Comment on the subject's physical appearance
- Say something that is untrue
- Attempt to diminish the seriousness of the offense, issue, or topic of discussion

Now the interviewer is ready to obtain an admission. This is done methodically and carefully. It typically involves asking three simple questions in a very precise order. Using the facts of the case appropriately, the questions unfold as follows:

- When did you first realize other employees were doing _____?
- When was the first time you had the opportunity to join them (*or some variation of this*)?
- When was the first time you participated?

The first two questions are designed to allow the interviewee to acknowledge the offense or offenses in question occurred, without incriminating himself or anyone else. The third question calls for the actual admission. If he hesitates to answer it, the interviewer can assist him by stressing the need to understand the motives behind the subject's every action; the interviewer can adhere to his conviction of the subject's guilt without being accusatory. While understanding motive and intent are not necessary for the employer to achieve a standard of proof, asking questions about the subject's thought processes and intentions allows him the opportunity to save face by rationalizing his behavior. The interviewer can even help in this regard. The interviewer might suggest:

> *I have no reason to believe you did this to hurt _____. Sometimes people do things they later regret. I think the reason this happened was because you did not think it through. You had good reason to be angry and just made a bad decision. Is that not correct?*

Another approach I often use at this critical moment during the interview is to ask this question:

> *Would I be truthful if I told management that you only _____ one time?*

Insert into this question the appropriate offense. Note that if the interviewee answers affirmatively, he has made a significant admission. If he answers *no*, the immediate response is to ask: *What number would be more accurate?* If he offers the unlikely response, *never* immediately move his attention back to the two commitments and indicate that his response *never* was not consistent with those commitments. Do not tell him that he is a liar or that he is lying. If he claims that you are, remind him the question was not regarding his truthfulness, but instead asked only: *Would I be truthful* if I told management ..." [emphasis added].

Once an admission is made, ask these important follow-up questions:

- *When was the last time you _____?*
- *How many times did you _____?*

Dos and don'ts:

- Do not exaggerate the quality or quantity of evidence you have.
- Do not claim to have evidence you do not.
- Do not show your proof or reveal the identity of any sources.
- Discourage the subject from challenging your evidence or the quality of your investigation.
- Do not threaten, coerce, or attempt to intimidate.

- Demonstrate confidence and do not allow challenges to cause you to doubt the accuracy of your information.
- Do not allow the subject to think you are a decision maker.
- Do not make promises you cannot keep.
- Do not offer immunity.
- Demonstrate compassion, not arrogance.

Throughout, manage your tone and body language, remain firm and confident. Demonstrate empathy and avoid any appearance of being judgmental. Look the subject in the eye. Use body language that is sympathetic, but confident. Observe the body language and behavior of the interviewee. Move into his intimate space in order to communicate your compassion. However, do not touch him. Do not pat his knee, put your hand on his shoulder, or touch his hands. Some interview methods call for this form of intimacy at this moment. DO NOT do it. Unwanted touching may later be regarded as battery. Battery in many jurisdictions is considered both a crime and tort. To commit it exposes the interviewer to both prosecution and a lawsuit. DO NOT touch the interviewee.

During this entire exchange, the interviewer and his witness should be taking notes. The date, start time, and the time of any breaks should be documented. All notes should be neat and legible. They should be retained and become part of the permanent case file. Even if one's notes are used to generate a report and then destroyed, the interviewer or fact finder could face the claim of spoliation. If your organization has a policy of not retaining investigative notes, change the policy. Destroying one's notes also creates the appearance that the interviewer/fact finder is hiding something. It also could give rise to the claim the interviewer is unprofessional and acted unethically. Here's how.

Suppose the interviewee cooperated fully, made an admission, but did not provide a written statement regarding his guilt. After the interview, the interviewer prepares his final report and destroys his notes. Postdiscipline, the interviewee recants his admission and claims he's innocent. He asserts the interviewer also thought he was innocent and was observed documenting it in his notes. He now demands the interviewer produce his notes to prove it. Do you see the problem? Without his notes, the interviewer has only his final report. Absent other circumstance (a witness for example), the matter is reduced to deciding who to believe, the accused or the unprofessional, paid fact finder.

4.2.5 Phase V: Discussion

Next, the interviewer needs to develop the admission. It sometimes can be difficult. For example, most employees know that theft is a terminable offense. Most know that to admit to it almost assures termination. So, instead, ease into it. Get the subject to identify the things he took without permission by offering a rationale for the behavior:

- *Taking office supplies is something everybody does. When was the last time you took some _____ home?*
- *It is not uncommon, for employees to borrow things from work. One of the more common things we have learned that employees borrow around here is _____.*
- *What was the smallest thing you ever borrowed from work?*
- *Would I be truthful if I told management that the smallest thing you have ever taken without permission was a _____?*

Tip: Note that the interviewer did not use the word "theft" or "steal." Instead, he uses terms such as "took without permission" or "borrow." Words matter, so choose them carefully.

Depending on circumstances and the fact pattern of the case, the interviewer should employ a variety of question types to develop additional information. Examples include:

- Open-ended questions: *Tell me what happened next?*
- Closed-end questions: *Exactly how many did you actually take?*
- Expansion questions: *You said you left the office at noon. Were you alone?*
- Directive questions: *Wouldn't you agree with me that honesty is the best policy?*
- Leading questions: *Did you see him touch her and then remark about her blouse?*
- Final questions: *Is there anything else we should discuss?*

Tip: Contrary to popular belief, leading questions are permissible. When used properly, they can expand the amount of information developed and sometimes take the interview in an entirely new and useful direction.

The interviewer also should seek the following information:

- Why did the subject do it?
- Was it his idea or was it suggested by someone else?
- What else did he do or say?
- Were there any witnesses?
- Who else was involved?
- Who else knows about it?
- Can the items taken be returned?
- Get the subject to name names.

Note that once the subject has made his admission and provided all of the pertinent details surrounding his misconduct, he should be questioned regarding the misconduct of others. If he is knowledgeable of others and their transgressions, he should be thoroughly questioned about them. The interviewer should systematically document the who, what, when, where, how, and why regarding each individual of whom the subject has knowledge. Use Appendix 5 to capture that which you are told regarding others. This information can then be added to that already developed during the second phase of the investigation. In doing so, the investigative team can make real-time decisions regarding the interview of others and continue to build its information base.

Here are few questions the interviewer should always ask:

■ *Who else should we talk to (and why)?*
■ *Who should we talk to next?*
■ *Who else knows about this?*
■ *How can you (we) prove that?*
■ *Do you have any physical evidence (email, photos, images, notes, cards, gifts)?*
■ *How might have we conducted a better investigation?*
■ *Does your supervisor know about this?*
■ *Who in management knows about this?*
■ *Did management ever engage in this?*
■ *How could we have learned about this sooner?*
■ *Do you think it will happen again, and, if so, why?*

Are here are a few questions the interviewer should never ask:

■ Coercive questions: *Would you be willing to cooperate in exchange for leniency?*
■ Intimidating/coercive questions: *Would you rather tell the truth or go to jail?*
■ Inappropriate questions: *Why didn't you tell your wife you wanted to leave her?*
■ Ignorant questions: *Do you think all people from _____ behave that way?*
■ Stupid questions: *Who do you think is going to win the game Sunday?*

Once the interviewer is satisfied that he has obtained all the information he is able to get, he should move closer to the desk at which he and the interviewee are sitting. Confidently, he should ask the interviewee two more questions: Are you prepared to make a commitment that, as long as you work here, you will never do these things again, and, if so, are you willing to put that commitment in writing? Revealing his written statement checklist (see Appendix 6, Written Statement Checklist), he will now walk the interviewee through it.

4.2.6 Phase VI: Written

Written statements play an important role in investigatory interviews. If the interviewer has been gentle and empathetic, most interviewees will not resist when asked to provide a written statement. Those that object should be asked why. In some instances, the interviewee is afraid of how the statement will be used or if others, including co-workers, will see it. Avoid these difficulties by communicating a little encouragement. The tools I have used include saying things such as:

■ While we cannot change the past, one can always alter the future.
■ If you are sorry, you should be given the chance to say so.
■ Putting your apology in writing will ensure that it is not misunderstood or forgotten.
■ Your statement will not be shared with your peers. Only the fact finders and decision makers will have access to it.
■ Without a statement by you, the decision makers will be left with only the results and my investigation and that which we discussed today.
■ There is no better way to affirm that you have been honest today than to put the truth into writing.

In other instances, the subject may simply be unable to write. It is acceptable for the interviewer to write or prepare the statement for the subject if asked. Doing so does not diminish the value of the statement or its usefulness. Even statements that are written by the subject, but unsigned, are useful. Statements written or prepared by the interviewer and read by the subject, but unsigned are still useful. Even a statement torn up by the subject is useful and should be retained.

> *Tip: Casually display your written declaration checklist and preprinted statement form (Appendix 7) and ask the subject: "How's your penmanship?"*

For those of you who haven't yet looked at Appendix 6, here are the elements that the interviewer should encourage the subject to include in his written statement:

1. A description of the precise nature of the misconduct.
2. Details of when, where, and last time the event in question occurred.
3. The known or observed misconduct of others.
4. The motive for subject's actions.
5. The motive for the subject's cooperation and participation in the interview.
6. An acknowledgement that subject understands that he violated company policy and/or the law.

7. An acknowledgement that the subject understands that because of his actions he may be disciplined or discharged (or prosecuted, if applicable).
8. Document why the subject has decided to be honest knowing the possibility of discipline (or prosecution).
9. The subject's opportunity to add anything to the statement in his own words.
10. An affirmation as to the truthfulness of the statement and the reliability of its contents.

In the event the subject is completely opposed to a written statement in any form, the interviewer should prepare an *addendum*. An addendum is a statement prepared by the interviewer (or any fact finder, for that matter) detailing a particular occurrence or event. This underused tool is particularly suitable for investigative interviews in situations where a written statement cannot be obtained from the subject. It permits the contemporaneous capture of information not possible by other means. What's more, addenda can be used as admissible evidence. For example, suppose the interview begins very cordially, the subject readily makes an admission, and then suddenly has a change of heart. He becomes belligerent and even abusive. Before the interview has been completed, the interviewee summarily leaves the interview and walks off the job. The interviewer would document this in detail. It would include all of the information the decision makers would need to appreciate what took place, what was said, and who said it.

> *Tip: If the subject refuses to provide a written statement, offer to prepare one for him. If that is refused, the interviewer can prepare an addendum and document what took place and the subject's admission if provided.*

As noted, the last list item to be included in the written statement is any comment or added information the subject wishes to incorporate. This is the best place for the subject to offer an apology or say he is sorry. Here are a few more tips:

■ Do not allow the subject to offer a conditional apology. (*If given a second chance, I promise never to _____ again.*)
■ Take each page of the statement from the subject as he completes it.
■ Return the statement one page at a time for the subject to sign.
■ When finished, make three copies and put the original in a secure place.
■ Obtain permission from the decision makers before providing the subject a copy of his written statement.

Once the statement is signed by the interviewee, both the interviewer and the witness should sign it. Once everyone present has signed each page the interviewer and the witness should politely excuse themselves, telling the interviewee that they are going to take a break and, when they return, they will be accompanied by the individual who introduced them at the beginning of the process or someone else in a decision making capacity. If not done so previously, it is appropriate to allow the interviewee to take a break or use the restroom if necessary. He should be instructed that should he leave the interview room, he is not to return to his work area and must return immediately once he has used the restroom. He should be told as well that, if he runs into someone outside the interview room, he is not to discuss the interview or reveal that an investigation is underway.

4.2.7 Phase VII: Oral

The oral portion of the interview involves a management representative or a decision maker, if available. That person will now participate in the interview in a scripted and concise manner. Begin this phase by providing a copy of the interviewee's statement to the management representative. Share with her the subject's level of cooperation, remorsefulness, and that which she admitted. Ensure the management representative also has a copy of Appendix 4. At the bottom of that document are instructions that must be followed. Things to consider before the interview resumes include:

■ Is the management representative properly briefed and does she know her script?
■ Is there enough seating for everyone in the interview room?
■ Does the subject know the management representative and, if so, what is their relationship?
■ Are there any problems that should be anticipated?

I frequently use this opportunity to digitally record this portion of the interview and attempt to have the interviewee repeat his admission so that it may be recorded. This enables me to capture the mood and tone of the interview and eliminate a future claim that the admission was made under duress or obtained improperly.

> *Trap: Recording any portion of an interview has its risks. Interviewers should not record their interviews unless they have been properly trained and have the requisite experience to do it properly. As such, the practice of recording this or any other portion of the interview should be very carefully examined before deciding to do so. A bad recording is worse than no recording at all.*

Again, using a preprepared checklist (see Appendix 8—the Oral Statement Checklist), I attempt to engage both the interviewee and the decision maker. Here are some of the more critical items on my checklist:

1. Have everyone else present identify his or herself by name, position, and employer.
2. Establish that the subject understands English and is aware that he or she is being recorded.
3. Establish that the subject understands why he has been investigated and/or being interviewed.
4. Establish that the subject was treated fairly.
5. Establish that the interviewer is an information gatherer not a police officer.
6. Establish that the subject was not imprisoned and that he could leave at any time.
7. Establish whether the subject requested a representative.
8. Establish that subject was not denied use of the telephone, food, drink, or the restroom.
9. Establish why the subject did/did not want representation.
10. Review the methods of investigation that could have been used and that one or more of them were used to gather information about the subject.
11. Establish that subject agreed to two conditions in order to participate in the interview and ask that he repeat them.
12. Establish that the interviewer is only an information gatherer, not a decision maker.
13. Establish that no threats or promises were made.
14. Establish possibility of termination and/or prosecution or other action as appropriate.
15. Establish that the subject understands that his cooperation did not (or does) guarantee favorable treatment or continued employment.
16. Establish why the subject has been honest.
17. Have the subject identify his signature on his written statement and then read the statement to the management representative.
18. Review information provided by the subject regarding others.
19. Allow the decision maker to ask questions.
20. Allow the subject to ask any questions or add anything to his or her statement that he wishes.
21. If the interview goes beyond a reasonable length of time, state why.
22. Ask the subject not to discuss the investigation or his interview with others that may be involved.
23. Ask the subject if everything he has just stated in the presence of the management representative is true and correct.
24. Establish date and time, and that the recorder (if used) was not turned off during the recorded portion of the interview (or, if it was, why).
25. Offer the subject the last word.

My questions are asked so as to allow the subject to answer without a simple yes or no response. I attempt to obtain as much dialogue between me and the subject as possible. I want the management representative (or listener, if it has been recorded) to have a very good appreciation for the atmosphere in which my interview took place. Here are a few more tips:

- Ask that the subject direct his answers to the management representative instead of you or the witness.
- Pay close attention to the subject's answers to the questions on your checklist. If answered incorrectly or inconsistently, politely correct him or ask for an explanation.
- Help the subject with the answers to your questions, but do not spoon-feed him.
- When asking the subject to read his written statement to the management representative, provide him only a copy, not the original. Read along with him to ensure he reads what is written and does not ad-lib.

> *Tip: If a witness is present, in the presence of the management representative ask if they have any questions or have something to add. Know in advance if they intend to ask or add something. During this critical portion of the interview, the last thing the interviewer wants is surprises.*

4.2.8 Phase VIII: Conclusion

Following the oral phase, arrangements are made to have the decision maker place the interviewee on administrative leave. Instead of deciding discipline on the spot, the decision maker is permitted time to analyze what was said by the interviewee and the totality of the information gathered during the entire investigation. Additionally, other interviews may be necessary. Those interviews may produce additional information regarding the subject and may impact any disciplinary decisions. Delaying the decision to discipline also allows the employer the opportunity to examine all of the evidence and make fairer, less disparate decisions. Postponing the disbursement of disciplinary action following the completion of the entire investigation also allows the employer time to prepare final checks, draft discharge notices, and make the appropriate internal disclosures.

Conclude your process by:

- completing all of the items on your oral statement checklist
- providing the subject your contact information and final instructions
- arranging to obtain the subject's personal effects (keys, jacket, purse, etc.) so that he may go home
- not allowing the subject to return to his work area
- disabling access card, codes, passwords, and, if appropriate, collect any organization items
- arranging for the subject to safely leave the premises

Tip: Ensure the subject leaves the premises by having someone watch him. If stolen property is to be returned, arrange for delivery of it away from the workplace.

4.3 Summary

There are few skills more important to the modern fact finder than the ability to obtain information through effective interviewing. However, many methodologists offer methods and techniques that are not appropriate for use in the private sector. Their style is accusatory and harsh; it assumes guilt and is largely contradictory to the best practices used by those outside law enforcement.

Investigatory interviews are different. They are always noncustodial, voluntary, and nonconfrontational. The interviewer always treats the interviewee with respect and dignity. However, interviews nonetheless are complex and fraught with unseen liability and risk. Like their law enforcement counterpart, they are psychologically demanding and require a high level of mental concentration. However, they also require more planning and preparation and typically culminate the fact finding and information gathering phase of most workplace investigations. They are conducted for the purpose of learning the truth and obtaining an admission. An admission is a simple statement of guilt. For disciplinary purposes, an employer needs only make a reasonable determination of guilt. The employer need not prove all of the elements of the crime in order to impose corrective action. Therefore, a properly obtained admission from the offender meets the employer's burden of proof. The Investigative Interview Method (I2M), as described in this chapter, was developed to meet this need. However, most critically, and unlike law enforcement's interrogations, investigatory interviews are nonaccusatory. Typically, the subject is either known to have committed the offense in question or the interviewer has very good reason to believe that he has. Coercion, intimidation, and psychological abuse are never used by the investigative interviewer.

Is summary, when used properly, I2M has several distinct benefits over other methods. They include:

- A nonaccusatory approach
- No use of intimidation or coercion
- A highly structured and process-driven technique
- An easily learned and replicated methodology
- Consistent results with admission rates typically exceeding 90 percent
- Significant reduction in the likelihood of false confessions
- Results that are court admissible
- A time-tested and proven process

4.4 Frequently Asked Questions

If you did not before, you now realize that successful investigative interviews are complicated. In spite of our best intentions and the amount of process we impose on our effort, investigative interviews sometimes encounter wrinkles. I will cover the most complex of them in Chapters 6 and 7. In those chapters, we will examine deception detection and how to deal with objections and denials as well as many of the legal issues and challenges associated with conducting investigative interviews in the workplace. For now, let's attempt to answer a few questions you likely have and smooth out a few of those wrinkles.

1. When should the interviewee be notified of his intended interview?

   This is a common question and it is surprising how few answer it correctly. The interviewee or subject, if you may, should not be told of his pending interview until he meets the interviewer. Without the element of surprise, the interviewee is able to:

   a. *Prepare for the questions he will likely be asked*
   b. *Destroy or alter evidence*
   c. *Intimidate or hurt witnesses or themselves*
   d. *Flee*
   e. *Engage in acts of vandalism or sabotage*
   f. *Warn accomplices*
   g. *Notify the press and others eager to damage the reputation of the organization*
   h. *Get a lawyer*
   i. *And, given enough time, initiate preemptive litigation*

   I have had cases in which my customer insisted the subject be told of his interview in advance. In some cases, it was debated as to whether the subject be given as much as a month's notice. The reason for this inanity was usually something to do with culture or employee expectations. If these are the reasons your decision makers insist your subject should be tipped off, ask them if the subject extended the same courtesy to them before he plotted and committed his crimes against his victims. If you agree to prenotification of your subject, also be sure to ask them to provide you a Kevlar vest—you might need it.

   The other common reason for early notification of the interviewee is scheduling. While it is often a challenge, organizational decision makers need to manipulate and manage the schedule of the subject without tipping him off. In doing this, obvious and inappropriate deceptions should not be used. Do nothing that will allow the interviewee to later claim he was deceived and, thus, justify his refusal to cooperate in the interview. Use your imagination and be careful.

2. When should others be notified?

This question goes to when we notify the subject's supervisor, manager, the legal department, or parties outside of the organization that the subject will be interviewed. Regarding the interviewee's supervisor, I offer the same reasoning as stated above. I also would add to my list of concerns the possibility that the supervisor knows of or has involvement in the problem. That is the reason we have the management representative introduce the interviewee to the interviewer, not his supervisor (see section 4.2.2 above). Regarding notification of the other parties, the decision should be made based on:

a. *Organizational needs*
b. *Past practices, precedents, and existing policies*
c. *The requirement to do so according to governing regulations and law*

It is helpful to remember that the more people who know that employees will be interviewed pursuant to an internal investigation, the greater the likelihood of it being compromised. I always suggest that my customers err on the side of caution and involve as few people as possible.

3. Is it permissible to interview those who are not employees?

It is permissible to interview nonemployees. How and when to interview them will be largely determined by the facts of the case and circumstances. Contractors are the most common nonemployee interviewees, though vendors and customers are sometimes interviewed as well. Unless contractually obligated, the fact finder does not need the permission of the contractor to interview his employees. Past practices and precedent aside and unless absolutely necessary, neither the contractor nor his employees should be notified prior to an investigative interview. To do otherwise invites unnecessary complications and problems. Here are a few of them. The contractor:

a. *May refuse to make the employee available*
b. *May insist he or his attorney participate*
c. *Might insist to see the evidence before cooperating further*
d. *Might notify government regulators, law enforcement, or the press*
e. *Might destroy evidence, intimidate witnesses, or fire the subject*

Unless absolutely necessary, do not notify the contractor of your intention to interview one of his employees. Similar caution should be used when deciding to interview customers and vendors. Often these situations pose a public relations problem, not a tactical one. Think it through, exercise caution, and prepare for the unexpected.

Another group to consider are family members of the subject. The first and foremost considerations when deciding to interview a family member are privacy and confidentiality. The fact finder should not rely on the insistence the family member keep his or her interview or that which is discussed during it confidential. The family member could easily (and will most likely) compromise the investigation upon learning of it. The damage could be irreparable.

4. When should recommendations be provided?

The temptation to provide recommendations should be resisted. Instinctively, most fact finders conclude their process by providing recommendations to whom they report. Many very experienced investigators do this as a natural course of business. However, by offering recommendations regarding discipline, the fact finder has the ability to influence the decision maker. In doing so, the fact finder places his credibility in jeopardy.

At first blush, this assertion is counterintuitive. A reasonable person could easily contend that by his very position, the fact finder is influential. The fact finder enjoys great autonomy and is able to take his investigation wherever he wishes and include or exclude whatever evidence he sees fit. Furthermore, it can be argued that of all of the interested parties, the fact finder is the most qualified to make recommendations, for it is he (and his team) who is closest to the facts. All of these propositions may be true. However, a proper investigation should have engineered safeguards into the process to ensure that the fact finder's efforts are focused and reasonable. Here are a few of those safeguards:

a. *The fact finder and project team are driven by established process, not personal agendas (review the first chapter for more details).*

b. *The Process of Investigation clearly defines the fact finder's role and the limits of his authority.*

c. *From the onset, the investigative effort is driven by clearly articulated and well defined objectives.*

d. *The fact finder and the entire investigative effort are overseen by a designated higher authority (very possibly outside counsel). As such, the fact finder is responsible to him, not necessarily the decision maker.*

e. *The decision maker is bound to a standard of proof established before the investigation began.*

These safeguards diminish the fact finder's ability to pursue his own agenda, spin facts, and influence the decision maker. This construct may appear contrived, however. Absent some sort of structure and defined process, including the delegation of responsibilities, the acting parties may indeed be defenseless. Only with a well-conceived and defined process can the participants assert impartiality and fairness. Good looks and a bright smile won't do it. Experienced employers will agree that, in the end, it is the process that will be challenged at a trial not the malfeasant employee who brought the suit.

Another problem arises when a fact finder makes recommendations. As the title suggests, the fact finder is one who seeks out and uncovers facts. His work product should be factual and grounded in objective determinations. Conversely, recommendations are subjective. By combining objective findings with subjective recommendations, the fact finder's work product can no longer be claimed as purely factual. In effect, it is tainted. Not intentionally, but nevertheless, it is tainted. Of course, the fact finder could clearly segregate his findings of fact from his recommendations, but when pressed while under oath, he might have to admit that the totality of his work product was not entirely factual. Albeit, with hesitation he would have to admit that he had been somewhat subjective and not all that he had provided the decision makers were facts. This damaging testimony could be cleaned up during cross-examination. However, regardless of the qualifiers added, it still does not play well. The point I am making is simple, there is no need or advantage in providing recommendations. When the fact finder makes recommendations, it tends to diminish his credibility by questioning his impartiality.

Possibly the biggest problem recommendations create are instances when the recommendations are not acted upon or rejected. If the recommendations are not protected by an attorney work product privilege, they are subject to discovery. Later, long after the investigation has been concluded, recommendations can come back to haunt an organization. Here is a good example.

Suppose the postinvestigation recommendations made by a fact finder included improvements to exterior lighting. Say the fact finder concluded that better lighting in the employee parking lot would reduce the chance of future vandalism to both the company property and employee vehicles. However, because of cost or other priorities, the improvements are never made. Then, sometime later, tragedy strikes. A female employee is brutally attacked in that same parking lot while leaving the facility late at night. She then sues alleging that the organization did not do enough to protect her. Her causes of action might include: inadequate security, negligent security, and employer negligence. During the discovery phase of the litigation the long-forgotten recommendations of our otherwise well-meaning fact finder are uncovered. Among his recommendations, of course, is the recommendation to improve the lighting in the very parking lot in which the attack took place. The report and its recommendations would support her allegations and further demonstrate that the attack was even foreseeable. Foreseeability would point directly to her employer's negligence. For the theory propounds that the employer knew of the risk and ignored it. In doing so, it was negligent and thus liable.

When proven, negligence and foreseeability impart huge exposure to the employer. The exposure is expanded further when the plaintiffs' demands include compensatory and punitive damages. As the name suggests, punitive damages are awarded to punish the defendant. It is not uncommon that punitive damages are awarded in large multiples of the compensatory damages. Making the matter even more painful, some states, such as California, prohibit insurance companies from paying punitive damages. In such states, these damages are paid directly by the defendant. See Appendix 8 for an example of properly crafted recommendations.

Trap: Allowing, asking, or insisting the fact finder make recommendations. The fact finder should resist the temptation to make recommendations. The tradition of providing the decision maker recommendations is unnecessary and tends to diminish the credibility of the fact finder and increases the employer's liability.

5. Should the interviewer use props during his interview?

   The answer is no. Interview props include stacks of documents or files, recording devices on the interviewer's desk, a computer screen visible to the interviewee with his or her image displayed or other items marked or appearing to be evidence. Some interview methodologists encourage the use of props and others are silent on the issue. Because of the potential for administrative or legal challenges to both the process and its outcome, props should not be used. If challenged, the interviewer will have to produce them and explain their purpose to the trier-of-fact. He ultimately will have to admit they were used to deceive the interviewee by creating the appearance that he had more evidence than he really had. The admission of deception will bring new light on the entire investigative interview process and the two commitments regarding honesty the interviewer imposed on the interviewee. Do not use props.

6. How does one go about recovering physical evidence from the interviewee?

   Carefully. If the interviewee offers or admits to having evidence in his possession, the interviewer should not attempt to recover it until the interview is entirely completed. Doing otherwise breaks momentum and allows the interviewee time to ponder his commitment to cooperate. I have made this mistake and it was devastating. During the Oral phase of the interview, the interviewer should ask the interviewee if he is willing to remand the evidence he disclosed in his possession. If he agrees, allow him to describe it in detail and obtain his commitment to surrender it at a time and location to be determined at a later date. From an evidentiary perspective, even if it is never surrendered, the admission of its existence (and full description of it) is almost as valuable as the physical evidence itself. Prior to the disbursement of disciplinary action contact the interviewee and arrange recovery of the evidence. At the place it is exchanged, properly inventory it, photograph it, and provide the subject a receipt after he has signed it.

7. What if the interviewee insists on providing a written statement after his interview?

   Discourage it. Tell the interviewee that the process requires a statement be provided during the interview. If the subject refuses and insists he provide it later, the interviewer may have no choice, but to accept it. However, rarely will they provide it and, if they do, it will likely have little or no value. What's more, it could possibly contain information or alleged evidence suggesting the subject's innocence. It also could contain allegations of interviewer and/or witness misconduct or worse. If the subject refuses to provide a written statement during the interview for whatever reason, the interviewer should write an addendum memorializing the interview and what took place during it as soon as the interview is finished.

8. Can an investigative interview be conducted electronically?

Yes. The need to conduct electronic interviews (those using the telephone or video conferencing) is growing. Today, more and more interviews, both administrative and investigatory, are being done electronically. The following are several issues the interviewer should contemplate before initiating a telephone interview of any type:

a. *How will confidentialities be assured?*

b. *How will the interviewer know if the subject or others are listening in on the interview?*

c. *Should the interviewer record the conversation?*

d. *Should the interviewee be notified that the interview is being recorded?*

e. *How does the interviewer deal with not being able to see the interviewee and his body language?*

f. *How does the interviewer deal with getting a written statement from the interviewee?*

g. *How should the interviewer respond if the interviewee wants to prepare a statement after the interview and email it to the interviewer?*

Each interviewer will have to address these questions based on the circumstances and challenges he faces. Though electronic interviews are often economical and convenient, they are not typically practical. Whenever possible, investigative interviews should be conducted in person.

9. Are there any other safety issues to consider?

Yes. Safety should be everyone's priority. The safety of all participants in the investigative interview process should be considered. Though I have never had an incident during or following one of my investigative interviews, I know of others who have. Safety begins with assessing and anticipating the risks. Once identified, the fact finder should engineer and install mitigating safeguards and precautions around those risks. When in doubt, err on the side of safety. If the risk is too great and cannot be adequately mitigated, do not conduct the interview.

Endnotes

1. Fred Inbau, John E. Reid, Joseph Buckley, and Brian Jayne, *Criminal Interrogations and Confessions*, 4th ed. (Gaithersburg, MD: Aspen Publishers, Inc., 2001), 5.
2. Ibid., 4.
3. Ibid., 6, 8.

4. In *Cotran v. Rollins Hudig Hall International, Inc.,* 1998 Cal. LEXIS 1 (January 5, 1998), the California Supreme Court joined the majority of other jurisdictions in holding that good cause existed for terminating an employee for misconduct if an employer had a reasonable and good faith belief that the employee engaged in misconduct. It was ruled that the employer does not have to convince the court or jury that the employee, in fact, committed the misconduct, only that the employer honestly believed that the employee engaged in misconduct based upon substantial evidence obtained through an adequate investigation that included a fair opportunity for the employee to respond to the charges. The court further defined the term *good cause* as a "reasoned conclusion … supported by substantial evidence gathered through an adequate investigation that includes notice of the claimed misconduct *and a chance for the employee to respond.*" So, while the employees of employers in the private sector do not enjoy constitutionally protected due process rights, the California Supreme Court holds that an accused employee indeed has the right to respond.

5. There are exceptions. Employers whose employees are members of a collective bargaining unit (members of a recognized employee union) are often required to meet a higher standard of proof.

6. Nina Moore, *Nonverbal Communication: Studies and Applications* (New York: Oxford University Press, 2010).

7. Edward T. Hall, *The Hidden Dimension* (New York: Anchor Books, 1990).

8. *NLRB v. J. Weingarten, Inc.*, 420 U.S. 251 (1975), was a case decided by the U.S. Supreme Court that ruled that employees in unionized workplaces have the right under the National Labor Relations Act to the presence of a union representative during any management inquiry that the employee reasonably believes may result in discipline. The decision, however, did not stipulate that the employer (or his agent) must notify the employee of this right. The decision also stipulated that the representative provided could not disrupt the process or otherwise interfere with the interview.

9. ASIS International, *Workplace Violence Prevention and Intervention* (ASIS/SHRM WVPI.1-2011, 2011).

10. J. S. Cawood, and M. H. Corcoran, *Violence Assessment and Intervention: The Practitioner's Handbook,* 2nd ed. (Boca Raton, FL: CRC Press, 2008).

Chapter 5

Administrative Interviews and Communicating Our Results

Key learning points:

1. Administrative interviews are designed for the purpose of gathering information. Generally they are reserved for those who are not materially involved in the matter under investigation, but are tangentially associated with it.
2. Before conducting administrative interviews, determine who likely has the information you seek and, among them, who is most likely to provide it. Remember, even innocent people will not always be cooperative or tell the truth.
3. All interview notes should be retained. Do not destroy notes, documents, evidence, or case files until the matter has been completely adjudicated and all possible opportunities of appeal have expired.
4. If an interviewee refuses to provide a statement or sign one prepared for them, they should be asked why. Often their concerns can easily be addressed and an otherwise hesitant interviewee will become agreeable.
5. The lay witness may express an opinion on matters of common observation where an opinion is the only logical way to convey the information. These opinions are permitted only concerning subjects of which the average person has considerable experience and knowledge.

6. Spontaneous declarations (*res gestae*) are declarations that are spontaneous utterances or statements, made in response to some sudden and shocking event, such as an accident or horrific crime.
7. Before testifying, the investigator should be aware of the probable line of questioning he will face and how all of the evidence he has gathered will be introduced and used at the trial.

"Though administrative interviews are for the purpose of gathering information, the one asking the questions should still be the smartest guy in the room."

E. F. Ferraro

5.1 Introduction

For the purposes of workplace investigations in the private sector, there are two types of interviews. The first and most basic is the *administrative* interview. Though we examined investigative interviews (the second type of interviews) in the prior chapter, administrative interviews, like the Reid Technique˚ *interview*, typically occur before any investigative interviews take place. I chose to present these interview types out of order because I have found that my students often fail to appreciate the importance of administrative interviews and to understand how investigative interviews use the information they potentially yield. Moreover, the format and structure of these two interview types are very similar. If one learns the intricacies of investigative interviewing, understanding and conducting administrative interviewing should be a snap.

5.2 Purpose of Administrative Interviews

The purpose of administrative interviews is to gather information otherwise not available by other means. Administrative interviews are a method of investigation and provide insight into a process, situation, or event. Generally, administrative interviews are casual, yet professional. As with all workplace interviews, the subject should be treated with respect and dignity. The tone should be polite and conversational. Because the subject is asked to cooperate and volunteer information, the interviewer should not fire questions at the interviewee. Instead, the interviewer should ask open-ended questions and allow the subject to provide explanatory responses in a conversational manner. The interviewee should *explain* more than just offer answers. The interviewer should be seeking insight as well as facts.

Administrative interviews are generally reserved for the following:

- Witnesses
- Stakeholders
- Process owners
- Anyone with information (other than the subject)

5.3 Administrative Interview Process

Similar to our investigative interview method, our administrative interviews involve process and will unfold iteratively. However, the administrative process is simpler. The methodology has only six distinct phases:

Phase I: Preparation
Phase II: Introduction
Phase III: Presentation
Phase IV: Discussion
Phase V: Written
Phase VI: Conclusion

And, like the Investigative Interview Method™ (I²M) it is structured, but flexible. However, it is designed to easily transition to an investigative interview when necessary. Because it is possible that the interviewee is culpable of an actionable offense unknown to the interviewer, the interviewer needs the ability to change his approach upon its discovery. This is more common than many fact finders anticipate. When it happens, the interviewer needs to be prepared and seamlessly transition an investigative interview, obtain an admission, and properly move on. A loose, ad hoc administrative interview methodology will not allow this. Thus, going forward, I want you to think of the administrative interview as an investigative interview without the benefit of knowing the full involvement or culpability of the interviewee before you. To facilitate our examination of this method I will forego much of what was discussed in the prior chapter and instead focus on the differences between the two methodologies. Let's begin with a few general considerations.

5.3.1 Determining Who Should Be Interviewed

Determining who should be interviewed is sometimes more complex than it might first appear. Employers often want everyone interviewed. Interviewing *everyone* is not a strategy, it's a fishing expedition. As mentioned in Chapter 4, it consumes time and valuable resources. The investigative team should consider the project's objectives, time restraints, and budget, and decide what information is needed and then interview those that possess it. As a general rule, start with those who are expected to be the most cooperative, not necessarily with the most information. In complex matters, the learning curve can be steep. By starting with those who will likely be talkers, the fact finder will more rapidly come up to speed and better prepare himself for interviewing those less cooperative or hesitant.

> *Tip: Before conducting administrative interviews determine who likely has the information sought, and, among them, who is most likely to provide it. Remember, even innocent people will not always be cooperative or tell the truth.*

Additional considerations include:

- How soon in advance should the interviewee be notified?
- How much should be the interviewee be told about the investigation's purpose?
- How best can confidentialities be protected?
- What can be done to prevent the perpetrator from learning of the investigation and the administrative interviews planned?
- Should anyone else be notified or involved?

5.3.2 Selecting the Interviewer

As with investigative interviews, selecting the right interviewer for the right reason is critical. However, because administrative interviews are not used for the purpose of obtaining an admission, interviewers with less skill and experience easily can be used. These interviews also serve as excellent training opportunities for new members of the team or investigative interviewers in training. To the extent possible, match the interviewer's skill and experience to the complexity of the matter in question. Administrative interviews are capable of producing information that can instantly break an investigation wide open. Do not undervalue a subject or his potential for providing useful information.

5.3.3 Location of the Interview

The location and interview room set up for administrative interviews is not as critical as they are for investigative interviews. However, remember at any moment an interviewee could make an admission against interest (incriminating himself) and the dynamic of the interview change accordingly.

5.3.4 *Introduction*

Like investigatory interviews, administrative interviews are best begun with a structured introduction. Here's the one I typically use:

> _____, *my name is* _____. *My team recently assisted your (or our) organization to look into* _____. *We have not yet completed that effort; however, today I would like to share with you some of what I and my team have learned so far. As you would image, we expect and appreciate your cooperation.*

Note the similarities to the introduction used for investigatory interviews. Also note that the word *investigation* is again not used. It should not be used at this point unless absolutely necessary or it is somehow widely known that an investigation is underway. And, again, like the investigative interview, I tell the interviewee he can do any of the following:

- Take a break
- Use the restroom
- Use the telephone
- Discontinue the meeting at any time, with or without my permission or that of management

5.3.5 *Presentation*

The interviewer should then disclose the genesis and purpose of the investigation. At a minimum, the interviewer should reveal the following:

- Context and ground rules (if any)
- That an investigation, in fact, is underway
- Generally, the purpose of that investigation
- Something about the information he is seeking and why

You should recall that this monologue is called the theme. The interviewer should know it cold. He also should disclose that he is only a fact finder and not a decision maker. He should explain that at the end of the process, his results will be provided to the decision makers, and only they will decide the outcome. He should then develop the theme by:

1. offering a general explanation of how an investigation is typically conducted and methods that are used; and
2. revealing that, by using one or more of those methods, it was learned that the interviewee *may have information that might be useful.*

Note that instead of telling the interviewee *we know he was involved* as in an investigative interview, we instead say that he *may have information that might be useful*. This is a key differentiator between this type of interview and an investigatory interview. Here is an example:

> *Let me begin by sharing with you a little bit about how an investigation of this type is conducted. Effectively, we have only six methods of investigation available to us. The first method is something we call physical surveillance. Physical surveillance is nothing more than watching people, places, and things. In this particular case, early on we discovered* (a few hints are dropped and the other methods explained with more hints).

Using one or more of these methods, we learned you *may have information that might be useful*. Today, what we hope to accomplish is *find out that which you know and how you might be able to assist us.*

Just like the investigative interview, the interviewer describes all six methods. He intertwines some facts from the case with the explanation of each method whenever possible and/or appropriate.

Next, in order to move the interviewee to providing the information in his possession, the interviewer needs to impose some conditions. The conditions create the appearance of an obstacle of which the interviewee must overcome in order for the interview to go forward and he be allowed to participate. Appropriately, those conditions involve honesty. And just like investigative interviews, the conditions are framed like this:

> *In order for us to discuss this matter and for you to have the opportunity to share with us that which you know, you need to agree to do two things. Both have to do with honesty. The first is to agree to be honest with me and the second is to agree to be honest with management (the decision makers).*

Once again, here it is, the first question asked during the interview: Can you promise to be honest with me? Notice that up to this point the interview has been a monologue. The interviewer has asked no questions or prompted the interviewee to respond to his statements. The first question asked is if the subject can be honest; when delivered properly, it is almost impossible for the interviewee to answer *no*. Moreover, should it be necessary to transition the interview to an investigative interview, the interview already has the two commitments in place.

If necessary, it is permissible for the interviewer to tell the interviewee that lying is the more serious offense if, in fact, it is. The interviewer also can remind the interviewee that the interview cannot continue unless the interviewee is truthful. The dialogue should go like this:

If you cannot be truthful about that which you know, this interview cannot take place. We will have no choice but to move our investigation along without you … and you may not have the chance to provide input later.

Again, without being accusatory, the interviewer tells the interviewee that he knows he has information concerning the issue in question. Experience shows that most administrative interviewees at this point will agree to cooperate and answer any questions posed to them.

5.3.6 Discussion

Suggesting the subject start at the "beginning," the interviewer can methodically move from the events leading up to the incident to the actual incident. At a minimum, the interviewer should seek answers to the following:

- What is it that the interviewee knows?
- Were there any witnesses?
- Who else was involved?
- Who else knows about it?
- Get the interviewee to name names.

This approach may seem overwrought or heavy handed, but remember the interviewee may be the person who committed the offense. By properly laying a foundation in this fashion, the interviewer is afforded the benefit of changing the interview from one seeking information to one seeking an admission.

The interviewer should next ask: "Are you willing to help us and put that in writing?" Casually, he should display his written declaration checklist and pre-printed statement form. If necessary, it is permissible to tell the interviewee that providing a written statement is a normal part of the process and that it is expected that a statement be provided by all those interviewed.

5.3.7 Documentation

Because the principal purpose of an administrative interview is to collect information, the interviewer should take notes. Like all interview notes, that which the interviewer documents should be accurate and concise. Notes should include the date of the interview, its start and finish time, and the name of the interviewer. As a matter of practice, some interviewers document their questions as well as the subject's answers. I have not found that to be necessary. In most instances, by accurately documenting the subject's answers, the questions that preceded them are obvious. The questions can be structured and, in some instances, prepared in advance. Sexual harassment investigations generally lend themselves to structured questions prepared in advance. Accident investigations on the other hand may not.

The fact finder's preinvestigation will help determine the line of questioning and the order of the questions to be asked. Helpful to the interviewer will be an outline containing some case facts and some information about the person being interviewed. The outline does not need to be formal and might contain the following:

- Name of the interviewee
- Date and time of interview
- Location of interview
- Type or description of incident in question
- Location of incident
- Known witnesses
- Relation of those witnesses to the subject
- Interviewee's job title
- Interviewee's known location at the time of the incident

Like all investigative notes, the notes of the interviewer should be written using a black ink pen on white lined paper (black ink photocopies better than blue ink on yellow paper). They should be neat and legible. The interviewer's notes should not contain any subjective comments or observations. The notes should be an objective reflection of what the subject said. At the completion of the interview, the notes should be kept in a safe place and retained. No notes (unless copies of originals) should be destroyed. Although many in public sector law enforcement destroy their notes after they have rendered their report, doing so in the private sector is bad form and should not be done. Destroying notes tends to raise questions later and make it appear that whoever destroyed them might be hiding something.

> *Tip: All interview notes should be retained. Do not destroy notes, documents, evidence, or case files until the matter has been completely adjudicated and all possible opportunities of appeal have expired.*

When appropriate, the interviewee should be asked to provide a statement. The statement may be prepared by either the interviewer or the interviewee. It may be handwritten or prepared using a computer. Regardless, the document should be authenticated by the interviewer and interviewee (and witness, if present) and dated. Authentication may be achieved with a signature or, more formally, with a notarized signature. The nature of the matter under investigation and importance of the statement should determine the appropriate protocol. If the subject is unwilling to provide a statement, one should be prepared for him and then be asked to sign it. If he refuses, ask that he read it and determine if it accurately reflects that which he said. If he agrees that it is accurate and yet still refuses to sign it, the interviewer should annotate such and sign it himself.

> *Tip: If an interviewee refuses to provide a statement or sign one prepared for him, he should be asked why. Often the subject's concern easily can be addressed and an otherwise hesitant interviewee will become agreeable.*

Important elements in an administrative statement include:

- Subject's name
- His position or job title
- Location of the interview
- Acknowledgement that the statement was voluntary
- The relevant facts, including the who, what, when, where, and how of the incident or matter in question
- Why the interviewee cooperated and was truthful
- An affirmation of the accuracy of the facts provided
- The signature of the interviewee
- The signature of the interviewer and witness, if present

The affirmation of the accuracy of the facts provided might read as follows. *I have written, read, and understand the above _____ number of lines and declare that they are true and correct. If later called upon to verify the information set forth in this statement, I will do so accurately and confidently.*

5.3.8 Confidentiality

Confidentiality is important to most workplace investigations. At the beginning of an administrative interview, the interviewer should tell the interviewee that the matter to be discussed is confidential and that it and the interview should be treated as such. Most interviewees will understand the need for confidentiality and will be agreeable to these terms. If they are not, they should be asked why. In matters such as the investigation of a sexual harassment allegation, confidentiality is almost always necessary. If so, it is acceptable for the interviewer to insist on it. If the interviewee is still hesitant, the interviewer should consider terminating the interview until a later time.

> *Trap: While an employer can consider the refusal to cooperate or keep a matter confidential to be insubordination, it is not advisable to discipline for it. Best advice: discontinue the interview and develop another investigative strategy.*

Conclude the interview by completing all of the items on your checklist, providing the interviewee your contact information and any final instructions. Then arrange for the interviewee to safely return to work if appropriate. A few final thoughts:

- SAFETY IS YOUR FIRST PRIORITY.
- Your work will affect the lives of those you interview and those they touch.
- Treat the subject as you would wish someone treat you or a family member.
- Respect the rights of those you interview.
- Treat all people with respect and dignity.

5.4 Communicating Our Results

Of all of the methods of communication, fact finders find report writing the least enjoyable. I tend to like it. Many tell me that the more they write, the more they seem to like it. Regardless of one's preference, report writing is a necessary requirement of the job. In this section, I will provide the fundamentals of basic report writing and review what I consider to be best practices. As most fact finders know, good reports evolve from good notes. Notetaking is a learned discipline. Accurate and complete notes allow the report writer the ability to write clear, concise, and complete reports. As you will read in the next chapter, notes frequently become part of the investigative case file and should be retained. One's notes should be written in black ink and be legible. The use of shorthand or symbols is acceptable as long as the notetaker can later accurately decipher his work. Destroying notes after a report has been rendered is not advisable and may lead to questions regarding the investigator's motives later. The same is not so for report drafts. Attorneys will occasionally recommend all drafts be retained. In all the years I have been in practice, I have not once been asked to produce a draft report of any kind. On the other hand, the request for notes is rather common and should be anticipated.

5.4.1 Bulletized Summary Reports

For many years, I prepared my reports in narrative form. With practice and considerable diligence, one can produce easy-to-read, well-written narrative reports. However, narrative reports are tedious and time consuming to write. Narrative reports also tend to lend themselves to inclusion of subjective remarks and the occasional conclusion. Alternatively, today, most of my reports are in the form of bulletized summations. I have found this format easy to write and easier for my reader to read and use. Figure 5.1 is a good example:

Notice, if you will, how easy this reads. It is fluid and easily tells the story. Additionally, the reader can quickly and efficiently find and extract what he wants. Also notice that this format eliminates the common redundancies of the typical narrative report, such as the subject's name, place, and date. Figure 5.2 is another example.

Interview of Mr. Erik Spicer

Saturday, August 21, 2011

Mr. Spicer stated:

- He is the Vice President of Finance and has been an employee of Marathon Press ("Marathon") since August of 1983.

- He currently works at the Houston, Texas office located at 1541 Wilshire Boulevard, Suite 150.

- Before joining Marathon he worked for Random House as an auditor for approximately fifteen years at its New York, New York headquarters.

- He reports to Mr. Charles L. Davidson, President and C.E.O. and has done so for the past eleven years.

- On Monday, August 16, 2011, he arrived at work at approximately 7:30 a.m. and opened the office for he was the first to arrive (see Exhibit C, Access Control Log dated August 16, 2011).

- Upon entering the business's executive office area in order to go to his office he noticed Mr. Davidson's office door was open and his desk lamp was on.

- Looking into Mr. Davidson's office expecting to see him, he saw instead, Ms. Rene Williams at his credenza with what appeared to be a contract file in her hand.

Figure 5.1 Sample of bulletized report.

The presentation is tight and to the point. Overwhelmingly, my clients have grown fond of this format as well. Moreover, it can be used for nearly any type of investigative report and any type of situation. I strongly recommend you try it if you are currently not using it. The bulletized summary reports also easily lend themselves to the insertion and use of references, exhibits, and footnotes. Because I like to use footnotes in my reports, the bulletized summary report allows me to quickly insert a few words that otherwise might not fit or flow smoothly in the body of the report. For example, see Figure 5.3.

Neatly, the footnote allows me to quickly provide additional information and context to what may appear to be an otherwise ordinary piece of information. Footnotes used in this fashion make the report interesting and more readable. Attorneys have used footnotes for years; isn't it about time professional investigators and fact finders do also?

Interview of Ms. Mary Brown

Tuesday, June 14, 2011

Ms. Brown stated:

- She has been an employee of XXX since July 2001, and is currently a maintenance clerk.

- She knew Ms. Snell from her previous place of employment, Hills Pet Nutrition and that Ms. Snell was known as a liar there, just as she is known to be one now.

- Ms. Snell hired her son-in-law (name unknown) at a wage, which exceeded his skills and experience.

- She was resentful that Ms. Snell rated her performance substandard and Ms. Brown intends to appeal it.

Figure 5.2 Sample of bulletized report 02.

Bulletized summary reports also allow reports to be quickly and easily redacted. Redacted reports are sometimes required when providing information to the authorities or others who are not members of the investigative team. In order to protect confidentialities and, in some cases, privacy, redacted reports are sometimes necessary. Deleting individual bullets or groups of bullets is easy and fast. The same cannot be said when redacting narrative reports.

> *Tip: Select a report format that best serves your purpose. Use a format that you find easy to prepare and your customer finds easy to use.*

Here are a few additional suggestions regarding reports:

- Ensure every report is clear, concise, and complete. The report should be a stand-alone document that can be read and understood by anyone.
- Prepare your report so that it tells a story. It should have a beginning, middle (or body), and an ending. Make sure your story is complete and precisely expresses that which is being reported upon.
- Ensure that your report objectively represents your investigative result. Subjective commentary and recommendations, even when appropriate, do not belong in an investigative report.

Interview of Ms. Susan Snell

Tuesday, June 22, 2013

Ms. Snell stated:

- She has been an employee of XXX since August 2013, and is currently a scheduling supervisor.

- She knew Ms. Brown from her previous place of employment, Hills Pet Nutrition and that they worked together closely for many years.

- Ms. Brown frequently complains about the performance of others and often distracts others with her constant griping.

- She hired her son-in-law, David Long approximately one year ago after receiving management approval from Stan Smith, Facility Superintendent.

- Mr. Smith decided both the pay rate and job title of Mr. Long at the time he was hired and that she had no influence over either decision.*

* This assertion is in direct conflict with the statements of Ms. Brown (dated June 14, 2013) and the first interview of Mr. Smith (dated June 15, 2011). It should also be noted that the employment application of Mr. Long dated April 1, 2010, indicates that it was Ms. Snell who decided Mr. Long's starting wage and it was she who approved a waiver for a pre-employment drug screening of Mr. Long (See report Exhibit Q).

Figure 5.3 Sample of bulletized report entry with footnote.

- Do not use military time. Other than those with military or law enforcement experience, most people are unfamiliar with military time. It is professionally arrogant to use it when your customer cannot translate it.
- Do not use law enforcement terminology. Do not use terms such as agent, suspect, perp, busted, or any other form of cop-speak. It is unprofessional and makes for lousy reading.
- Do not opine on the subject's credibility, truthfulness, or character.
- Do not offer a legal opinion or draw a legal conclusion.
- Do not use abbreviations or acronyms unless properly explained.
- Do not address the subject solely by his or her last name. Address the subject properly in the body of your report, and use Mr. and Ms.
- Use footnotes to provide supplemental information or context.
- Use footers on all of your reports. It looks professional and helps identify pages that have been separated from the original document.

- Clearly mark the classification (i.e., COMPANY CONFIDENTIAL (or its equivalent), ATTORNEY WORK PRODUCT) on each page of your report.
- Consider writing your reports in the third person, past tense. The use of first person should be reserved for statements, addenda, and affidavits.
- Spell-check and proofread all reports before submission.

The most frequent shortcomings I see include:

- The report writer has a poor understanding of facts and/or topic.
- Disorganization.
- Communicating in the wrong language (using industry vernacular or acronyms no one knows).
- A general failure to meet needs or expectations of the reader.

5.4.2 Findings of Fact

For several years my firm has added another section to its reports. We call that section *Findings of Fact*. The information is provided in tight, easy-to-report snippets with one fact following that which preceded it. When done properly, it tells a story and the reader, when finished, should have no questions as to what the investigation revealed. Here is an example:

- Ms. Snell provided Ms. Brown the combination to the company safe in the finance office on October 21, 2012, via email (See Exhibit G).
- Ms. Snell did not have the authority to share the safe combination with Ms. Brown (see Exhibit L, PNNL Safe Security Policy).
- Ms. Brown used the combination to open the safe and took without permission, $47,000 from it on the evening of October 22, 2012 (see Exhibit R, Ms. Brown's Written Statement).

Notice how one fact seems to build on the one that preceded it. The reader is easily able to see how the pieces fit together and from where the information came.

Another interesting feature that has been added to some of our reports is a timeline. It dawned on me one day that I often used timelines when assembling the various pieces of an investigation. So, I decided to add a version of one to a report. The result was stunning. Visually, it is pleasing to the eye, but, at the same time, it was very functional. Try adding a timeline to your next report.

5.4.3 Executive Summaries

Another component of an investigative report is the executive summary. All of the interim and final reports my firm produces include an executive summary. The executive summary is a concise synopsis or snapshot of the entire contents of the

EXECUTIVE SUMMARY

On December 15, 2013, Mr. John Smith of XYZ Company ("XYZ"), Denver, Colorado contacted Convercent, Inc. and requested investigative and consultative assistance in a matter involving alleged employee and vendor misconduct at the newly opened box plant in Anytown, California. According to Mr. Smith, several employees at the Anytown facility had alleged the plant manager and his plant superintendent had knowingly authorized contractor overcharging and were engaged in other inappropriate activities, much to the determent of the organization. Mr. Smith also stated that independent financial analysis of the box plant's start-up costs and other indicators (see Exhibit A) suggested something was terribly wrong.

The resultant investigation involved on-site information gathering, employee and contractor interviews and the detailed analysis of hundreds of records, invoices, purchase orders and requisitions. During the process, plant manager, Mr. Paul Jones admitted he had accepted personal services from a painting contractor for which he did not pay and authorized the overpayment of several hundred thousand dollars in invoices (see Exhibit M). His superintendent, Mr. Robert Miller admitted to have accepted $2,200.00 in cash from one contractor (Mr. William Redkin of Handy Services), who himself admitted paying it (see Exhibit J). Additionally, two other contractors admitted they had overcharged for their services to varying degrees or failed to maintain adequate records to justify their invoices.

The total economic impact and scope of the fiscal misconduct uncovered at the Anytown facility has been impossible to determine. The lack of proper record keeping, internal process failures and managerial negligence at the location has frustrated any effort to accurately quantify the damage. However, demonstrably the loss exceeds $500,000.00.

Figure 5.4 Sample of executive summary.

report. It might include the identity of the person who requested the investigation and why they requested it, who performed the work and some indication of the overall result. I insist that my firm's executive summaries not exceed one page. Figure 5.4 is an example.

By holding the report writer to one page, the executive summary is forced to be concise, complete, and correct. I know from experience that clients and decision makers often haven't the time or inclination to read a comprehensive report. A report produced as the result of a complex fraud or substance abuse investigation can sometimes exceed several thousand pages. We have produced reports exceeding 15,000 pages. Busy people haven't the time to read a report of this size. What's more, large reports are difficult to use. They are tough to lug around and it is hard to find the information one wants in a large report. Most decision makers want to get to the bottom line. The best way to do it is by way of an executive summary. Respect your reader; include an executive summary in your next investigative report.

5.4.4 Electronic Communications

Electronic communications are a growing part of today's workplace. The use of email is nearly universal and as important as the telephone to many organizations. Email is efficient and free, and is perfectly suited as a communication tool in most workplace investigations. For all of its benefits, email also has some disadvantages:

- ◼ It is not always secure. Unless precautions are taken, it is subject to potential interception and being read by other people.
- ◼ Unwanted distribution is difficult to manage. A recipient may forward email to unauthorized parties if precautions are not taken.
- ◼ It is discoverable. In the event of litigation, all electronic communications (and records thereof) exchanged during the investigation may be subject to possible discovery and production.
- ◼ Deleted email can often be recovered.

Precautions can be taken to minimize some of these risks. For example, encryption technology can be employed to reduce the potential of unwanted reading of email. Additionally, email retention and management protocols can be established to ensure the timely elimination of unwanted email. A client of mine recently learned the value of such a protocol. According to my client, his firm was forced to produce nearly 500,000 emails; one copy of each in both paper and electronic form for discovery purposes in litigation the firm was in.

Electronically transmitting reports is another problem. It is common practice to simply attach a report to an email message. This exposes the report to the same risks described above. Protecting the document with a password or by other means is helpful, but by no means a perfect solution. A better solution is to store the report on a secure server with restricted access. A link to the report can be sent via email and upon receipt, the recipient follows the link and uses a user name and password to access the document. My firm uses this technology and our clients are very satisfied with it. Additionally, with a little programming, processes can be established that record when the report was accessed and by whom. Our system additionally tells us if the client copied or printed the report. A log is permanently created to detail who, when, and what actions were taken every time a report on system had been accessed.

Every email should contain a confidentiality notice. The purpose of the notice is to warn those who view the email that it is indeed confidential and intended only for a particular recipient. Here is the confidentiality warning that you might consider:

CONFIDENTIALITY WARNING: This email is for the confidential use of the intended recipients only, and may be protected by the attorney work-product privilege. Any unauthorized review, access, copying, dissemination, distribution, or use of the content of this message/information is strictly prohibited by Federal Law. Anyone who attempts to intercept this message or distribute it without authorization is in violation of 18 U.S.C. 2511(1) of the Electronic Communications Privacy Act (ECPA). Fines, imprisonment, and/or civil damages may be imposed for violations.

Every email leaving our offices from our professional services group includes this warning.

Tip: Electronic communications are efficient and economical. However, users of this technology need to take the necessary precautions to protect the communication from interception and unauthorized use while preserving it for evidentiary purposes.

5.5 Testifying and the Preparation for Testimony

All fact finders must be willing and prepared to testify. Witness testimony is a critical component of our legal system. Its use is common in both criminal and civil proceedings. Regardless of how compelling some piece of evidence may be, its value can always be affected by testimony. For this reason, witness testimony is one of the most important elements of any proceeding. However, witnesses can only testify to what they have observed directly through the medium of their senses: sight, hearing, touch, taste, or smell. With few exceptions, evidence that is opinion is not admissible. It is, in part, for this reason that reports should be factual and objective. Generally, witnesses may testify only to facts, not to their effect or result, or to their conclusions or opinions based on the facts. Accordingly, fact finder testimony should not contain opinions or conjecture. The rules of evidence, however, make two major exceptions. The first involves the lay (ordinary, nonexpert) witness and the second applies to the expert (specialist) witness.

5.5.1 Lay Witnesses

The lay witness may express an opinion on matters of common observation where an opinion is the only logical way to convey the information. These opinions are permitted only concerning subjects for which the average person has considerable experience and knowledge. Some examples of matters of common observation, in which an opinion may be expressed by a lay witness, are physical properties, such as weight, size, approximate age, race, color, emotional state, physical state, and approximate speed of a vehicle.

5.5.2 Expert Witnesses

Expert witnesses may testify as to their opinion on evidence. An expert is a person skilled by means of education, training, and experience in some art, trade, or science to the extent that he or she possesses information not considered common knowledge among ordinary people. Expert testimony is not proof, but rather evidence that can be accorded its own credibility and weight by the judge and any other trier-of-fact. Expert witness testimony helps the trier-of-fact understand things that are not common knowledge or otherwise known only by experts in a particular art, trade, or science. An example might be testimony regarding the functioning of disk brakes in an automobile, how an airfoil produces lift, or the intricacies regarding how a proper investigative interview is conducted. Experts also write reports. Their reports are the basis of their testimony at trial. Thus, at trial, they may not offer opinions that were not expressed in their report.

5.5.3 Hearsay Rule

Hearsay can be considered a rumor or secondhand information. It is information that has been told to a witness by someone else. Hearsay evidence is generally considered not admissible or competent, and applies to verbal statements and written material as well. Thus, an investigative report and the statements provided by interviewees are considered hearsay. Therefore, for these documents to be admissible, they must be entered into evidence (at trial) by way of a witness who is competent and credible. For our purposes, it is either the investigative interviewer or the subject. Remember, hearsay is anything that is not within the personal knowledge of the witness or interview.

There are several exceptions to the hearsay rule. One is the dying declaration. A dying declaration is evidence resulting from an act or declaration made under a sense of impending death that relates to the declarant's cause of death. In order to be admissible, the victim must have believed that he or she was dying, must, in fact, have subsequently died, and must have been competent at the time the statement was made. Spontaneous declarations (*res gestae*) are declarations that are spontaneous utterances or statements made in response to some sudden and shocking event, such as an accident or horrific crime. Testimony of a witness who heard the defendant exclaim, "My God, I shot him," might qualify under this exception. Another exception is former testimony. This is testimony given by a witness at a prior proceeding. This exception requires that the person who gave the prior testimony is unavailable.

Additionally, the *past recollection recorded* exception is a memorandum or record concerning a matter about which a witness once had knowledge, but now has insufficient recollection to allow her to testify fully and accurately. Investigators referring to their notes is a good example of past recollection recorded. Business records that are created and maintained in the normal course of business can be exceptions as well. Examples include records of a telephone call, invoices, check registers, billing statements, and personnel files. The last exceptions are confessions and admissions. Fact finders may testify about a person's confession or any admission made by another person—his interviewee, for example. Because confessions and admissions are acknowledgements of guilt, the presumption exists that it is not likely that a person would voluntarily confess unless guilty.

Investigators are often called into court or before other official bodies to present testimony, and juries are often influenced by their appearance and demeanor on the witness stand. Upon being notified of an impending court appearance, the investigator must ensure that the case is complete and a final report prepared. A pretrial conference with the attorney calling him as a witness is to prepare the investigator and organize the facts and evidence in the case. The investigator must provide the attorney with all reports and other relevant documents or exhibits in order for the attorney to assess the strengths and weaknesses of the case.

5.5.4 Presenting the Evidence

Before testifying, the fact finder should be aware of the probable line of questioning he will face and how all of the evidence he has gathered will be introduced and used at the trial. The fact finder's appearance in court is an important component of his preparation.

How the jury will perceive the investigator's credibility will be determined in part by her appearance, demeanor, and professionalism. To that end, John Dempsey recommends the following:[1]

■ Know precisely when and where you will be testifying.
■ Do not discuss anything about the case in public.
■ Treat people with respect. Your professionalism, politeness, and courtesy will be noted and remembered.
■ Do not discuss your personal life, official business, biases, prejudices, likes or dislikes, or any controversial subjects in a place that they can be overheard.
■ Be on time.
■ Dress and groom appropriately.
■ Avoid contact with defense (opposing) counsel.

5.5.4.1 Testifying

At trial, the fact finder will be subjected to direct examination by the attorney calling them, and cross examined by the opposing attorney. Direct examination is the initial questioning of a witness (or defendant) by the attorney who is using the person's testimony to further his case. Cross examination is questioning by the opposing attorney for the purpose of assessing the validity of the testimony. Some of Dempsey's more useful advice for witnesses includes:

- Be prepared to be "sworn" or take an oath before testifying.
- Bring any notes or reports to the witness stand and refer to them when necessary.
- Answer with a simple "yes" or "no" whenever possible.
- Hesitate before answering a question in order to permit an objection.
- Always ask that a question be repeated if it is not understood.
- Don't offer opinions or make statements about a defendant's character or reputation.
- State only facts that he knows.
- Never fabricate, exaggerate, or speculate.

5.5.4.2 Dempsey's Ten Commandments of Courtroom Testimony[2]

1. Relax and be yourself
2. Answer only questions that are before you
3. Refer to your report only when allowed
4. Paint the crime scene just as it was
5. Be ready to explain why you are remembering details in court if they are not in your report
6. Avoid using jargon or unduly difficult language
7. Avoid sarcasm
8. Maintain your detachment
9. You don't need to explain the law
10. Explanation of what you said is possible on rebuttal

5.5.4.3 Impeachment

At trial, a witness that does not testify consistently, or alters his testimony from time to time and is contradictory, will not be credible. The opposing attorney will attempt to cast doubt on the witness's credibility and discredit him. That process is known as impeachment. Several methods are used to impeach or attack the testimony and credibility of a witness. They include:

- Showing that the witness's previous statements or conduct of the investigation are inconsistent with the witness's testimony.
- Showing that the witness is biased or prejudiced for or against the defendant.
- Attacking the witness's character by revealing prior criminal convictions or other irrefutable characteristics.
- Showing the witness's capacity to observe, recollect, or recount due to mental weakness, a physical defect, or influence of drugs or alcohol.
- Showing that the witness is in error; that the facts are other than as testified.

> *Tip: The best testimony is accurate, truthful, and in accordance with the facts.*

5.6 Frequently Asked Questions

In anticipation that you may have some questions, allow me to answer some of the more frequent ones I ask during my investigative interview trainings.

1. Ought an organization have an investigations policy?

   Yes. Investigations policies are becoming more common. However, by their very nature, policies tend to be rigid and inflexible. Better than a policy is to have an investigations protocol. The protocol should detail when, how, and for what purpose internal investigations should be conducted and by whom. The protocol also should contain similar guidance relative to the interviews pursuant to those investigations. Those that I build for our customers include forms, checklists, and other tools that both the fact finder and the interviewer might use for their projects. Investigation and interview protocols should not contain words such as: shall, always, or never. These words are too restrictive and diminish the fact finder's ability to adjust and improvise when necessary. At the same time, the document should not be so fuzzy that it is effectively useless.

2. Should the interviewee be allowed to take notes or record the interview?

   "Yes" to the question of notetaking and "no" to the question of recording. It would appear unfair and suspicious not to allow the interviewee to take notes while the interviewer did so. I always allow it and so should you. It is permissible to ask the interviewee for a copy of his notes; however, if you do, you can be assured he will ask for copies of yours. As mentioned in Chapter 4, I do not recommend anyone other than professional interviewers to record their interviews. The effort involves too many technical and legal complexities that it is not worth the few benefits it provides. If one is to follow my processes for investigative and administrative interviews, electronically recording your interviews will not be necessary.

3. How should one respond if the interviewee asks to see the interviewer's notes? *Show them to the interviewee, but do not put them in his hands. Do not allow the interviewee to handle any original documents. Doing so creates the risk that the interviewee not return them. It has happened to me. In one memorable instance, an interviewee, who had admitted to an immense fraud, asked to see the "smoking gun." Without thinking, I handed him the document. He said, "Yep, that's it," and proceeded to shred it and stuff in his underwear. He then summarily concluded our interview and walked out. I should have been fired for the mistake. Don't commit the same one yourself.*

4. How should the interviewer handle questions regarding his use of one or more of the investigative methods? *After explaining the methods of investigation, it is not uncommon for the interviewee to ask questions such as: "Do you have photographs of me?" or "Did you search my email account and find evidence?" These questions should be answered with a pat answer. Here's mine: "I am sorry, but given the nature of the issue and the expectation of privacy of those involved, I cannot answer that question at this time. Upon the completion of our investigation you are welcome to submit a written request to examine any evidence we have gathered or ultimately used. Right now I must fulfill my commitment to those who have cooperated and provided us assistance and not disclose their identity." The caveat, of course, is that this, in fact, is true and one or more individuals cooperated or assisted me. But, as we will learn in the next chapter, this type of question when posed to the interviewer is what we call a* tacit admission. *Most reasonably intelligent people who are innocent do not ask to see evidence implicating them in an alleged offense—because they know none exists. For them, the question is rhetorical and absurd and, as such, it is rarely asked by innocent people. I have gone so far as to tell this to an interviewee. The response I get is usually, "Really?" Their head then drops and they mumble something to the effect: "If I did, it was a mistake." This is also a tacit admission. When given this reply, the interviewer should immediately respond with the question: "Was it a mistake, or did you do it intentionally?"*

5. How should the interviewer respond if an administrative interviewee suddenly admits to wrongdoing of some sort? *The interviewer should casually acknowledge the admission and suggest that before going into it, the interviewee take the interviewer back in time and share what led up to the offense. This approach does two things. First, it does not alert the interviewee that they have suddenly revealed something that was previously unknown. Second, it gives the interviewee the opportunity to rationalize the transgression. By inviting them to go back in time and provide background, the interviewee is able to provide context and justification for his behavior. This technique is disarming and allows the interviewer to collect his thoughts and consider next steps.*

6. Should the interviewee's written statement be included in the fact finder's final report?

Yes. Written statements, interview, and witness notes and addenda are evidence and most likely relevant to the matter in question. As such, like all other relevant evidence, copies should be included in the fact finder's final report.

Tip: A written statement is useless until it is necessary to use it.

Endnotes

1. John S. Dempsey, *Introduction to Investigations,* 2nd ed. (Farmington Hills, MI: Cengage Learning, 2002).
2. Ibid.

Chapter 6

Deception Detection and the Process of Overcoming Objections and Denials

Key learning points:

1. Because some interviewees are, in fact, smarter than others, the professional investigative interviewers should never, ever underestimate the cognitive abilities of those they interview.
2. People lie because they believe that lying provides more benefits than telling the truth. The interviewer needs to appeal to the interviewee on the conscience and subconscious level and convince them that telling the truth is more beneficial than lying.
3. The use of rationalization or projection is a means by which the subject attempts to make their behavior understandable and socially acceptable. Assisting the interviewee find a suitable rationalization or project blame on someone else is often critical in obtaining an admission.
4. Contrary to the myth, those who commit workplace violence don't simply snap without warning. Abundant research has shown that aggressors tend to exhibit inappropriate and disruptive behavior prior to committing an act of violence.

5. Exceptional interviewers are as aware of their body language as they are aware of their interviewee's.

6. The best fact finders are active listeners who use both verbal and nonverbal means to show the interviewee they are listening and that what they have to say is important.

7. Lying is learned while honesty is earned.

"The question: What will happen if I tell the truth, *is an admission disguised as a lie and the answer:* If I did it, it was a mistake, *is a lie disguised as an admission."*

E. F. Ferraro

6.1 Introduction

Some students are smarter than others. During a recent two-day advanced interviewer training course, my co-instructor engaged one of the students in an attempt to demonstrate the use of questions to determine the cognitive skills of an interviewee. The instructor requested a volunteer and invited him to the front of the class and to sit with him at a table staged for an interview. Once seated, the instructor told the student, "I will ask you a question and if you don't know the answer, you pay me $5. Then you ask me one, and if I don't know the answer, I will pay you $500." With the class cheering him on, the student eagerly accepts the challenge.

The instructor smiles and asks the first question. "What's the distance from the Earth to the Moon?" The student squirms in his seat and tugs his ear. Without saying a word, he reaches into his pocket, pulls out a $5 bill and hands it to the instructor. Rooting for their classmate, several in the class offer mock boos and toss jeers at the instructor. Now it's the student's turn. He collects himself and confidently leans back into his chair. In proper interviewer style (notepad at the ready, pen in hand), he asks, "What goes up a hill on three legs and comes down on four?"

This time the instructor squirms. Rubbing his forehead, crossing his arms, then gazing up as if the answer was somehow written on the ceiling, he tells the student he doesn't know the answer. He digs five crisp Franklins from his pocket and begrudgingly hands them to the student. As he does and with complete loss of any semblance of professionalism, he snaps, "Well, smarty-pants, so what goes up a hill on three legs and comes down on four?" Without saying a word, the still smiling student hands the instructor another $5 bill and leaps from his chair with clenched fists thrust high over his head. The class goes nuts. With high fives and laughter everywhere, we broke and took a well-earned 15-minute break.

Tip: Because some students (interviewees), in fact, are smarter than others, the professional investigative interviewer should never, ever underestimate the cognitive abilities of those they interview.

6.2 Why Most People Tell the Truth

It is human nature to resist doing something that is uncomfortable. Even under the best of circumstances, admitting one's transgressions to a stranger or someone of authority is uncomfortable. Whether the stakes are large or small, it is not fun to admit one's mistakes. Fortunately, for most people, telling the truth is instinctual. On the other hand, lying seems to be learned. One learns to lie through conditioning. For example, a child frequently disciplined for misbehaving after admitting his/her offense might equate punishment with telling the truth. In the same fashion, a child might eventually learn that lying tends to prevent punishment. If this conditioning continues, we could expect the child to eventually conclude that lying is an acceptable behavior and, when used properly, it can prevent undesirable outcomes in some circumstances. This is not the type of person one would hope to marry or employ.

Although it may sound a bit trite, fortunately most of us in our Western society have learned that honesty is the best policy. Intellectually, we know that sometimes telling the truth can hurt and inflict emotional harm on both the truth teller and his victim. On other occasions telling the truth may result in severe punishment and very undesirable consequences. However, experience shows that all things equal, most people in our society choose to tell the truth. That is a good thing. Much of the normalcy in our lives depends on us and others consistently telling the truth. Be it personal relationships, interactions with our employer and co-workers, our criminal justice system, our tax system, or everyday commerce, exchanging the truth with those we interact with enables our society to function properly. Truth telling builds trust and improves the quality of our lives. It makes our life and interaction with those around us predictable. That predictability improves the efficiency of society. In contrast, imagine a society where the words of no one can be trusted; one in which every communication, message, label, advertisement, every spoken or written word could not be trusted and had to be vetted. What an awful, wasteful place that would be to live.

From the investigative interviewer's perspective, one should assume the following:

- Most people are honest.
- Most people want to tell the truth.
- Most people know that those that are untruthful cannot be trusted.
- Most people know that those that are untruthful are punished.

It may appear these assumptions are naïve; however, remember our topic is investigative interviewing in the *private sector*. And, although occasionally the fact finder will investigate matters that are both allegations of policy violations and crimes, the criminal aspects of the offense are typically secondary. In most circumstances, the worst tangible punishment that the transgressor can receive is termination. While harsh, it is magnitudes less than life in prison or execution. Thus, comparatively, the price for admitting a workplace offense is less than that one would pay for that of admitting a crime. Secondarily, the people under investigation in a private sector matter are for the most part screened, tested, carefully selected, and demonstrably honest and trustworthy. As a result, there is a disparate impact on those who are not. In essence, those who are honest and of good character are hired and those who are (were) not, are turned away. All the good reasons one was hired are the same reasons we should expect our investigative interviewees to be honest when confronted. Granted, many of the transgressions we investigate deals with the absence of integrity. However, in the final analysis, they are proved to have been transgressions involving the *suspension* of integrity. That is, the transgressions are not the product of a defect in character, but merely lapses of judgment—and poor decision making. Resultantly, the offender is more likely to be truthful and admit guilt when properly confronted. However, there are some disturbing exceptions.

6.3 Why Good People Sometimes Do Bad Things

6.3.1 Guiltlessness and the Enemy Within

Many organizations mischaracterize charm and charisma as leadership traits. They like leaders with confidence and demeanor. In selecting them, they often fail to recognize their anointed leaders' most deceptive skill—the ability to plausibly describe the opposite of their real intentions. Here's such a case.

Bain skated through high school.[1] With grades good enough to attend almost any college, he chose a midtier state school. Rarely attending class and never appearing to study, he earned the name Bain the Brain. He was indifferent to the women he dated. He drank alcohol when served at parties and experimented with drugs. His father, an accomplished lawyer, encouraged him to pursue a career in law. What excited him, however, was money.

Misleading the headhunters and the HR professionals who interviewed him, he was offered an entry-level position at a large investment bank on Wall Street. Quickly he rose up through the organization and became a partner at the age of 30. He married Sara the same year. Soon they had children. However, Bain was always distant. He blamed the demands of his job for not spending more time with his family. While on travel, he lived large and recklessly. He over-imbibed, abused his expense account privileges, and slept with whoever would have him. Bain was also ruthless. Backstabbing his colleagues, undercutting his competitors, and swindling unsuspecting investors came natural to him. He peddled influence and bartered with information. At the age of 45, he was at the top of his game—and then he made a mistake.

Using what regulators later described as insider information, he invested his organization's money on a $150 million bet. He was caught, tried, and convicted. He was ruined. But, during his sentencing, he smirked and whispered in the ear of his attorney, "What disappoints me most is your inability to set me free."

Bain is a sociopath. Sociopaths are known for their shallowness of emotion, and the hollow and transient nature of the affectionate feelings they claim to possess. They are risk-takers and adventure seekers. They possess no empathy, guilt, or remorse. Sociopaths may feel anger, but never experience sadness or shame. They have no conscience.

Are all malfeasants sociopaths? No. Most transgressors are not as complex as Bain nor can they be clinically diagnosed as sociopaths. However, clinicians estimate that about 4 percent of the population are sociopaths or exhibit sociopathic behaviors.[2] In comparison, the Centers for Disease Control and Prevention reports that colon cancer rates in the United States are "alarmingly high" with roughly 40 individuals per 100,000 afflicted each year—a rate 100 times lower than those with an antisocial personality disorder.[3] Arguably, those who wish to do us harm are all around us. In fact, many organizations unintentionally recruit them. There are four possible reasons for this.

1. The talents of many sociopathic wrongdoers often seem valuable to employers. Many are charming, seemingly gracious, polite, and considerate. They are able to turn on their charm and use their charisma to disarm even the most experienced professional. They are skilled at social manipulation and a job interview is the perfect place to ply those talents.
2. Many organizations mischaracterize charm and charisma as leadership traits. They seek talent that is able to think on its feet. They like leaders with confidence and demeanor. In selecting them, they often fail to recognize the ability of these individuals to plausibly describe the opposite of their real intentions.
3. In the race to embrace change, many organizations (and nations for that matter) willfully overlook obvious character flaws and the shallowness of those who promise to delivery that change. Desperate for the change they seek, they assume the best of people and put aside their instincts and natural aversions.
4. Sociopathic wrongdoers are characteristically rule breakers. They like fast-paced, competitive, and transitional organizations. By their very nature, this type of organization actively seeks individuals who are risk-takers and easily motivated by opportunity and reward. A more perfect match for the malfeasant sociopath is not possible.[4]

6.3.2 The Ability to Rationalize

What distinguishes our species from all others is its capability for rational thought and conscious decision making. However, it is the ability to distinguish right from wrong that uniquely makes us human; the guardrail that provides that ability is our conscience. The late Dr. Donald Cressey was the first to recognize the relationship between transgression and the ability to rationalize. As a sociologist and criminologist, Cressey expressed his theory in what has become known as the fraud triangle (Figure 6.1).[5]

Cressey points out that even the best systems of internal control cannot provide absolute safeguards against irregular activities perpetrated by malfeasants. According to Cressey, of the three elements—opportunity, motivation, and rationalization—under most circumstances, society can only control opportunity. Though created to assist in the design of organizational internal controls, this model is overly simplistic; however, it is still useful in understanding the mind of the malfeasant and the significance of his ability to rationalize. Let's take a closer look.

Manipulation and deceit are essential components in almost all forms of workplace misconduct. Barring unintentional negligence, malfeasant behavior requires the perpetrator to possess the ability to rationalize. Often this is a simple cost-benefit analysis. Most perpetrators rationalize the intended behavior by consciously minimizing the cost and exaggerating the benefit. Common rationalizations include thoughts such as, "everybody does it, so why shouldn't I," or more pathetically, "I earned it and they owe it to me." In doing so, the malfeasant uses rationalization to overcome the confines of his conscience. Sociopaths, on the other hand, intellectually recognize the true cost and value of the benefit, but simply do not care. For them, they are the center of the universe. They are unable to view their behavior as unethical, selfish, or immoral because they lack a conscience. Rationalization for them is merely a distraction.

Figure 6.1   The fraud triangle.

6.3.3 Motive and the Consciencelessness of Greed

Rationalization does not occur in a vacuum. In order for one to rationalize an intended behavior, he must first have a motive. Simplistically, motives can be placed into one of three categories: greed, need, and stupidity.

6.3.3.1 The Greedy

The foundation of greed is envy. Envy breeds contempt, and contempt is a tool that disassembles our conscience. Most often, greed manifests itself in small ways. Using rationalization, employees tempted by greed first see themselves as victims. Victimhood leads to vengeance and vengeance leads to action. In the final analysis, the greedy often conclude that their misconduct is permissible given their condition and desires. Ethical lapses and frauds most often start here.

6.3.3.2 The Needy

The needy usually transgress because of perceived or real needs. This individual may steal so they can support a drug habit, pay off a debt, or support a family. The need can be perceived as so urgent that the benefit derived from the act outweighs any comprehensible risk. Pilfering, theft, and petty schemes start here.

6.3.3.3 The Stupid and Foolish

The stupid is typically one who succumbs to temptation. Given sufficient opportunity, they are able to justify their behavior and whisk away their values and principles during a moment of emotional weakness. The stupid often commit crimes of opportunity. The foolish, on the other hand, are slightly more complex. Their behavior might be driven by anger or disappointment. Deeply seated in their psyche is the desire to get even or punish. The progression toward acts of violence invariably starts here.

6.3.4 Importance and Influence of Opportunity

Cressey argued that in order to prevent fraud (malfeasance of any sort, actually) an organization must control opportunity. Of the required three elements, he said only opportunity was manageable. His conclusion was logical given the worldview of his times and the limitations of his research. In fact, to this day many lawmakers believe the laws and regulations they promulgate will diminish the opportunity to commit the very behavior they intend to regulate. This approach is wrong-minded, however. Most laws and regulations do not limit behavior; they instead provide punishment for those who misbehave. Consider for a moment your own organizational policies and work rules. How many can you identify that have the ability to actually stop the behavior they prohibit?

A better, more useful approach is to seek out and identify vulnerabilities and address them before an otherwise dishonest employee does. Once identified, the organization can intelligently build controls around these vulnerabilities. The sum of these controls is called governance. When the organization aligns its culture with properly measured governance, it achieves a state of compliance. Those in my organization and I have to call that state, Principled Compliance™. However, for most organizations, culture management is a passive activity. It is typically delegated to an array of tacit assumptions, unspoken rules, and traditions. Only those with sufficient organizational experience or history comprehend this aspect of the culture. Though intangible, it still holds a powerful influence on organizational values and behavior. In summary, opportunity is a manageable risk factor. In order to prevent temptation and allowing good people to sometimes do bad things, opportunity must be reduced to its smallest denominator, if not eliminated. Good governance is the only means by which that is possible.

6.3.5 But for Bad Decisions and Mistakes

Anthony Catanese takes another view.[6] With over 30 years in academia and study in the field of public planning and development, he believes good people are not only capable of doing bad things intentionally, but also because of susceptibility to common human foibles. Catanese cites five possible factors:

1. Timing and the push toward deadlines. Urgency breeds mistakes because decision makers value the importance of time more than outcomes.
2. Distractions: The cause of most accidents and mishaps also influence our decision making. When we allow them, distractions divert our attention and energy.
3. Bad information often leads to bad decisions. If our assumptions are inaccurate, our ability to make good decisions is greatly diminished.
4. Poor advice: Combining bad information with poor advice multiplies the probability of ruin.
5. Satisfizing.

According to Catanese, decision makers often make profound decisions not based on the best information available, but in the pursuit of outcomes that will satisfy the largest number of constituents. Thus, they opt to *satisfize* and, in doing so, compromise the inner voice of their conscience and sometimes even their personal ethics.

Mistakes play a role as well. Consider the condition known as innumeracy— the unfamiliarity with mathematical concepts and methods. Even the brightest people suffer from this common malady. Unfortunately, innumeracy can lead to

Answer: The probability of at least two students with the same birthday in a group of 30 is a whopping 70%. In fact, we find that in a group of 23 students, the odds are better than 50% to find at least two with the same birthday. Here's the formula:

$$\frac{365!}{(365-n)!}$$

The exclamation point means "factorial." Factorials are defined as n*(n-1) *(n-2)... (3)(2)(1). For example, 6! = 6*5*4*3*2*1. In this example, n is the number of students.

Figure 6.2   The birthday paradox.

disastrous outcomes. The bias it fosters provide its victims a false sense of assurance when making decisions. To make the point, consider your understanding and appreciation of simple probability. *In a class of 30 students, what is the probability that two or more will share the same birthday?*

While an approximate answer to this seemingly simple question may appear intuitively obvious, only the decision maker who has exceptional intuition will likely answer correctly. Intuition is an expression of probability and reflects the current state of knowledge about the problem being worked. This sort of leader sees things others do not; that is, he demonstrates that unique creativity we sometimes call genius. What's more, intuition is an attribute that is usually derived from life-long personal experiences and not necessarily from formal education. As such, incisive insight is a corresponding attribute that allows the prediction of events and the ability to visualize unexpected patterns, periodicity, or structure amid apparent chaos. It is likely your intuitive answer to the birthday paradox is surprisingly wrong (Figure 6.2).

Thus, if our initial presumptions are not accurate or contain imperfect data, the final conclusion we draw will likely be inaccurate. Innumeracy and other inherent biases are the bane of many fallen leaders.

6.3.6 Prevention and the Path to Better Guardrails

The simplest path to prevention of bad things is to not hire those who have a propensity to do bad things. A task that is easier said than done. Among the tools available, is Robert D. Hare's Psychopathy Checklist Revised (PC-R) (see www.hare. org). Widely considered the foremost reliable diagnostic tool available to identify clinical psychopathy and its attendant personality disorders, it is up to the task.[7] However, most employers haven't access to the PCL-R or the means to properly administer it. Moreover, a host of federal and state employment laws make the path to preemployment diagnosis nearly impossible. Thus, the use of diagnostic screening to prevent hiring potential problems (or people capable of creating future problems) is neither practical nor likely lawful. Instead, prevention is a matter of building more sensible guardrails. Here are a few to ponder:

1. Set the tone at the top and make culture management a top priority. This involves role-modeling and active culture management across the enterprise where eliminating bad behavior becomes everyone's responsibility.
2. Screen all employment applicants using all of the tools lawfully and practically available. Be consistent and treat all applicants similarly and don't be afraid to ask tough (lawful) questions. For example, request applicants provide proof of prior earnings or wages and carefully verify all prior employment and references.
3. Properly train those who screen and interview applicants and those selected for promotion. Empower those involved in the selection process by allowing their input in hiring and promotion decisions and put qualifications and experience before the immediate need to fill vacancies.
4. Establish clear expectations regarding workplace performance and behavior. Create policies and protocols that manage behavior instead of those that simply prescribe discipline or corrective action when transgressions occur.
5. Embrace the concept of culture management and retain only those employees who share the organization's culture.
6. Inspect that which you expect. Constantly assess, audit, and evaluate all of the elements contributory to the organization's pursuit of principled compliance.
7. Provide employees the means by which to safely and anonymously (if they desire) report issues of concern, bad behavior, and retaliation.
8. Establish reward and recognition programs that allow the celebration of proper and ethical behavior.

Of all of the sciences, human behavior is the least understood. The ancients pondered the origins of good and evil and modern psychologists are still seeking the foundation of our conscience. What is known, however, is that regardless of our rules, laws, ethos, and the infinite boundaries man has attempted to place on his behavior, good people sometimes still do bad things.

6.4 Why Some People Lie

It is not a secret that the outcome of the investigatory interview is likely to result in discipline. This potential outcome is not lost on the interviewee. Even the most honest and well-meaning offender may be tempted to lie in order to avoid punishment. To be successful, the interviewer must be able to provide the interviewee a credible reason to believe that cooperating and telling the truth will benefit him. That is, the interviewee must be motivated to tell the truth. That motivation or incentive must be sufficient to overcome the potential benefits of lying. On both a conscious and subconscious level, the interviewee conducts a risk-benefit analysis. If the benefits of telling the truth outweigh the benefits of lying, the subject will tell the truth. Classic responses indicating just the opposite include:

■ "The way I was raised …"
■ "My Daddy told me to never …"
■ "You know, I've got a family to feed."
■ "Why would I lie?"
■ "You haven't shown me anything. Where is the proof?"
■ "If I did it, prove it."

These responses provide incredible insight into the mind of the interviewee. Notice that the interviewee does not offer anything useful that might prove their innocence. Instead, he demands proof of his guilt. Here is what is likely not said when these responses are offered:

■ "The way I was raised … I am guilty and learned that lying works. People who tell the truth always get punished."
■ "My Daddy told me to never … I am guilty, but my Daddy taught me to never tell the truth, truthful people are stupid."
■ "You know, I've got a family to feed … I am guilty, but, if I tell the truth and lose my job, feeding my family will be more difficult."
■ "Why would I lie? Let me count the reasons: save my job, avoid punishment, protect my reputation, stay out of jail, keep my kids, keep the money I've stolen, save my marriage, and get over on a chump like you."
■ "You haven't shown me anything. Where is the proof? I am guilty and I am stalling. Even if you show your proof to me, I'll claim it proves nothing. Moreover, if you show me your evidence now, I will be able to fabricate a better alibi and lie my way out of this mess later."
■ "If I did it, prove it. I am guilty and I know you know it. But, I suspect your proof against me is weak and you need me to confess. I've learned that challenging my accuser, I almost always go unpunished."

In other words, it is often useful to listen to what is not said as much as one listens to that which is said. Here is something else to ponder—innocent people very rarely ask to see the *evidence*. They recognize such a question is rhetorical because if they are indeed innocent, they know that there is no evidence. Generally the request to see the evidence is made only by guilty people. The guilty want to see the amount and quality of proof that has been gathered against them in order to more effectively challenge it. They know from experience that their failure to know the evidence possessed by their accuser makes effective lying very difficult. By saying too much without knowing all of the evidence gathered, it is too easy to say something wrong and be trapped. Thus, very often the guilty will confront their accuser with: "I'm not going to answer another question until you show me some proof."

Tip: People lie because they believe that lying provides more benefits than telling the truth. The interviewer needs to appeal to the interviewee on the conscience and subconscious level and convince them that telling the truth is more beneficial than lying.

Warning signs of deception include:

- Using language to mask an untruth, such as "to tell the truth" or "honestly speaking"
- A selective memory
- The inability to recall even nonincriminating facts or circumstances
- Avoiding eye contact or appearing to be visually looking for an answer
- Offering useless and irrelevant comments or details
- Inconsistent, evasive responses
- Body language and mannerisms that are inconsistent with one who is telling the truth

Tip: The use of rationalization or projection is a means by which the subject attempts to make their behavior understandable and socially acceptable. By assisting the interviewee find a rationalization or to project blame onto another person is often critical in obtaining a confession.

Deceptive behaviors include:

- Overly anxious: tapping feet, clicking teeth, bobbing knee, constantly looking at the clock
- Unconcerned: the lint-picker, whistling, rolling eyes, grooming self, inspecting nails
- Defensive: demanding proof, evidence, or the identity of witnesses
- Evasive: memory loss, vague, aloof
- Guarded: uses qualified answers, suspicious, questions interviewer's intentions
- Complaining: room too hot, too cold, thirsty, body pain, headache
- Angry or arrogant: in your face, disrespectful, argumentative

It is well established that the greater the consequences, the greater the temptation to minimize one's guilt or deny guilt completely. Those who are guilty frequently try to psychologically distance themselves from the offense. They will frequently refer to the victim in the third person, awkwardly avoiding the use of their name or revealing their connection with them. For example, Patsy Ramsey, the mother of murdered child celebrity JonBenet, repeatedly referred to her slain daughter as *that child* when speaking in public. Curiously, Mrs. Ramsey seemed unable to bring herself to say *my baby* or *my JonBenet*. Subsequently, we saw Mark Peterson, the philandering cad accused of murdering his pregnant wife and unborn son, when talking to the media said of his wife, "A lot of people want her to come home." Peterson also seems to have difficulty saying, *I want my wife to come home.* Killers like Peterson can be so consumed by guilt that they are unable to personally identify with those who were once the most important people in their lives. In another murder case involving a child victim, the stepfather suspected of molesting and then killing the toddler told the police, "I would never hurt that child." Notice that the suspect substitutes the word *hurt* for *murder* and words *that child* for the child's name.

In a recent case of mine, an office manager suspected of stealing an envelope stuffed with cash that had been pushed through a door slot after the close of business, repeatedly told my interviewer, "I did not *see* the money on the floor." A curious answer for anyone asked *did you* take *the money*. Again, analyze what the subject is saying. First, he was not asked if he saw the money, he was asked if he *took* the money. Second, the money was never on the floor, the *envelope containing the money* was on the floor. Factually, the manager's response was truthful. However, he failed to answer the question. Figure 6.3 shows a few of the more common psycho-linguistic differences frequently encountered when dealing with truthful and deceptive individuals.

People lie for another reason as well. They lie because of fear. That fear includes the fear of losing one's job, punishment, humiliation, embarrassment, and castigation. Fear can be a terrific force. It can either motivate us or inhibit us. The investigative interviewer's job is to assist the interviewee overcome that fear and share the truth.

6.5 Confront Objections and Overcome Denials

Admitting one's guilt often involves the loss of face as well. When other people know we have done bad things, we are embarrassed. We know people will think differently of us if they know the bad things we have done. As such, there are enormous pressures to hide the truth, minimize our malfeasance, and lie. It has been my experience that in workplace investigations, most people lie because they are afraid. In order to obtain an admission from these individuals, one must determine what they fear.

Truthful	Deceptive
Rich in details.	Vague, few details.
First person singular, past tense.	Inconsistent first person singular. Speaks in both present and past tense.
Uses possessive pronouns such as, "My daughter."	Lack of possessive pronouns. Instead says, "The child."
Proper characterization of the victim…"My daughter."	Improper characterization of the victim…"She…"
Appropriate emotions at the right time.	Inappropriate emotions. No emotions at all.
Wants truth known. Actively seeks to find it.	Wants truth hidden. Claims to seek the truth, but actions indicate otherwise.
Tries to assist and focus the investigation.	Provides little useful information; attempts to broaden the investigation. Casts a wider net than is necessary.
Committed to innocence and alibi.	Not committed to innocence or alibi. Will offer multiple alibis. Passive when asked tough questions.
Expressive and speaks with conviction.	Detached and evasive.
Admits the opportunity to commit the crime.	Denies the opportunity. Overstates inability to commit the crime.
Argues actual innocence. Identifies facts which support innocence.	Argues legal innocence. Raises legal defensives, while ignoring the facts.

Figure 6.3   Comparison of truthful and deceptive behaviors.

In the context of investigatory interviews, the best way to learn what one is afraid of is to ask. The question might be proposed as follows. "Bobby, it is not uncommon in these circumstances that people are afraid of losing their job, going to jail or being shunned by their friends. However, most often our worst fears never come true. Are you afraid you will be fired?"

By approaching the obstacle in this fashion, I have articulated some of the common fears people face in these circumstances. Even if my suppositions are incorrect,

I will likely draw the interviewee out and encourage him to tell me his fear. Once the fear is identified, in most instances, it can be addressed. While it is improper to minimize the seriousness of the offense or the possibility of punishment, the interviewer can put these matters into proper perspective. For example, the fear of losing one's job is not as frightening if one knows other employment is readily available. Alternatively, the fear of going to jail may be exaggerated and not even a mere possibility. Only talking about it can the interviewer address the interviewee's fears and possibly overcome them.

A denial also can be overcome by appealing to the subject's sense of integrity. A rational person knows that lying often makes matters worse. They know that lying ultimately complicates things and, in the end, the truth almost always prevails. Here is one approach to overcome this challenge:

> *While I cannot tell you what will happen when this investigation is over, the worst mistake someone can make is lying when others know they are guilty. Your decision not to tell the truth will not minimize what you have done. It will not make it go away or remove your guilt. In addition to what you already have done, you will have to deal with the prospect of being known as a liar. Which behavior do you think management least likes, _ or lying?*

This creates a fascinating psychological dilemma for the interviewee. It is similar to what I refer to as my *liar's paradox.*[8] My version of the liar's paradox goes like this:

> *In order to avoid punishment for breaking one policy, you have chosen to break another. Giving your choice more thought, which policy do you believe to be more important, the one you broke or our policy against lying?*

Another question to ask someone who clings to their innocence in the face of considerable evidence against them is: "How is it we can know with certainty you are not lying today?"

This question causes the subjects to ponder the gravity of their guilt without calling them a liar. If the response questions whether the interviewer is calling the interviewee a liar, the response to him might be: "No. However, in light of the amount of evidence that points to your guilt, it is impossible to understand how you are innocent."

This line of questioning will frequently elicit a tacit admission. This type of admission comes in a variety of forms. Within the answer provided by the interviewee, he only will imply or infer guilt. For example, the interviewee might use one of the phrases in Figure 6.4.

The last question I ask someone who cannot find the ability to tell the truth begins with a statement:

"O.K., then show me the evidence."	An innocent person knows there is no evidence and would not ask to see something which does not exist.
"If I am guilty, then why haven't they fired me?"	This question tests the interviewer's confidence in his evidence. It also suggests that the interviewer has not convinced the interviewee of the quality of his investigation or the evidence it produced.
"Show me what you've got and then I will tell the truth."	This is a trap. The interviewee has no intention of telling the truth but wants to see the evidence against him. No quantity of evidence will cause this interviewee to provide an admission.
"Tell me the names of the people who talked about me and then I will cooperate."	This is also a trap. The interviewee wants to know the interviewer's source of information in order to size up the quality of evidence against him. He may also want the information in order to intimidate witnesses.
"I am not going to say anything because I don't trust the company."	This is likely a lie. What the interviewee is really saying is that he is certain that the only thing between him and the prospect of discipline is his admission.
"I'd like to cooperate but I need more time to think about it."	Innocent people do not need time to formulate a statement of innocence, only guilty people do.
"I did not do this. But if it makes any difference, I will repay the money."	An innocent person rarely will say this. An innocent person finds it unconscionable to pay for something they have not done. In fact it is one of the reasons a truly innocent person is often so cooperative. They will generally provide the interviewer assistance hoping to demonstrate their innocence and avoid undeserved punishment.

Figure 6.4 Deceptive responses.

In spite of the evidence against you, by maintaining your innocence you give up three very valuable things. They include (1) the opportunity to offer any mitigating circumstances that might help understand your action and, in turn, potentially reduce the punishment; (2) the opportunity to ask for a second chance; and most importantly (3) the opportunity to say you are sorry. Most troubling to management is your failure to say you are sorry.

Then the question:

If you were a decision maker, in this instance, who would you forgive— the person who admitted he had made a mistake and said he was sorry, or the person who hid behind a lie?

An answer of "I don't know" is a tacit admission of guilt, and the interviewee should be told so. If the subject answers correctly and says, "The person who told the truth," the interviewer should ask: "Then, why haven't you told the truth?" For some employers that may be too close to offering leniency in exchange for an admission. Some employers may even think it is patently coercive. However, I think the approach and question is legitimate. It contemplates human nature's distinction between right and wrong and our compulsion to say we are sorry when we have indeed made a mistake. To blunt the assertion that the question is coercive, the interviewer should make it clear that he is not offering leniency in exchange for an admission. Instead, the interviewer should tell the interviewee that all he is seeking is the truth.

6.6 Indications of Deception

6.6.1 Lack of Self-Reference

It is well established that truthful people make frequent use of the pronoun "I" to describe their actions: "I arrived home at noon. The phone was ringing as I unlocked the front door, so I walked straight to the phone and answered it. It was my girlfriend and we talked about 10 minutes. I hung up and went to the kitchen to feed my dog. I then went into my office and discovered that both my TV and computer were missing." This brief statement contains the pronoun "I" four times in five sentences. On the other hand, deceptive people often use language that minimizes references to themselves. They commonly use what is called a passive voice.

- "A lot of people want her to come home," rather than, "I want my wife to come home."
- "No saw the envelope," rather than "I didn't see the envelope."
- "The safe was left unlocked," rather than "I left the safe unlocked."
- "The expense was authorized," rather than "I authorized the expense."

Another common way self-references are reduced is for the subject to substitute the pronoun "you" with "I."

Question: "Can you tell me how purchase orders are approved?"
Answer: "You know, you try to look at the requisition, approval signatures, but sometimes when you're really in a hurry, you just approve them."

Deceptive interviewees sometimes omit all self-referencing pronouns and torture themselves and the English language to do so. Consider this statement by a suspected embezzler: "So, at work early, no one is in yet. A little coffee, some paperwork and BANG, there it is, the safe is wide open. Who knew? You gotta think there is a problem. You know, people just don't leave safes open at night. Hey, you don't think you know who had something to do with it, do you?" Notice first the absence of "I" and the lack of general specificity. The hour of the morning is not mentioned, the type of paperwork performed is not mentioned, yet he says, "People just don't leave safes open at night," when, in fact, it is discovered open in the morning. The astute interviewer would ask how did he know the safe was left open at night?

6.6.2 Verb Tense

Truthful people typically describe historical events in the past tense. Deceptive people sometimes refer to past events as if the events were occurring in the present (like the example above). Describing past events using the present tense suggests that people are rehearsing the events in their mind. Skilled investigative interviewers pay particular attention to points in a narrative when the speaker shifts tense inappropriately. Consider the following statement made by a supervisor claiming that a pouch containing $5,000 in cash was stolen before he could deliver it to a drop box.

> After closing, I put the pouch in my truck and drove to the First Bank branch on State Street. At the bank *you enter the parking lot and drive around back* to the drop box. When I get to the back and park, this guy jumps out and comes toward me. *He has a gun, see, and grabs the pouch just like that. In seconds he is gone.* I wasn't scared but I called the police anyway. On the way home, I called my boss and told him what happened" (emphasis added for the reader's benefit).

Notice the mixed use of past and present tense. At the moment the crime allegedly occurs, the interviewee switches from past tense to present tense. This likely occurs because this portion of the story is false. Also note the additional suspicious failure to self-reference in: "… *you enter the parking lot and drive around back.*"

6.6.3 Answering Questions with a Question

For some of the reasons mentioned earlier, even liars prefer not to lie. Outright lies carry the risk of detection. Before answering a question with a lie, a deceptive person usually will try to avoid answering the question with a question of his own. Often these questions contain a veiled threat or an accusation of their own. Here are a couple of examples:

- "You really think I'm stupid, don't you?"
- "Are you crazy, that's against the law?"
- "If you knew you would get fired, why would somebody do that?"
- "You better not be calling me a liar."

These responses are intended to both deceive and intimidate the interviewer. Also notice that the responses reveal a pseudo-pride. A pride that is fabricated and based on the assertion that being called a liar is an insult of intolerable proportion. It is phony and the technique is obvious.

6.6.4 Equivocation

Using this technique, the subject avoids the interviewer's questions by filling his or her responses with expressions of uncertainty, confusion, and vagueness. The interviewee includes words such as: think, guess, sort of, maybe, might, approximately, about, or perhaps in their response. This vagueness is an attempt to create the appearance of lack of memory while seeming agreeable. If boxed in, it allows the interviewee to later modify or alter their assertion as more evidence against them is revealed. Using equivocating (noncommittal) verbs and adverbs such as: think, believe, guess, suppose, figure, assume, almost, and mainly are indicators of deception.

6.6.5 Oaths

The most classic deception is the use of oaths. Oaths are used to reinforce a statement of guiltlessness. Users of this technique want the interviewer to believe they are innocent and what they say is true. Deceptive subjects often use oaths to try to make their statements sound more convincing. Lacking their own credibility, they attempt to use that of others, such as parents, God, or any higher power. Users of this technique say things like: "I swear to God," "God is my witness," "On my children's grave," or "I cross my heart." Truthful individuals are more confident that the facts will prove the veracity of their assertions of innocence and feel less need to fortify their statements with oaths.

6.6.6 Euphemisms

Most languages, English included, offer alternative terms for almost any action or situation. Statements made by those who are guilty often use alternative terms to describe their behavior in an attempt to lessen its seriousness. Euphemisms portray the subject's behavior in a more favorable light and minimize the apparent harm his actions might have caused. Here is a short list of synonyms I have seen frequently used:

- Borrowed or took in place of stole
- Bumped, in place of hit, slapped, or inappropriately touched
- Warned or told, in place of threatened or insulted.

6.6.7 Lack of Narrative Balance

A narrative consists of three components: a prologue, event description, and epilogue. The prologue contains background information and describes events that took place before the event in question. The event description is the most important component of any narrative. The epilogue describes what happened after the event. It is used to tie up loose ends and complete the narrative. In a complete and truthful narrative, the balance will be approximately 25 percent prologue, 50 percent event description, and 25 percent epilogue. Typically, if one component is significantly shorter than these percentages, it can be assumed important information has been omitted. If one component of the narrative is significantly longer than expected, it may contain additional information that is false or misleading. The following statement is suspiciously out of balance. It is a case involving the disappearance of cargo:

> *The truck was loaded by the night crew. I would assume Bobby and Jose did most of the loading because they always load my route. I arrived exactly at 8 a.m., punched in and picked up my route slip in shipping. Tom and I chatted a minute about the game and his fishing trip last weekend. I did a walk-around on my truck and checked the tires, cargo doors, spare tire, you know the usual stuff, and left the terminal heading north on Interstate 25 at exactly 8:47 a.m. When I got to my first stop, I noticed the load was light. I called dispatch immediately and reported it. I then returned to the terminal and got in at about 2:30 p.m. That's about it, what else do you want to know?*

Notice the amount of detail early in the narrative. Without accusing anyone, the driver even identifies for the interviewer people that he should interview (Bobby and Jose). But, the driver fails to say where and when he arrived at his "first stop." He states that he noticed the load was "light," but fails to even suggest what or how much of the load is apparently missing. Then, without providing another useful detail, he states he arrives at the terminal at 2:30 p.m. Effectively, all that takes place between 8:47 a.m. and 2:30 p.m. is a mystery and left unexplained. Merely from this narrative a good fact finder should suspect the driver, not the night crew, of involvement in the missing cargo.

6.7 Deception Detection Technology

Man's pursuit of the truth and the detection of deception has been an endless endeavor. Recorded history reveals that the ancients employed ingenious methods to separate truth-tellers from liars. Some methods, such as the dunking of suspected witches, were simply cruel and illogical. Others carefully leveraged the human psyche and exploited the subconscious inability to maintain innocence when guilty. A good example is ancient India (500 BCE) where it is said a priest put lampblack on the tail of a donkey in a dark room. One at a time, suspects were to enter the room and pull the magic donkey's tail. They were told that when the one who was the thief pulled the magic donkey's tail, he would speak and be heard throughout the temple. Fearing detection, rarely did the real thief ever pull the donkey's tail. He, of course, would have clean hands when exiting the room, pronounced the thief, and he would be punished.

Of all of the forensic deception detection tools available today, the most well known is the polygraph. Similar to the methods employed by our ancestors, the polygraph allows a peak into the subject's mind as well as his body. According to Dictionary.com:

> [The polygraph is an] instrument designed to record bodily changes resulting from the telling of a lie. Cesare Lombroso, in 1895, was the first to utilize such an instrument, but it was not until 1914 and 1915 that Vittorio Benussi, Harold Burtt, and, above all, William Marston produced devices establishing correlation of blood pressure and respiratory changes with lying. In 1921, an instrument capable of continuously recording blood pressure, respiration, and pulse rate was devised by John Larson. This was followed by the polygraph (1926) of Leonarde Keeler, a refinement of earlier devices, and by the psychogalvanometer (1936) of Walter Summers, a machine that measures electrical changes on the skin.

Since its invention, the polygraph and its use have been controversial. The polygraph is most widely used today by law enforcement. More than one half of the large police departments in the United States use polygraph for preemployment screening.[9] For decades, the law enforcement community has successfully used polygraph testing as an investigative tool. Here are the ways law enforcement has traditionally used the polygraph:

- Verify the statements of witnesses and victims
- Establish the credibility of witnesses
- Evaluate truthfulness

In the private sector, the polygraph is most effectively used to help exonerate an innocent person suspected as the result of circumstantial evidence. In fact, this is the only way I use polygraph testing today. For example, instead of testing the most obvious suspect, I typically would test everyone else in the possible pool of suspects. This strategy will likely accomplish several things: (1) exonerates the innocent, (2) help achieve the standard of proof necessary to take disciplinary action absent an admission, and (3) removes the possibility that the suspect will refuse a polygraph test and subsequently claim the discipline he received was not because of his guilt, but instead, because he had refused to take the test. To appreciate the latter, the reader should know that disciplining an employee for refusing to submit to a polygraph exam is unlawful.[10]

Trap: Requesting an employee, on whom one already has sufficient evidence to justify discipline, submit to a polygraph exam is very risky. Should the individual refuse and then be disciplined, he may claim his treatment was unlawful. It would appear that he was disciplined for refusing the exam, not his misconduct. The employer would then need to explain why it wanted the test, when it already had sufficient evidence to justify and sustain the discipline. Under these circumstances, the discipline would likely appear retaliatory and thus unlawful.

6.7.1 Employee Polygraph Protection Act

The Employee Polygraph Protection Act of 1988, 29 U.S.C. §§ 2001-2009 virtually prohibits all private sector preemployment polygraph testing. The Act (sometimes referred to as the EPPA) bars most private-sector employers from requiring, requesting, or suggesting that an employee or job applicant submit to a polygraph or lie detector test, and from using or accepting the results of such tests.[11] The Act further prohibits employers from disciplining, discharging, or discriminating against any employee or applicant (a) that refuses to take a lie detector test, (b) based on the results of such a test, or (c) for taking any actions to preserve employee rights under the Act.

The Act contains several limited exceptions to the general ban on polygraph testing, one of which permits the testing of prospective employees of security guard firms. A second exemption is for employers that manufacture, distribute, or dispense controlled substances. The third exemption is the most important to private employers. It permits the testing of current employees who are reasonably suspected of involvement in a workplace incident that resulted in economic loss or injury to the employer's business.[12] Thus, in situations involving a *specific issue* of economic loss or injury wherein an employer has reasonable suspicion of a particular employee, the employer may test. In order to do so, however, the employer must:

- be engaged in an ongoing investigation involving economic loss or injury to its business
- be able to show that the employee to be tested had access to the property in question
- show it has a reasonable suspicion that the employee to be tested was involved in the incident

The Act goes further. In part, it requires the employee be given written notice of the date, time, and location of the test and what is to be asked at least 48 hours before the examination. The examiner must not deviate from the questions originally proposed and may not offer conclusions or opinions that are not relevant to the purpose and stated objectives of the test. Furthermore, neither the polygraph test results nor an employee's refusal to submit to an exam can provide the sole basis for discharge, discipline, a refusal to promote, or any other form of adverse employment action.

Given the complexities of the Act and the negligible utility of the polygraph, I have used it fewer than six times in my 29-year career. Although, some of my colleagues swear by it and use it frequently, I think it is more trouble than it is worth. However, there is one way it can be used very effectively and with very few complications. Here is how.

Suppose the matter under investigation is the unexplained disappearance of several hundred dollars from the company safe. Also, suppose our preliminary investigation has revealed that five employees had access to the safe during the time in question. However, for various compelling reasons, four of the five can be eliminated as suspects and two of them have credible reasons to suspect the fifth. The fifth employee for additional reasons is also our primary suspect. Instead of proposing our suspect submit to a polygraph exam, ask the other four to do so. We explain that they are not suspects, but that we want to affirm the suspicions they have regarding the actual subject and exonerate them if possible. As would be expected, all four provide nondeceptive responses with two confirming their original suspicions. We then interview our subject. Using the findings of our investigation and the results of the polygraph tests, the subject may have little choice but to admit (assuming, of course, he, in fact, is guilty) to the theft. The psychological burden of guilt and knowing the other four "passed" exams will likely be too much for him and he will be unable to maintain his innocence. However, even if he does, our hypothetical employer can still easily justify the discipline of him. The employer has met a good faith investigation/reasonable conclusion standard, by clearing four of the five individuals who had access to the safe. Confident that no one else had access, it is now obvious the one who was not polygraphed is the guilty party.

Under the circumstances, as unfair he may think his employer's process was, *failing to polygraph someone* is not a recognized cause of action. Thus, the angry employee who desired to sue would be left with asserting that his employer did not meet the standard of a good faith investigation/reasonable conclusion *and* the polygraph exams it had administered were unreliable. The employee, however, before getting an attorney, probably demanded that he, too, be allowed to take a polygraph to prove his innocence; creating the ultimate dilemma for himself—why he once thought it reliable and demanded to sit for an exam and then later assert it to be unreliable when administered on other people.

> *Tip: The polygraph should never be offered to those we suspect of guilt; only to those we are sure of their innocence. If we terminate parties that refuse to take a polygraph when our investigation points to their guilt, they may claim they were disciplined for unlawful reasons, while an employer's decision* not *to administer a polygraph is not a recognized cause of action.*

The polygraph's accuracy and determinations made by the examiner can be influenced by the emotional state of the examiner, the examinee's psychological and medical state, and the contemporaneous use of drugs or alcohol by the examinee. Because of these complexities and others surrounding the use of the polygraph, the investigative team should seek the advice of competent employment law counsel before deciding to use the polygraph.

6.7.2 Voice Stress Analyzer

The subject of voice stress analysis as a tool to detect deception has been the subject of study for years. The National Institute for Truth Verification claims to be the manufacturer and sole source of the Computer Voice Stress Analyzer.[13] The CVSA is only sold to law enforcement agencies and, according to the Institute, more than 1,200 public agencies use the CVSA. However, the use of this technology has been limited in the private sector. The EPPA and the state laws that mirror it place significant restrictions on lie detector "or similar" tests.[14] Accordingly, employers and private sector fact finders should use caution when considering the use of any deception detection technology.

It should be remembered, that while seemingly powerful technologies might exist, there are no *silver bullets* for those undertaking a workplace investigation. Extreme care should be used when deciding if a new or unproven technology should be utilized. Do your homework and seek the advice of counsel before deciding your final course of action.

6.7.3 *Kinesics*

Kinesics is the interpretation of body language, such as facial expressions and gestures or more formally, nonverbal behavior related to movement, either of any part of the body or the body as a whole. The term was first used in 1952 by Ray Birdwhistell, an anthropologist who wished to study how people communicate through posture, gesture, stance, and movement. Part of Birdwhistell's work involved filming people in social situations and analyzing them to show different levels of communication not clearly seen otherwise. The study was joined by several other anthropologists, including Margaret Mead and Gregory Bateson. Drawing heavily on descriptive linguistics, Birdwhistell argued that all movements of the body have meaning (i.e., are not accidental), and that these nonverbal forms of language (or paralanguage) have a grammar that can be analyzed in similar terms to spoken language. Thus, a "kineme" is "similar to a phoneme because it consists of a group of movements that are not identical, but which may be used interchangeably without affecting social meaning."[15] Today it is widely held that kinesics can and should be used during most investigative interviews.

My first exposure to this fascinating subject occurred while attending a training seminar offered by D. Glenn Foster over 25 years ago. Foster offered that, by recognizing behavior and interpreting body language, one could detect deception and emotion. He demonstrated that both verbal and nonverbal communications could be used by investigative interviewers to obtain information from an interviewee who was reluctant to reveal it. Today Foster offers one-, two-, and three-day seminars teaching his methodology.[16]

Before we go farther and examine how kinesics can be used, let's first examine the types of lies the investigative interviewer might typically encounter.

6.7.3.1 *Types of Lies*

Given adequate time to prepare, a guilty subject will sometimes enter an interview with the intention of withholding the truth. This is not necessarily lying, but it still obstructs the opportunity to obtain an admission. During the interview, the mindset of the interviewee in this state undergoes several stages before voluntarily providing an admission. Those stages typically include:

■ Defiance
■ Neutrality
■ Acceptance
■ Cooperation
■ Admission

During the defiance stage, the interviewee may be inclined to deceive the interviewer and withhold information. A common tool to accomplish this is use of lies. It is generally agreed that there are five types of lies:

- *The Simple Denial* is simple and to the point—"I didn't do it."
- *The Lie of Omission* is the most common lie used by deceptive individuals. To use it, the liar offers only the facts and details that are not incriminating, while withholding those which are just that.
- *The Fabrication* is a lie that contains elements that have been fabricated. It requires inventiveness and a good memory in order to remain consistent.
- *The Minimization* is a lie that contains a small admission in the hopes the fact finder will accept it and discontinue his questioning.
- *The Exaggeration* is a lie that uses the truth as a foundation, then exaggerates some aspects in order to deceive the fact finder.

6.7.3.2 Body Language of the Guilty

As these lies are employed, the interviewee will often provide indications of his intention to deceive. Both his words and body language betray him. Although we examined a few of these earlier in this chapter, here is a complete list of those I think are most common:

- Using language to mask the truth, such as "to tell the truth" or "honestly speaking"
- A selective memory
- The inability to recall even nonincriminating facts or circumstances
- Offering useless and irrelevant comments
- Inconsistent, evasive responses
- Avoiding eye contact or appearing to be visually looking for an answer
- Body language and mannerisms that are inconsistent with one who is telling the truth

Of these, the last two are non-verbal. Birdwhistell would call them *kinemes*. Attempting to withhold the truth, the interviewee might appear overly anxious, unconcerned, defensive, evasive, and even angry or arrogant. Communicating both verbally and nonverbally, the interviewee is sharing information with the interviewer. The correlation between these forms of communication might include:

- Overly anxious: Tapping feet, clicking teeth, bobbing knee, constantly looking at clock
- Unconcerned: The lint-picker, whistling, rolling eyes, grooming self, inspecting nails
- Defensive: Demanding proof, evidence, or the identity of witnesses
- Evasive: Memory loss, vague, aloof
- Guarded: Uses qualified answers, suspicious, questions fact finder's intentions

Figure 6.5   Contemplative.

- Complaining: Room too hot, too cold, thirsty, body pain, headache
- Angry or arrogant: In your face, disrespectful, argumentative

Further messaging, the interviewee squirms, crosses his legs or arms tightly, covers his mouth, or tugs at his ears. Figure 6.5 to Figure 6.13 illustrate some these expressions.

While these images are of an actor and the poses are somewhat exaggerated for illustrative purposes, it is easy to understand the emotions of the subject. When

Figure 6.6   Closed.

these visually expressive emotions are responses to specific questions, the skilled interviewer will be able to detect not only the intent to deceive but also the mindset of the interviewee and the stage that he is in. You may find some of these humorous, such as the "lint-picker." Here the subject is more concerned with the lint clinging to his socks than questions posed by the interviewer. In the image labeled "Fetal," we see the interviewee curled on the floor in a tight fetal ball. Though amusing, I included this image because more than once in my career, an interviewee did just this. Do you suppose he was guilty of the offense in question?

Figure 6.7   Uninterested.

In addition to the more obvious expressions using his body, the subject will sometimes offer lesser visual cues without even recognizing them. Professional gamblers call these cues *tells*. Here are few of the more common ones:

■ Looking away when asked an incriminating question
■ Looking away when lying or withholding the truth
■ Harshly staring at an object or nothingness

Figure 6.8 Anxious.

- Impulsively pursing his lips when asked a difficult or incriminating question
- Cringing or inhaling through his teeth before answering an incriminating question
- Putting fingers to his forehead as if in deep thought before uttering an untruth
- Templing or assuming other dominant body language
- Shaking his head no, before the question is fully asked

Figure 6.9   Lint-picking.

6.7.3.3 Body Language of the Interviewer

Just as a good interviewer observes his subject, the exceptional interviewer knows the interviewee is observing him. And, as such, he is conscious of his every movement and mannerism. An interviewer who appears nervous is nervous, an interviewer who appears unsure of himself or his facts will appear unsure and an interviewer, who is clueless, will appear both clueless and pathetic. The best and most successful interviewers appear confident, relaxed, professional, and at ease

Figure 6.10   Templing.

with themselves and the interviewee. They are not easily intimidated or thrown off balance. They come to the interview prepared and are able to demonstrate it. However this confidence should not be confused with arrogance. No one likes arrogance and an interviewer who is arrogant will be able to empathize with his subject and the subject will know it.

I also use something called *mirroring*. I will sometimes emulate the body language or mannerism of the interviewee. If he is templing, I, too, will temple. If he notices it, I will casually change my body language to something more compliant.

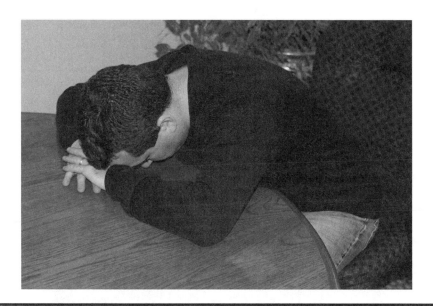

Figure 6.11   Surrendering.

Often the interviewee will then unconsciously mirror me. The effect alters not only his posture, but his mindset as well. I use this technique frequently when an interviewee is hesitant to commit to a written statement. In such circumstances, I will not question his hesitation or even look at him. I will simply begin filling out my written statement checklist in full view of him, with my form only inches from the blank statement form I presented him. Often my writing seems to give him permission to write and he does so. Similarly, if for some reason I want him to stop writing, I might put my pen down and cross my arms. Subtly this signals something is wrong or I am somehow dissatisfied. The behavior should cause him to stop writing and ask me "what's wrong?"

Another way I use my body language to influence an interviewee is with head movements. Try this, shake your head as if in agreement with me while saying "no." Now shake your head as if disagreeing with me and say "yes." If you simply did what I told you, without thinking about it, you likely found this exercise difficult. Most interviewees will also. So, when asking a question of which you want an affirmative answer, nod your head as if you are in agreement. Do the opposite if you want the interviewee to disagree with your statement.

> *Tip: Exceptional interviewers are as aware of their body language as they are aware of their interviewee's.*

Figure 6.12   Looking for answers.

6.7.4 Statement Analysis

First a disclosure. I do not use this technology (a method, to be more precise) nor have I ever attempted to use it. I share this with you so that you know I am not attempting to influence your decision to use it or learn more about it. Many find it extremely valuable and rely on it extensively. I do not because it is largely incompatible with the investigative interview method. First a little insight.

Figure 6.13   Fetal.

Statement analysis, also called *investigative discourse analysis*, and scientific content analysis (SCAN) is a technique for analyzing the words people use. Proponents claim this technique can be used to detect concealed information, missing information, and whether the information that person has provided is true or false.[17] Related to statement analysis is a different technique for analyzing the words people use called *statement validity assessment*, which uses something called *criteria-based content analysis*. According to Wikipedia, CBCA has been accepted as evidence in courts in Germany as early as 1954. Statement analysis involves the fact finder searching for linguistic cues and gaps in a subject's testimony or preliminary statements. Ideally, the technique guides the fact finder to ask follow-up questions to uncover discrepancies and inconsistencies. These irregularities are then used as the basis for more targeted questions.

Creator of SCAN, Avinoam Sapir gives the example of someone saying, "I counted the money, put the bag on the counter, and proceeded to go home." Sapir says the statement was literally true: "He counted the money (when you steal you want to know how much you are stealing), and then the subject put the bag on the counter. The subject didn't say that he put the money back in the bag after counting it, because he didn't; he left the empty bag on the counter and walked away with the money." Sapir says that a fundamental principle of statement analysis is that "denying guilt is not the same as denying the act. When one says 'I am not guilty' or 'I am innocent,' they are not denying the act, they are only denying guilt." Sapir claims that it is almost impossible for a guilty person to say, "I didn't do it." He asserts that guilty people tend to speak in even greater circumlocutions by saying things like: "I had nothing to do with it" or "I am not involved in that."[18]

SCAN's most ardent supporters are those in law enforcement. His proponents say statement analysis has proven highly effective as a police interrogation technique. I do not doubt this as many of my law enforcement students rave about its usefulness and reliability. However, if you have studied Chapter 4, The Investigative Interview Method (I2M), and understand its function and intricacies, you know it offers little room to obtain a preinvestigation statement from a suspected wrongdoer. I2M's success is based on a proper and thorough investigation. Only after the investigation is complete do investigative interviews take place. That said, I encourage the reader to explore statement analysis further if they find the concept intriguing. Who knows, you may find it a better method than mine.

6.8 Final Thoughts

I thought this would be a good place to tie up a few loose ends. Not that I have skipped over anything or left something out, but instead offer some thoughts about dealing with those who simply will not offer an admission. My employees, inclusive of our trainees, who adhere to the investigative interview method and use the scripts I have provided you, yield admissions in over 90 percent of the investigative interviews they conduct. Because I will not be with you and hold your hand, your results might be different. Regardless, we (you and I) need tools to deal with the most challenging interviewees. Here are some of the best I can offer.

6.8.1 Providing the Interviewee a Reason to Be Truthful

Sometimes an interviewee simply needs a reason to be truthful. Indications of this are typically very obvious. He might ask, "Why should I tell you what happened?"

On other occasions, his desire for a reason will be far less obvious. Figure 6.10 is a good example. An experienced interviewer would instantly realize the interviewee has surrendered; however, he has yet found the words to communicate his admission. He is asking for reason to answer the question truthfully. Recognizing this, the interviewer should offer it. Here are few of the more common reasons to tell the truth:

- ■ … Stop the shame
- ■ … Stop the pain
- ■ … Change the future
- ■ … Stop living a lie
- ■ … Start fresh
- ■ … Start over
- ■ … Get this fixed
- ■ … Get it behind you once and for all

Using that which has already been discussed or shared during the interview, the interviewer with full appreciation for the facts of the case (called *the fact pattern*), would offer a reason best suited for the circumstances. Upon offering the reason to be truthful, I would immediately follow it with: "(insert the subject's first name) would I be truthful if I told management you (insert offense, [i.e., took the cash]) and (insert rationalization, [i.e., but intended to return it as soon as you could])." Take a close look at this approach. I start with a reason to be truthful, described the offense, and then closed with a rationalization. But I posed the question asking him only to agree with me. I am not asking the interviewee to make an admission, I am only asking if *I would be truthful*.

> *Tip: The best fact finders are active listeners who use both verbal and nonverbal means to show the interviewee they are listening and that what they have to say is important.*

6.8.2 Failure to Assign Guilt

I am going to close this chapter by sharing with you a tool I hope you never have to use. It is not a tool to obtain an admission from a reluctant interviewee or reveal something that he does not want to disclose (although, it is capable of doing so, as you will see). It is a tool to restore your confidence in your investigation's findings and affirm for you that your subject is guilty of the offense in question. It is a tool to be used when your subject has emphatically and unequivocally stood on his denial. So strong is the denial, that you begin to doubt your investigative results and yourself. I call the tool, *the failure to assign guilt*. Here is how to deploy it. At the point you are about to cave, ask this:

> You said repeatedly that you had nothing to do with this. I think that is untrue, but assume for a moment it is one of the others. Who then, out of the three who had the combination, do you think did it?

A guilty person will almost always answer like this:

> You know I have been thinking about that and for the life of me, I just don't know. I mean I know these guys. One has a family and the other just sticks to himself. I don't know. I would hate to guess; maybe you should ask somebody else.

Notice that while up to this moment the interviewee may have been very convincing, I do not budge on my assertion that he is guilty. For his part, however, the subject is unable to accuse someone else. He knows just as I do that he is the only one with the motive and capacity to have committed the offense. Ah, you say, an innocent person not knowing the identity of the guilty would be very hesitant to implicate someone who is innocent as well. I agree. So, if necessary, I follow his response with a very similar question using the same technique:

> Let me put it another way, though you have said repeatedly that you had nothing to do with this, I still think that is untrue. But, assume for a moment we identify the real person responsible. Given the circumstances as you know them, what do you think is the appropriate punishment?

A guilty person will *always* answer with something similar to this:

> You know I couldn't really say. I mean, you're the guy who did the investigation. I've never worked in Human Resources. Geez, you're the guy that makes the big bucks around here. What do you think? Heck, maybe if the guy could prove he never did it before, he should be given a second chance.

Notice that again, I do not budge on my assertion that the subject is guilty. However, now the subject is unable to assign punishment. He fears that whatever punishment he suggests, it might be the punishment he gets. Thus, he hedges, and makes a very phony suggestion that the offender be given a second chance. The guilt of the subject could not be more evident. I would immediately follow this response with:

I agree; I think a second chance should be considered. (Insert the subject's first name), would I be truthful if I told management you took the cash, but intended to return it as soon as you could. You did intend to return the money, didn't you?

I have yet to encounter a better tool to restore interviewer confidence and obtain an admission than this. But like I said, I hope you never have to use it.

6.9 Frequently Asked Questions

1. Do most people really tell the truth?

   Yes. In our Western society truthfulness is still an important virtue. In other parts of the world this is not so, and the investigative interviewer should be aware of cultural differences when interviewing those outside Western society.

2. What is it about sociopaths that make them so dangerous?

   Their failure to have a conscience. The absence of remorse and compassion for others is the hallmark of all serial killers and most terrorists. These animals stop only when they have been killed or confined.

3. Is it proper to offer the rationalization that the victim deserved the treatment they received from the accused?

   Not in private sector investigations or the investigative interviews that accompany them. Though law enforcement sometimes uses this rationalization to obtain a confession, in the private sector its use is inappropriate and often unethical.

4. Speaking of ethics, it seems that the some of the techniques in this chapter are a little heavy-handed, possibly even unethical. Do those techniques cross the line?

   No. None of that which is offered in this chapter or anywhere else in this book is unethical. All of the techniques, methods, and scripts offered have been tested, challenged, and used. All of them have withstood legal and ethical examination and have been proved to be acceptable. They are fair and appropriate when used properly.

5. In Chapter 4 you mentioned the use of truth-tellers. How can they be used to detect deception?

   Truth-tellers are simple, nonincriminating questions. The best truth-tellers are questions of which the interviewer already knows the answers. Asking truth-tellers, the interviewer attempts to build rapport, relax the interviewee, and observe him when responding truthfully. Lying causes physiological stress. If the interviewee lies the interviewer should expect his physical behavior, body language, and mannerisms to be different than when truthful. The objective and subjective differences should be apparent to the interviewer and often are.

6. I have heard that the intensity profile of a denial when offered by an innocent person is different than that of someone who is guilty. Can you explain that?

Yes. The intensity profile of a denial of an innocent person begins with a gentle and polite denial of guilt. As the interviewer continues to press, the intensity of the denial increases. The opposite profile is typically exhibited by those who are guilty. This is because a guilty person knows that the more he talks the more difficult it is to sustain his innocence. He hasn't the will to argue his innocence because he lacks conviction. On the other hand, the innocent argue their innocence with greater passion as time passes because their integrity is at stake. They want to be believed because they know what they are saying is true and become increasingly frustrated with the interviewer who isn't listening to them.

7. Are false confessions a concern and how can they be avoided?

   Yes. Every professional interviewer should have some concern regarding a false confession or admission. There has been much written on the topic and a substantial amount of case law has addressed the topic. However, because this book addresses the subject of interviewing in the private sector, confessions and false confessions are not a concern, per se. Investigative interviews are instruments of the private sector and by definition are, among other things, for the purpose of obtaining an admission. As I have mentioned at length throughout this book, a successful investigative interview (one yielding a proper admission) rests on the foundation of a good investigation. According to protocol, one should not undertake an investigative interview of anyone unless he knows the subject is guilty of the offense in question or has a very good reason to believe so. Thus, a false admission is nearly impossible. In my 30+ years, I have yet to encounter one or am I aware of one of my team producing one. That said, often I have encountered, no, make that witnessed, a disciplined employee who had freely made an admission against interest subsequently recant it. In roughly 10 percent of the 300 odd arbitrations I have participated in, the interviewee that had made a full written admission recanted it during his testimony at the hearing. Regrettably for him, however, he then had to explain why he had lied, during his interview or during his testimony. Regardless of his answer, his credibility was severely damaged and, in most cases, fatally.

8. Do you offering training on the topic of investigative interviewing and, if so, where can I learn more about it.

   Yes. For more details, go to Convercent.com or email me at gene.ferraro@Convercent.com

Tip: The weakness of one's denial is typically proportional to their guilt.

Endnotes

1. The people and events depicted in this case study are fictional. They and the behaviors described are composites of individuals and events examined by the author during one or more investigations he performed in this career. Any similarity to real people or actual events is purely coincidental.

2. Martha Stout, *The Sociopath Next Door* (New York: Three Rivers Press, 2006), 8.

3. Ibid.

4. The dynamic of rule-breaking and creative leadership was recently celebrated in Buckingham and Coffman's bestselling book, *First Break all the Rules: What the World's Greatest Managers Do Differently* (Simon & Schuster, 1999). A marketing piece for the book states, "[G]reat managers share one common trait: They do not hesitate to break virtually every rule held sacred by conventional wisdom. They do not believe that, with enough training, a person can achieve anything he sets his mind to. They do not try to help people overcome their weaknesses. *They consistently disregard the golden rule.* And, yes, they even play favorites" [emphasis added].

5. For a more detailed examination of fraud and fraud prevention, see my book: *Investigations in the Workplace,* 2nd ed. (Boca Raton, FL: Taylor & Francis, 2012), 392–394 and 399–402.

6. Anthony Catanese, and A. W. Steiss are the authors of *Systemic Planning: Theory and Application* (Heath Lexington Books, 1970). Catanese is currently the president of the Florida Institute of Technology in Melbourne.

7. R. D. Hare, and P. Babiak, *Snakes in Suits: When Psychopaths Go to Work* (New York: HarperCollins Publishers, Inc., 2006), 24–28.

8. In philosophy and logic, the original liar's paradox is the statement: "This sentence is false." You will note that trying to assign to this statement a binary truth value leads to an irresolvable contradiction, thus making it the classic paradox.

9. John J. Fay, *Encyclopedia of Security Management,* 2nd ed. (Woburn, MA: Butterworth-Heinemann, 2007), 170–174.

10. Employee Polygraph Protection Act of 1988, 29 U.S.C.

11. *The National Employer* (San Francisco: Littler Mendelson, P.C., 2002), 730.

12. Ibid.

13. Online at: http://cvsa1.com/index.php (August 2002).

14. Employee Polygraph Protection Act, §§ 2001–2009.

15. Online at: http://en.wikipedia.org/wiki/Kinesics (accessed November 21, 2013).

16. Online at: http://www.dglennfoster.com/training#KIT

17. Online at: http://en.wikipedia.org/wiki/Statement_analysis (accessed November 22, 2013).

18. Ibid.

Chapter 7

Legal Challenges and Litigation Avoidance

Key learning points:

1. Law is most easily defined as a system of standards and rules of human conduct that impose obligations and grant corresponding rights in which the rules provide for the creation, modification, and enforcement of those standards.
2. From the onset, the fact finder and investigative interviewer must be thinking of one destination and one destination alone: the courtroom.
3. The first and foremost legal consideration when contemplating a workplace investigation is the right of privacy. That right extends to everyone the investigation touches, including the accused *and* accuser.
4. Workplace privacy rights when not statutorily protected nevertheless exist in the form of a "reasonable expectation of privacy."
5. Investigatory interviews, while never custodial, can nevertheless give rise to claims of false imprisonment, assault, battery, and the infliction of emotional distress.
6. In the private sector, the burden of proof necessary to discipline an employee, in most instances, is that of a good faith investigation and reasonable conclusion. However, the standards and burdens of proof for other actions shift and vary depending upon the action and jurisdiction that action takes place.

"The truth is only theory until it is proved."

E. F. Ferraro

7.1 Introduction

Given the nature and complexity of this chapter's topic, I thought the reader deserved some explanation regarding its enormity. While no single chapter, or book for that matter, could possibly cover all of the legal challenges facing fact finders or investigative interviewers in the private sector, this chapter is an attempt to cover that which the practitioner should have some command. Because of the litigiousness of today's society, no one should undertake an internal investigation without some familiarity of the law. In order to achieve that, one needs knowledge. This chapter contains that knowledge and that which is necessary to navigate the legal minefields that lay before the modern fact finder and investigative interviewer. It is written to be used as a standalone treatise or a reference. Regardless, I encourage every reader to read it in its entirety before conducting their next investigative interview.

7.2 Jurisdiction over Workplace Investigations

Traditional private sector fact finders conduct investigations for their employers or contract for a fee to conduct investigations for others. The types of investigations conducted and the legal constraints upon private sector fact finders are often different from those of public sector investigators acting with police powers. Whereas public sector investigators are primarily concerned with violations of criminal codes, private sector investigators conduct a wider variety of workplace investigations, including internal, administrative, civil, and criminal investigations. These investigations fall under the jurisdictions of various federal and state courts and agencies, and there are a variety of evidentiary tests used in these different proceedings to determine the reasonableness of the investigative processes, the merits of the information gathered, and the justifications for adverse actions taken against employees based upon the investigative outcomes.

7.2.1 Origin and History of Law

One of the earliest known systems of law was the Code of Hammurabi, which was established by King Hammurabi of ancient Babylon in about 2000 BCE. Later, the Egyptians, Hebrews, Greeks, and Romans all established systems of governance and law. Following the fall of Rome, Emperor Justinian of Constantinople carried on the Roman legal traditions and, in 528 CE, established the Justinian Code. The Justinian Code is the foundation of today's system of civil law for most of the civilized world. The most significant exception is English common law, which is the basis of our legal system today.

English common law was codified by King John of England upon his signing of the Magna Carta in 1215 CE. The Magna Carta became the basis for most of that contained in the first package of amendments to the U.S. Constitution, better known as the U.S. Bill of Rights. The Bill of Rights includes 10 amendments. In summary they include:

1. Freedom of religion, speech, press, assembly and petition
2. Right to keep and bear arms
3. No quartering of soldiers in time of peace
4. No unreasonable search and seizure
5. No unlawful imprisonment; double jeopardy, self-incrimination; taking of private property without just compensation
6. Speedy trial, opportunity to confront witnesses
7. Trial by jury
8. No excessive bail, no cruel or unusual punishment
9. Preservation of states' rights, residual rights to the people
10. Federal preservation of rights, residual rights to the state or people

These rights protect citizens against intrusions and abuses by government. They do not protect citizens from the behavior of one another. For that we have criminal and civil law. Civil law recognizes an assortment of torts (civil wrongs) that are actionable. The most common of these tort claims of which the investigative interviewer is exposed includes:

- Assault
- Battery
- False imprisonment
- Malicious prosecution
- Defamation, slander, libel
- Invasion of privacy
- Extortion
- Negligent hiring, supervision, retention, and investigation
- Wrongful discharge
- Intentional (and unintentional) infliction of emotional distress

Before we examine these torts and their potential for arising from our workplace investigations, let's first discuss the concept of jurisdiction and some of the other legal aspects associated with them that influence when and where they may be brought.

7.2.2 Jurisdiction

Jurisdiction refers to the authority of a state or federal court to hear a case. In order to preside over a case, a court must have both subject matter and *in personam* jurisdictions. Subject matter jurisdiction refers to authority over the matter in dispute, and *in personam* jurisdiction refers to authority over the person. For example, assume a warehouse employee who worked for a Jacksonville, Florida, company injured his back at work and pursued a workers' compensation claim. Subsequently, his employer's investigator trespassed upon the employee's property, in Jacksonville, while attempting to video the employee digging a trench in his backyard. If the employee filed suit for $100,000 against the investigator and company for invasion of privacy, he would do so in the Florida courts because they have subject matter jurisdiction over a wrongful trespass committed within the state, and in personam jurisdiction over the employee, investigator, and employer. Of course, the courts of other states have neither jurisdiction over the trespass or parties in this case.

The state and federal courts have exclusive jurisdiction over many areas of law and concurrent jurisdiction over areas of mutual interest. Of interest here, the federal courts have jurisdiction over cases involving the federal government, constitution, and laws; and concurrent jurisdiction over civil cases involving state law issues between parties from different jurisdictions (such as states) that involve damages greater than $75,000. Under the doctrine of pendant jurisdiction, the federal courts, in the interest of judicial efficiency, may decide cases that involve both state law issues and substantial federal issues when the parties and facts are the same. When deciding state law issues, the federal courts follow the laws of the states. The state courts exercise exclusive jurisdiction over legal disputes involving state law issues regardless of the magnitude of damages when there is no diversity of jurisdiction. State courts also have exclusive jurisdiction over state law issues when there is diversity of jurisdiction and damages are less than $75,000, and concurrent jurisdiction with the federal courts when there is diversity of jurisdiction and damages are greater than $75,000.

Returning to the case study, assume the employee's home was in Georgia rather than Florida and the employee was still seeking $100,000 in damages. Because the requested damages are greater than $75,000, and the plaintiff employee is from Georgia and the defendant company is from Florida, there is now diversity of jurisdiction and the state and federal courts have concurrent jurisdiction. The employee could file the lawsuit in Georgia because it has *in personam* jurisdiction over the employee and store investigator in the state and subject matter jurisdiction over wrongful trespass committed within the state. Or, the employee may elect to file the case with the federal courts. The defendant, if sued in Georgia, may accept the jurisdiction of the Georgia state courts or he may file a motion to have the case transferred to the federal courts. If the case is tried in the federal courts, it will apply the state law of Georgia to decide the issues in any cases filed under state law.

Jurisdiction also refers to the authority of an agency, board, commission, department, or other public administrative body to initiate, investigate, or review a complaint. Different federal and state administrative bodies have jurisdiction over the conduct of private sector investigators and private employers. For example, the National Labor Relations Board (NLRB) and Equal Employment Opportunity Commission (EEOC), respectively, have the authority to review charges against employers and their agents of unfair labor practices and discriminatory practices.

State human rights commissions also may review discrimination complaints. State workers' compensation commissions and unemployment boards routinely analyze the adequacy of evidence derived from workplace investigations when deciding the merits of employee benefit claims. Federal and state labor departments, too, may investigate claims against employers and fact finders for violating labor codes. Decisions rendered by administrative bodies are subject to judicial review by appropriate federal and state courts.

7.2.3 Evidentiary Burdens and Standards

Every federal and state judicial and administrative tribunal has established burdens and standards of proof. Here, burden of proof refers to the duty of a party to present evidence, whereas standard of proof refers to the level of evidence that must be presented to prevail. The elements of proof are the specific facts that must be proved for each cause of action.

In criminal proceedings, for example, the police must show probable cause to obtain a search warrant or make an arrest, and prosecutors must establish guilt of an accused beyond a reasonable doubt. Probable cause means evidence sufficient for a reasonable person to believe a crime has been committed and that the subject committed it. Guilt beyond a reasonable doubt is the highest standard in the judicial system. It means there is certainty in the minds of jurors and judges. The elements that must be proved are those of the alleged crimes as set forth in the penal codes of the jurisdictions.

In order to prevail in a civil case, the plaintiff must establish fault by only a preponderance of the evidence. This means when the competing evidence of the parties is weighed it must tilt in favor of plaintiffs. If the evidence tilts the other way, the defendants prevail. The elements of proof are those of the alleged wrongful acts (e.g., invasion of privacy, malicious prosecution) as set forth in the judicial decisions and statutes of the jurisdictions. By understanding the elements of the actions that might be filed against them (discussed throughout this chapter), fact finders can conduct themselves in an appropriate manner and minimize their liability exposures.

In a discrimination lawsuit there is a confusing series of shifting burdens. First, the employee must establish prima facie discrimination, which means he is a member of a protected class and adverse employment action was taken against him. Second, the employer has the option to articulate a legitimate business reason for the alleged adverse employment action. If it does, the burden shifts back to the employee to show by a preponderance of the evidence the reason set forth by the employer is a pretext to hide the alleged discriminatory action. For example, assume a company fired a female production employee for subjected theft of company tools. The employee filed a sex discrimination complaint. She alleged she was discharged [the adverse employment action] because of her status as a female [membership in a protected group]. In response, the company introduced testimonial evidence by co-workers who observed her taking the tools. In response, the employee claimed she borrowed the tools. Further, she introduced evidence that male employees routinely took tools home to work on personal projects and they were never disciplined. Was the firing justified or was it really a pretext by the company to cover up discrimination?

These shifting burdens are especially confusing in discrimination claims because they actually do not shift the burden of proof. The burden of proof remains at all times on the plaintiff. These are instead the steps that a judge should go through to decide if the case warrants trial.

Although the evidentiary standards in workers' compensation and unemployment hearings vary by state, the initial burden is generally upon employers to prove employees are disqualified from receiving benefits. One level of proof in some states is substantial evidence. This means facts sufficient to support a reasonable conclusion, although others might reach a different conclusion. In workers' compensation hearings, for example, employers in these states are required to provide substantial evidence that an injury did not arise out of and in the course of employment, the benefits were procured by fraud, or some other disqualifying conduct. Similarly, employers need to produce substantial evidence showing willful misconduct or just cause to disqualify unemployment applicants. Interestingly, parties that lose at the agency level and appeal to the courts often must satisfy higher standards of proof. For example, they may have to prove the agencies' decisions were clearly erroneous or outside their statutory authority. The reason is the courts give deference to the expertise, interpretation of facts, and decisions of the agencies.

In addition to knowing the burdens and standards of proof necessary when bringing actions, employers and their fact finders need to know what level of evidence will enable them to successfully defend their conduct. For example, in malicious prosecution lawsuits, fact finders may defend their actions by showing they acted upon probable cause. They and their employers may defend against discrimination complaints by showing they acted for legitimate business reasons. Parties may defend against defamation lawsuits by showing their comments were privileged and the communication had a legitimate business purpose. Because there are so many different claims that may be raised (many discussed in this chapter), the key issue is that fact finders understand these claims and understand the burdens and standards the courts and regulatory agencies will impose to evaluate their evidence and their conduct.

7.2.4 Multiple Agency and Court Review

It is important to remember that the vast majority of workplace investigations are never contested and, therefore, are not reviewed by outside agencies and courts. Nonetheless, one cannot forget that any investigation may be subject to review if an aggrieved employee files an administrative complaint or lawsuit. Further, depending upon the facts, a single investigation and resulting disciplinary action may be reviewed by multiple agencies and courts.

Hypothetically, assume a white male, union employee, 47 years of age with 25 years of service, was terminated after a lengthy investigation for theft of company property. Further, the employee was not given notice of, nor provided union representation during a confrontational investigative interview. The employer signed a criminal complaint and the ex-employee was found not guilty at his criminal trial. Based upon these facts, the employee could file a union grievance that he was terminated without cause, an unfair labor practice charge that he was not provided union representation, and an age discrimination complaint that the criminal charges were trumped up as a pretext to discharge him. He also might file a claim for workers' compensation benefits for emotional distress suffered when he was unjustly accused, and a separate claim for unemployment benefits on the grounds he did not engage in disqualifying misconduct. Finally, he might sue for false imprisonment, defamation, malicious prosecution, emotional distress, and assault had his interview been conducted improperly.

This is not to say the employee would win any or all of the charges, but the employer and fact finder would have to respond to each agency and court per the respective charges. In response to the union grievance, the employer would have to convince an arbitrator that it had just cause to terminate. Regarding his right of representation complaint before the NLRB, the employer would need to show it did not violate his right to representation on the grounds the employee never requested representation. Addressing the EEOC issue, the employer would have to prove it had a legitimate business reason to terminate and did not engage in age discrimination. Before the state unemployment board, it would have to establish employee willful misconduct to prove ineligibility to collect unemployment benefits, as well as establish that the misconduct was sufficiently egregious so as to harm the interests of the employer. Regarding the workers' compensation claim, the employer would need to prove any emotional distress suffered was a self-inflicted result of the employee's misdeeds or beyond the scope of statutory protection. To defend against the false imprisonment and assault claims, the employer must prove that it did not detain the employee against his will, nor did its agents do or say anything that constituted assault. It also may need to substantiate that it acted in good faith and had probable cause to sign the complaint to defend against the malicious prosecution claim. Regarding the emotional distress allegation, the employer would need to show it did not act in an extreme and outrageous manner during the investigation, interview, and termination. The actual responses of the fact finder before the different agencies and courts might range from providing investigative documents to testifying at official hearings and proceedings.

The harsh reality of the situation is that even a simple case may be very complex when all the underlying variables and liabilities are examined. Although few workplace investigations result in administrative complaints and lawsuits, the potential exists in every investigation. Thus, it is imperative that fact finders understand their rights and duties, respect the rights of those they investigate, and understand the standards and burdens of proof used in the different proceedings.

Regardless of the standards or burden of proof necessary to prevail in court, the experienced fact finder (and his counterpart: decision maker) knows the standard of proof will drive his process and significantly determine the resources necessary to obtain the stated objective. If only an employment action is sought, the standard of proof should be that of good faith investigation/reasonable conclusion. As discussed in several of the preceding chapters, in *Cotran v. Rollins Hudig Hall International, Inc.*, the Supreme Court of California held that good cause existed for terminating an employee for misconduct if an employer had a reasonable and good faith belief that the employee engaged in misconduct. It was ruled that the employer does not have to convince the court or jury that the employee, in fact, committed the misconduct, only that the employer honestly believed that the employee engaged in misconduct based on substantial evidence obtained through an adequate investigation that included a fair opportunity for the employee to respond to the charges. The court further defined the term good cause as a "reasoned conclusion … supported by substantial evidence gathered through an adequate investigation that includes notice of the claimed misconduct and a chance for the employee to respond." Thus, the importance, if not necessity, of the fourth phase of investigation, the verification and analysis phase, which involves interviewing the subjects of one's investigation.

In conclusion, both federal and state courts and administrative agencies have exclusive and concurrent jurisdictions over various aspects of workplace investigations. Investigators, in order to perform their duties effectively, should become familiar with the courts and agencies that have jurisdictions over their investigations and learn about the different burdens and standards of proof. To do otherwise is unprofessional and potentially expensive.

7.3 Preparatory Legal Considerations

From a liability risk management perspective, the "preparation and planning phase" of an investigation is a critical stage. It is the foundational stage. If not properly set, there is a greater probability the investigation may not achieve its objectives, but will waste time and resources. As a review, the following critical issues should be, at a minimum, addressed during this phase: (1) the legal duty to investigate, (2) investigator selection, (3) investigative objectives, (4) evidentiary burdens, and (5) documentation controls.

7.3.1 Legal Duty to Investigate

One of the first issues an employer should address is to determine whether it has a legal duty to conduct the intended workplace investigation. In most circumstances, the decision to investigate employee misconduct in the workplace is left to the discretion of the employer. The underlying reason is that the victim of the misconduct in the majority of cases is indeed the employer. Whether the loss is of a type or magnitude that concerns the employer sufficiently enough to allocate resources to investigate is a business decision left to the discretion of the employer based on its calculation of return on investment (ROI), as discussed in Chapter 1.

There are circumstances, however, where an employer may have a legal duty to investigate employee misconduct. That is, in these cases, the decision to investigate is no longer discretionary. A duty to investigate, for discussion purposes here, may arise from statutes and regulations, contracts with employees, and common law duty to properly screen and supervise employees.

First, for example, a few statutes and regulations impose a duty upon most employers to investigate under limited circumstances. Civil rights laws prohibit various forms of workplace discrimination. This general duty includes the right of employers to investigate allegations of discrimination, harassment, and retaliation. Because a prompt investigation, combined with a response that stops the misconduct, generally bars a claim for the original violation, employers have a substantial incentive to investigate all such allegations. While this is technically not a duty to investigate, since a failure to investigate does not necessarily give an employee the right to sue, it is a practical matter often the equivalent of a duty for employers, because a failure to investigate can cause an employer to lose one of its most effective tools for limiting exposure to claims under the civil rights laws.[1] Also, the general duty clause of the Occupational Health and Safety Act (and similar clauses under state plan programs) requires employers to maintain an environment "free from recognized hazards that are causing or are likely to cause death or serious physical harm to their employees."[2] If an employee demonstrates a propensity toward violence and the employer fails to investigate, the employer might be cited for violation of the general duty clause if the employee later injures another. For those interested in more details, go to OSHA's Fact Sheet on workplace violence at http://www.osha.gov/OshDoc/data_General_Facts/factsheet-workplace-violence.pdf. In a situation where the organization is the alleged perpetrator, e.g., defrauding the government or investors, and is facing criminal prosecution in federal court, under the Federal Sentencing Guidelines, the court may reduce the severity of its penalty if the employer investigated the alleged misconduct in a timely manner.[3]

Further, employers in certain regulated industries have a duty to investigate specific types of incidents. For example, healthcare providers must investigate cases of patient abuse; pharmaceutical companies must investigate missing controlled substances; financial institutions must report certain financial transactions, losses, and irregularities; and officers and boards of public trade corporations now have a greater duty to ensure the accuracy of their financial statements.

Second, employers have an implicit duty to conduct reasonable inquiry when investigating suspicious behavior of union and possibly other not-at-will employees. Union and personal contracts of employment usually contain clauses that stipulate discipline, and termination must be based on cause, just cause, good cause, or other similar standards. These contracts place the burden upon employers to produce sufficient evidence to sustain the appropriate disciplinary actions. Implicit in this condition is the requirement of a reasonable investigation. Failure to do so may leave an employer in a position where it loses a grievance hearing or breach of contract lawsuit because it cannot meet its contractual evidentiary burden.

Third, many courts recognize common law claims of negligent hiring and negligent supervision. Negligent hiring occurs when an employer hires an untrustworthy employee into a position of trust and the employee subsequently injures another. A position of trust is one where others are highly dependent upon the employee to perform his duties in a reasonable and safe manner. Negligent supervision occurs when an employer has or should have knowledge that an employee is unfit for duty or for performing his duties in an unsafe manner. For example, allowing an intoxicated employee to operate a company vehicle or failing to properly intervene when an employee threatens another may expose employers to liability based on their failure to investigate further and take appropriate remedial measures.

In *Salinas*, the Supreme Court of Texas affirmed a jury verdict in excess of $3 million against a taxi company held liable for negligent hiring of a taxi driver who had been given a taxi permit by the police.[4] The firm failed to do a separate criminal background check. If it had, the background check would have revealed multiple felonies. The driver sexually assaulted a female customer. Because of the high trust customers place in taxi drivers, the company was held to an ultrahigh duty of care in hiring and was not permitted to shift its responsibility and liability to the police. In *Saine*, the Supreme Court of Arkansas held a cable company could not be sued for negligent hiring, but could be sued for negligent supervision and retention.[5] The company hired a cable installer who brutally sexually assaulted and attempted to murder a customer in her home. The company did check with two past employers, verified he had an honorable military discharge, and administered a drug test prior to hiring. But, the company did not follow up on an earlier female customer's complaint that the employee made sexual advances and her allegation that he left windows unlocked and later attempted to break into her home.

In *Yunker*, the defendant company rehired a man who had spent five years in prison for the murder of another employee (the circumstances of this case were never set forth).[6] He was twice transferred to new facilities after he had some encounters with co-workers. At the last facility, he was terminated for threatening a female subordinate. He murdered her a few days later in her front yard. The Appeals Court of Minnesota affirmed the dismissal of the negligent hiring claim on the grounds it would undermine the public policy of rehabilitation to find an employer was negligent for hiring a felon. But, it reinstated the family's negligent retention claim because it was based on more than the mere fact the employee had a felony history; it was based on "several workplace outbursts" by the employee "specific(ally) focus(ed)" on the victim, including one in which the words "one more day and you're dead" were scratched on her locker door.

In conclusion, the decision to investigate must be made based on a determination of whether the employer owes a legal duty to investigate or, in the absence of a legal duty, on a determination of ROI as discussed elsewhere in the text.

7.3.2 Investigator Selection

As discussed at length in Chapter 4, the selection of the right fact finder/investigative interviewer is critical. The fact finder and his team should have a combination of experience, education, and continuing professional development sufficient for the level of sophistication of the investigation. An experienced individual, with a successful record of prior investigations of similar nature and complexity, is more likely to appreciate the time and resources necessary to complete the project properly; be more familiar with the appropriate agencies and courts that may review the investigative process; and possess more insight as to the legal duties owed, standards of proof required, and overall liability risks. This is not to say that employers cannot call upon less experienced fact finders, for it may be very appropriate to use less seasoned investigators so long as they are properly supervised. Selection of an investigator or investigative team, either employee or outside contractor, is an important decision that employers should make with care.

7.3.2.1 Liability for Employee Fact Finder/Interviewer Misconduct

What is the liability of an employer for the misconduct of its fact finder? Under the doctrine of respondeat superior, a principal is vicariously liable for the actions of its agent that are committed within the scope of employment or engagement. An employer–employee relationship is a principal–agent relationship because the employer has control over the methods of work and performance outcomes. An employee investigator conducting a workplace investigation on behalf of the company is an agent of the company, and the employer may be held liable for any misconduct.

7.3.2.2 Liability for Contract Fact Finder/Interviewer Misconduct

A contract investigator is, in most cases, an independent contractor of the client principal. An independent contractor does work for a principal, and the principal controls the performance outcome. However, unlike with an agent, a principal does not exercise the same degree of control over the methods of performance. An independent contractor performs the work according to his methods or the methods of his trade or profession. Under the independent contractor rule, a principal is not liable for the conduct of the independent contractor on the premise the principal does not exercise substantial control over the contractor's methods.

For example, in *Paradoa*, the plaintiff, a worker on disability benefits, sued an insurance company for the alleged verbal abuse of investigators working for the private investigative firms it retained to conduct routine activities checks.[7] The Appeals Court of Massachusetts affirmed the insurance company was not liable for conduct of the independent investigators because the insurance company

> provided no instruction or protocol to … the investigators as to the manner it wanted work on its behalf conducted … did not supervise the … investigations or ask for amplification of reports that were filed by … the investigators … and the investigators billed the agencies that hired them, not CNA (the Defendant), and were paid by those agencies … the conclusion compelled by the evidence is that CNA contracted out work to them when needed and left to them the manner and means.

However, a principal may be held liable for the acts of an independent contractor if the principal retains control over the contractor in the contract for service or actively exercises control over the activities of an independent contractor. A principal also might be held liable if it knows the contractor is engaged in misconduct and ratifies this conduct by not taking appropriate action to stop further similar conduct. In *Greenbaum*, when interviewing an employee subjected of theft, a private investigator placed his chair in front of the door in the manager's office, twice told the employee he could not leave, and even once shoved him back into the chair.[8] The Court of Appeals of Georgia, in affirming a judgment for false imprisonment against the company, noted the defendant could be held liable for the conduct of the investigator on the grounds the "defendants actually exercised a power of direction and control over the interrogator at the time of plaintiff's detention." Specifically, the court commented on the fact noted that the store manager and investigator had planned the interrogation together, and it was the manager who had determined when it was over.

7.3.2.3 Contractual Shifting of Liability Risk

As a means of managing liability risks, principals and independent contractors may include certain provisions in the contracts for service. For example, a contract may require the independent contractor to carry a specified amount of general liability, errors and omission, or other insurance coverage. Further, the principal may require proof of insurance and notification of cancellation. Either party may require the other to indemnify the other for any third-party claims and lawsuits arising out of performance of the contract. If there is a dispute over proper performance of the contract, the parties may stipulate the maximum damage exposure to each other. From the perspectives of the employer and contract investigator, the more clearly the roles, objectives, and risks are defined at the beginning of the relationship, the more probable the investigative process will be conducted in a reasonable and professional manner.

7.3.3 Investigative Objectives

The investigative objectives set the focus and tenor of an inquiry. The objective of an investigation is not to get the money or the subject to show who runs the business, or to make an example of the subject. In *Kelley*, for example, the Massachusetts Court of Appeals, in affirming a $36,000 judgment for abuse of process against a company, was not impressed with the company investigator, who testified "his job was to make sure he got the $96 and 9 cents."[9] This and similar statements are the antithesis of a professional investigation and set the stage for unnecessary liability.

The objectives of an investigation must be lawful in purpose, scope, and methods. An employer should have a clear, legitimate business purpose for launching a workplace investigation. The scope of the inquiry, too, should be limited to the legitimate purpose of the investigation. The methods of investigation must be lawful as well. For example, while an employer may have a right to conduct criminal background checks on job applicants, a decision to investigate the criminal backgrounds of only minority applicants is a discriminatory and unlawful purpose. Similarly, during an undercover investigation into subjected employee on-the-job illegal drug use, it may be within the scope of the investigation to observe and report on the subject's union employee involvement, but it would clearly be outside the scope of the investigation to also report on his lawful union activities. Finally, the philosophy "the ends justify the means" is not acceptable. The methods of inquiry must be reasonable. Employers may have the right to conduct investigative interviews with their employees, but regardless of how serious the offense, it would be clearly unlawful to physically or coercively detain the employees against their will in order to interview them.

> *Tip: A professional workplace investigation is a tool. It is a lawful inquiry, reasonable in scope and methods, conducted by a qualified individual or team to systematically identify, collect, and document material evidence about a legitimate workplace concern. Like most tools, a workplace investigation is something that should never be misused.*

7.3.4 Identifying Standards of Proof

Inherent in the issue of determining the investigative objectives is identifying the applicable burdens and standards of proof to be placed upon the process. For example, if an organization's investigation is noncriminal in nature, it makes little business sense to devote extra resources necessary to achieve the criminal burden of proof beyond a reasonable doubt. As noted earlier, a decision to terminate a union employee may, depending upon the language of the bargaining agreement, be satisfied by showing cause, just cause, or good cause. If an employee files a claim for unemployment benefits, the company may prove ineligibility by merely establishing the employee's willful misconduct. The key point is that, at the beginning of an investigation, the employer should be cognizant of the standards and burdens of proof that it may need to prove: to bring an action against the employee and to defend its conduct should the employee later make a claim against it. One overlooked and sometimes costly risk in this process is an employer will assume a higher standard of proof than necessary to achieve the legitimate objectives of the business.

For example, assume a manufacturer receives an anonymous tip on its hotline that a few employees at a small facility are taking inventory from the plant after hours. It is a violation of company policy to be onsite during nonoperating hours without authorization. It is also a violation to remove property without authorization. The manufacturer conducts a routine inventory audit and discovers an unexplained 10 percent inventory variance at one of its small plants. The company president tells the corporate security manager to investigate. When asked, he states he does not want to prosecute the employees. The security manager contracts with an experienced licensed private investigator in that state to conduct video surveillance of the plant after hours. Three days later, the investigator provides video evidence of three persons entering the plant after hours and removing several cartons. All three are readily identifiable as employees. Their duties do not entail being onsite after hours nor the removal of property. Herein lies the issue, should the company spend further funds to gather more video evidence, to track the property removed, to catch the employees in the act, and to prove employee theft beyond a reasonable doubt? Or, should the company cease the video surveillance, interview the employees to verify their unauthorized presence and removal of boxes, and terminate them for violation of company policy? An intelligent response to this situation can only be made if the fact finder understands the legitimate intent of the president and applicable burdens and standards of proof necessary to protect the interests of the company should the employees file wrongful discharge and other civil actions, or seek unemployment benefits.

7.3.5 Documentation Control

Almost every investigation will produce some records even if it is as simple as a note on a calendar about a call from a concerned employee or verbal disciplinary meeting with an employee. Records produced during workplace investigations and resulting disciplinary actions are often discoverable during administrative and judicial proceedings. This includes notes on calendars, field notes, e-mail messages, investigative reports, conference notes, disciplinary actions, and other documents produced as the result of the investigation, disciplinary action, and postinvestigative analysis. Proper documentation control procedures for creating, labeling, copying, tracking, distributing, and retaining investigative documents should be established. Without such ground rules, there are risks. Documentation may be produced that is immaterial or even harmful to an investigation; investigative documents may be inadvertently intermixed with other records and create problems locating and editing them when requested in litigation; vital evidence may not be properly documented; sensitive information may be too broadly distributed; and critical documents may be lost. Ideally, documentation controls should be established before any specific investigation and reviewed in the preparation and planning phase. In the alternative, ground rules should be established in this phase before the information and fact-finding phase begins.

7.3.6 Confidentiality

It is a recommended practice in the planning stage of an inquiry to remind all of the participants, especially those who do not normally participate in investigations, that the information uncovered and discussed is to remain confidential; shared with only those who need to know in performance of their duties. The accidental exposure of an employer's investigation or investigative results is almost always undesirable. If employees become aware of critical information or investigation before its completion and some form of formal communication by management, it may adversely impact morale and productivity. Customers or suppliers also may feel resentful of having been a part of the investigated activity and may choose to discontinue their relationship or patronage. Public exposure of a compromised investigation may spark resentment, an onslaught of painful adverse publicity, and law suits. The failure to timely remind all parties, at the outset and throughout the inquiry, of their duty to retain confidentiality can only harm the investigative process and enhance the liability risks.

7.4 Information Gathering and Fact-Finding Considerations

The confluence of federal and state laws, regulations, and judicial decisions makes the information gathering and fact finding phase the most dynamic and complex, and the highest risk phase of the investigation. Fact finders must be sensitive and responsive to a complex mixture of constitutional, administrative, civil, and criminal laws that proscribe behavior, standards, and burdens of proof. Uninformed fact finders may unduly restrict their methods of investigation, expend unnecessary time and resources to achieve an unnecessary standard of proof, or engage in high-risk conduct that increases their employers', their clients', and their own personal liability exposure. The next several sections address fact-finding liability concerns in more detail.

7.5 Constitutional Considerations

The Fourth Amendment of the U.S. Constitution guarantees "the right of the people to be secure in their persons, houses, papers, and effects, against unreasonable searches and seizures." The Fifth Amendment guarantees the right against self-incrimination, and the Sixth Amendment provides the right of legal counsel in criminal proceedings. Under the exclusionary doctrine, evidence obtained in violation of these constitutional rights may be ruled inadmissible in criminal proceedings. Employers and employees are often confused about the constitutional protections afforded employees during workplace searches and investigations. Employees often believe they enjoy constitutional protections against workplace searches and are entitled to be advised, based upon the landmark U.S. Supreme Court decision in *Miranda*, of their constitutional rights to remain silent and to have legal counsel present when interrogated.[10] Collectively these rights among others constitute the right of due process. Employers, on the other hand, are frequently uncertain whether they are bound by the prohibitions of the Constitution and precisely whether due process rights should be afforded a subject employee.

The federal and state courts (which are obligated to abide by the decisions of the federal courts in this area of law) have been petitioned by numerous criminal defendants to apply federal constitutional rights to private sector investigatory matters. The courts have consistently held that there must be state action (government involvement or entanglement) to invoke the protections of the Constitution. As a rule, private parties are not viewed as state agents nor is their conduct viewed as state action. The courts, under most circumstances, view corporate and private investigators as private parties engaged in private actions.

7.5.1 Self-Incrimination

In *Antonelli*, a contract security officer searched the car of a dock worker and found stolen imported merchandise worth thousands of dollars.[11] The employee made several self-incriminating statements at the scene. He was convicted at trial and appealed the use of the self-incriminating statements to the security officer. The appeals court stated:

> there was no governmental knowledge or instigation of, influence on, or participation in any of the actions surrounding the taking of appellant into custody, which produced the statements unsuccessfully sought to be suppressed prior to trial … the Fifth Amendment privilege against self-incrimination does not require the giving of constitutional warnings by private citizens or security personnel employed thereby who take a subject into custody

The U.S. Court of Appeals affirmed the admission of the incriminating statements and the conviction.

Similarly, in *Green*, an employee made several incriminating statements when "interrogated" by a company investigator without being advised of his constitutional rights. He objected to the use of the statements at his criminal trial.[12] The Court of Common Pleas of Pennsylvania noted:

> The overwhelming authority from other jurisdictions supports the position that "Miranda" warnings need not be given by a private security officer prior to questioning a subject taken into custody. This Commonwealth has never squarely decided the issue. "We believe ... the guarantees of the Fifth Amendment are intended as limitations upon governmental activities and not on private individuals," thus the "Miranda" warnings need not be given by persons other than governmental officials or their agents.

7.5.2 Search and Seizure

In *Simpson*, a union employee refused to open his lunchbox for a routine search by plant security at the end of the workshift.[13] He was resultantly suspended. He requested unemployment benefits for the time of his suspension. The referee granted him benefits on the grounds he had "good cause" to refuse the search based upon his belief the search violated his federal and state constitutional rights against unreasonable searches. On review, the full board reversed the decision and the employee appealed. The Commonwealth Court of Pennsylvania rejected the circuitous logic of the employee who argued the board's denial of benefits was "state action" because it deprived him of his constitutional right against unreasonable search. The court stated:

> It is firmly settled that the Fourth Amendment of the United States Constitution applies only to the actions of governmental authorities, and is inapplicable to the conduct of private parties ... The same is true of the search and seizure provision in the Pennsylvania Constitution ... It follows, then, that the right the claimant seeks to establish against his employer, a private entity, is not a right that arises from the constitutional provisions.

The court affirmed the employer's search did not violate either the federal or state constitution.

When acting as private parties in private matters, private sector investigators are not engaged in state action and, thus, are not governed by the constitutional prohibitions against unreasonable searches, self-incrimination, and right to counsel. But, there are exceptions to this general rule.

7.5.3 *Joint Action and Public Function Exceptions*

The courts have stated a private party may be held to constitutional standards when acting jointly with a public party to perform a public function. Hypothetically, assume a fact finder had uncorroborated information that an employee was dealing drugs out of his company locker. Now, consider two alternative scenarios. First, assume the fact finder, per company policy, directed the employee to open the locker and found what were later proved to be controlled substances. The fact finder then conducted an investigative interview, never advised the employee of his constitutional rights, and the employee provided a full admission. The fact finder called the police to the facility and turned over the drugs and the details of the signed admission. In the second alternative, assume the fact finder called the police and together they opened and searched the employee's locker and found the subjected drugs. The fact finder and detective jointly interviewed the employee, never advised the employee of his constitutional rights, and he admitted the drugs were his. In this alternative, will the drugs and admission be admissible at the employee's criminal trial? How would a court make this determination? One way is to look at the level of government knowledge and involvement before and during the time, and to look at the motives of the private party.

In the first alternative, the government was unaware of and played no role in the search or subsequent interview. Further, the company fact finder acted to protect the interests of the employer. His turning the evidence over to the police did not make him a state actor or agent. Therefore, there is no government action and the evidence and admission should be admissible. In the second scenario, the government played a very direct and active role in both the search and interview that followed. Also, although the investigator was acting to protect the interests of the employer, it appears that he was concurrently acting in a public capacity. Because the fact finder was an active participant and effectively acting as an agent of the government, there is a significant probability that many courts would apply constitutional prohibitions when evaluating the admissibility of evidence under the second scenario.

Note that there is a difference between the police directing or participating in workplace searches and interviews versus being apprised of lawful private sector investigations or standing by as witnesses.[14] Private sector investigators also need to recognize that there is an enhanced probability, but not certainty, that their conduct may be subject to constitutional prohibitions if they are off-duty police working security or have special police commissions.[15]

> *Tip: Fact finders, as private parties engaged in private action, are not normally subject to federal constitutional prohibitions. But, these prohibitions might apply if they have special police commissions or are off-duty police officers conducting the investigation.*

As discussed later, the proper remedy for unreasonable searches by private parties is a civil suit for invasion of privacy. Similarly, if an employee is unable to leave an interview conducted by a fact finder, the appropriate remedy is a civil suit for false imprisonment.

7.5.4 State Constitutional Issues

A state constitution may set forth similar prohibitions to the federal constitution regarding unreasonable search and seizures, and the right against self-incrimination.[16] The states almost universally follow the lead of the federal courts in requiring state action to invoke these protections.[17] However, a state Supreme Court may interpret a state constitution as granting greater rights than provided under the U.S. Constitution. For example, in evaluating whether to suppress the admissions and evidence obtained from a shoplifting subject after he had requested to talk with a lawyer and refused to waive his constitutional rights, in Muegge, the Supreme Court of Appeals of West Virginia found the state shoplifting detention law vested private merchants with state powers.[18] It stated: "[W]e find that the security guard was not acting in a purely private fashion, but under the mantle of state authority and that, therefore, the protections of … the West Virginia Constitution apply to her dealings with the appellant."

Three states have held that private security personnel acting under merchant detention statutes were vested with state power. But, two of the three have since reversed their stance. There is debate whether the remaining state, West Virginia, has or has not.[19] Nonetheless, workplace searches and employee interviews are not normally conducted under specific state statutory authority and are not viewed as state action.

It also should be noted that a few state constitutions provide a specific right of privacy. As shown in the following examples, this right may be worded independently of or incorporated in the state prohibition on unreasonable search and seizure. Here are two examples:

California Constitution, Article I, §1
All people are by nature free and independent, and have certain inalienable rights, among which are those of enjoying and defending life and liberty; acquiring, possessing, protecting property; and pursuing and obtaining safety, happiness, and privacy.

Hawaii Constitution, Article I, §5
The right of the people to be secure in their persons, houses, papers, and effects against unreasonable searches, seizures, and invasion of privacy shall not be violated.

An important issue in the few states that recognize a state constitutional right of privacy is whether it protects against both unreasonable government and private party intrusions. In *Hill*, a collegiate diver challenged the National Collegiate Athletic Association drug-testing program on the grounds it violated her state constitutional right of privacy.[20] The Supreme Court of California affirmed that the provision applied to intrusions by private parties because the constitution has been amended, in part, to protect against businesses collecting and misusing personal data. It adopted a shifting burden test to determine if the invasion was unreasonable. First, the plaintiff must show a legally protected privacy interest, a reasonable objective expectation of privacy under community norms, and a serious breach of that privacy. The burden then shifts to the defendant to establish that it had a legitimate competing interest or justification for the intrusion. The burden then shifts back to the plaintiff to show a less intrusive means available to achieve the competing interest. Applying this test, the court ruled the NCAA had a legitimate interest in requiring college athletes to submit to drug testing, and the program was not unreasonably intrusive because it contained many procedural safeguards. The exact effect of this decision on workplace investigations in unknown, in part, because the objective expectations of privacy in the workplace might be somewhat reduced. Nonetheless, of relevance here, fact finders need to be aware of and sensitive to investigate procedures that may violate an applicable state constitutional right of privacy.

7.6 Federal Law and Employee Rights

The U.S. Congress has enacted several labor laws in order to reduce labor strife and promote national economic welfare. Of special interest here, the National Labor Relations Act (NLRA) guarantees employees the right to engage in "concerted activities" that foster labor organization and collective bargaining.[21] The NLRA defines and prohibits "unfair labor practices" by employers and unions, and vests the National Labor Relations Board (NLRB) with authority to receive complaints, investigate, hear, and decide alleged violations under the statute.[22] The Labor Management Relations Act (LMRA) places exclusive jurisdiction over labor disputes in the federal courts.[23] State courts are preempted from deciding disputes that fall under the jurisdiction of the NLRB. Rulings of the NLRB may be appealed to the federal appellate courts.

7.6.1 Unfair Labor Practices

The NLRB has identified two broad workplace investigative practices it considers unfair labor practices, under section 8(a), that are in violation of employee rights, as set forth in section 7 of the NLRA. Specifically, section 7 guarantees employees the "right to self-organization; to form, join, or assist labor organizations; to bargain collectively through representatives of their own choosing; and to engage in other concerted activities for the purpose of collective bargaining or other mutual aid or protection." These practices deal with the employees' right of union representation during disciplinary hearings and employer investigations into protected concerted activities.

7.6.2 Union Representation

The landmark case affecting workplace interviews is *Weingarten*.[24] It is based upon an unusual set of factual coincidences. Here is what happened. Based on a report that a food counter employee was stealing cash, a company investigator, without advising store management, watched the food service operation for two days. He observed no thefts. The investigator introduced himself to the store manager and told him of his investigation. Coincidentally, the manager stated another employee just reported the subject had just paid only $1, the price of a small box of chicken, for a $2.98 large box of chicken. The investigator interviewed the subject employee. Her requests for a union steward to be present were denied. The investigator confirmed her explanation that the company was out of small boxes and that she had used a large box for her order. He apologized for any inconvenience and prepared to leave. The employee then started to cry and spontaneously said the only thing she had ever taken were her free lunches. She had been with the company for approximately 11 years and had worked 9 of those years at a store that provided free lunches. The last two years she had worked at a new store that, by company policy, did not provide free lunches. The investigator began to question her further and calculated she owed about $160 for lunches she had taken. Her requests for a union steward to be present were denied in this session as well. The investigator ended his investigation after he checked with the corporate office and could not verify the no free lunch policy had ever been communicated to the employees at the current store. The investigator and store manager told her the matter was closed; no disciplinary action was taken against her; and she was asked not to discuss the matter with anyone. A short while later, she revealed the entire matter to a union representative. The union, concerned about the chain of events, filed an unfair labor practice complaint on the grounds the employer had refused her requests for a steward to be present during the interviews. The NLRB held that union employees upon their request are entitled to union representation during interviews that they reasonably believe might lead to discipline. The denial of this representation was an unfair labor practice. On appeal, the U.S. Court of Appeals disagreed and reversed the decision.

The case was appealed. On appeal, the U.S. Supreme Court affirmed the NLRB decision that union employees are entitled upon request to union representation during investigative interviews that they reasonably believe might lead to discipline. The Court found, however, a fact finder is not bound to advise the union member of this right. If the employee requests and insists upon representation, the investigator may advise the employee that the interview may be discontinued. The employee may waive this right and participate in the meeting without representation, or forego the interview and the opportunity to present his side of the matter.

The Court said that in such circumstances, the employer is free to continue its investigation, with or without the interview, and to take appropriate disciplinary action based upon the information it is otherwise able to derive. The Court also said if an interview is conducted with a representative present, the interviewer is not obligated to bargain with that representative, and that the role of the representative is to assist the employee, but not to answer the questions.

However, the role of the representative is not one of a "passive observer." In *Pacific Telephone and Telegraph*, the NLRB ruled it was an unfair labor practice for the company to not advise two employees (who were to be disciplined for the unauthorized installation of a telephone in one's home) and their union steward the purpose of the meeting after they requested to know before it was conducted.[25] Further, the court held it was an unfair labor practice to deny the employees and steward (and two other employees and steward in a companion case) a preconference meeting once a steward requested it. The request did not have to come directly from the employee. But, in *Southwest Bell*, the U.S. Court of Appeals held the right of representation was not violated when a union steward was asked not to interfere with the questioning, but was permitted to consult with an employee before the investigatory meeting and was free to make comments, suggestions, and clarifications after the interview.[26]

By permitting union representation in investigatory interviews while restricting the role of the union representative, the NLRB and courts are attempting to balance the right of employees to engage in concerted activities for mutual protection with the right of the employers to investigate and to take reasonable measures to protect their properties and businesses.

Before concluding this section, it should be noted the right of nonunion employees to co-employee representation can quickly change. In 2000, the NLRB ruled nonunion employees were entitled to co-worker representation; the U.S. Court of Appeals upheld this decision in 2001; but, in 2004, the NLRB reversed its position and returned to the long-standing view that the right of representation did not extend to nonunion employees. Because this is not the first time the NLRB has briefly flirted with granting nonunion employees a right of co-employee representation, fact finders should note the NLRB often reflects the labor policy of the president and this issue might arise again when changes in administration occur.[27]

> *Tip: While nonunion employees are generally not entitled to co-employee representation, employers should contemplate such request during the planning and preparation phase. Refusing representation can be risky. It can raise other issues about motive, methods, and trust. If it is granted, there are other issues. Is it a co-employee of choice? What if the co-employee is also a subject? What is the role of the co-employee? These are decisions best answered before raised in an interview.*

7.6.3 Investigations into Protected Concerted Activities

The NLRB and the courts fully recognize the right of employers to take reasonable measures to protect their businesses and to investigate suspicions of misconduct by all employees, but such investigations may not include overly broad or intrusive surveillances, interviews, undercover operations, and other investigative inquiries that infringe upon or "chill" the employees' rights to organize, collectively bargain, and engage in other protected concerted activities.

In *Parsippany*, the U.S. Court of Appeals concurred that a hotel had a "legitimate business interest" in protecting its guests; however, it affirmed that it was an unfair labor practice for an employer during a labor organization drive to beef up its security staff and then have those officers conduct surveillance in the workplace on the employees that advocated the union.[28] In *Unbelievable*, the U.S. Court of Appeals affirmed it was an unfair labor practice when the chief of security eavesdropped on a conversation between an employee and union representative talking in a breakroom that was an authorized area for visits.[29] Further, it was an unfair practice when the employer expelled the representative based upon what was overheard.

When employees engage in protected organizational and protest activities, the documenting of these activities by video recording of participants may be viewed as an unfair labor practice to coerce or intimidate employees from exercising their rights. When those activities include threats, vandalism, violence, or other unlawful activities, employers are justified in enhancing surveillance activities. But, enhanced surveillance activities should not focus on or be overly inclusive of lawful activities of union members.

In *Horsehead Resource Development Company*, the company, based on volatile contract negotiations and in anticipation of a lockout or strike, installed a camera at its front gate and in two vehicles that were used for interior patrols.[30] The evening after the last negotiation session, the hotel where the company negotiators were staying received a bomb threat. Later that evening the plant mysteriously lost its power and lights on two occasions, and the old office trailer was set on fire. On the first day of the lockout, the company discovered several acts of sabotage and a drawing of a rifle scope aimed at a man labeled "Yankee Scab." The front gate camera was left on the first day and thereafter it "was turned on whenever company personnel … crossed the picket line to enter or leave the plant." After someone attempted to run a manager off the road, the cameras in the vehicles were used during the escorting of the shuttle vans between the plant and hotel. These cameras also were used to observe union members who were peaceful and off company property as "they parked their cars, gathered to talk in the shade, or moved to and from the picket shack and the portable restroom." The cameras also documented acts of "misconduct on the part of four employees that was sufficiently serious to justify their discharge."

The misconduct involved placing "jackrocks" (six-pronged objects constructed from bent nails) and roofing nails in the road to puncture tires, using a slingshot to shoot ball bearings at a truck and through the windshield of a car, and spitting in the face of a security guard as he drove through the picket line.

The union filed unfair labor charges against the company for its use of the cameras. The U.S. Court of Appeals held:

> It was clearly not an unfair labor practice to photograph the four miscreants. Likewise, the videotaping of company vehicles crossing the picket line and the use of camera cars to patrol the plant perimeter and escort replacement employees did not interfere with employees' protected concerted activity. These were justified precautions against potential violence.
>
> For the most part, however, the picketing seems to have been peaceful. To the extent that the Board's finding of an unfair labor practice was based on surveillance that went beyond videotaping the access to front gate, the plant perimeter, and the company cars, we conclude that it was supported by substantial evidence. The surveillance of union members who were in no way engaged with company personnel or property, but were merely talking among themselves or moving to and from the picket shack and the portable restroom, was unjustified. We are satisfied that it was within the Board's province to find that [the company] went too far in its surveillance.

In *California Acrylic Industries*, the U.S. Court of Appeals held it was an unfair labor practice for an employer to videotape a lunch hour meeting between employees and union representatives talking on a public sidewalk.[31] Allegedly, the company felt "something might happen" and videotaped to protect against possible union vandalism and trespass. The court affirmed this was insufficient justification in light of the chilling effect of videotaping upon employees in the exercise of their protected rights.

In *National Steel and Shipbuilding Co.*, the company placed a camera on a tripod on top of a building to monitor a gate and large parking lot where the unions, which were working without a contract, conducted rallies every morning with about 100 persons present.[32] The company monitored these rallies for approximately four months. Even though there were three to four security officers stationed at a guard station next to the gate and there were two permanent cameras, the company tried to justify the decision to install the extra camera based on a history of strikes every 4 years for the past 12 years and acts of violence during those strikes.

The U.S. Court of Appeals affirmed the NLRB ruling that the use of this extra camera was an unfair labor practice because the incidents of violence cited were too remote in time and occurred during strikes, and the union was actually working without a contract and was not out on strike. The court and NLRB rejected the company's argument there was no tendency to coerce by its use of the camera on the grounds that at least 100 employees showed up every morning and the company had never taken any reprisal action against any employees. The court stated this did not prove the other 2,900 employees didn't feel coercion and the lack of disciplinary action did not prove there was no fear of reprisal.

In conclusion, video surveillance is often most appropriate for documenting destructive and unlawful employee activities in progress. Also, when there is a reasonable objective basis for anticipating disruptive behavior, a company may engage in limited videotaping of protected activities; for example, video recording a truck entering a plant when employees in the immediate past have blocked the entrance or video recording managers entering a plant when they have been threatened or attacked in the recent past. Care should be taken to avoid videotaping protected concerted activity.

7.6.4 Federal Preemption and State Tort Actions

As noted, federal labor law preempts state courts from deciding issues that fall under the jurisdiction of the NLRB. One such situation is when the employer and an employee's union have entered into a collective bargaining agreement that covers the nature of the employee's complaint. In that situation, section 301 of the Labor Management Relations Act (LMRA) allows the union to sue for breach of the collective bargaining agreement. The U.S. Supreme Court has said that is to the exclusion of the worker; in other words, only the union, not the worker, can sue, except in some limited circumstances (see *Allis-Chalmers Corp. v. Lueck*, 471 U.S. 202, 220 (1985)). The deciding factor in this type of case is whether the collective bargaining agreement does or does not need to be interpreted to determine whether the alleged tortuous conduct was committed (see *Lingle v. Norge Div. of Magic Chef, Inc.*, 486 U.S. 399, 405-06 (1988)). If the union contract does not need to be interpreted, then the aggrieved employee will be permitted to proceed with the state tort claim(s). This might mean, as discussed above, that he could sue his employer for some type of wrongful discharge claim, or even the investigator for claims related to the investigation. However, if the collective bargaining agreement does need to be interpreted, his claims are preempted and decided under federal labor law. The answer to whether a collective bargaining agreement does or does not need to be interpreted depends on the alleged tort(s) and the contract language.

In *Hanley*, a cashier failed to properly enter seven of eight transactions in a blind security test where money was left on her register.[33] After signing an admission that she often saved the money for the end of her shift and used it to balance the register, but never for personal gain, she was terminated. She filed suit. She claimed she was "interrogated" in a backroom, verbally detained even though she wanted to leave, threatened with arrest, and promised no other action would be taken if she confessed. The Supreme Court of Montana held the LMRA §301 did not preempt her state tort claims because it was not necessary to interpret the union–management contract to decide the issues of false imprisonment, intimidation, emotional distress, slander, and employer negligence. It reinstated the suit against the company.

In *Blanchard*, the company, based on information provided by employees and police, hired an outside firm to conduct an undercover investigation.[34] Months later, two other investigators were retained to interview employees implicated in the investigation. The employees were interviewed in an office where all the windows were covered with paper. Allegedly, each was falsely told that there was substantial evidence of their individual drug use, advised they would be terminated if they left the interviews, promised they would not be discharged if they confessed, and told they had the right to union representation. Twelve employees, who made self-incriminating statements, were discharged. Four of the employees, whose discharges were affirmed in binding arbitration, filed suit. In part, the suit contained state tort claims of intentional infliction of emotional distress, false imprisonment, invasion of privacy, and fraud (false promise that no other action would be taken against them). The company argued the tort claims were preempted by the LMRA. The U.S. District Court held the privacy claim was preempted because the labor contract contained language pertinent to the use of controlled substances. The false imprisonment claim also was preempted because the alleged threat of termination for failing to answer questions pertaining to violations of work safety rules required an examination of the company authority under the labor contract to direct the activities of the employees and to investigate and take appropriate disciplinary actions for violation. The court also ruled the allegations of fraud and emotional distress, if fraud was first proved, might be decided without reference to the labor contract, and it permitted plaintiffs to continue with these two claims.

In *Cramer*, the employer, a large trucking company concerned about driver drug use and dealings, installed cameras in the restrooms used by its drivers, both female and male.[35] Employees in two separate lawsuits, one a class action and other with 282 plaintiffs, filed invasion of privacy and emotional distress claims in state court. The company removed the cases to federal court on the grounds they were preempted under the LMRA because the company was allowed under the collective bargaining contract to use cameras in employee theft and dishonest cases. The U.S. Court of Appeals held it was not necessary to interpret the labor contract to decide these cases. The conduct of the company was in violation of the state criminal code. Further, the collective bargaining agreement could not make illegal conduct under state law legal. Absent any federal question, the appeals court remanded the consolidated cases back to state court for further adjudication on the merits of the claims.

7.6.5 Union Contract Restrictions

Fact finders in unionized environments should review the applicable collective bargaining agreement(s) before undertaking an investigation. It will often set forth the burden that the employer has agreed is necessary to justify discipline. Common requirements set forth in these contracts include such terms as cause, just cause, good cause, and other similar language. Although the exact meaning of these terms may vary, all of them place a burden upon the employer to produce evidence to support the discipline. A termination may be subject to arbitration if the union appeals.

Other restrictions may be placed on workplace investigation in a unionized environment. For example, an employer and union may contractually agree that organizational interviewers will advise union members of the right to union representation prior to investigatory interviews. Further, both parties may agree that no investigative disciplinary interviews will be conducted without a representative and even a stenographer being present. A union and employer may agree that a union member cannot be questioned about the conduct of another union member. Further, a union and company may agree whether drug testing or use of drug dogs will or will not be permitted. The important point is that workplace fact finders must be aware of and abide by any pertinent conditions negotiated into the collective bargaining agreements.

7.6.6 Arbitration

Binding arbitration is a process where two or more parties (usually management and union, but such clauses are being inserted with more frequency into management and professional contracts) contractually agree to use an independent party to review and decide disputes between the parties. Arbitration decisions are generally final and may be appealed to the courts only on very limited grounds. Usually, arbitrators are not bound by earlier decisions of other arbitrators on the same issues, and, thus, arbitration decisions are sometimes quite unpredictable.

Employers and unions use this process to settle grievances under the management–union contract. Most disciplinary arbitrations focus not upon the methods of investigation, but upon whether the company met the necessary standard of proof. Nonetheless, these decisions may affect how workplace investigations are conducted. An arbitrator, for example, may influence an investigative method by finding a company did not have sufficient evidence, based upon a single documented incident of property removal, to prove the employee stole rather than borrowed the equipment. As a result, company investigators may alter their investigations to include multiple observations of property removal in order to meet the standard of proof established by the arbitrator. Where applicable, company investigators should take time to review past arbitration decisions for guidance on acceptable practices and burdens of proof.

7.6.7 Civil Rights Law

A number of federal laws prohibit various forms of workplace discrimination and harassment. The major act is the Civil Rights Act of 1964 (often referred to as Title VII).[36] It prohibits employers from engaging in unlawful employment practices relating to hiring, firing, promoting, and altering the terms and conditions of employment because of race, color, religion, sex, or national origin. It also vested enforcement authority in the Equal Employment Opportunity Commission (EEOC), but did not preempt state law. Other important federal laws include:

The Civil Rights Act of 1866
Age Discrimination Employment Act
Equal Employment Opportunity Act
Rehabilitation Act
Pregnancy Discrimination Act
Americans with Disabilities Act
Civil Rights Act of 1991

Collectively these laws prohibit other forms of discrimination and harassment, strengthen the enforcement authority of the EEOC, and authorize compensatory and punitive damages, and attorney's fees in certain instances. In addition to the federal laws, all 50 states and many local authorities have similar antidiscrimination laws, and some of these laws may include other categories of protected persons.

At the fact-finding stage of an investigation, the major impact of civil rights laws that prohibit employment discrimination and harassment is twofold upon workplace investigations. First, as explained, the practical effect of the civil rights laws is that employers should generally investigate all employee allegations of discrimination and harassment. Second, fact finders must be careful not to engage in or use discriminatory methods of investigation.

7.6.7.1 Duty to Investigate

EEOC guidelines provide that employers should "investigate promptly and thoroughly" all credible allegations of sexual harassment.[37] This statement balances and puts equal value on two competing criteria that employers should consider for all discrimination and harassment investigations. It does not permit an employer to sacrifice timeliness for thoroughness, nor to sacrifice thoroughness for timeliness. Instead, the burden is on an employer to initiate the investigation in a timely manner and to keep it moving forward to a timely conclusion. But, the conclusion must be based on a reasonably thorough investigation into the facts. This normally includes interviewing the complainant, witnesses, and alleged harasser, and reviewing other relevant documents and available evidence. It also may include identifying other complainants or witnesses who have not stepped forward. More complex allegations and number of persons involved, variations in work schedules, and other factors will, in part, determine the length of an investigation.

For example, in *Fuller*, the U.S. Court of Appeals found that an employer's investigation of a sexual harassment complaint was seriously deficient in several respects. The employer failed to timely interview the harasser, giving him time to prepare his defense, and the investigator often accepted the harasser's side of the issue without taking reasonable steps to confirm, including failing to check telephone records available to him. The employer disregarded evidence in support of the complainant, and failed to interview a key witness in favor of the complainant.

Similarly, in *Valdez*, the court was critical of the "remarkably shoddy" internal company investigation. The company received an anonymous EEOC complaint of sexual harassment by "top management" at one of its stores. The personnel manager who received the complaint assigned it to the zone manager who himself had a questionable history involving alleged sexual harassment. He, in turn, assigned the investigation to the manager of the store where the harassment had allegedly occurred. In the analogy of plaintiff's counsel, it was as if the fox was guarding the hen house. The store manager never contacted the law firm representing the complainant and named on the EEOC complaint for more details; when he interviewed employees, he asked only about the conduct of his assistant manager; and he never allowed the assistant manager to respond to the allegations in writing. The assistant manager was terminated within two days of the start of the investigation. The assistant manager, who was a Salvadorian, filed a national origin discrimination complaint. Although the case facts were very complex, the U.S. District Court sharply criticized the shoddiness of the employer's investigation. It disapproved of the decision to assign the investigation to the zone manager who had a questionable history and, as it came out in trial, who also had stated on two occasions a desire to fire the plaintiff because there were too many "wetbacks" working for the company. It also doubted the selection of the store manager, who was a prime subject himself, to conduct the investigation. It wondered about the manager's thoroughness and objectivity for focusing only on the assistant manager and failing to gather more facts. And, it criticized the company for terminating the assistant manager when he didn't even work at the store at the same time the complainant worked there. The court found the company had discriminated against the manager when it terminated him.

As a final comment, an important consideration for employers is that a prompt and thorough investigation of a harassment complaint, accompanied by appropriate and timely remedial action, can provide the employer an affirmative defense in subsequent litigation. But note, the issue of whether temporary remedial measures need to be taken before or during the investigation is a separate issue. Depending on the severity of the allegations, sensitivities of the parties, and level of immediate supervision, an employer may need to take temporary measures before an investigation is completed.

7.6.7.2 Discriminatory Practices

Discriminatory investigative practices include those that are discriminatory on their face and those that are neutral on their face while discriminatory in impact. For example, it would be discriminatory practice on its face for a company to check for criminal histories of only minority job applicants. Similarly, all factors being the same, it would be a discriminatory practice for a company to interview only white males and not minority employees who had access to stolen company property. But, this does not mean everyone has to be interviewed if there is legitimate evidence for interviewing some and not others. Similarly, if, as part of an internal investigation, an employer searched only the purses of women employees and not the briefcases of male employees, this may be a discriminatory investigative practice unless there was a legitimate reason for such a search pattern. The simple fact of the matter is that investigative methods should not on their face be discriminatory.

Other investigative practices may be neutral (nondiscriminatory) on their face, but may have a discriminatory impact. A workplace investigation procedure that is neutral on its face might include something so simple as interviewing only hourly employees and not management staff who had access to missing property or areas where subjected illegal drugs were found. The distinction between hourly employees and salaried managers is not discriminatory on its face. But, hypothetically, what if all the managers were white males and all the hourly employees were female minorities? Further, assume the investigation was inconclusive and the company elected to terminate all the hourly employees. If a complaint was filed and the employer (and his fact finder) could not articulate a legitimate reason for interviewing only minority hourly employees, the underlying investigation and subsequent adverse employment action might be vulnerable to claims of discrimination. Investigators need to remain sensitive to the potential for engaging in direct and indirect discriminatory investigative practices.

> *Tip: Fact finders need to be sensitive to the totality of the investigative environment as not to be influenced by or to engage in practices that are discriminatory on their face or impact, including bias remarks, selection of subjects, and investigative reporting.*

7.6.8 Select Federal Statutes

The following statutes have been discussed elsewhere in this text. The purpose here is to provide a brief foundation in each and to highlight their relevancy to fact finders.

7.6.8.1 Employee Polygraph Protection Act

The Employee Polygraph Protection Act (EPPA) prohibits private sector employers from administering polygraph examinations, creates limited exemptions where it may be used, and sets forth very specific rights of employees who refuse or agree to take the test.[38] Specifically, it is illegal under the act for a private employer to "require, request, suggest, or cause any employee ... to take or submit to any lie detector test," or to "discharge, discipline, discriminate against in any manner ... or threaten to take any such action" against any employee who "refuses, declines, or fails to take or submit to any lie detector test." Thereafter, it creates a few specialized exceptions for businesses dealing with national security, pharmaceuticals, and protection of key public facilities. It also permits private employers to use the polygraph for "ongoing investigations involving economic loss to the employer," where the employee had access to the missing assets and the employer has other "reasonable suspicion" that the employee was involved. The act also places certain conditions upon employers and details rights of the employee, including the right to refuse and withdraw permission, notification of the specific grounds for reasonable suspicion, and other rights.

For example, in *Wiltshire*, the defendant bank conducted an extensive investigation into the unauthorized wire transfer of $1.5 million.[39] It recovered the funds only because another bank intercepted the transfer when it became suspicious. But, the defendant bank had to pay a few thousand dollars in administrative fees for the transaction. Based on information provided by the FBI, access to funds, use of an outdated time stamp, and knowledge of fund transfer protocol, the bank narrowed its investigation to a manager, the plaintiff. During employee interviews, the manager was the only subject who stated it was necessary to put a date stamp on a debit transfer. The bank asked the manager to take a polygraph. Per the statute, he was allowed 48 hours to decline and he did so on the second day. Approximately two weeks later, based on existing information, the bank terminated his employment for lack of confidence in his ability to protect bank assets. He claimed his termination was based on his refusal to take the polygraph, and he filed suit for violation of the EPPA. The bank countered that he was fired based on the information it had and not his refusal to take the polygraph. The court, per the statute, found it was an ongoing investigation, he had access, and there was economic loss (the loss of use of funds for a few days and the fee). Further, the court concluded the bank had reasonable suspicion to request that the manager take the polygraph test. But, the court found the notice provided the manager was deficient because it didn't adequately describe with "particularity" the bank's basis for its suspicion. The notice for reasonable suspicion stated: "You were present on December 7, 1990, when the wire transfer was sent. You had access to all necessary documents and stamps to create item and place it in basket for transmission." The bank argued that there was sufficient particularity and notice principally based upon the multiple interviews that it had had with the plaintiff.

The Supreme Court of New York County, New York, disagreed and held the verbal notice was insufficient because Congress was specific that the reasonable suspicion notice must be set forth in writing. Because the bank failed to comply fully with the notice requirement, the court found the bank violated the EPPA when it requested the plaintiff to take the polygraph. Addressing the issue of his termination, the court added: "Citibank's suspension and termination of plaintiff were barred by EPPA §3 (29 U.S.C. § 2002[3]) unless Citibank can prove at trial that plaintiff's failure to take the polygraph test played no part in the decision either to suspend or fire him." The court denied the bank's motion for summary judgment.

In another interesting case, *Lyle*, the U.S. District Court held the defendant hospital did not qualify for the ongoing investigation exemption for economic loss.[40] The hospital vice president who was investigating the theft of funds from a doctor's locker asked the plaintiff, a technician in the surgical area where the theft occurred, to take a polygraph. He refused and subsequently was terminated. He sued for violation of the EPPA. The hospital filed for summary judgment on the grounds it qualified for the ongoing investigation exemption. The court held it did not because the doctor, not the hospital, had suffered economic loss. In addition to the federal statute, employers and fact finders need to recognize that many states have laws that restrict the use of polygraphs as well.[41]

7.6.8.2 Fair Credit Reporting Act

The Fair Credit Reporting Act was enacted by Congress to place reasonable procedural controls on Consumer Reporting Agencies (CRAs) that balance the needs of commerce for fast and reliable consumer information regarding a consumer's credit worthiness and character versus the rights of individual consumers to accuracy and confidentiality.[42] A CRA refers to a person or business that engages in the "practice of assembling or evaluating consumer credit information or other information on consumers for the purpose of furnishing consumer reports to third parties." It is important to note that a public agency, such as a police department or court that keeps public records, is not a CRA.

There are two types of consumer reports: a consumer report and an investigative consumer report. A consumer report pertains to a person's "credit worthiness, character, general reputation, personal characteristics, or mode of living ... which is used or expected to be used in establishing the consumer's eligibility for [among other things], employment purposes." An investigative consumer report expands this information to include "personal interviews with neighbors, friends, or associates ... or who may have knowledge concerning any such items of information." The term *employment purposes* means "a report used for the purpose of evaluating a consumer for employment, promotion, reassignment, or retention as an employee."

In order to obtain and use information from a CRA for employment purposes, an employer must give notice to the consumer, obtain the consumer's written permission, and verify this information to the reporting agency. If it is an investigative consumer report, the employer must also identify it as such, provide an explanation why the information is sought, and give notice that the consumer may submit a request for a complete disclosure about the nature of the investigation and its methods. If an employer takes adverse action based on a consumer report, the employer has further duties prior to the action including providing the consumer with a copy of the report and a document that again outlines his or her rights. After the adverse action, there are further notification requirements placed upon an employer. Of interest here, the Fair Credit Reporting Act (FCRA), as amended in 2003, excludes certain communications between a CRA and employer regarding investigations into employee misconduct, breaches of written policy, and compliance with regulations, and rules of self-regulated organizations. If adverse action is taken upon the communication there is a duty to provide a summary of the "nature and substance" of the report. It is essential that employers and CRAs abide by the FCRA.

7.6.8.3 Federal Sentencing Guidelines

In order to reduce the disparity of sentences defendants received for similar offenses by the federal courts, the Federal Sentencing Commission was established to provide uniform guidelines.[43] Of interest here, the Federal Sentencing Guidelines provide guidance on how the culpability score of a convicted organization (e.g., business) is to be calculated. The higher the culpability score, the greater the severity of the financial penalty assessed against the organization. The score is increased if "high-level personnel … participated in, condoned, or were willfully ignorant of the offense." Further, it may be increased if the organization has a prior history of similar offenses, it violated a court order, or it obstructed the government investigation. An organization may lower its culpability score if it has an "Effective Program to Prevent and Detect Violations of Law." The score also may be lowered if the organization self-disclosed the offense, cooperated in the government investigation, and accepted responsibility.

Employers should enact corporate codes of ethics, provide all employees appropriate training, and provide internal reporting mechanisms for employees to report concerns, including suspicions of criminal conduct by high-level personnel. Further, employers should conduct reasonable follow-up investigations when presented with credible accusations. The failure to implement these countermeasures and the failure to investigate high-level misconduct can expose an organization to severer penalties in the federal courts.

7.7 State Tort Law Issues

The majority of workplace, investigation-related lawsuits are civil tort actions under state law. However, fact finders should be aware that, although very similar in nature, there are variations in the laws of the 50 states, the District of Columbia, Puerto Rico, and other territories. When crossing jurisdictional lines, investigators should be sensitive to these variations.

7.7.1 Assault and Battery

Workplace investigations do not usually involve the use of force by the fact finder. Nonetheless, if private sector investigators unnecessarily threaten to or use unnecessary or unreasonable force, they may be sued for assault and/or battery.

An assault occurs when one party creates a reasonable apprehension in the mind of another of a forthcoming, imminent offensive touching. An assault does not require that there be any contact. An assault may be physical, verbal, or a combination of both. A verbal threat combined with apparent capability to hit, slap, shove, or smash, or a similar threat can certainly be sufficient behavior by a fact finder to constitute an assault. Making a fist, glaring, lunging, swinging, grabbing at, and other similar body motions also may constitute an assault. Of course, verbal threats coupled with aggressive body motion make for an even stronger impression of an assault.

Battery is the intentional touching of one party by another that is offensive in nature. The touching may be either directly or indirectly upon the other. For example, it would be battery if a frustrated fact finder directly slapped an uncooperative employee. Likewise, even though the investigator never touched the employee, it would be battery if the investigator kicked the chair out from underneath an uncooperative employee, causing him to fall to the floor.

For example, in *Warren*, a company security representative and private investigator "interrogated" an employee for failing to properly enter a $1 transaction during an anonymous honesty and efficiency check.[44] The two men questioned the plaintiff about the incident and continued to press the issue of whether she had taken other money. They threatened her with arrest if she did not sign an admission with an estimate of the amount she took. They told her the arrest would be an embarrassment for her family, on several occasions refused to let her leave, and, on one occasion, the private investigator grabbed her on the arm to prevent her from leaving. She wrote an admission as dictated by the private detective, but never entered the amount. Later, she claimed she did so under duress in order to be allowed to leave the interrogation. The Court of Appeals of Texas held the "findings of the trial court clearly establish ... assault and battery as against the defendant, private investigator."

7.7.2 False Imprisonment and False Arrest

When conducting workplace interviews, fact finders need to be sensitive to the issues of false imprisonment and false arrest. False imprisonment occurs when one denies another the voluntary freedom of movement. The denial may be by verbal or physical means.

For example, in the aforementioned *Warren* case, both of the investigators involved denied the plaintiff's requests to leave, and the private investigator grabbed her arm to prevent her from leaving.[45] Not only did the private investigators commit assault and battery, the evidence clearly showed that both of them falsely imprisoned the employee against her wishes.

False arrest is arrest without legal justification. Whenever there is a false arrest, there is false imprisonment. Workplace investigators rarely make citizen's arrests of employees. But, nonetheless, they need to avoid creating an impression that the subject is under arrest by claiming to have police authority, stating the subject is under arrest, or unnecessarily restraining the individual.

7.7.3 Defamation

Defamation is the single most frequently cited complaint in civil lawsuits against employers. A defamatory statement is a false statement of fact published by one party, either by spoken or written means or conduct, to a third disinterested party that impugns the community, business, or professional reputation of another. A false allegation that a party committed a crime is such a grievous act that it is considered defamation, per se. That is, the remark is presumed to be so injurious to one's reputation that damages need not be proved.

There are two types of defamatory statements: slander and libel. Slander refers to defamation by the spoken word or conduct. For example, an employee might claim he was slandered when he was handcuffed or verbally accused of dishonesty in front of co-workers. Further, a subject employee might claim defamation when a fact finder made inquiries of co-workers about him that inferred he was involved in the alleged incident. Libel refers to written statements or pictures that are defamatory. An employee, for example, might claim he was libeled in the fact finder's report to his employer's managers.

Defendants may raise several affirmative defenses to suits for defamation. First, truth is a defense as defamation entails the publication of a false statement. Assume an employee was arrested in the workplace and sued for defamation; a showing that the arrest was lawful would defeat the allegation of defamation. Second, non-publication is also a defense; in other words, the alleged defamatory statement was never communicated to a third disinterested party. For example, if an investigator accused an employee of selling drugs during an investigatory interview with just the two of them present, in a suit for defamation, the investigator could defend on the grounds there was no publication to a third party. In some states, intraorganization communications (communications within a business) are considered nonpublished on the premise a business is a single legal entity.

The third defense, the one most commonly used in workplace investigations, is privileged communication. Privileged communications are either absolute or conditional/qualified. As a matter of public policy, to protect the interest of the public at large over the interest of the individual, absolute privileged communications are protected even if false and made maliciously. Statements made in legislative and judicial proceedings usually enjoy an absolute privilege. Assume, at a criminal trial, a fact finder accused an employee of stealing funds or assets, the employee was found "not guilty," and the employee sued for defamation. Because the accusation was made in a criminal trial, it would be an absolute privileged comment. However, note that there may be other sanctions taken if a witness lies under oath (perjury), lies in an official report (false statement), or maliciously initiates criminal prosecution (malicious prosecution).

Conditional or qualified privileged communications are protected if made in good faith to an interested party. An interested party, in the context of workplace investigations, is someone who needs to know in performance of his duties. For example, if a fact finder told an employee's superior that an employee was using illegal drugs while on the job, in most jurisdictions, this statement would be considered a conditional privileged communication so long as the fact finder was acting in good faith. But, the statement would no longer be privileged if the investigator told his family and friends (clearly disinterested parties) or acted maliciously (intentionally lied about the truth of the allegation).[46]

An employer, in *Nipper*, received an employee hotline tip that a store manager was flashing a gun, working under the influence of drugs, allowing her boyfriend to stay in the store for hours at a time, and permitting birthday parties in the store.[47] A company investigator interviewed store employees based on this tip and a documented $30,000 loss of inventory. The interviews were conducted in a back room with an open door; employees were told the information was confidential and told the scope and nature of the inquiry. After confirming in the employee interviews the information set forth in the hotline tip, the investigator interviewed the manager. After the manager admitted to allowing her boyfriend to visit, bringing a gun to work, and taking medication that made her sleepy, the company terminated her. She sued. In part, she claimed she was defamed when the investigator interviewed the other employees. The Supreme Court of Alabama noted communications between employees acting within the proper scope of their duties "do not constitute a publication." Here, the investigator was acting within the scope of his employment; he spoke only with employees "only to the extent reasonably necessary to investigate the hotline complaints and the inventory loss." Therefore, there was no publication and no defamation. It affirmed judgment for the company.

In *Gaumont*, the Court of Appeals of Ohio held a contract investigator enjoyed a qualified privilege to discuss an employee subjected of theft of company tools with a deputy sheriff from another county.[48] The sheriff was an interested party because he had previously investigated a burglary of tools at the employee's home and the contract investigator wanted to know if the deputy had noticed any company tools during his search of the residence. Of note, the states are split on whether statements made to law enforcement personnel are absolute privileged communications or are conditional privileged communications.[49]

Defamation lawsuits are sometimes based more on office rumor than the words or conduct of the investigators. As a rule, companies are not responsible for office gossip and rumors. For example, in *Ashcroft*, a private duty nurse was arrested in a hospital gift shop for shoplifting.[50] She claimed that she lost referral business because of alleged defamatory statements by the security officers. However, she cited "no specific statement published by defendants to her prospective employers." Rather, she admitted to basing her allegations on speculation and "rumors by way of the grapevine." The Ohio Court of Appeals affirmed summary judgment for the hospital.

In *Paolucci*, the Court of Appeals of Ohio held a nurse discharged for violation of work rules was not defamed when two security officers escorted her off hospital property in plain view of others.[51]

Crump is an unusual case that illustrates the need for investigators to be careful not only with whom they speak, but in what they say.[52] Crump worked as head receiver for dry goods at the defendant's warehouse. His job was to verify proper delivery of ordered goods and to reject unordered and defective goods. Rejected goods were to be returned to the delivery driver or placed in the company salvage pile where they might be repackaged or given to the warehouse employees. Company policy held that if property was removed, the employee taking it had to obtain a property pass signed by a supervisor. The plaintiff had been with the company 18 years when he was terminated for breach of company policy. Specifically, he rejected two cases of breakfast food; the driver refused to take the goods back and told the plaintiff to take them for his grandchildren. The plaintiff offered to share the items with co-employees and kept them by his desk to take home. He admitted he violated company policy by not placing the merchandise in the salvage area and properly obtaining a property pass, instead he had issued himself one. He sued for defamation on the grounds he was called a "thief" in a meeting attended by the company director of warehousing, director of loss prevention, and a loss prevention specialist. Further, in two written reports prepared after the incident, he was referred to as a "problem employee." The trial court awarded the plaintiff both compensatory and punitive damages for defamation. The company appealed.

The Supreme Court of Vermont affirmed that the company enjoyed "a conditional privilege for intracorporate communications to protect its legitimate business interests." But, the court noted this privilege might be lost if the company acted with reckless disregard for the truth or acted with ill will in violation of the discharged employee's rights. Here, the court affirmed there was reasonable evidence to support the verdict. The court noted the rejected merchandise did not belong to the company, since it did not have to pay for it, therefore, the company's characterization of the plaintiff's conduct as theft might reasonably be interpreted by a jury as showing a "reckless disregard both for the truth and for plaintiff's rights." Further, the court noted the company acted outside its privilege when it made an oral report to the security manager for the trucking company and spoke with the driver and another employee of the trucking company.

> *Tip: Exercise care when communicating the results of an investigation to others. Prior to dissemination, be certain it is made in good faith, without malice or careless disregard for the facts, and there is a justifiable business purpose for the recipient to know.*

7.7.4 Invasion of Privacy

The right of privacy emanates from three sources of law: constitutional, statutory, and common law. Having previously discussed federal and state constitutional privacy rights in workplace investigations, this section addresses statutory and common law rights of privacy enjoyed by those in the workplace.

7.7.4.1 State Statutes

State statutes and case law, in some form or another, afford the right of privacy in all 50 states. There are essentially two types of privacy laws: (1) those that protect a general or specific right of privacy and (2) those that restrict different methods of intrusion or investigation. Typically, all of these laws provide individuals with greater privacy rights as against a public entity or other governmental actor, than as against a private employer or nongovernmental investigator. This section focuses on the latter, with an eye toward giving a sense of how privacy statutes vary from state to state.

For example, under the laws of Massachusetts, a person has "a right against unreasonable, substantial, or serious interference with his privacy."[53] Similarly, Rhode Island by statute guarantees four specific rights of privacy (three of interest here) that are often guaranteed under the common law of other states.[54] These rights include the right to be secure from unreasonable intrusion upon one's physical solitude or seclusion, unreasonable publicity given to one's private life, and publicity that reasonably places another in a false light before the public.

In *Williams*, a payroll clerk was terminated after an investigation into the cashing of forged payroll checks.[55] The investigation included both private and federal investigators. During the course of the investigation, she was asked to account for her activities on the day when some checks were cashed. She had had an abortion and some complication thereafter, and this fact came to light in response to this inquiry. She sued under the general privacy statute of Massachusetts. First, she claimed her privacy was invaded by the accusations of theft against her. The court rejected this claim on the grounds the defendants had conducted a good faith inquiry that warranted further investigation. Second, she claimed publication of a private fact. The Superior Court of Massachusetts noted this statute covered the publication of highly personal or intimate information to an employer, but this disclosure had to be weighed against the employer's legitimate business interests. Here, the court held there was no publication of private fact because it was reasonable for the employer to question her regarding her activities on the day the checks were cashed and the employer had no idea this inquiry would elicit personal information of this nature. The court granted summary judgment to the defendants with regard to all privacy claims.

In California, in addition to a state constitutional right of privacy as discussed earlier, there are numerous statutes that protect specific information. For example, the Labor Code of California provides employers "shall make reasonable efforts to safeguard the privacy of the employee as to the fact that he or she has enrolled in an alcohol or drug rehabilitation program"[56] or "has a problem with illiteracy."[57]

California (as in many states) also prohibits or restricts certain methods of investigation. For example, the Civil Code of California specifically prohibits the physical trespass upon the land of another with the intent to capture visual, sound, or other impressions of the plaintiff engaged in personal or familial activities where the trespass is "offensive to a reasonable person." The same law also restricts the use of a "visual or auditory-enhancing device" without any trespass to capture visual or audio impressions of a person engaged in similar activities where the plaintiff had a reasonable expectation of privacy and the attempt is "offensive to a reasonable person."[58]

Similarly, under the Penal Code of California, it is a crime to intentionally amplify or record confidential communications of others without the consent of all parties, and it is unlawful to install a "two-way mirror permitting observation of any restroom, toilet, bathroom."[59,60] In *Cramer*, for example, the United States Court of Appeals ruled that federal labor law, LMRA §301, did not preempt the more than 280 plaintiffs from pursuing their privacy claims under California law against the company for violating state law by installing two-way mirrors and video–audio recorders in men's and women's restrooms to detect drug usage.[61]

The intent here is not to attempt to cover the multitude of statutes that guarantee general or specific rights of privacy, nor is it to discuss all the different statutes that restrict various methods of gathering information. The purpose is to alert fact finders (and those who employ them) that they need to understand the privacy-related statutes of the jurisdiction in which they operate.

7.7.4.2 Common Law Right of Privacy

Employees also enjoy various degrees of common law right of privacy under the judicial decisions of the respective state courts. There are three different tort actions for invasion of privacy of interest to workplace fact finders: invasion of privacy—false light; invasion of privacy—publication of a private fact; and invasion of privacy—intrusion upon seclusion. The first two actions deal with how investigative information is managed, whereas the third tort action deals with the method of gathering information.

7.7.4.2.1 False Light

False light invasion of privacy is similar to defamation. But, there are differences. Defamation involves injury to one's reputation, whereas a false statement involves emotional distress suffered by the party. Defamation may occur with publication to just one other party, whereas a false statement involves publicity.[62] A false statement is one made with reckless disregard for the truth that attributes highly objectionable characteristics, beliefs, or conduct to an individual and places him before the public in a false position.[63] Publicity means the statement was made before the public or shared with a sufficient number of persons that it is likely to become public knowledge.

In *Aranyosi*, several employees were terminated when the company elected to contract out their duties.[64] During an exit meeting, a few of the employees made modestly veiled, threatening remarks. That evening two intruders, dressed in camouflage, confronted a plant security officer, placed a gun at the officer's head, made threats against the plant manager, and stated there was a bomb in the plant. The police were contacted. The police learned from the plant manager and other employees about the threats of a few terminated and even remaining staff, such as:

- *What goes around, comes around*
- *You will reap what you sow*
- *Y'all [sic] better watch your backs*
- *I will make sure the same thing happens to you … and your family*

One employee was even quoted as saying that "he received a vision about the warehouse blowing up." The local newspaper, based on information provided by the police, reported the incident and bomb threat (no bomb was found) and published: "Company officials said they had been threatened earlier that day by several of the 14 employees who officials laid off." The plaintiff–employees filed suit, in part, alleging false light invasion of privacy, because the information made it appear that they had participated in the threats and attack. The court held there was no false light publication on the grounds the company did not act unreasonably in relating the comments of the employees and events of the day to the police who were summoned to investigate the aggravated battery and bomb threat. It granted summary judgment on this issue for the company.

The outcome was different in *Lee* where a long-term employee was accused of being involved in theft.[65] Two company investigators and police detectives went to search his home. Ultimately, three other police detectives, an officer, and 12 to 15 employees were involved. More than 400 items valued at over $50,000 were taken from the home, placed in the yard, inventoried by the police, and put in a truck rented by the company. The company kept the items in secured storage, but somehow items not listed on the police inventory were co-mingled with the items seized.[37] Several persons saw the search in progress and the local papers covered the story. Ultimately, the county prosecutor refused to prosecute the case. Lee filed civil suit. In court, the items that Lee identified as his were returned and the 37 co-mingled items were returned to the company. The court awarded Lee over $1.6 million in damages, in part, for false light invasion of privacy. The Supreme Court of Arkansas affirmed.

Most cases, of course, do not involve the public media. But, it is not necessary for the media to be involved for a plaintiff to file a false light claim. In *Bine*, an employer installed a camera in its parking lot after reported acts of vandalism and stationed an officer with a handheld camera in the lot.[66] The officer observed a suspicious person around a vehicle that had been previously vandalized. He checked the car and noticed it had been recently scratched. The officer identified the plaintiff as the suspicious person (the record was not clear whether any of the incident was recorded on videotape). The plaintiff denied any involvement, but was terminated.

In order to deal with rumors about the termination, the plant management told a number of employees that the plaintiff, in fact, was terminated for vandalism. The plaintiff filed suit, in part, for false light invasion of privacy. The trial court granted summary judgment to the employer. The Supreme Court of West Virginia held there was a dispute of material fact as to the truth of the allegation. It noted: "The spreading of such information, if false, could constitute a valid false light claim." The court remanded the case to the trial court.

In *Smith*, discussed earlier, a purchasing agent was suspended pending her decision to resign or take a demotion for her abuse of vacation leave.[67] At that time, she was escorted off company property by the investigator. Smith claimed false light invasion of privacy on the grounds it "left her co-workers free to speculate that Smith had been disciplined for something more egregious than vacation day violation, such as fraud or graft." The court rejected this circuitous argument that she was placed in a false light because the company did not publicize the true reason for her demotion or escort off its property.

7.7.4.2.2 Publication of a Private Fact

There are facts (truths) about people that are private and the law recognizes a tort action for invasion of privacy when such facts are given publicity and such disclosure is highly offensive to a reasonable person.

In *Johnson*, the employer, based upon reports of employee drug use and large inventory losses, hired a contract investigative firm to provide undercover operatives in its warehouse.[68] The agents, based on what they saw and heard, reported on the personal lives of some of the employees, including information about children, domestic violence, pending divorces, sexual partners, personal health, future employment plans, and even characterizations of some employees as alcoholics. The employees filed suit, in part, for publicity of a private fact. The trial court entered summary judgment for the defendants. The Appellate Court of Illinois stated the information could be viewed as private because the agents obtained it through deception, communication to the employer could be considered publicity, and its disclosure might be highly offensive to a reasonable person. The appellate court reversed and remanded the issue to the trial court.

Note that the commenting about a private fact in front of others does not always mean the speaker has given publicity to the matter. In *Dietz*, a jewelry clerk was "interrogated" about an unauthorized discount provided a customer who was upset about the length of time it took to be served.[69] During her interview, the company investigator stated that Dietz had personal credit problems. Present in the room was a female manager who was serving as a witness and a security officer who was monitoring the CCTV (closed circuit television) system and was not a party to the session. The court denied that the reference to her credit difficulties with the two employees present amounted to publicity of a private fact. The Court of Appeals of Indiana affirmed summary judgment in favor of the defendants on this issue.

In *Shattuck*, the plaintiff, who worked at a resort, was raped while on break and the attack was captured on video.[70] The company immediately reported the incident to the police. In order to determine if the rapist was an employee, the company showed the video to select managers. It also showed the tape to another rape victim (who was not attacked at the resort) and the police officer investigating that case. The plaintiff claimed this showing was an unreasonable publication of a private fact. The Supreme Court of Utah ruled the company's showing of "the video to a discrete number of persons for the legitimate purposes of a criminal investigation" did not qualify as a public disclosure.

7.7.4.2.3 Intrusion upon Seclusion

Intrusion upon seclusion refers to an intentional intrusion by another upon the physical solitude or private affairs of another that is unreasonable and highly offensive to a reasonable person.[71] Employees enjoy a degree of privacy in the workplace, but the level of privacy afforded them must be balanced with the legitimate interest of the employer in running its business. There is a long list of intrusion of seclusion cases on a variety of issues that impact workplace investigations. The following cases cover traditional off-premise and onsite cases, and more recent cyber privacy issues.

In *Johnson v. Corporate Special Services, Inc.*, a contract investigator staked out the plaintiff's house to observe if the plaintiff was engaging in any physical activity that would disqualify him from receiving benefits under workers' compensation.[72] As the court noted, at no time did the investigator try to observe or peek into the home. One evening, during the surveillance, the investigator was questioned by the police. He was asked to explain his presence, which he did. The plaintiff noticed this encounter and continued to watch the investigator who relocated to another close-by spot. The plaintiff, subsequently, pulled his car in front of the investigator's vehicle and confronted the investigator, who pulled his weapon and withdrew. The plaintiff sued for assault and battery, and invasion of privacy. The trial judge granted summary judgment on the invasion of privacy claim in favor of the defendant and the jury found in his favor on the assault and battery claim. The plaintiff appealed the invasion of privacy claim. In affirming judgment for the investigative firm, the Supreme Court of Alabama used a two-part test: it looked at the "means" of intrusion and "purpose" of the intrusion. It stated parties to personal claims should expect some investigation into their claims and loss of privacy related to the claim. It found that the purpose of the investigation was lawful and the outside surveillance did not intrude into the privacy of his home.

However, not all outside investigations are reasonable or lawful. In *Souder*, the Court of Appeals of Louisiana held the plaintiff, who had filed a workers' compensation claim, did state a privacy cause of action against investigators for the constant surveillance of his home, use of binoculars, trespass to property, and peeping into windows.[73] The last conduct was in violation of the state "Peeping Tom" statute and the court noted that any investigation outside the lawful bounds of state law is unreasonable.

The Georgia Court of Appeals, in *Stevens*, found similar conduct by detectives, conducting surveillance of a plaintiff in an automobile accident case, actionable.[74] The investigators peeped through hedges adjoining her property, trespassed upon her property, peeped into windows, eavesdropped upon conversations, and cut a hole in the hedges, and closely followed her about in public areas. They were so aggressive and blatant in their tactics that her neighbors became suspicious of and shunned her. Even after being advised by legal counsel for plaintiff of the emotional duress caused, the intensity and tactics of the investigators did not change.

But, in *Saldana*, the Court of Appeals in Michigan ruled it was not an intrusion upon the privacy of an employee, who was subjected of malingering on disability, when investigators watched his home, walked by the house to look in open windows, observed the home with a telephoto camera, talked with the garbage pickup crew, and pretended to be a process server to look inside the home.[75] One justice on the three-judge panel dissented on the issue of the camera use, as he felt it created a triable issue of fact. Interestingly, the investigator sent a letter to the employee's physician, but, fortunately for the investigator, the doctor never replied.

In another off-premise case, *Sowards*, the Court of Appeals of Ohio affirmed it was an intrusion of privacy when an employer searched a hotel room it had reserved for an employee–driver who used the same room on a regular basis.[76] The court noted the employee had a reasonable expectation of privacy because he was the only person in the room, he had a key to it, and it was not used for company business. The court also rejected the good faith investigation defense of the company because an invasion of privacy need not be made maliciously or intentionally to be actionable.

Fact finders also need to be sensitive to their activities in the workplace. The seminal office search case is not a private sector case. In fact, the case is based upon the Fourth Amendment of the U.S. Constitution (which we know does not apply to private sector searches unless there is state action). But, it was decided by the U.S. Supreme Court and the underlying logic of the case has been used as a frame of reference by many courts.

In *O'Connor*, a state hospital searched the desk, filing drawers, and office of a physician who had used the office for over 17 years.[77] There was debate whether it was investigative (into professional improprieties including sexual harassment) or noninvestigative (inventorying state property). The U.S. Supreme Court noted the protections of the Fourth Amendment apply to noncriminal searches. However, it ruled the requiring of public employers to obtain a warrant and to establish probable cause to conduct workplace searches was too cumbersome. Instead, in order to balance the government employee's "not insubstantial" expectation of privacy with the "substantial government interests in the efficient and proper operation of the workplace," the court adopted a two-part reasonableness standard:

Under this reasonableness standard, both the inception and the scope of the intrusion must be reasonable; Determining the reasonableness of any search involves a twofold inquiry: first, one must consider "whether the ... action was justified at its inception," ... second, one must determine whether the search as actually conducted "was reasonably related in scope to the circumstances which justified the interference in the first place."

Although this decision dealt with the application of the Fourth Amendment to government employer searches, the logic of the U.S. Supreme Court provides strong guidance toward determining the reasonableness of private sector searches as well.

In *Simpson*, discussed earlier, an employee refused to participate in a lunchbox inspection because he strongly felt it violated his human and constitutional rights of privacy.[78] After having rejected the constitutional arguments, the Commonwealth Court of Pennsylvania looked at his property right of privacy in his lunchbox versus the reasonableness of the employer's request. Concluding the request to inspect was reasonable, based upon past practice even without a written policy, the court stated Simpson had a duty to cooperate and his failure to do so could not "be predicated upon asserted common law personal and property rights ... the employee has waived those rights as a basis for noncompliance; he waived them when he voluntarily assumed the legal relationship with his employer."

In *Clement,* the defendant company, without admission of fault, settled a claim that it had invaded the privacy of plaintiffs when it, based upon rumors of employee drug use, placed a concealed camera in a men's locker room.[79] In *Trotti*, managers opened an employee's locker and searched her purse while looking for a missing watch, which they had no reason to believe she had taken, and a missing price-marking gun.[80] Because the employee was allowed to put her lock on the locker and the company did not advise employees the lockers were subject to search, despite the manager's claim it did, the court felt there was sufficient evidence the employee had a reasonable "expectation that the locker and its contents would be free from intrusion and interference." The Court of Appeals of Texas further affirmed there was sufficient evidence the employer acted with malice when the manager originally denied the search and misrepresented that employees were advised of the search policy. (Note, the court reversed the trial court judgment in favor of the plaintiff on grounds the jury instructions were deficient and it remanded the case for a new trial.)

In *Johnson v. K Mart*, also discussed earlier, the undercover agents reported on the personal lives of the employees, and the court held they had stated a cause of action for publication of a private fact.[81] The court also found that the employees had a cause of action for intrusion upon seclusion. It felt there was sufficient evidence that a jury might find the methods and scope of the investigation to be an offensive intrusion. Specifically, the court expressed concern about personal information being gathered on and off company property, about it being gathered by deception, its lack of relevancy to the legitimate interests of the business, and the company never stopped this practice. It reinstated the employees' privacy claim.

McLaren is one of the first email cases to deal with employee privacy as it relates to an internal company investigation.[82] The company suspended the employee pending a sexual harassment and inventory investigation. He requested access to his email to gather evidence to disprove the allegations against him. He also asked that the company not tamper with his workstation and email files. Subsequently, he filed suit for invasion of privacy. He claimed the software allowed him to password protect his email files (separate from the network password protection) and that this protection gave him an expectation of privacy, symbolically speaking, similar to the expectation Trotti enjoyed in a company locker once she put her personal lock on it. He argued that the decryption of his password and distribution of it (presumably to other company employees) by the employer represented a serious intrusion and interference with his privacy. The Court of Appeals of Texas rejected the locker analogy, noting that the locker was specifically for the employee to store personal items, whereas the computer was provided by the employer for his work, and "the email messages contained on the company computer were not McLaren's personal property, but were merely an inherent part of the office environment." The court added that even if he had a reasonable expectation of privacy it would be outweighed by the company's compelling interest in investigating and resolving the accusations of sexual harassment and inventory issues given that he had indicated some of the email messages were relevant to the investigation. The Court of Appeals of Texas affirmed the trial court's dismissal of the case for failing to state a cause of action.

> *Tip: There are three different tort actions for invasion of privacy. Fact finders must understand how each might affect an investigation and interviews.*

7.7.5 Emotional Distress or Outrage

Many cases against investigators contain claims of emotional distress or outrage. In general, in order to prevail on a claim of this nature, the plaintiff must prove the defendant acted in an outrageous and highly offensive manner that was highly probable of inflicting severe emotional distress upon another. In some states, plaintiffs may have to show physical manifestations of the duress.

In *Agis*, a restaurant manager called a staff meeting, told everyone that there was stealing going on, and stated he was going to fire everyone present starting with the letter "A" until the thief stepped forward.[83] In a misguided move, using discipline in lieu of fact finding and verification, he summarily fired Agis who immediately became hysterical. She suffered anguish and lost wages. She filed suit for intentional infliction of emotional distress, but the court granted summary judgment to the defendant because the state did not recognize a cause of action for emotional distress without physical injury. The Supreme Court of Massachusetts reversed. It held the plaintiffs, the waitress and her husband, did state, even without physical injury, a cause of action for intentional or reckless infliction of emotional distress and it reinstated their claims.

In *Bodewig* a customer accused the plaintiff, a young sales clerk, of taking four $5 bills she left on the checkout counter while she went to get a sale item. The manager intervened. He pulled out the clerk's apron pockets, checked the area around the register and found nothing. He offered to check her register and the customer demanded he do so. The register balanced perfectly. The customer continued to cause a commotion and would not leave. Finally, the manager told a female assistant manager to take the clerk to the restroom and search her. The assistant manager offered to allow the customer to watch the search. The clerk stripped to her underwear with the two watching her. The customer, when asked, said the clerk did not have to remove her underwear since she could see through it. That evening the customer found the money in her purse, called the mother of the clerk [whom she knew], and called the store. Plaintiff sued for outrage. The trial court granted summary judgment for the store and customer. The Court of Appeals of Oregon found there was sufficient evidence that a jury might find the manager, "after concluding that plaintiff did not take the customer's money, put her through the degrading and humiliating experience of submitting to a strip search … that the manager's conduct exceeded the bounds of social toleration and was in reckless disregard of its predictable effects on plaintiff." It also held there was sufficient evidence a jury might conclude the customer intended to humiliate plaintiff. It remanded the case for trial.[84]

In *Olivas,* an employee's missing paycheck was cashed at a local liquor store. Co-workers accused the employee's brother who also worked for the company. An employee made copies of some employee pictures, showed them to the liquor owner, and accused the brother of theft and forgery. The owner signed a criminal complaint against the brother. Other employees accused the brother in their conversations, with the victim and brother's landlady. The brother was fired. The criminal charges were dismissed. The brother filed suit. The Superior Court of Connecticut denied the company's motion to strike plaintiff's claim for emotional distress. The court held that the discharge, taken with the accusation of theft and forgery, could amount to "extreme and outrageous conduct."[85]

In *Tenold,* the plaintiff worked for the defendant's railroad company that was part of its forestry operation. Plaintiff obtained approval from the site security supervisor to remove some railroad ties. The site security supervisor told him to check the price with the company. Plaintiff assumed this meant he could pay for the items later. The next day, the same supervisor gave him permission to use company equipment to remove the ties. A week later, a contract security officer, who lived onsite, told the site security supervisor the plaintiff had delivered some railroad ties to a ranch. The site security supervisor reported it to his superior and a company security supervisor. The company security supervisor directed a deputy sheriff (the company paid the county for the deputy to be assigned full-time to patrol the company's property) to investigate. The deputy sheriff told the ranch owner that the plaintiff had taken 600 ties. The site security supervisor interviewed two employees who stated they had helped deliver the ties and reported that plaintiff told them that he intended to pay for the ties. The site security supervisor did not pass the later remark on to his company superiors or the deputy.

A union representative, the site security supervisor, and his manager met with plaintiff who admitted taking the ties, but stated he had permission from the site security supervisor. The manager reported to his superiors that the plaintiff admitted taking the ties and "he really offered no excuses or reasons for taking the ties without paying for them." The company terminated plaintiff's employment. The deputy sheriff cited plaintiff for criminal theft. His report did not indicate plaintiff's claim he had permission to take the ties and intended to pay for them. Plaintiff was indicted but the district attorney dismissed the charges after he learned some of the confiscated ties did not belong to the company and had been paid for by plaintiff. Plaintiff filed civil suit against the company. Evidence was presented that the site security supervisor bore ill will toward plaintiff. An employee testified that two years earlier the site security supervisor had stated, "There's more than one way to get rid of [plaintiff]." The company security supervisor testified another manager involved in the investigation had stated, "I don't care what the court system does or anything else, that I—I will have the man's job." He also noted the site security supervisor had stated plaintiff was a drug addict and he had caught plaintiff with marijuana two years earlier. The site security supervisor's foster son even testified he overheard his father state plaintiff was a drunk, a drug user, and had a methamphetamine lab in his home. The jury awarded damages of approximately $2.4 million against the company for defamation, malicious prosecution (discussed later), and intentional infliction of emotional distress, and $150,000 in damages against the site security supervisor for defamation and intentional infliction of emotional distress. The Court of Appeals of Oregon affirmed there was sufficient evidence for a jury to conclude defendants engaged in an extraordinary and intolerable campaign to defame, terminate, and prosecute plaintiff.[86]

In conclusion, investigators must be careful to not engage in outrageous conduct that is highly likely to inflict severe emotional distress upon subject employees. Unreasonable investigative methods and interrogations include such activities as gathering immaterial personal information on employees, threatening employees with arrest, shouting at and physically threatening employees during interrogations, and similar conduct.

Clearly, fact finders must be careful not to engage in intentional outrageous conduct that is highly likely to inflict severe emotional distress upon an employee. Unreasonable investigative methods and interrogations are unacceptable. This includes such activities as gathering immaterial personal information on employees, threatening employees with arrest, shouting at employees during an interrogation, and similar conduct. Also, an employee might file suit against an investigator and employer for negligent infliction of emotional distress where the employer failed to reasonably train and supervise the employee in performance of the investigation. Here, too, the conduct of the defendant must be extreme and highly probable of inducing severe emotional distress.

7.8 Negligent Investigation

7.8.1 A New Tort Action

Most lawsuits against fact finders and their private employers involve specific claims of injury, such as defamation, invasion of privacy, wrongful discharge, malicious prosecution, and emotional distress. In recent years, plaintiffs have added a new tort action for negligent investigation. The courts have not universally endorsed this concept because it often conflicts with the employment at-will doctrine and other available legal remedies. For example, assume an at-will employee (see Section 7.10.2) is subjected of criminal conduct. The company conducts a shoddy investigation, terminates the employee, and unsuccessfully prosecutes. Further, the company tells co-workers he was fired for theft. Should he be able to sue for negligent investigation when the company could have terminated him under the employment at-will doctrine without ever investigating the matter? Also, because he can sue for defamation and for malicious prosecution, many courts question the need to recognize a new tort action for negligent investigation.

In *Sears*, the plaintiff worked as an independent insurance agent.[87] He had been with the company several years when a policyholder wrote to the company and stated the agent, an insurance adjuster, and a local contractor were engaged in a fraudulent kickback scheme. The company looked at his files, determined a few might be suspicious, and hired a private investigator. The investigator never obtained any direct evidence against the plaintiff, but still advised the company he should be considered a subject because of two suspicious claims. The company fired the plaintiff, and it reported him to several federal and state law enforcement and regulatory agencies. The adjuster and contractor were indicted, and the contractor was convicted. The authorities never pressed charges against the plaintiff, and the insurance licensing board refused the company's efforts to have his license suspended.

Sears, who claimed the investigation destroyed his local reputation, sued and won damages for negligent investigation and emotional distress. The appellate court affirmed damages for emotional distress, and it affirmed a cause of action for negligent investigation, but overturned the judgment for insufficient evidence. The Supreme Court of Texas stated the conduct of the defendant in conducting the investigation and reporting its suspicions to the authorities did not amount to outrageous behavior. There was "certainly no evidence that (defendant) knew the reports to be false or manipulated the findings so that Sears would be subject to criminal or other liability." The court, in a case of first impression, also declined "to recognize a negligent-investigation cause of action in this circumstance, because to do so would substantially alter the parties' at-will relationship."

The Appeals Court of Massachusetts affirmed the denial of a negligent investigation claim in *O'Connell*.[88] The plaintiff, a former bank teller who had left to take a higher paying position with a new company, was charged sometime afterward with theft of $4,800. The theft involved a single transaction posted, in her last few days, to two different accounts. The transaction occurred at the window of a teller trainee working adjacent to plaintiff. The investigation of the theft was difficult because the plaintiff's daily journals for the day of the theft were missing (misfiled by the bank with the trainee's records) and the time clocks on the bank videotapes were out-of-synch with the transaction logs. As a result, the investigator did not further analyze the video. When interviewed by the bank, she stated she did not work the teller line where the checks were cashed, but the video showed she did. The bank concluded she was the only person on that line who had enough knowledge to make the transactions. After she was charged, her attorney prevailed upon the bank to retain a handwriting expert. He concluded the writing on the documents was not the plaintiff's. A municipal judge found her not guilty. The plaintiff sued. During the civil trial, the videotape, which the bank denied having, resurfaced, and the plaintiff and bank together carefully synched the film with the teller's transactions. It showed a hand, not the plaintiff's, reaching in to enter the fraudulent transaction. Regarding the plaintiff's negligent transaction claim, the court held the duty of investigation ran to the party requesting the investigation and not the party under investigation. Although the party under investigation might be injured, the appeals court stated, "… the law makes remedies available—actions for defamation, malicious prosecution, and tortuous infliction of emotional distress." (Several months later the bank filed charges for other thefts against the male supervisor of the teller trainee.)

In *Devis*, a bank called the police in the belief that the plaintiff was attempting to cash a stolen check on the account of a customer who had posted a warning about stolen checks.[89] The customer had written separate checks to a Davis and a Devis, and Davis stole some blank checks. When Devis attempted to cash a lawful check, he was arrested. Based on the bank's failure to properly check his identification, he sued for negligent investigation and defamation. The California Court of Appeal affirmed summary judgment for defendant bank. Under state law, reports to the police are part of a judicial proceeding and privileged communications when made in good faith. The appeal court, in a case of first impression, stated, "The privilege must extend to actions based on negligent investigation, for if it did not, the privilege for reports to the police would be eviscerated."

In conclusion, the courts have been reluctant to recognize a new and distinct common law cause of action for negligent investigation on the grounds that it conflicts with the employment at-will doctrine, and that there are other established legal remedies available to plaintiffs.

7.8.2 Implicit and Explicit Duties to Investigate

Although the courts have been reluctant to recognize a new common law action for negligent investigation, there are circumstances where employers have overarching duties that contain explicit or implicit duties to investigate. A duty to investigate, for discussion purposes here, may arise under statute, regulation, employment and labor contracts, and tort law governing the duty to hire and supervise employees. Further, as noted, a failure to investigate may enhance liability exposure for other tort actions.

First, for example, civil rights statutes and regulations prohibit various forms of workplace discrimination. This broad duty includes the obligation to investigate complaints of harassment. As noted in *Fuller* and *Valdez*, the courts were critical of defendant employers for their deficient investigations. In *Fuller*, because of a lack of investigative thoroughness and timeliness, the employer was unable to show it took appropriate remedial measures.[90] In *Valdez*, the shoddy investigation resulted in the wrong employee being terminated.[91] When coupled with other facts, the court found the company had engaged in national origin discrimination. Also, for example, the general duty clause of the Occupational Health and Safety Act (and similar clauses under state plan programs) requires employers to maintain an environment "free from recognized hazards that are causing or are likely to cause death or serious physical harm to his employees." If an employee demonstrated a propensity toward violence, which the company did not investigate, and later the employee injured or killed another employee, the employer might be cited for violation of the general duty clause. The failure to investigate or to do a reasonable investigation may be an explicit or implicit issue in administrative and judicial proceedings when an employer owes a broader statutory duty to employees.

Second, regarding the duty to properly hire and supervise employees, in *Salinas*, the employer was found liable for the negligent hiring (i.e., failing to do a reasonable background investigation) of a taxi driver who had a felony record and later assaulted a customer.[92] In *Saine*, the Supreme Court of Arkansas held a cable company could be sued for negligent supervision and retention based on its alleged failure to investigate a female's complaint about a cable installer who subsequently assaulted and attempted to murder another female customer.[93]

Third, regarding the issue of a contract duty to investigate, employers need to remember that not all employees are at-will. There are countless arbitration decisions under collective bargaining agreements against employers who have failed to properly investigate and satisfy their burden of establishing cause, good cause, or similar standard when seeking to discipline and terminate employees for their misconduct. Fourth, the case of *Mendez* illustrates the enhanced risk of employers being held liable for other torts based upon a failure to reasonably investigate workplace incidents.[94] Here, the Appeals Court of Massachusetts affirmed a defamation judgment against the defendant employer based on its failure to "verify its truth, in circumstances where verification was practical."

In conclusion, the courts have been reluctant to recognize a separate cause of action for negligent investigation when plaintiffs are at-will employees and where other remedies are readily available. However, employers and investigators must remain sensitive to the fact that there may be an explicit or implicit duty to investigate under certain statutes and regulations, contracts of employment, and common law torts for negligent hiring and supervision.

Tip: Failure to conduct reasonable investigations might lead to lawsuits for negligent hiring and supervision, and increase the risk of defamation, emotional distress, and other tort claims.

7.9 Claims Arising from Employee Interviews

The verification and analysis phase is still an inquiry phase, but it is different in the sense that it is based on previously gathered information and its primary focus is on the subjected wrongdoers. Before conducting investigative verification interviews with employee subjects, fact finders need to understand the following issues:

Constitutional warnings
Labor law right of representation
False imprisonment
Assault and battery
Defamation
Emotional distress
Admissibility of admissions

Further, fact finders should be open-minded and recognize that the beginning of the verification process does not necessarily mean the fact-finding phase is completely concluded, for any verification process has multiple possible outcomes. It may not provide any additional material and relevant information; it may produce evidence that confirms known information; it may provide information that contradicts known information; it may provide information that may or may not need further investigation or corroboration; and it may provide a combination of the aforementioned outcomes. Investigators must be sensitive to the possibility that further fact finding may be necessary after conducting verification and analysis investigative interviews. Since the first six issues listed have been previously discussed, generally only the key points will be summarized here.

7.9.1 Constitutional Warnings

Generally, as noted earlier, private sector investigators acting as private parties in private matters are not required to advise employee subjects of the constitutional Miranda rights to remain silent and to legal counsel. As the Court of Common Pleas of Pennsylvania stated in *Green*, "… the overwhelming authority from other jurisdictions supports the position that 'Miranda' warnings need not be given by a private security officer prior to questioning a subject taken into custody and the guarantees of the Fifth Amendment are intended as limitations upon governmental activities and not on private individuals, then the 'Miranda' warnings need not be given by persons other than governmental officials or their agents."[95]

Although it happens infrequently, if fact finders operate as agents of or jointly with law enforcement, the courts may find their conduct to be state action and impose constitutional protections.

In *Tarnef*, the Supreme Court of Alaska held that a signed admission obtained by a private arson investigator working for an insurance company was governed by the Fifth Amendment right against self-incrimination.[96] Prior to interviewing the subject, who was in prison for another crime, the arson investigator met with the authorities and promised to provide them a copy of any statement obtained. The authorities aided the private investigator in gaining access to the correctional facility. The subject signed a five-page admission. Immediately afterward, the investigator reported back to the authorities. The arson investigator, who was a former police officer, claimed he advised the subject of his constitutional rights, but the waiver was defective because it did not contain this notice. In the words of the court, "… we hold under the facts of this case that [the insurance arson investigator] was required to give a Miranda warning and secure the defendant's waiver of rights before undertaking interrogation of appellant." Note, unlike most workplace investigations, here the subject was clearly in custody.

In *Elliott*, a hospital security officer, who was a retired city police officer, was dispatched to a car in the hospital parking lot that was reported to contain a gun.[97] He was told the city police also had been dispatched. The security officer was the first to arrive on the scene. He observed the gun in the locked car. At the same time, the vehicle owner, who was also a security officer, arrived. The security officer asked the owner if it was his car and gun. The owner replied in the affirmative, opened the car, and gave the gun to the security officer. At that time, a police officer arrived and the hospital security officer turned the gun over to him. The police officer asked the owner if it was his gun and whether he had a permit. The owner replied it was his gun and he did not have a permit. The police officer arrested him. The Supreme Court, Queens County, New York, held the hospital security officer's conduct was governed by the constitution because he acted in "coordinated private–public law enforcement … investigation of a crime incident. The parking lot investigation and response here, by the hospital security officer, did accommodate police objectives." However, the court found the owner voluntarily turned the gun over to the security officer. It also ruled his statements were admissible in court because the owner was not in custody at the time he was questioned and the security officer's questions were routine field investigative inquiries. Therefore, the hospital security officer was not required to advise the owner of his Miranda rights.

7.9.2 Assault and Battery

An assault occurs when a party, who has apparent capability, creates a reasonable apprehension in the mind of another of an imminent and offensive forthcoming touching. For example, if an investigator made verbal or physical gestures to intimidate or threaten an employee during an investigative interview, this conduct may be sufficient to support a claim of assault. A battery is an intentional touching that is highly offensive in nature to a reasonable person. There is no requirement that there be physical injury. The injury is the offensive touching. If an investigator bumped, pushed, jabbed, grabbed, or threw an object at an employee, a court might find such conduct sufficient to support a battery claim. Most workplace assault and battery claims involve the shoving or pushing of employees into meetings or the grabbing and holding on to prevent employees from leaving investigative interviews. It should be noted, too, some courts use the terms *assault* and *battery* interchangeably.

In *General Motors Corp.*, the security staff at a plant entrance stopped an employee, who was subjected of stealing small radio components, in order to question him.[98] The employee testified that an officer reached out and grabbed his arm and he pulled it away; a second officer grabbed his arm and he twisted away again; and he was finally detained "by a number of guards, 'and, you know, like nudging me through the door or shoving me,' I guess what you call nudging or shoving, blocked his path." The security supervisor testified that he asked the employee to enter the security office; the employee responded with profanity and protests that the company was calling him a thief; that neither he nor any of the officers touched the plaintiff; and that it was against company policy to do so. The trial court found the plaintiff's testimony to be more persuasive and found that the officers assaulted the plaintiff. The Court of Special Appeals of Maryland affirmed both compensatory and punitive damages.

In *Blailock*, the Supreme Court of Mississippi ruled an employee could sue her employer and supervisor for assault and battery based on the allegation that the employee was grabbed on the arm and pushed toward an office by her supervisor who wanted to conduct a disciplinary interview.[99] Similarly, in the previously discussed case of *Warren*, the Court of Civil Appeals of Texas affirmed an assault and battery claim against a defendant investigator when he reached out and grabbed the plaintiff's arm to prevent the plaintiff from leaving the interrogation.[100]

7.9.2.1 Sympathetic Touching

The potential liability for assault and battery raises the issue of whether an investigator should reach out in sympathy and touch a subject during an interview, such as patting a subject's hand, knee, or shoulder. Indeed, touching may be a powerful means of communicating empathy and willingness to listen. But, it also may be perceived differently. The key issue may not be what the investigator intended, but how the employee perceived the touch. When an investigator touches an employee, even with a sincere intent of expressing sympathy, in a manner that goes outside of normal business physical contact, such as a handshake, the employee may interpret or at least allege that it was an unreasonable and offensive touching amounting to battery. Investigators should carefully weigh the risks.

7.9.3 False Imprisonment

False imprisonment, as defined earlier, occurs when one person denies another by verbal or physical means his voluntary freedom of movement. For example, in the previously discussed case of *Warren*, the investigator falsely imprisoned the plaintiff when he denied her requests to leave and grabbed her arm to prevent her leaving. In *Caldor*, a juvenile employee was detained in an interrogation room with two investigators.[101] One stood behind the employee blocking his access to the door. When he attempted to leave, he was told to "sit down or we'll help you sit down." When he attempted to use the phone in the room, he was told "to put the damn phone down." The interrogation lasted from approximately 6:45 p.m. until sometime past 11 p.m. The Court of Appeals of Maryland affirmed judgment for false imprisonment.

In *Hampton*, one investigator bumped the employee while another investigator stood in front of the door to prevent him from leaving.[102] The Court of Appeals of Georgia noted that a false imprisonment did not have to be by physical restraint, but also could be by "words, acts, gestures, or the like, which induce a reasonable apprehension force will be used if plaintiff does not submit." The appeals court reinstated the claim of false imprisonment and derivative claims for punitive damages and attorney fees.

In *Smith*, a purchasing employee went skiing while claiming to be on a vendor call that had been canceled.[103] She was interviewed for approximately three hours by two company investigators for vacation abuse under company policy. She was given a notice that she was not supposed to discuss the investigation with anyone other than authorized parties. Smith denied the abuse and noted that upon her return to the office she had sent a note to payroll to record the day as a vacation day. About two weeks later, she had lunch with a co-worker who was also a subject of the investigation and the vendor they were to visit, and they discussed the investigation. The next day she was reinterviewed and she walked out of the meeting. About a month later, the company gave her the choice of resigning or accepting a demotion for violation of the vacation policy, failing to cooperate in the investigation, and discussing the case with unauthorized persons. She accepted the demotion and filed suit against the company. In part, she claimed the two investigators falsely imprisoned her because one of the investigators "yelled at her and repeatedly called her a liar ... slammed the note on the table at one point." The United States District Court thought the alleged conduct of the investigator was "disagreeable," but noted Pennsylvania law required there be "verbal threats" if there was no violence in the confinement. Because the room was unlocked, she was never threatened or physically restrained, never asked to leave, and had walked out of the second interview, the court granted summary judgment for the company.

7.9.3.1 Economic and Moral Compulsion

An interesting issue is whether an employee may be falsely imprisoned if he stays out of concern about losing his job (economic necessity) or feels a need (moral compulsion) to stay and clear his name. Although one's reputation is important and the loss of a job may inflict serious economic harm, the general rule is that these factors alone are insufficient to support claims of false imprisonment.

For example, in *Wright*, a loss prevention agent interviewed an employee subjected of underringing items.[104] The employee never attempted to leave and he was never threatened. He felt compelled to stay to clear his name and he was concerned that if he left he might be arrested. The U.S. District Court rejected these facts as being sufficient to support a claim of false imprisonment and granted summary judgment for the defendant.

In *Johnson v. United Parcel Services, Inc.*, an employee was interviewed for approximately three to four hours concerning theft and drug dealings.[105] He was not physically detained, verbally threatened, or confined in a locked room. Nor did the investigators act in any way to block an escape. He stayed based on "a statement leading plaintiff to fear that he might lose his job should he leave." He filed suit, in part, for false imprisonment. In granting summary judgment for the defendant corporation, the U.S. District Court stated, "The restraint that resulted simply from plaintiff's fear of losing his job is insufficient as a matter of law to make out a claim of false imprisonment."

7.9.3.2 Precautionary Protocols

Fact finders can easily decrease the risk of successful suits for false imprisonment by taking certain precautionary measures. They should be able to show the employee was given notice that he was free to leave at any time; the employee was seated closest to the door and had unobstructed access to the door (provided safety of the interviewer is not an issue), which was unlocked; there were not an excessive number of company representatives present; and the investigative interview was conducted in a reasonable manner and voice without threats, yelling, profanity, and similar conduct. It is important that an investigator properly document an interrogation, not only the content of the interview, but also the process, such as room, location of parties, start and end times, persons present, breaks and amenities, and other material information.

> *Tip: When conducting an investigative interview, the fact finder should allow the employee unobstructed access to the door, speak in a moderate tone, and avoid physical gestures that infer the employee is not free to leave.*

7.9.4 Defamation

Defamation, as described earlier, refers to a false statement of fact published by one party to a third disinterested party that impugns the business, professional, or community reputation of another. Libel refers to written defamation, and slander refers to defamation by the spoken word or conduct. Defenses to defamation lawsuits include truth, nonpublication, absolute privileged communication, and qualified/conditional privileged communication.

7.9.4.1 Precautionary Protocols

In order to minimize their risk exposure, fact finders need to exercise prudent common sense prior to, during, and after investigative verification interviews. In the preinterview stage, requests to meet with subject employees should be neutral or nonaccusatory in nature to minimize the risk of premature publication of the accusations to disinterested parties. Hallway, lunchroom, and other public area conversations regarding the investigations and with subjects should remain neutral in nature. In the interview phase, whenever reasonably possible, investigative interviews should be conducted in private offices or work areas where other disinterested employees cannot overhear the discussions. The number of company agents present during an investigative interview should be restricted to persons who serve a necessary function, such as the investigator and witness, to minimize the risk of excessive publication.

In the postinterview phase, notes, written reports, and oral briefings should similarly be shared with only interested parties. This often includes the employee's superiors and select staff, such as human resources and security, if necessary to perform their duties. Investigators should be careful to avoid personal conclusions (which is different from accurately reporting and properly crediting statements of persons interviewed) and to use terms in all reports that accurately describe the subject's conduct and that can be proved. This will reduce the risk of a court finding an investigator acted with malice and lost either the intraorganizational or qualified privilege defenses to communicate derogatory information with interested parties.

7.9.4.2 Escorting of Employees

Fact finders should conduct themselves in a normal, reasonable manner when escorting employees to and from investigative interviews, off organizational property, and when inspecting employee possessions. The following cases highlight a few of the risks.

In *Uebelacker*, a manager and two large subordinates confronted an employee in his office cubicle.[106] The manager told the employee that he was fired and to clean out his belongings. When the employee attempted to go to the personnel office, the manager blocked his path, grabbed him by the arm and spun him around, and later pushed down the phone disconnect button to prevent him from calling the personnel office. The manager even refused the employee permission to use the restroom. Subsequently, he relented, but had the employee escorted. The encounter lasted approximately an hour and was witnessed by co-workers. The Court of Appeals of Ohio affirmed judgment for false imprisonment, emotional distress, and defamation.

Similarly, in *Caldor*, the Court of Appeals of Maryland affirmed a store security manager, who lacked probable cause to arrest, defamed a juvenile employee who he had handcuffed and paraded through the store before patrons and other employees.[107] If an employee is to be handcuffed, a practice that has liability risks, the investigators should have probable cause to arrest or lawful need to restrain (e.g., the employee was violent).

It should be noted, however, that the courts have generally held the reasonable escorting of employees off premises and searching of their possessions are not defamatory acts. In *Paolucci*, the Court of Appeals of Ohio held a nurse discharged for violation of work rules was not defamed when two security officers escorted her off hospital property in plain view of others.[108] In *Rolsen*, a store loss prevention manager and detective escorted an employee, who was eating lunch in the mall, through the mall and through the store where she worked.[109] Many employees in the mall and store knew the loss prevention staff even though they were nonuniformed. She was interviewed for subjected theft of a watch that she wore to lunch, suspended, and escorted off the property by the human resource manager and store detective. Later that evening she was fired. She was kept under surveillance when she returned that night to pick up her possessions. She sued, in part, claiming defamation based on this conduct. The Ohio Court of Appeals held the security and management staff did not act in an outrageous manner to support a claim that she was defamed. The rationale behind this and other similar decisions is the court's view that the reasonable escorting of employees offsite and the inspecting of employees' packages as common security practices do not infer the employees were engaged in criminal conduct.

7.9.5 Duty to Investigate an Alibi

The alleged failure to verify an alibi is in actuality an allegation the fact finder was negligent in conducting the investigation. As discussed earlier, the majority of courts are reluctant to create a new tort action for negligent investigation. Such a tort action conflicts with the widely accepted doctrine of employment at-will. In addition, many other tort actions are available to plaintiffs who allege wrongful investigator conduct, including defamation, malicious prosecution, emotional distress, and wrongful discharge.

Nonetheless, as a practical matter, fact finders should be sensitive to the need to conduct additional fact finding when subjects offer reasonable alibis or verifiable information. The failure to do so may not expose an investigator and employer to new liability, but may add validity and strength to other claims for defamation, emotional distress, wrongful discharge, and malicious prosecution. A failure to conduct further reasonable inquiry also may lend credence to a plaintiff's claim for punitive damages based on the reckless or malicious conduct of the investigator.

For example, the court, in *Mendez*, held an employee accused of theft was defamed by the company, an alcohol beverage distributor, when the plant manager, at the direction of the company president, fired the employee for theft and advised the employee's supervisor and union steward.[110] Prior to firing the employee, the president, on his way to breakfast, drove by the plant before it opened and saw the employee, a janitor, loading a box into the trunk of his car. The box was a type used by the company. After breakfast, the president told the plant manager he had observed the employee stealing and to "take care of the matter."

Hereafter, the facts are in dispute. The employee claimed he was called by the plant manager to the president's office and told he was being fired for theft. He further stated that he attempted to explain he took an empty box from the trash to hold the tools in his car, and he offered to open his car to be inspected. The executives declined. In contrast, the plant manager stated he fired the employee shortly after leaving the president's office, and it was sometime afterward that the employee offered to have his car searched. Regardless of the sequence of events, without any further investigation, the employee was discharged per company policy. The plant manager told the reason why to the supervisor and union steward. The employee sued the president and company for defamation. The jury found the president had not defamed the employee, but the company did. The company appealed on the grounds the verdicts were irreconcilable.

The Appeals Court of Massachusetts affirmed judgment for the plaintiff employee. It held both the president and plant manager were privy to discuss the sensitive allegation, but it went on to state:

> We think that the evidence warranted a finding that broader dissemi-
> nation of the charge against [the employee] without an effort to verify
> its truth, in circumstances where verification was practical, amounted

to a "reckless disregard" of [the employee's] rights and of the consequences that [might] result to him.

The conditional privilege to disseminate a serious charge may be
lost, not only by knowledge of its falsity, but also by reckless disregard
whether it is true or not. Reckless disregard does not necessarily imply
that the charge has a flimsy base. Here, clearly, it did not. Recklessness
can also be shown by a failure to verify in circumstances where verification is practical and the matter is sufficiently weighty to call for
safeguards against error.

Further, as discussed earlier, when an employment relationship is not at-will, the
duty to verify an alibi or other evidence favorable to a subject might be implicit in a
contractual relationship such as a collective bargaining agreement. Likewise, there
might be an implicit duty to verify alibis and other information in select statutes
and regulations, such as antidiscrimination laws. The duty to investigate an alibi
may include the obligation to properly document it as well. In *Tenold*, the Oregon
Court of Appeals awarded about $2.5 million against the defendant for malicious
prosecution, defamation, and emotional distress because, in part, the security staff
did not properly report plaintiff's alibi to upper management or authorities.[111]

7.9.6 Allegations of Discrimination

The potential for employees to claim discrimination raises other management
investigative issues. For example, assume a subject employee claims he is the victim
of discrimination because his conduct is no different from the conduct of other
employees. Notice the subject did not claim innocence, but merely that others have
engaged in similar conduct without being confronted or disciplined. How should
an employer handle this allegation? Should the employer ignore or investigate the
allegation? Should it continue to move forward with the investigation and corrective action, and treat the allegation as grounds for a separate investigation? Or,
should the employer delay corrective action and conduct further investigation of
the allegation?

There is no simple answer. The decision must be made on a case-by-case basis
by weighing the totality of information available. Regardless, when counterclaims
of discrimination or similar claims are made, employers must recognize that the
dynamics of an investigation may have changed and it may well be the company
that will have to show it acted reasonably (e.g., it had a legitimate business reason
for taking corrective action). A legitimate business reason may include the duty
to investigate an alibi or other relevant information before taking the investigation further.

Nonetheless, employers and investigators should be cautious not to feel compelled to investigate every conceivable piece of evidence regardless of how remote.
For example, in *Stockley*, the court refused to find a manager was defamed in an

internal investigation when the company allegedly failed to interview a witness favorable to him.[112] The court noted the company had interviewed approximately 20 other persons. Relevant factors in deciding when a reasonable investigation has been conducted include the status of the employee (at-will versus employment contract), the possibility of an implicit statutory or regulatory duty, the applicable burdens and standards of proof, the thoroughness of the current investigation, the strength of the existing evidence, the ease and convenience of follow-up investigation, and similar factors.

7.9.7 Admissible Admissions

The admissibility and evidentiary value of any signed admission may be challenged in a courtroom of law. In order to be admissible, a signed admission must be made knowingly and voluntarily without undue duress, coercion, threat, or promise. A court may exclude an admission or admission that was obtained by duress, deceit, or false promise. Even if admitted as evidence, a jury may give little credence to the admission if it feels the plaintiff signed it as a result of abusive interrogation tactics, such as the interviewer yelling, threatening, intimidating, demanding an admission, or even dictating the wording of an admission. Because an admission may be extremely damaging to an employee's case, interviewers should assume all plaintiffs will challenge the admission or credibility of their admissions.

A coerced admission may actually backfire on the investigator. In *DeAngelis*, the plaintiff, a 17-year-old cashier, sued her employer for false imprisonment.[113] Based on the accusation of another employee who claimed the two split a false refund, the loss prevention district manager interviewed the employee for four hours in the evening. During the interview, the plaintiff "was lectured about theft, shouted at, frightened, charged with theft, and forced to admit to a crime she did not commit." The New Jersey Superior Court, Appellate Division, expressed its view of the investigator's conduct and the value of the admission when it stated: "The coerced false admission, the evil that concerned the Miranda court, evidences the outrageous nature of defendants' conduct." The appeals court affirmed punitive judgment for false imprisonment.

There are many factors that influence the admissibility and credibility of admissions, including age (e.g., youth and old age), experience, language skills, mental health, intelligence, conduct, and even requests of an employee. The number of management and investigative staff present, demeanor of the investigator, seating arrangements, location and room conditions, time of day, length of interrogation, breaks, and communications with outside parties also may be factors. An admissible and credible admission is the product of a reasonable investigative environment and process. The process may not be duress free, nor should it include undue coercion, trickery, or false promises.

Tip: Investigations can take quick turns. An alleged failure to investigate an alibi, a discrimination claim, or an allegation of a coerced admission can undermine the credibility of a fact finder and the investigative findings. Be professional, be prepared, be objective, learn the facts, document the facts, report the facts, and let the facts speak to the allegations.

7.10 Claims Arising from Employee Disciplinary Actions

Liability risks associated with the discipline or corrective action phase of the investigative process include the continuing risks of defamation (and the newly established risk of self-published defamation), emotional distress, wrongful discharge, and malicious prosecution. In addition, fact finders must be prepared to meet the evidentiary burdens of arbitration, unemployment, and workers' compensation hearings.

7.10.1 Defamation

Employees may try to claim they were defamed based on false and excessive publication internally within a company and for false and derogatory reports made externally to outside parties, such as the police, unemployment boards, workers' compensation commissions, and media. However, as noted earlier, internal company discussions and reports regarding employee misconduct are usually protected by the intracorporate publication rule or a conditional privilege. Remarks and documents provided to government agencies are usually viewed as absolute or conditional privileged communications. Intraorganizational and conditional privileges may be lost if a communication is not made in good faith (e.g., communications made with malice or reckless disregard for the truth of the matter) or if communicated to a disinterested party. Not to be overlooked, alleged defamatory comments must first be published.

In *Chappelle*, the defendant company initiated an investigation of an employee based on an unusual pattern of no sales and voids.[114] He was interviewed for slightly over one hour by a regional loss prevention investigator with the store's loss prevention manager as a witness. He was advised the meeting was voluntary and that he was free to leave at any time. The door was left unlocked. The subject verbally confessed, signed a promissory note, and wrote the following admission:

> Over the last 5 or 6 months I have rang 5 transactions where I have rang the transaction for myself in order to generate a receipt so I could leave the store with unpaid merch[andise]. The approximate loss to

Robinsons May by doing this is 500 dollars. I knew what I did was wrong[,] so I am willing to pay back the company for the loss. I am terribly sorry for what I have done and feel terrible[,] that is why I feel it is right to pay this back to the company.

After he affirmed his admission with the human resource manager, his employment was terminated. He filed suit, in part, for defamation. The plaintiff alleged he was defamed when an investigative report was forwarded to the Store Protection Association. The trial court held the evidence of defamation was insufficient to send to a jury and granted nonsuit in favor of defendant store. The plaintiff appealed. The Appeals Court of California noted: "Here it was uncontroverted that appellant stole merchandise. The only dispute was the amount taken." It stated: "The trial court ruled that appellant failed to meet his burden of proof for defamation. We agree. Appellant claimed that an internal case report was forwarded to the Store Protection Association, but there was no evidence that defendants actually transmitted the report. Defamation requires a publication." The trial court further ruled that the claim for defamation "is barred by the defenses of truth and qualified privilege. It did not err. Truth is an absolute defense to defamation." The Appeals Court of California affirmed judgment for defendant merchant.

Crump, as noted earlier, illustrates the need for employers to be careful about using unsubstantiated conclusions in internal discussions and reports.[115] Crump was the warehouse receiver who was terminated for taking defective goods home in violation of company policy. He successfully sued for defamation based on the allegation that he was called a "thief" in an internal meeting involving the warehouse director and two loss prevention personnel. Further, in two postincident reports, he was labeled a "problem employee" despite the fact he had been with the company for 18 years and had no other personnel actions taken against him. The Supreme Court of Vermont affirmed judgment against the company. It found the company lost the intracorporate publication privilege based on evidence showing a "reckless disregard for the truth or ... ill will in violation of the plaintiff's rights."

In *Present*, the plaintiff, a brochure production manager, was terminated after a thorough internal investigation initiated by his new director based on complaints of the manager's subordinates.[116] Separate employees explained how the plaintiff divided large vendor invoices into smaller invoices to bypass audit controls, took a leather jacket, developed personal film at company expense, and directed a subordinate to have a vendor buy the plaintiff a $900 watch and bill it to the company. The vendor confirmed it had done so for fear of losing business. After the director made his report, in-house legal counsel reinterviewed and took affidavits from the parties. The plaintiff was confronted. He offered no reasonable explanation and was suspended. After two other vendors confirmed that they falsely billed the company to cover for items they bought the plaintiff, the company terminated the plaintiff's employment. Corporate security and internal auditors then conducted independent investigations. Security presented its findings to the police. The plaintiff was charged with seven misdemeanors. He was acquitted on one count and the jury could not reach a verdict on the other six charges. The district attorney dismissed the charges rather than retry the case. The plaintiff filed suit for defamation and malicious prosecution (to be discussed later).

In part, he claimed the employees and vendors lied and defamed him, and the company defamed him when it reported the allegations to the police. The trial court denied defendants' motion for summary judgment. The Supreme Court, Appellate Division, New York stated:

> As defendants asserted in their summary judgment motion, all of the challenged statements are undoubtedly covered by a qualified privilege. This being the case, it was incumbent upon plaintiff to raise an issue of fact as to whether defendants acted with constitutional or common law malice, which he failed to do.
>
> A good faith communication upon any subject matter in which the speaker has an interest, or in reference to which he has a duty, is qualifiedly privileged if made to a person having a corresponding interest or duty. The common interest privilege covers statements by employees to management about another employee's job-related misconduct. The same is true of statements by an outside vendor or independent contractor. This qualified privilege also extends to reports to the police or the district attorney's office about another's subjected crimes. If the person passing on the information has a good faith belief in its truth, he is shielded from liability for defamation, even if a more prudent person would not have reported it or the information turns out to be false.
>
> Essentially, to overcome the privilege, the plaintiff needs to challenge the good faith of the defendants by showing that they acted with malice. A speaker exhibits constitutional malice when he makes a defamatory statement while knowing that it is false or recklessly disregarding whether it is false. The plaintiff must set forth evidence to support the conclusion that the defendants entertained serious doubts as to the truth of the statement.

The court went on to compliment the thoroughness of the investigation, the direct knowledge of the employees and vendors, the cross-checking and consistency of evidence from the different sources, and the extensive documentation. Based on the good faith shown by defendants, the Supreme Court, Appellate Division, New York, granted summary judgment to defendants.

In *Kelly*, the plaintiff was accused of assisting the spouse of another employee to steal merchandise and was terminated.[117] After the company dropped the criminal charges and she was awarded unemployment benefits over the objection of the company, the plaintiff sued her employer, manager, and co-workers for defamation. She argued the outcomes in the criminal and administrative proceedings were proof the defendants lost any qualified privilege they had to share the allegations against her. The Court of Appeal of Louisiana affirmed summary judgment for the defendants except for the alleged statements by one co-worker. It held the manager did not lose his qualified privilege because he communicated in good faith with persons who participated in the investigation, were in the plaintiff's chain of command, the company's lawyer, and its unemployment representative. Absent any evidence other than the plaintiff's speculative allegation that the employees conspired to "frame her to divert suspicions [of theft] from themselves," the court also affirmed the employees who reported the alleged misconduct of plaintiff did not abuse their privilege when they spoke with management, police, and unemployment representative. However, the court did find the alleged comments, if proved, of one employee to her mother and roommate would fall outside the conditional privilege.

In *Layne*, the Appellate Court of Illinois affirmed an employer's statement to the police that an employee had threatened, harassed, and assaulted a co-worker was an absolute privileged communication.[118] In *Beauchamp*, a company terminated all five store managers for "failure to protect company assets" after it conducted a three-month investigation and could not isolate the cause of a $150,000 inventory shortage.[119] One manager filed for unemployment benefits. The company contested on the grounds he was "not a prudent manager" and his "failure to protect company assets." Because the company did not establish the manager was at fault for the losses, he was awarded benefits. He claimed he was defamed in the unemployment hearing and filed suit. The appeals court affirmed the accusations by the company were not defamatory per se (note, the company did not accuse him of theft) and the employee failed to show the statements were false or the company acted with malice. It noted the company acted under a "qualified business privilege" and:

> the statements made by [the company] to persons at the Department of Employment Security were certainly relevant to the determination of unemployment compensation and made to persons with a legitimate interest therein. The testimony at trial concerning the defendant's extensive investigation as to the lost inventory provides the required element of good faith.

In conclusion, most communications to police, unemployment boards, workers' compensation, and similarly interested outside parties are privileged communications. In some jurisdictions, statements in judicial and administrative agency proceedings are absolutely privileged communications, whereas, in other jurisdictions, these statements are conditional privileged communications. So long as employers act on a good faith belief of the truth of the matter and not with careless disregard for the facts or reasonably discoverable facts, employers should be protected when sharing information with interested external agencies. Second, employers generally have a conditional internal privilege to share adverse employee information with union stewards, supervisors, managers, and select staff, such as security and human resources, if this information is needed by them to perform their duties. In the alternative, employers may defend on the grounds of truth or nonpublication for intracorporate communications. Nonetheless, investigators should be careful to avoid prematurely labeling subjects as having engaged in criminal conduct. Instead, investigators should report the allegations as reported and the facts as documented, and refrain from reaching unsubstantiated conclusions in their oral and written investigative reports.

7.10.1.1 Self-Published Defamation

There is a little-known tort action for self-published defamation. These cases normally involve employees who have been terminated for misconduct and who repeat the reasons for their discharges to potential employers. In order to prevail, a plaintiff must show a defamatory statement, compelling facts that made it reasonably foreseeable that the plaintiff would republish the derogatory statement, and actual self-publication to a third party.

The majority of states that have reviewed this doctrine have rejected it primarily because it conflicts with the at-will employment doctrine. That is, discharged at-will employees could tell potential employers the stated reasons they were fired and then sue their former employers. There are other concerns, too. Employees might purposely repeat such allegations; statutes of limitations might be extended with each republication; and employers might feel compelled to fire employees without comment rather than use constructive discipline to improve employee performance.

For example, in *Sullivan*, the plaintiff was a part-time neonatal nurse at defendant's hospital and at another hospital that was setting up a neonatal unit.[120] The plaintiff told a co-worker that she had taken some new angiocaths, used to start infant IVs, from the defendant's hospital to the other hospital. The co-worker reported her. She denied the allegations. The hospital terminated her. She applied for positions with two other hospitals and revealed the reason for her discharge. She was not hired. She filed suit for self-published defamation. The trial court granted summary judgment to defendant hospital on the ground the plaintiff failed to prove publication. The appeals court reversed. It held the state would recognize the tort of self-publication defamation in the employment context. The hospital appealed.

The Supreme Court of Tennessee rejected the self-publication doctrine because it would chill employer–employee communications, negatively impact grievance procedures, cast an unfair doubt of silence over persons who were discriminatorily discharged, create a cause of action of negligent investigation in conflict with at-will employment, and unreasonably stretch the state statute of limitation. The court also concluded the lower standard of proof used in the self-publication doctrine conflicted with the higher standards in the state statute governing the right of employers to share employee information. Under the self-defamation doctrine, an employer might be held liable for its negligence in failing to uncover the truth, whereas the state statute shielded employers from liability except in circumstances where an employer shares information that is "Knowingly false, Deliberately misleading, Disclosed for malicious purpose, Disclosed in a reckless disregard for its falsity … , or Violative of … employment discrimination laws."

A few states have recognized self-publication defamation.[121] Many, perhaps all, of these have retained the qualified/conditional privilege of employers to communicate in good faith with their employees. In *Theisen*, for example, the plaintiff was a security director who was terminated for leaving a sexual harassing phone message on the voice mail of a nurse.[122] He claimed self-publication defamation in that he felt compelled to tell his family, friends, and potential employers the alleged reason for his discharge to get their support for his personnel appeal and to obtain future employment. In the words of the state Supreme Court, the trial court granted summary judgment to the defendant hospital on the grounds "an employer is entitled to qualified immunity for statements made to an employee to protect the employer's interest, and that the privilege extends to situations in which the employee feels compelled to repeat such statements." The Supreme Court of Iowa affirmed the hospital had not acted outside its privilege. It found the original communication:

> was made in good faith, based on the identification of [plaintiff's] voice by four persons. [The hospital] had an undisputed interest in the subject of the statement, which was made as part of a sexual harassment investigation. And the statement was made during a closed-door meeting with [plaintiff's] supervisor and the director of employee services, a proper time and place to discuss such an accusation with limited parties. Thus, [the hospital's] statement easily falls within the criteria necessary to establish a qualified privilege as a matter of law.

In *DeWald*, the employee plaintiff put some loose wood in two shopping carts, showed it to the assistant department manager, paid the reduced price he was told to pay by the assistant manager, and loaded it into his truck.[123] The store loss prevention manager saw him loading the wood, spoke with an assistant manager, and then told the plaintiff to pay more for the excess wood he had beyond three bundles, or unload it from his truck. Later, the employee left without unloading or paying for the alleged excess wood. He returned the next morning with the wood still in his truck. The loss prevention manager and two store assistant managers interviewed the employee. He was terminated. The loss prevention manager walked him out of the store through the front door even though an employee exit was closer, unloaded the wood from the truck, and refunded the employee's money. At this time, co-workers overheard the loss prevention manager state the plaintiff was fired for taking more wood beyond that which he paid. The assistant managers stated in his personnel file that the plaintiff was discharged for "theft of firewood and a fraudulent act." About a month later, the loss prevention manager and assistant store manager in an employee meeting stated the plaintiff was "terminated for stealing firewood and had to be dealt with in the same fashion as [the company] dealt with other shoplifters." The latter comment meant he was escorted out the front door as other shoplifters to make an example of him and to intimidate fellow employees. In subsequent job interviews, the plaintiff, in response to the question why he had left his former employer, stated he had been fired for theft and fraud.

He filed suit for defamation, including compelled self-publication defamation. The trial court granted summary judgment for defendant employer and employees. The plaintiff appealed. The appeals court reversed. It noted that, when job applicants are asked why they left their former employment, there is compulsion to reveal the reasons for failure to do so or lying could be grounds for denial of employment or termination. The court held the plaintiff offered evidence on each element of his defamation claim and the company did not "conclusively establish[ed] that the defamatory statements were either substantially true or that their publication was a privileged communication." The Court of Appeals of Texas remanded the case for further proceedings on the issue of self-publication defamation.

> *Tip: When responding to employee complaints and claims for benefits, employers enjoy a good faith privilege to share investigative information with government agencies, including state unemployment and workers' compensation commissions, and federal agencies, such as the NLRB and EEOC.*

7.10.2 Wrongful Discharge

The vast majority of private sector workers are at-will employees. Under the employment at-will doctrine, which is recognized in all jurisdictions, an employee may accept and leave a position at anytime, and an employer may hire and discharge an employee at anytime for any reason, no reason, or even a bad reason. This doctrine is a major, but sometimes surmountable, barrier for employees who believe they were unjustly discharged. As discussed here, not all employers serve at-will, and there are several exceptions to the employment at-will relationship.

7.10.2.1 Union and Personal Employment Contracts

Not all employment relationships are at-will. Union members, for example, work under collective bargaining agreements, and an employer must show cause, just cause, good cause, or similar evidence to terminate. Failure to satisfy the requisite burden may result in an arbitrator directing the company to reinstate a terminated union employee with or without back pay and benefits. Similarly, some executives and professionals have personal contracts of employment that restrict the rights of employers to cause discharges. A terminated employee may file an arbitration grievance or a breach of contract lawsuit against the employer and force the employer to show cause or pay the full benefits of the contract.

7.10.2.2 Implied Contract of Employment

One exception to the at-will doctrine is an implied contract of employment. In union and personal contracts of employment, the terms and conditions of employment have been negotiated and agreed to by all concerned parties. In contrast, an implied contract is one that arises based on facts that would lead a reasonable party to conclude a contract right exists. Many of these cases involve oral statements by managers and the disciplinary procedures and standards set forth in employee handbooks and personnel manuals. Sometimes at-will employees claim these unilaterally issued publications by employers are binding contracts of employment and they were fired outside the disciplinary provisions. Employers may defeat these claims by inserting appropriate notices in the documents (e.g., the manuals are not contracts of employment and the employment relationship remains at-will).

7.10.2.3 Whistleblower and Similar Statutes

Many states have whistleblower statutes that prohibit retaliatory discharges against employees who report illegal company acts (e.g., tax fraud and illegal dumping). The breadth and depth of protection varies by statute. Some protect only employees who actually report the criminal conduct to the authorities. Other statutes, as a means of shielding employees from preemptive terminations by their employers, also protect those employees who were about to report the criminal conduct. Some statutes protect employees when reporting violations of a specific law, whereas other statutes protect employees for reporting a wide variety of employer criminal conduct under the penal code. These statutes may not apply when employees report criminal acts that are unknown to company executives. When an employee qualifies for protection under a statute, the burden usually shifts to the employer to show the termination was for reasons separate from the employee's protected status.

7.10.2.4 Public Policy

Many states recognize an action for wrongful discharge in violation of public policy (i.e., the discharge is harmful to the larger interests of the public). In order to prevail, employees must often prove a clear and compelling reason the discharge violates the public interest. Usually this interest must be based on the constitution or statutes of the state, although a few states recognize judicial public policy. This doctrine allows the courts to intervene when other remedies may not be available. For example, assume an employee filed a workers' compensation claim and was shortly thereafter falsely terminated for theft, the employee might argue the discharge violated public policy because it was a pretext to deny him benefits and to deter co-workers from filing for workers' compensation benefits.

7.10.2.5 Discriminatory Discharges

Terminated at-will employees might claim their discharges were illegally based on race, nationality, color, sex, religion, age, disability, or other protected classification. Once an employee shows *prima facie* discrimination (member of a protected class and adverse employment action), the burden shifts to the employer to show a legitimate business reason for the discharge. The burden then shifts back to the employee to prove the proffered reason is a pretext. At-will employees who are members of protected groups may claim their discharges were discriminatory, shifting the burden to the employers to show legitimate business reasons (facts supported by the investigations) for the terminations, thereby shifting it back to the employees to show the investigative findings were pretexts.

7.10.2.6 Covenant of Good Faith and Fair Dealings

The covenant of good faith and fair dealings is a contract law doctrine. It implies all parties to a contract have a duty to act accordingly. A small minority of states have applied this doctrine to wrongful discharge cases to prevent employers from unfairly denying employees benefits they have or are near earning. For example, assume a sales representative made a large sale and was entitled to substantial upfront and continuing commissions and he was shortly thereafter fired for embezzlement. He might file a wrongful discharge suit claiming his discharge was a pretext by the company to avoid paying his commissions in violation of the covenant of good faith and fair dealings.

7.10.2.7 Additional Cases to Consider

In *Dewald*, an employee was terminated for alleged theft of firewood. He had paid the reduced price for the unbundled firewood (a common practice by the store) that he was told to pay by the assistant department manager.[124] Later that day, the loss prevention manager, at the direction of the assistant store manager, told him to pay more or unload it. He left work and returned with the wood the next day. The company gave him his money back and fired him for theft. Although the Court of Appeals of Texas reversed the summary judgment in favor of the defendant store on the issue of defamation, it affirmed judgment on the issue of wrongful discharge. The employee argued he had an expressed agreement based on a company policy of providing three warnings prior to termination. The court held employee practices and employee handbooks standing alone without expressed agreement do not alter an at-will employment relationship. Here, the company had disclaimers that the handbook was intended to provide only guidelines, it was subject to change, and it did not create any contract rights.

In *French*, the plaintiff employee, an inventory stocking crew leader, was discharged after he signed an admission to knowingly eating a small amount of food and not paying for it.[125] He alleged his admission was coerced by a private investigator. The company fired him. He filed suit claiming the company "breached an express contract of employment … an implied-at-law covenant of good faith and fair dealing," and tortuously discharged him in violation of public policy. The trial court granted summary judgment for the company. He appealed. The Iowa Supreme Court, first, noted an exception to the employment at-will doctrine arises "when a contract created by an employer's handbook or policy manual guarantees an employee that discharge will occur only for cause or under certain conditions." But, it rejected the employee's claim because the handbook contained language that was for "information only," the company "reserves the right to change or terminate any or all of [policies, procedures] at any time," and "Just as you retain the right to terminate your employment at any time, for any reason, [the company] retains a similar right." Second, the Iowa Supreme Court stated the plaintiff "urges us to adopt a cause of action for breach of an implied covenant of good faith and fair dealing, a theory that we expressly rejected. In rejecting this theory, we joined the majority of jurisdictions that have considered it." Third, the employee argued the coerced admission violated "Iowa's policy against suborning perjury and the prohibition against making a false charge of dishonesty" and the policy that "every person is presumed innocent until proven guilty." The court did not discuss the alleged coercion, instead it rejected his public policy argument on the grounds the case did not involve a criminal charge, perjury, or the presumed innocent doctrine. The Iowa Supreme Court affirmed judgment for the company.

In *Mead*, the defendant company terminated an employee over an unspecified incident at a convenience store and the employee filed suit.[126] She claimed, in part, breach of an implied contract of employment. The company responded that its employment application governed the case and she was an at-will employee. It filed a motion for summary judgment. The Superior Court of Connecticut denied the motion on the grounds there were material facts in dispute about the nature of the employment. Specifically, it stated the manager's alleged remarks "about security, longevity, and promotion opportunities, which, factually, contradicts the at-will employment relationship."

In *Theisen*, discussed previously, a director of hospital security was subjected of making an obscene phone call that was left in the voice mailbox of a nurse.[127] After four employees identified the voice as the director's, the hospital requested he submit an exemplar of his voice for voice pattern analysis. He refused based on an attorney's advice that it violated the state polygraph statute. The hospital terminated his employment. The director filed suit, in part, alleging his discharge was in violation of public policy because it violated the state polygraph act that prohibited employers from requesting or requiring an employee to submit to a polygraph examination. The court granted summary judgment to the defendant hospital. The director appealed. The Supreme Court of Iowa found the voice pattern analysis as requested was not to detect deception. Instead, the device was to be used as a means of identification, much as fingerprints and photographs. Because he was not going to be asked specific questions for determination of truth, his discharge did not violate the public policy of the state. The court affirmed judgment for the hospital.

In *Wholey*, a long-term at-will store security manager filed a lawsuit for wrongful discharge in violation of public policy.[128] After having given the security manager permission to install a camera in the office of the store manager who was subjected of theft, the security director told him to remove it before it was activated. Shortly thereafter, the store manager fired him. He filed suit and won damages of $166,000 for wrongful discharge. The Court of Special Appeals of Maryland reversed. It held there was no clear legislative or judicial mandate that an employee investigate or report a co-employee's criminal conduct, therefore, his discharge did not violate the public policy of the state.

Similarly, in *Morris*, a long-term at-will employee claimed he was wrongfully terminated in violation of public policy.[129] He argued the company failed to conduct a reasonable investigation and it falsely accused him of misappropriating funds. The Supreme Court of Connecticut affirmed he failed to state a recognized cause of action because a mere negligent false accusation did not violate a clear constitutional, statutory, or judicial public policy.

In *Koller*, a nurse on separate occasions reported two doctors for abusing patients.[130] She threatened to report the abuse to the state if the hospital did not address the issues. Over the next 18 months, she reported retaliatory abuse by the physicians. The hospital proposed to initiate a staff training program in response to her complaint. She quit. She filed suit for wrongful discharge under a constructive discharge argument (i.e., working conditions were so bad a reasonable person would feel compelled to quit). She argued her constructive discharge violated the "about to report" section of the state Whistleblowers' Protection Act. The Court of Appeals of Michigan affirmed judgment in favor of the hospital on the grounds the plaintiff could not show with clear and convincing evidence she was protected under the statute given the long lapse of time, 18 months, between her first statement that she would report the abuse until the time she resigned.

In *Vaillancourt*, an assistant store manager with a bipolar disorder was granted a leave of absence.[131] Later, she returned to work on a reduced work schedule to accommodate her disability. Due to staffing shortages, she frequently worked over her scheduled hours. One day when working late, she was told by an associate that two customers had just shoplifted. She and a security officer followed the subjects outside the store and told a police officer who detained the subjects and recovered the items. She was terminated for violating the "Four Steps of Proof" policy of the company that required a manager to witness the theft. She filed suit for failure to accommodate and wrongful discriminatory discharge. The trial court granted summary judgment for the store.

The appeals court reversed. It found there was sufficient evidence to go to trial to determine if the store did offer reasonable accommodation in light of the fact that accommodation is an ongoing requirement (i.e., the question of whether her working longer than approved by her doctor was a triable issue). Reference the discriminatory discharge claim, the appeals court noted her manager reported she did not train the plaintiff on the policy until after the incident. There was testimony that the regional manager had been condescending and hostile to her accommodation needs. Further, the regional manager did not inform the management staff that reviewed the incident that plaintiff had not been trained prior to the incident. In addition, there was evidence the company had not fired other assistant managers who violated the policy. The Court of Appeals of California remanded the case to the trial court.

In conclusion, although most employees are at-will and may be terminated at anytime for any, no, or poor reasons, fact finders still must be cognizant of wrongful discharge claims. When employees establish that their services are not at-will or they qualify under an exception to the employment at-will doctrine, wrongful discharge claims shift the burden to the employers to offer sufficient evidence to sustain the terminations.

> *Tip: Under the employment at-will doctrine, employees may be fired at any time for any reason. However, there are exceptions to this rule that employers need to understand and to consider before discharging employees.*

7.10.3 Malicious Prosecution

Before deciding to bring criminal charges against an employee, an employer should understand the civil tort action of malicious prosecution. It is a civil action designed to protect persons from being unjustly prosecuted. In order to prevail on a malicious prosecution claim, the plaintiff employee must prove the defendant employer or investigator initiated or continued a criminal proceeding without probable cause and for a malicious purpose, and the criminal proceeding terminated in favor of the accused employee.

When analyzing these cases, the courts focus on the issues of initiation and continuation, probable cause, malice of the accuser, and decisions in favor of the accused. In addition to a not guilty verdict, possible verdicts in favor of the accused cover a wide range of actions, including a dropping of charges by the employer, a decision to not prosecute by the district attorney, and a dismissing of the charges on merit by a judicial officer. The existence of probable cause is often based on the good faith belief of the employer or investigator at the time or it may be based on the beliefs of a reasonable person in the same situation at the time. If a grand jury indicts the employee on the same evidence and not evidence later acquired, this is a very strong but refutable presumption of probable cause. Malice is closely linked with but separate from the issue of probable cause. The absence of probable cause supports a conclusion of malice by an employer, but malice must be further proved by a showing of a reckless disregard for the facts to a specific ill will directed at the accused employee.

The time when a criminal proceeding is actually initiated also varies by jurisdiction. Generally, the reporting of information to the police is not an initiation of a criminal proceeding if the police have the opportunity to conduct an independent investigation. However, the known inclusion of false information or the withholding of material information from the police may convert the reporting party's action into an initiation. The signing of a criminal complaint by an employer and the insistence of having an employee arrested on the scene by a police officer are acts that increase the probability the courts will find the employers initiated the criminal proceeding. Finally, the continuation of a criminal proceeding refers to an employer's ongoing duty after initiating a criminal proceeding to timely disclose to the authorities any subsequently discovered material information that favors an accused and diminishes existing probable cause. Failure to do so may be viewed as evidence of malice toward the accused.

In *Wright*, a customer was stopped leaving a store with approximately $50 of merchandise for which she had paid only a $1.05.[132] The customer signed a statement that the employee (plaintiff) who underrang the items had participated in prior misconduct. This later part of the statement was based on information the customer's husband, who worked at the store, told her. The husband later denied making such a statement. The employee was interviewed for approximately one and a half hours. The police were called. A detective took a statement of the store loss prevention agent. Without any further involvement by the company or further investigation by the police, 10 days later the police arrested the plaintiff for shoplifting. He was acquitted and sued, in part, for malicious prosecution. The company filed a motion for summary judgment. The U.S. District Court held the company did not initiate the arrest of the plaintiff. The company played no more active role than reporting the offense. The police elected to engage in no further investigation and to initiate charges. Further, it found the company had probable cause to report the incident to the police based on the merchandise recovered versus the purchase price paid. The probable cause was strengthened by the allegation of the customer against the plaintiff. The court granted summary judgment on the issue of malicious prosecution in favor of the company.

In *Binns*, the company appealed an award of $750,000 compensatory and $2 million punitive damages for malicious prosecution and abuse of process.[133] The company pressed criminal charges against the employee for theft of layaway payments. The evidence against the employee consisted of numerous cancellations of customers' final payments by the employee and the lack of overage in her cash drawer when she balanced the count. The company contacted the police. A detective reviewed the files, copied some transactions, and obtained an arrest warrant for the employee. A year later, the prosecutor nolle prossed the case for lack of evidence. The plaintiff successfully sued for malicious prosecution and the company appealed. The Supreme Court of Arkansas focused its analysis on the testimony of the employee's expert. He testified the company's computer software in use at the time would not have shown an overage in the system when the last payment was canceled even if she did not remove the payment. He also thought the two managers who investigated the problem probably believed they had probable cause to believe she stole the funds, and they probably did not act with "ill will, spite, or a spirit of revenge." The Supreme Court of Arkansas found the managers had "honest and strong suspicions" that the employee was taking funds from the register. It reversed the judgment against the company and it held the company was entitled to a directed verdict because the plaintiff failed to prove either the absence of probable cause or the existence of malice.

In *Sisney*, a company vice president had a check issued to himself, told the cashier to record it as a cash advance, and because the president was absent, signed the president's name followed by his name—"Ballou by Sisney."[134] The company contacted the police and reported the vice president was embezzling company funds because he did not have the authority to sign the president's signature, nor had he ever done so in the past. The prosecutor refused to prosecute the case when he found out the vice president on four prior occasions had issued and signed similar checks, a fact the company withheld. The court held there was sufficient evidence to prove the company maliciously initiated criminal proceedings against the accused.

When money turned up missing out of a cash register, a store manager filed an initial police report, followed by two company investigators, which named the plaintiff as the prime subject.[135] Subsequently, the company investigators learned another employee had access to the missing money, she had access to other missing funds, and creditors were calling her at work. The company investigators never shared this information with the police. The police arrested the first employee. She was found not guilty and sued the company for malicious prosecution. The trial court granted summary judgment for the defendants. The Maryland Court of Appeals reversed. It ruled there was sufficient evidence for the plaintiff to pursue a malicious prosecution claim against the company and remanded the case for trial.

When reporting subject employee criminal activities to the authorities, employers should make full and timely disclosure of all known facts and, subsequently, discovered facts material to the cases. Further, they should not hastily sign criminal complaints nor press the authorities (including officers on the scene) to make arrests in order to make examples of the employees. Employers should refrain from labeling employees as criminals; rather they should simply share known facts that the police may conduct independent investigations to determine if probable cause exists to arrest or obtain an arrest warrant. Before actually signing criminal complaints, fact finders should reaffirm they have conducted good faith investigations and reasonably believe they have probable cause to support the complaints.

7.10.4 Emotional Distress or Outrage

Employees who are terminated or prosecuted by their employers may reasonably be expected to add claims for emotional distress/outrage. As previously discussed, these claims may be for the intentional or negligent infliction of emotional distress. In order to prevail on a claim of intentional infliction of emotional distress, a plaintiff must prove the defendant acted in an outrageous and highly offensive manner that was highly probable of inflicting severe emotional distress upon another. In a negligence case, plaintiffs also may have to prove physical impact, risk of imminent physical impact upon themselves, or physical manifestations of the distress. These claims in investigation cases are usually based on abusive investigative interviewing practices and the reckless disregard for the truth of the information obtained during the investigation.

In *Agis*, as discussed earlier, a restaurant manager in response to employee theft terminated employees in alphabetical order in order to force the thief to confess. The Supreme Court of Massachusetts felt this action, even without physical injury, was sufficient to support a cause of action for intentional or reckless infliction of emotional distress. It reinstated the claims against defendant.

In *Olivas*, the Superior Court of Connecticut held an employee could sue his employer for emotional distress on the grounds the discharge taken with the accusation of theft and forgery could amount to "extreme and outrageous conduct."[136] Here, after a paycheck was stolen and cashed at a liquor store, an employee of the company made comments to the liquor store owner that the employee plaintiff stole the check and committed forgery. Allegedly, other employees accused the plaintiff and told his landlord. Later, the criminal charges against the plaintiff were dismissed.

In *Tenold*, the Court of Appeals of Oregon affirmed $2.4 million against the company for defamation, malicious prosecution, and intentional infliction of emotional distress, and $150,000 in damages against the site security supervisor for defamation and intentional infliction of emotional distress.[137] This case involved the employee who was arrested for stealing company railroad ties. The criminal charges were dropped after the company could not show evidence of ownership and the employee was able to produce receipts for some of the ties. The employee claimed he had been given permission to take the ties and pay for them later. There was evidence a site security supervisor and another manager bore ill will toward the employee. The manager had stated he wanted his job, and the security supervisor accused him of being a drunk and drug user, and operating a methamphetamine lab. The company investigative reports did not accurately reflect the exculpatory statement of the accused employee. The appeals court held these facts were sufficient evidence for a jury to conclude the defendants had engaged in an extraordinary and intolerable campaign to defame, terminate, and prosecute the plaintiff.

Disciplinary actions based on unreasonable investigative methods and interrogations expose businesses to the increased risk of lawsuits for infliction of emotional distress. Fair disciplinary actions that are based on reasonable inquiry are far less likely at the disciplinary phase to expose employers to claims of emotional distress.

7.10.5 Unemployment Claims

Unemployment compensation is a state-administered program designed to provide temporary financial relief for workers who lose their jobs through no fault of their own. If an employer wishes to challenge an employee's claim for benefits, the burden is generally placed on the employer to prove the employee's actions constituted misconduct, willful misconduct, or similar disqualifying conduct as defined by state statute.

For example, Florida defines misconduct as:

(a) Conduct demonstrating willful or wanton disregard of an employer's interests and found to be a deliberate violation or disregard of the standards of behavior, which the employer has a right to expect of his or her employee; or

(b) Carelessness or negligence to a degree or recurrence that manifests culpability, wrongful intent, or evil design or shows an intentional and substantial disregard of the employer's interests or of the employee's duties and obligations to his or her employer.[138]

In Illinois, misconduct is defined as "the deliberate and willful violation of a reasonable rule or policy by the employing unit."[139]

The degree of evidence required to be produced by an employer varies by state. A frequently referenced standard is substantial evidence.[140] Substantial evidence is sufficient to support a decision even though others might reach a different conclusion. Some courts will not overturn an unemployment board's decision unless it is clearly contrary to the overwhelming weight of the evidence[141] or against the manifest weight of the evidence.[142]

In *Cabreja*, the claimant was a hospital janitor.[143] A security officer observed her accepting an empty bag from a subject ex-employee under surveillance, going into a locker room, and returning the bag filled with hospital cleaning supplies to the subject. She was terminated and denied unemployment benefits. An appeals court affirmed there was substantial and credible evidence to support the unemployment board's decision that the claimant employee engaged in misconduct and was disqualified from collecting benefits. In the words of the board, as affirmed by the Supreme Court, Appellate Division, New York: "We find significant the credible eye-witness testimony of the security guard who personally observed the transfer of the shopping bag, which contained the stolen hospital property."

In *Hurlbut*, the Missouri Court of Appeals ruled a convenience store manager violated the reasonable rules of her employer when she and her subordinates failed to include a cash register tape with the daily count of the cash box.[144] The absence of the detail tape impeded the company from determining the actual date and time of a cash shortage. The appeals court affirmed there was sufficient evidence to support the denial of benefits.

Similarly, in *Frey*, the Commonwealth Court of Pennsylvania affirmed there was substantial evidence of willful misconduct by an employee who left a piece of paper with the combination on top of the office safe.[145] The fact she claimed that she left it for another employee and asked it be placed in her mailbox did not relieve her of her duty.

7.10.5.1 Off-Duty Misconduct

The general rule is that off-duty conduct of employees is not relevant to employers. But, when there is a nexus or connection with the duties of the employee, the off-duty conduct may be grounds for denial of unemployment benefits. These cases normally involve conduct that breaches a necessary trust or reflects negatively upon the reputation of the company.

In *Montellanico*, the claimant was the supervisor of hourly workers.[146] He scheduled workers and processed unemployment and other claims. He was also treasurer of the employees' credit union where he was arrested for making fraudulent loans. The credit union operated completely independent of the company. Upon hearing of his arrest, the company suspended and later terminated him before there was a conclusion of the criminal proceeding. Based on his admission to the authorities that he had made fraudulent loans, the unemployment board found this conduct related directly to his duties as hourly employee supervisor. Applying a two-prong test where the employer must show the employee's off-duty criminal conduct was inconsistent with acceptable behavior and it reflected upon his ability to perform his duties, the Commonwealth Court of Pennsylvania held that the claimant's conduct threatened, if not totally destroyed, the requisite trust between himself and the hourly employees. It affirmed the denial of benefits.

In *Conseco*, the employer, in response to thefts in the workplace, instituted a criminal records check of employees.[147] The claimant signed the authorization. She worked the midnight shift and had unrestricted access to five buildings. Her job entailed the printing of customer claim checks. Later, she was arrested for shoplifting. She pled not guilty. The company discovered the arrest when it conducted her background check. It terminated her employment. She filed for benefits. The company argued the employee breached a necessary trust. The hearing deputy denied her benefits. An administrative law judge reversed on the grounds there had not been a final adjudication and, therefore, no proven disqualifying conduct. The company appealed. It introduced evidence that the employee later pled guilty. Nonetheless, the board found the company's evidence was too attenuated to prove she was terminated for just cause related to work. The company appealed. The appeals court found there was substantial evidence to support the board's decision. It affirmed the company did not establish work-related just cause.

7.10.6 Workers' Compensation

The purpose of workers' compensation is to provide financial benefits and medical care for victims of accidental injuries arising out of and during the course of employment. At the time of discipline, employers should determine whether they will contest the awarding of benefits. If they do, the burden is generally upon an employer to establish that the injury did not arise out of and in the course of employment, an employee is malingering and able to return to work, or employee fraud. One popular investigative method in workers' compensation cases is surveillance with video cameras. Employers and investigators must recognize that, although video evidence is often invaluable, there are restrictions upon its use and limits to inferences that might be drawn from the evidence.

For example, in *Combined Insurance Company of America*, the employer had photographic evidence of an employee jumping into a pool and bending over a lounge chair.[148] This video evidence was reviewed by the employer's medical expert. He testified the employee was able to return to work. This evidence, however, was stricken from the record when the employer failed to authenticate it by having the photographer testify as the parties had agreed.

In *Anthony*, a private investigator observed a widow beneficiary of a deceased worker had an overnight male visitor.[149] A second investigator placed surveillance on the home and videotaped the widow (she was 60 years of age and her husband had died approximately 10 years prior) and the male early in the morning standing on the front porch hugging twice and kissing once. The employer requested the discontinuance of death benefits on the grounds she had entered into a meretricious relationship. The claimant testified that the male lived in her home while he was remodeling his home, a period that lasted for approximately 20 months, and that they did not have a sexual relationship. Further, medical testimony was introduced that the male was a diabetic and suffered from erectile dysfunction. The workers' compensation judge cut off benefits on the grounds the two lingering kisses were "not the type of kiss the majority of Pennsylvanians give to their platonic friends." Noting the parties did not admit to the relationship and there was no child conceived out of the relationship, the court held the video evidence was insufficient to establish substantial evidence of a carnal relationship. Even though it recognized employers were in a difficult situation, finding substantial evidence of such a sensitive nature without invading the privacy of the persons, it reversed the board's denial of benefits.

In seeking to use video evidence, investigators must be prepared to authenticate the evidence. They may enhance the strengths of their cases, although it may not always be practical or possible, by obtaining multiple videotapes of subjects engaged in disqualifying behavior before seeking to disqualify them.

In conclusion, the primary liability issues that arise from employee discipline are defamation including compelled self-published defamation, emotional distress, wrongful discharge, and malicious prosecution. Further, at this stage of the investigation, the burden is on the employer to produce evidence to prove disqualifying employee conduct to deny or terminate the awarding of workers' compensation and unemployment benefits.

Employers may minimize the liability risks and enhance their successes in administrative hearings by sharing adverse information in good faith on a need-to-know basis only, administering fair and impartial discipline, properly documenting all evidence and making full and timely disclosure to law enforcement authorities when filing criminal charges, and obtaining documentation of repeated or serious disqualifying behavior when challenging unemployment and workers' compensation benefits.

7.11 Prevention and Education

The final phase of the investigative process is prevention and education. When reaching out to inform and change employee behavior, an important question for employers is how much information regarding an investigation and disciplinary action should be shared with co-workers? The primary liability concerns are lawsuits for defamation, false light invasion of privacy, and emotional distress.

7.11.1 Defamation and False Light Invasion of Privacy

Both of these actions have been discussed earlier. In review, defamation occurs when one party publishes a false statement of fact to a third disinterested party and the statement is injurious to the community, business, or professional reputation of the named party. False light invasion of privacy involves the emotional distress suffered by the party based on the publicity of a false statement.[150] A false statement is one made with reckless disregard for the truth that attributes highly objectionable characteristics, beliefs, or conduct to an individual and places him before the public in a false position.[151] Publicity means the statement was made before the public or shared with a sufficient number of persons that it is likely to become public knowledge.

In *Bine*, previously discussed, the plant manager, in order to deal with rumors, told a number of employees the plaintiff was fired for vandalism. Plaintiff filed suit, in part, for false light invasion of privacy. The trial court granted summary judgment to the company. The Supreme Court of West Virginia held there was a dispute of material fact as to the truth of the allegation. It noted: "The spreading of such information, if false, could constitute a valid false light claim." The Supreme Court reversed and remanded the case to the trial court.[152] In *Garcia*, the human resource manager held two staff meetings and told co-workers of plaintiff that, based on a "thorough investigation" [an anonymous phone call], the plaintiff was observed shooting up cocaine. Plaintiff sued for both defamation and false light invasion of privacy. The jury found in her favor on both counts. The trial judge vacated the judgment. U.S. Court of Appeals reversed. It affirmed there was sufficient evidence to support both claims.[153]

Where these cases involved oral statements made by management, *Stock* involved two written statements released by management to employees. As noted earlier, plaintiffs were new contract security officers who were accused of cheating in their basic training class. They were denied access by the electric company to the nuclear facility where they were to be assigned. The company investigation did not conclusively prove which employees had cheated. Yet, the company released two statements to its employees. The first memo by the plant manager stated the 10 officers were denied access because they were involved in cheating while in training. It also stated the company would not tolerate such conduct and that this incident did not reflect upon the current security staff. The second statement appeared in the monthly nuclear department newsletter. It stated the company had rescinded the unescorted access of 10 security guards because they broke the bond of trust by violating the testing code. It added that it was a difficult situation for all; the company felt sympathy for the officers and families, but the rescission of access privileges was the right thing to do. The officers sued the company for defamation. Because the communications made it appear as if all the officers were cheating, the jury found the officers were defamed and awarded each officer $46,500. The Court of Appeals of Wisconsin affirmed the judgment.[154]

The risk for companies that attempt to explain or justify specific disciplinary actions to co-workers is that the underlying investigations will not support the alleged defamatory and false light statements. A safer alternative is to not make any internal public statements. For example, in *Smith*, the U.S. District Court rejected plaintiff's claim that she was put in false light when she was escorted off company property and the company "left her co-workers free to speculate that Smith had been disciplined for something more egregious than vacation day violation, such as fraud or graft." Similarly, in *Szot*, an insurance agent, who was terminated for falsification of applications for insurance coverage, claimed, in part, defamation based on the "rumor mill" among other agents regarding her termination. Because the plaintiff did not produce any evidence the company told the other agents of the reason for her discharge, the U.S. District Court granted summary judgment to the defendant company.[155]

It is more difficult to sue an employer for not saying anything than it is to sue for the confidential remarks published beyond a need-to-know basis. In the alternative, if an employer feels the information must be shared, before sharing it, the employer should carefully consider:

- Why it is necessary to share this information?
- Who will be told?
- What is the legitimate business reason for sharing this information with each employee?
- How will it enable each employee to better perform his duties?
- Will the investigative facts support the truth of any statements made?

From a business perspective, the employer should also ask: Will the benefit from this sharing exceed the liability risks to be incurred? In the final analysis, it is more difficult to sue for silence than for words spoken.

7.11.2 Emotional Distress

When organizations openly discuss employee misconduct and name the parties involved or give facts sufficient that co-workers may identify the involved employees, there always exists the possibility the named employees will claim defamation, false light invasion of privacy, and infliction of emotional distress. The claims may be for negligent infliction or intentional infliction. Assuming the plaintiffs can offer proof of severe emotional distress with physical manifestations if required, the focus at trial will be on the defendant's conduct and whether it was outrageous in nature. A determination of outrage might include review of the defendant's motives for releasing the information, the integrity and reliability of the information discussed, and the parties to whom it was released. Malicious or reckless motive, known falsity or reckless disregard for the truth of the information, and overly inclusive sharing of information are factors that may support findings of employer outrage. Good faith intent to educate employees to prevent future similar incidents, reliable and documented information, and focused training programs for concerned employees are factors that will mitigate the risks of adverse judgments for infliction of emotional distress.

In relaying case facts to co-workers, in order to prevent future problems, an organization may defend its action by showing the release of information was done in good faith and communicated to only those employees who needed to know in order to properly perform their duties. However, it is imperative that managers and investigators carefully consider the need to openly discuss case facts versus the risks of defamation, false light invasion of privacy, and emotional distress lawsuits. An employer's good intentioned release of information to quell employee rumors or to reinforce company values may expose the company to undue risk if the investigative foundation for the statements is incomplete or flawed. In the alternative, a company may ask an employee to voluntarily sign a release and waiver from liability for the company to share the case file with co-employees so they will not make similar mistakes.

7.12 Litigation Avoidance and Employee Dignity

Sound planning and superb execution are two key elements of a litigation avoidance strategy. As detailed at length in this chapter, poor planning, aggressive fact finding, careless communication, and poor disciplinary and corrective judgment frequently produce substandard results and litigation.

There is another equal, if not more important, critical factor that cannot be overlooked: the attitude of the fact finder. An objective fact finder who understands the liability risks and conducts an inquiry in a manner that respects the dignity of all employees is more likely to be respected and less likely to be sued.

7.12.1 Awareness and Liability Avoidance

Employers and their fact finders need to recognize the complexity of federal and state laws and regulations that are woven throughout every phase of modern workplace investigations. These laws impose affirmative duties upon employers to restrict the purposes of their investigations to lawful objectives, to confine the scope of inquiry to legitimate business interests, and to use only methods of investigation that are lawful in nature. When personal reputations, incomes, jobs, promotions, and personal freedom are at stake, the liability risks are real, and employers must properly identify and manage these overlapping risks.

7.12.2 Employee Dignity and Liability Avoidance

The Process of Investigation is an approach that is founded upon a balanced respect for employee and employer rights and dignity. It respects the right of the employer by providing a fair and equitable process to make reasonable inquiry into wrongful workplace behavior that is harmful to the interest of the employer and ultimately to the employees. The process respects the rights and dignity of all employees, not merely those who are the subjects of investigations, to a reasonable scope of inquiry, an objective inquiry, verification of facts, and fair discipline and corrective action when appropriate. The seeds of litigation will find it difficult to take root, grow, and spread in an investigative environment that is reasonable in scope, methods, and outcomes.

Tip: The most effective ways for fact finders to mitigate litigation and liability are to intelligently plan and carefully execute the plan, and at all times to be objective, straightforward, fair, and respectful of all employees, including their interviewees.

Endnotes

1. *Fincher v. Depository Trust and Clearing Corp.*, F.3d, 2010 U.S. App. LEXIS 9881 (2nd Cir. 2010).
2. Occupational Health and Safety Act, 29 U.S.C. §654.
3. Federal Sentencing Guidelines (§8C2.5)(f) and (g).
4. *Salinas v. Forth Worth Cab and Baggage Company*, 725 S.W.2d 701 (Tex. 1987).
5. *Saine v. Comcast Cablevision of Arkansas, Inc.*, Supreme Court of Arkansas, No. 02-1388, Oct. 23, 2003.
6. *Yunker v. Honeywell, Inc.*, 496 N.W.2d 419 (Minn. App. 1993).
7. *Paradoa v. CNA Ins. Co.*, 672 N.E.2d 127 (Mass. App. Ct. 1996).
8. *Greenbaum v. Brooks*, 139 S.E.2d 432 (Ga. App. 1964).
9. *Kelley v. Stop & Shop Companies, Inc.*, 530 N.E.2d 190 (Mass. App. Ct. 1988).
10. *Miranda v. Arizona*, 384 U.S. 436, 86 S.Ct. 1602, 16 L.Ed.2d 694 (1966).
11. *United States v. Antonelli*, 434 F.2d 335 (C.A.N.Y. 1970).
12. *Commonwealth v. Green*, 1973 WL 15308 (Pa. Com. Pl. 1973).
13. *Simpson v. Commonwealth*, Unemployment Compensation Bd. of Review, 450 A.2d 305 (Pa. Cmwlth. 1982).
14. For a short and insightful discussion of some of these points, see *U.S. v. Leffall*, 82 F.3d 343 (10th Cir. 1996).
15. *United States v. Dansberry*, 500 F. Supp. 140 (N.D. Ill. 1980).
16. For example, see West Virginia Constitution, Article III, section five (right not to be compelled to be a witness against himself) and section six (right to be free from unreasonable searches and seizures).
17. Simpson, supra at 13.
18. *State v. Muegge*, 360 S.E.2d 216 (W. Va. 1987), overruled on other grounds *State v. Honaker*, 454 S.E.2d 96, 59 (W.Va. 1994).
19. See California, *People v. Zelinski*, 594 P.2d 1000 (Cal. 1979); *Montana, State v. Helfrich*, 600 P.2d 816 (Mont. 1979); and *West Virginia, State v. Muegge*, 360 S.E.2d 216 (W. Va. 1987). However, two states have since reversed their positions: Proposition 8, passed by California voters in 1982; and Montana rulings, *State v. Long*, 700 P.2d 153 (Mont. 1985) and *State v. Christensen*, 797 P.2d 893 (Mont. 1990).
20. *Hill v. National Collegiate Athletic Association*, 7 Cal.4th 1 (1994).
21. National Labor Relations Act, §157. "Rights of employees as to organization, collective bargaining, etc. [Known as §7 rights] Employees shall have the right to self-organization, to form, join, or assist labor organizations, to bargain collectively through representatives of their own choosing, and to engage in other concerted activities for the purpose of collective bargaining or other mutual aid or protection."
22. 29 U.S.C. §158. Unfair labor practices [Known as §8(a) and §8(b) unfair labor practices]. (a) Unfair labor practices by employer. It shall be an unfair labor practice for an employer—(1) to interfere with, restrain, or coerce employees in the exercise of the rights guaranteed in section 7 [29 U.S.C. §157]; …(4) to discharge or otherwise discriminate against an employee because he has filed charges or given testimony under this Act; … (b) Unfair labor practices by labor organization. It shall be an unfair labor practice for a labor organization or its agents—(1) to restrain or coerce (A) employees in the exercise of the rights guaranteed in section 7 [29 U.S.C. §157]: …

23. Labor Management Relations Act: §301, as codified in [29 U.S.C. §185]: §185. Suits by and against labor organizations— (a) Venue, amount, and citizenship Suits for violation of contracts between an employer and a labor organization representing employees … may be brought in any district court of the United States having jurisdiction of the parties, without respect to the amount in controversy or without regard to the citizenship of the parties.

24. *NLRB v. J. Weingarten, Inc.*, 420 U.S. 251 (1975).

25. *Pacific Telephone and Telegraph Co. v. NLRB*, 711 F.2d 134 (9th Cir. 1983).

26. *Southwest Bell Telephone Co. v. NLRB*, 667 F.2d 470 (5th Cir. 1982).

27. Id. See: Epilepsy Foundation of Northeast Ohio, 331 N.L.R.B. No. 92, at 1, 2000 WL 967066 (July 10, 2000) ("Board Decision"); *Epilepsy Foundation of Northeast Ohio v. NLRB*, 168 L.R.R.M. (BNA) 2673, 144 Lab.Cas. P 11,129, United States Court of Appeals, District of Columbia Circuit, Decided Nov. 2, 2001; and IBM Corp., 341 NLRB No. 148 (06/09/2004).

28. *Parsippany Hotel Management Co. v. NLRB*, 99 F.3d 413 (D.C. Cir. 1996).

29. *NLRB v. Unbelievable, Inc.*, 71 F.3d 1434 (9th Cir. 1995).

30. *Horsehead Resource Development Co., Inc. v. NLRB*, 154 F.3d 1093 (6th Cir. 1998).

31. *California Acrylic Industries, Inc. v. NLRB*, 150 F.3d 1095 (9th Cir. 1998).

32. *National Steel and Shipbuilding Co. v. NLRB*, 156 F.3d 1268 (D.C. Cir. 1998).

33. *Hanley v. Safeway Stores, Inc.*, 838 P.2d 408 (Mont. 1992).

34. *Blanchard v. Simpson Plainwell Paper Company*, 925 F.Supp. 510 (W.D. Mich. 1995).

35. *Cramer v. Consolidated Freightways Inc.*, No. 9855657, No. 9856041, No. 9856154, (U.S.C.A. 9th Cir. En Banc), 2001 U.S. App. Lexis 19157.

36. 42 U.S.C. 2000e et seq.

37. Policy Guidance on Current Issues in Sexual Harassment, *Equal Employment Compliance Manual* No. 120 (Oct. 25, 1988).

38. Employee Polygraph Protection Act, 29 U.S.C. §§2001-2009.

39. *Wiltshire v. Citibank*, 653 N.Y.S.2d 517 (N.Y. Sup. 1996).

40. *Lyle v. Mercy Hospital Anderson*, 876 F. Supp. 157 (S.D. Ohio 1995).

41. For example, see Alaska [Alaska Stat. §20. 10.037] and Delaware [19 Del Code. Ann. §704].

42. 15 U.S.C. §1681 et seq.

43. 2001 Federal Sentencing Guidelines (§8C2.5).

44. *Kroger Company v. Warren*, 420 S.W.2d 218 (Tex. Civ. App., 1967).

45. Id.

46. Restatement (Second) of Torts, §§600-605A.

47. *Nipper v. Variety Wholesalers, Inc.*, 638 So.2d 778 (Al. 1994).

48. *Gaumont v. Emery Air Freight Corp.*, 575 N.E.2d 221 (Ohio App. 1990).

49. For an extensive discussion on this topic, see *Caldor, Inc. v. Bowden*, 625 A.2d 959, 330 Md. 632 (Md. 1993).

50. *Ashcroft v. Mt. Sinai Medical Ctr.*, 588 N.E.2d 280, 68 Ohio App.3d 359 (Ohio App. 8 Dist., 1990).

51. *Paolucci v. Robinson Memorial Hospital*, 1995 WL 236743 (Ohio App.) [Unpublished].

52. *Crump v. P & C Food Markets, Inc.*, 576 A.2d 441 (Vt. 1990).

53. Mass. Gen. Laws Ann. ch. 214 §1B.

54. General Laws of Rhode Island Annotated, 9-1-28.1

55. *Williams v. Brigham & Women's Hosp., Inc.*, 14 Mass.L.Rptr. 438, 2002 WL 532979 (Mass. Super.).

56. California Stat. Ann., Labor Code §1026.
57. California Stat. Ann., Labor Code, §1042.
58. California Stat. Ann., Civil Code, §1708.8 (a) and (b).
59. California Stat. Ann., Penal Code §632.
60. California Stat. Ann., Penal Code §653n.
61. Cramer, supra at 35.
62. Restatement (Second) of Torts §652D. Comment (a).
63. Restatement (Second) of Torts §652E.
64. *Aranyosi v. Delchamps, Inc.*, 739 So.2d 911 (La.App. 1 Cir. 6/25/99).
65. *Wal-Mart Stores, Inc. v. Lee*, 74 S.W.3d 634 (Ark. 2002).
66. *Bine v. Owens*, 542 S.E.2d 842 (W.Va., 2000).
67. *Smith v. Bell Atlantic Network Services, Inc.*, 1995 WL 389697 (E.D.PA.).
68. *Johnson v. K Mart Corporation*, 723 N.E.2d 1192 (Ill. App. 2000).
69. *Dietz v. Finlay Fine Jewelry Corp.*, 754 N.E.2d 958 (Ind. App. 2001).
70. *Shattuck-Owen v. Snowbird Corp.*, 16 P.3d 555 (Utah 2000).
71. Invasion of Privacy—Intrusion Upon Seclusion (Restatement (Second) of Torts, 2d. §652B). One who intentionally intrudes, physically or otherwise, upon the solitude or seclusion of another or his private affairs or concerns, is subject to liability to the other for invasion of his privacy, if the intrusion would be highly offensive to a reasonable person.
72. *Johnson v. Corporate Special Services, Inc.*, 602 So.2d 385 (Ala. 1992).
73. *Souder v. Pendleton Detectives, Inc.*, 88 So.2d 716 (La. App. 1956).
74. *Pinkerton National Detective Agency v. Stevens*, 132 S.E.2d 119 (Ga. App. 1963).
75. *Saldana v. Kelsey-Hayes Company*, 443 N.W.2d 382 (Mich. App. 1989).
76. *Sowards v. Norbar, Inc.*, 605 N.E.2d 468 (Ohio App. 10 Dist. 1992).
77. *O'Connor v. Ortega*, 480 U.S. 709 (1987).
78. Simpson, supra at 13.
79. *Clement v. Sheraton-Boston Corporation*, Commonwealth of Massachusetts, Superior Court Department, Civil Action No. 93-0909-F, settlement entered 1/8/98.
80. *K-Mart Corp. v. Trotti*, 677 S.W.2d 632 (Tex. App. 1 Dist.,1984).
81. Johnson, supra at 72.
82. *McLaren v. Microsoft Corp.*, 1999 WL 339015 (Tex. App.-Dallas).
83. *Agis v. Howard Johnson Co.*, 371 Mass. 140, 144 (1976).
84. *Bodewig v. K-Mart, Inc.*, 635 P.2d 657 (Or. App. 1981), overruled on other grounds *Mathieson v. Yellow Book Sales & Distrib. Co.*, 2008 U.S. Dist. LEXIS 55941 (D. Or. 2008), citing *Navarette v. Nike, Inc.*, 2007 U.S. Dist. LEXIS 6323, 2007 WL 221865, *3 (D. Or. 2007).
85. *Olivas v. DeVivo Indus., Inc.*, 2001 WL 282891 (Conn. Super.).
86. *Tenold v. Weyerhaeuser Co.*, 873 P.2d 413 (Or. App. 1994).
87. *Texas Farm Bureau Mut. Ins. Companies v. Sears*, 45 Tex. Sup. Ct. J. 1245 (Tex., 2002).
88. *O'Connell v. Bank of Boston*, 640 N.E.2d 513 (Mass. App. Ct. 1994).
89. *Devis v. Bank of America (1998)*, 65 Cal.App.4th 1002, 1008, 77 Cal.Rptr.2d 238.
90. Fuller, supra at 1.
91. Valdez, supra at 1.
92. Salinas, supra at 4.
93. Saine, supra at 5.
94. *Mendez v. M.S. Walker, Inc.*, 528 N.E.2d 891 (Mass. App. Ct. 1988).
95. Green, supra at 12.
96. *Tarnef v. State*, 512 P.2d 923 (Alaska 1973).

97. *People v. Elliott*, 501 N.Y.S.2d 265, (N.Y. Sup. Ct. Queens 1986).

98. *General Motors Corp. v. Piskor*, 340 A.2d 767, (Md. App. 1975).

99. *Blailock v. O'Bannon*, 795 So.2d 533 (Miss. 2001).

100. Warren, supra at 44.

101. Caldor, supra at 49.

102. *Hampton v. Norred & Associates, Inc.*, 454 S.E.2d 222 (Ga. App. 1995).

103. Smith, supra at 69.

104. *Wright v. Montgomery Ward & Co., Inc.*, 814 F. Supp. 986 (D. Kan. 1993).

105. *Johnson v. United Parcel Services, Inc.*, 722 F.Supp. 1282 (D.Md., 1989).

106. *Uebelacker v. Cincom Systems, Inc.*, 608 N.E.2d 858 (Ohio App. 1992).

107. Caldor, supra at 49.

108. Paolucci, supra at 51.

109. *Rolsen v. Lazarus*, 2000 Ohio App. LEXIS 4466.

110. Mendez, supra at 104.

111. *Tenold v. Weyerhaeuser Co.*, 873 P.2d 413 (Or. App.,1994).

112. *Stockley v. A.T. & T Information Systems, Inc.*, 687 F. Supp. 764 (E.D.N.Y. 1988).

113. *DeAngelis v. Jamesway Dept. Store*, 501 A.2d 561 (N.J. Super. A.D. 1985).

114. *Chappelle v. Robinsons-May, Inc., et al.*, California Court of Appeal, Second District, Division 6, 2d Civil No. B150130, Dec. 18, 2001 [Unpublished].

115. Crump, supra at 52.

116. *Present v. Avon Products, Inc.*, 253 A.D.2d 183, 687 N.Y.S.2d 330 (Sup. Ct. App. Div. 1st 1999).

117. *Kelly v. West Cash & Carry Building Materials Store*, 745 So.2d 743 (La. App. 4 Cir. 1999).

118. *Layne v. Builders Plumbing Supply Company, Inc.*, 569 N.E.2d 1104 (Ill. App. 1991).

119. *Beauchamp v. Eckerd's Drugs of Louisiana, Inc.*, 533 So.2d 390 (La. App. 4 Cir. 1988).

120. *Sullivan v. Baptist Memorial Hospital*, 995 S.W.2d 569 (Tenn., 1999).

121. Stephen P. Pepe and Scott H. Dunham, *Avoiding and Defending Wrongful Discharge Claims*, §2:09 Reference Checks—Defamation In Employment Setting. Callaghan & Company (1987–1991); Clark Boardman Callaghan, a Division of Thomson Information Services, Inc. (1991–1997); and West Group (1998–2000).

122. *Theisen v. Covenant Medical Center, Inc.*, 636 N.W.2d 74 (Iowa 2001).

123. *Dewald v. Home Depot*, 2000 WL 1207124 (Tex.App.-Dallas) [Unpublished].

124. Id.

125. *French v. Foods, Inc.*, 495 N.W.2d 768 (Iowa, 1993).

126. *Mead v. Deloitte & Touche LLP*, 2000 WL 1337662 (Conn. Super.).

127. Theisen, supra at 122.

128. *Sears, Roebuck and Co. v. Wholey*, 779 A.2d 408 (Md. App., 2001).

129. *Morris v. Hartford Courant Company*, 200 Conn. 676 (Conn. 1986).

130. *Koller v. Pontiac Osteopathic Hospital, et al.*, Court of Appeals of Michigan, No. 229630. May 21, 2002.

131. *Vaillancourt v. The Gap, Inc.*, Court of Appeal, First District, Division 3, California. No. A096201. (Marin County Super. Ct. No. 174776). Oct. 15, 2002. [Unpublished].

132. Wright, supra at 104.

133. *Wal-Mart Stores, Inc. v. Binns*, 15 S.W.3d 320 (Ark. 2000).

134. *Sisney v. Sha-Tec Foods, Inc.*, Pottwatomie County District Court, Okla., No. C-89-291 (Sept. 16, 1989), reported in 33 ATLA L. Rep. 74 (March 1990).

135. *Brown v. Dart Drug Corporation*, 551 A.2d 132 (Md. App. 1989).

136. *Olivas v. DeVino Indus., Inc.*, 2001 WL 282891 (Conn. Super.).

137. *Tenold v. Weyerhaeuser Co.*, 873 P.2d 413 (Or. App., 1994).

138. Florida, 443.036(26)(a) and (2).

139. Illinois Unemployment Insurance Act, 602A.

140. For example, see *Cabreja v. Mount Sinai Medical Center*, 535 N.Y.S.2d 149 (N.Y.A.D. 3 Dept. 1988) and *Frey v. Unemployment Compensation Review Board*, 589 A.2d 300 (Pa. Commw. 1991).

141. Hurlbut, supra at 91.

142. *Ray v. Department of Employment Security Board of Review*, 614 N.E.2d 196 (Ill. App. 1 Dist. 1993).

143. *Cabreja v. Mount Sinai Medical Center*, 535 N.Y.S.2d 149 (N.Y.A.D. 3 Dept. 1988).

144. *Hurlbut v. Unemployment Review Board*, 589 A.2d 300 (Pa. Commw. 1991).

145. *Frey v. Unemployment Review Board*, 589 A.2d 300 (Pa. Commw. 1991).

146. *Montellanico v. Unemployment Compensation Board of Review*, 558 A.2d 936 (Pa. Commw. 1989).

147. *Conseco v. Review Board of Indiana Dept. of Employment and Training Services*, 626 N.E. 2d 559 (Ind. App. 1993).

148. *Combined Insurance Company of America v. Workers' Compensation Appeal Board*, 754 A.2d 59 (Pa. Commw. 2000).

149. *Anthony v. Workers' Compensation Appeal Board*, 823 A.2d 1046 (Pa. Commw. 2003).

150. Restatement (Second) of Torts §652D. Comment (a).

151. Restatement (Second) of Torts §652E.

152. Bine, supra at 66.

153. *Garcia v. Aerotherm Corp.*, 202 F.3d 281, 1999 WL 1244486 (10th Cir. (N.M.)) [Unpublished].

154. *Stock v. Wisconsin Electric Power Company*, No. 93-0522, Court of Appeals of Wisconsin, March 9, 1994.

155. *Szot v. Allstate Ins. Co.*, 161 F.Supp.2d 596 (D.Md., 2001).

Chapter 8

The Future of Investigative Interviewing

Key learning points:

1. Investigations of all types will remain important well into the foreseeable future.
2. Those who conduct investigations will need greater legal and technological skills.
3. The safeguarding of the rights of suspected wrongdoers will grow in importance.
4. The public's preoccupation with privacy and its desire to protect it will birth new legislation and regulation.
5. The triers-of-fact, regardless of stripe, will increase their demand for higher quality investigations and better proof emanating from them.

"Inconvenient facts are always the most valuable."

E. F. Ferraro

8.1 Introduction

At those occasional casual settings, where my colleagues and I have a chance to congregate and relax together, the future of internal investigations and the importance of investigative interviewing is often debated. I find it interesting that those who don't use or have never conducted an internal investigation hold some of the strongest opinions. They support their claims or positions merely on what they think they know. Frustratingly, many lawmakers legislate in a similar manner.

283

Instead, my frame of reference is experience. While admittedly not all of it has been good, all of it was educational. That education leads me to believe that internal investigations and the investigative interviews that accompany them are here to stay. They are viable and effective tools. Specifically, investigative interviews enable the gathering of information not possible by any other means. Most importantly, investigative interviews are one of the few forms of investigation that is interactive. It not only permits one to learn what is going on, *but why it is going on*. Other than undercover, no other form of investigation is as revealing. So, while the other methods of investigation may come into and fall out of favor over time, I believe that investigative interviewing will remain the fact finder's most effective investigative tool in the private sector.

As stated in the first chapter, an investigation is best defined as the logical collection of information through inquiry and examination for the purpose of gathering reliable evidence in order to solve a problem. The problems investigations typically solve vary in complexity and magnitude. Regardless of their purpose, all proper investigations must have legitimate objectives, appear fair and impartial, and be conducted within the boundaries of the law. For today's ethical organization operating in the free, industrialized world, these fundamentals have changed little in the past 100 years. What has changed are the expectations of the benefactors of the modern internal investigation and those of the trier-of-fact. Modernity has raised the bar and there is no indication that the future will lower it.

Long gone are the days of the seedy private detective, agenda-driven HR manager, or heavy-handed audit team. Today's fact finders are almost exclusively an educated, disciplined, and professional class. Unarguably, command of current civil and employment law, a strong appreciation for civil rights and privacy, and a solid grasp of modern technology and science are essential attributes of the modern investigator. Recent history has shown that those who have been unable to adapt soon become obsolete. The future will be more of the same.

Foregoing an empirical analysis, a quick look at legislation and case law over the past two decades suggests the modern fact finder ought to conclude:

1. Investigations of all types will remain important well into the foreseeable future.
2. Those who conduct investigations will need greater legal and technological skills.
3. The safeguarding of the rights of suspected wrongdoers will grow in importance.
4. The public's preoccupation with privacy and its desire to protect it will birth new legislation and regulation.
5. The triers-of-fact, regardless of stripe, will increase their demand for higher quality investigations and more compelling proof emanating from them.

Predictably, these conclusions foretell the future. And, when collectively considered, it is reasonable to expect that the net effect will be more structured, technical investigations and the requirement for far more resources to conduct them. Simply put, investigations of the future will be more demanding and more expensive. Let's take a closer look and examine each of these elements.

8.2 Criticality

Private sector investigations of all types will remain important well into the foreseeable future. Because investigations serve a useful purpose and have become such an integral component of so many modern processes, it is unlikely that they will soon become obsolete. What's more, the civil and criminal legal systems of all of the free, industrialized nations rely upon fair, impartial, and professional investigations in order to properly function. Without an alternative means to gather facts, collect evidence, and solve crimes and other problems, modern societies depend on reliable and proper investigations at many levels. The absence of an effective method of fact finding and interviewing, for whatever purpose, is almost unimaginable. That said, internal investigations and the methods by which they are conducted will continue to evolve. The future will likely see all credible societies expand their use and increasingly benefit from them.

8.3 Skills

Those who conduct private sector investigations will need greater legal and technological skills. The societies of free nations understand and respect the rule of law. The laws of the land codify a society's rules of conduct and establish the boundaries of acceptable behavior. As societies evolve, so do their laws. In the United States, for example, we have seen the acceptance of slavery followed by its abolishment by proclamation and constitutional amendment. Years later, discrimination was outlawed with the enactment of the Civil Rights Act of 1964. Continuously since 1964, we have seen additional federal and state legislation protecting the rights of individuals and a plethora of case law interpreting that legislation. By design, law evolves. It is permitted to change as the needs of society change. Therefore, it is reasonable to expect this evolutionary process to continue and that the investigator of the future will need to augment his understanding and appreciation of the law as it changes. However, over time, the law will become more complex. There will be more rules, regulations, and case law to consider. The fact finder of the future will need to know more law and better understand that which applies to him.

Similarly, technology evolves. For several decades, technology has played an increasing role in the conduct of investigations. As a result, internal investigations and the investigative interviews that accompany them also have become more structured and complex. Even the types of things investigated have changed. It is sadly expected that new technologies are exploited almost as quickly as they are invented. To a large degree, the crimes of today rely increasingly on technology. As such, it is reasonable to conclude that the investigations of the future will also rely increasingly on technology. It is reasonable to expect tomorrow's fact finders and interviewers to use technology for more predictive modeling; link analysis, data mining, rules-based crime detection, computer forensics, and, of course, Big Data.

The fact finders of the future will be legal minded and technologically savvy.

8.4 Protecting the Rights of Others

The safeguarding of the rights of suspected wrongdoers will grow in importance. Consistent with the evolution of law is the expansion of the protections afforded suspected wrongdoers. A cursory review of the state and federal legislation and case law of the past 10 years fails to yield a single instance where the rights of the accused have shrunken (some would argue, *Hamdi v. Rumsfeld* to be a vivid acceptation).[1]

Over the years, we have witnessed the birthing of *Miranda*, *Garrity*, and *Weingarten*. These landmark decisions have altered the way fact finders conduct investigative interviews and interrogations, and, to a significant degree, how they *engineer* their fact finding. Additionally, we have witnessed more judicial sympathy for claims of defamation, discrimination, coercion, intimidation, and false imprisonment. There is nothing foreseeable to suggest that the direction of this trend will change. The trend, however, has given rise to a curious anomaly—America's apparent tendency to accept the erosion of individual property, free speech, and gun ownership rights, while seeming to favor the expansion of rights for those accused of serious wrongdoing.

At the expense of appearing to politicize the topic, it seems clear that we are witnessing a cultural shift in morals and values. Among the most disturbing is the growing sense that accepting personal responsibility and respect for the rule of law are choices. Consistent with this mindset is the proposition that those accused of wrongdoing deserve more legal protections—protections that often seem to be rendered at the expense of the victim. Given this tendency, fact finders of the future should fully expect that protecting the rights of those that they investigate will grow in importance.

8.5 Privacy

The public's preoccupation with privacy and its desire to protect it will birth new legislation and regulation. It is no secret that the concept of privacy and the necessity to protect it have become a public preoccupation. What's more, the issue of *privacy* is the perfect political football. Lawmakers of late have recognized that everyone can be made afraid of intrusions into their privacy. Regardless of age, race, color, or religion, everyone can be a victim who needs protection. This absurd conclusion has precipitated a legislative arms race in which lawmakers hastily craft one privacy bill after another in an attempt to out-protect one another's constituents. The result has created a tangled web of contradicting laws and regulations, each with its own set of unintended consequences. The U.S. Fair Credit Reporting Act (FCRA) is a perfect example. Originally signed into law in 1970, it has since been amended 20 times. Today, the FCRA has more to do with employment background screening than *credit reporting* and has long lost sight of its original intentions. While it covers approximately 330 million American consumers and over 150 million American workers, one would be hard pressed to fill a modest conference room with *consumers* who would assert its privacy protections are useful.

Elsewhere, we have witnessed bill after bill intending to restrict the use of Social Security Numbers, names, addresses, and all manner of public records in the name of privacy protection. The effect has reduced the public's access to public record information and made it more difficult to find criminals. The trend is as dangerous as it is irrational. No society can be free, if information is not accessible and criminals are allowed to hide behind a shield of privacy. Given the tenor of today's politics and our preoccupation with the make-believe threat to our privacy, the future will hold more of the same for future fact finders. As such, their work will be more difficult and less productive.

8.6 Higher Standards and More Proof

The triers-of-fact, regardless of stripe, will increase their demand for higher quality investigations and better proof emanating from them. Judges, juries, arbitrators, and administrative law judges of the future will demand higher quality investigations and better proof from the fact finders that come before them. Ironically, it was the Rodney King incident in Los Angeles, California, in 1991 that changed everything.[2]

Because the King incident (and several other instances similar to it) was so vividly recorded on video, both the triers-of-fact and the public came to assume all acts of injustice *and crime* could and should be video recorded. This assumption has created a significant legal dilemma. In another high-profile case, the fate of O. J. Simpson was divined by the absence of any video evidence, in spite of the overwhelming evidence against him.[3] For almost two decades the trend has continued. Not only have triers-of-fact demanded better quality evidence, they have demanded better quality investigations.[4] This is not a bad trend. Any reasonable person who might be the subject of a formal investigation, criminal or otherwise, would hope that the investigation surrounding him or her be proper and professional, and that any evidence gathered would be real and reliable. For reasons similar to those stated earlier, this trend is unlikely to reverse. If anything, the interest in better investigations and better proof should only increase over time.

8.7 Summary

Today's fact finders are educated, disciplined, and professional. Most possess a strong command of current civil and criminal law, and a solid appreciation for the civil rights and privacy of those they investigate and interview. Tomorrow's fact finders will possess more of the same skills. Additionally, the investigators of the future will need a solid grasp of modern technology and science in order to be successful. When all is considered, it is reasonable to expect that the investigations they conduct will be more structured and will require far more resources in order to conduct them. With little doubt, investigations of the future will be more demanding and significantly more expensive.

Endnotes

1. *Hamdi v. Rumsfeld*, 542 U.S. 507 (2004) was a U.S. Supreme Court decision reversing the dismissal of a *habeas corpus* petition brought on behalf of Yaser Esam Hamdi, a U.S. citizen being detained indefinitely as an "illegal enemy combatant." The Court recognized the power of the government to detain unlawful combatants, but ruled that detainees who are U.S. citizens must have the ability to challenge their detention before an impartial judge.
2. Rodney Glen King was an African American who, on March 3, 1991, was the victim of apparent excessive force committed by Los Angeles police officers following a high-speed chase and traffic stop. A bystander, George Holliday, videotaped much of the incident from a distance. Holliday's footage showed LAPD officers repeatedly striking King with their batons. A portion of the footage was later aired by news agencies around the world, causing public outrage that raised tensions between L.A.'s black community and the LAPD. The acquittals of the officers involved sparked the 1992 Los Angeles riots.
3. See Jeffrey Toobin's, *The Run of His Life: The People v. O. J. Simpson* (Random House, 1997).
4. Ibid.

Chapter 9

Improving Results

Key learning points:

1. A successful workplace investigation requires the investment of time, money, and patience.
2. All investigative efforts should be measured. Without some form of measurement, analysis, or critical review of the investigative effort, neither process improvement nor best practices development is possible.
3. A cooperative and remorseful interview is a perfect candidate to provide useful information and input about process and process failures.
4. Before undertaking any investigation, the fact finder must ask: Is the investigation necessary and is there a suitable alternative?
5. It is the responsibility of every employer to foster a safe and productive workplace. Workplace investigations and the investigative interviews that accompany them are essential tools that enable us to make that possible.

"All good fact finders know there is no such thing as coincidence."

E. F. Ferraro

9.1 Investment and Cost Management

A successful workplace investigation requires the investment of time, money, and patience. In addition to all of the other prerequisites, these three elements must be available in ample quantities if the investigation is to be a success. The size, scope, and nature of the problem will determine the amount the employer must invest. There is no formula. One thing is certain, the bigger the problem, the bigger the investment. However, employers can manage their investment in many ways. The experienced employer knows that the issue, which precipitated the investigation initially, is often not the only problem. Frequently, the initial problem is only the tip of the iceberg. Beneath the surface may loom other issues and problems, which may be significantly more serious. The best example is vandalism.

Over the years, I have been asked to conduct hundreds of investigations into apparent vandalism in the workplace. Frequently targeted were the vehicles and property of employees. For years, I handled these matters as routine investigations. And, while I contemplated motive to assist me in identifying a suspect pool, I rarely thought beyond it. Today, I know better. I know now that the vandalism of personal property does not occur in a vacuum. In fact, vandalism is frequently a critical component of a far greater problem—workplace violence. Workplace violence erupts after a progression of ever-increasing inappropriate behaviors is left unmanaged. Research and experience shows that the aggressor is typically a self-proclaimed victim who, over time, morphs into an avenger. One of the less recognized components of the progression is vandalism. Vandalism is an expression of anger; anger resulting from frustration. Instead of focusing on the source of that frustration, e.g., a supervisor, the aggressor attacks the property of the target. Characteristically, the victim's property is seen as an extension of him. Unable to yet muster the courage or determination to inflict bodily harm, the aggressor substitutes the property for the person. Having an acute appreciation for this phenomenon today, I approach every instance of workplace vandalism much as I would if it were workplace violence.

Anyone who has ever conducted a sexual harassment or discrimination investigation also knows that the initial allegations are often just the tip of the iceberg. Rarely do complainants of any type tell the whole story when they initially come forward. Some do this unintentionally, others do it purposefully. Some victims will only tell their employer that which they think they need to know in order for them to stop the undesired behavior or treatment. This is typical in domestic violence cases that spill into the workplace. In other instances, the victim is afraid or untrusting. In yet other instances, the victim may derive some psychological or personal benefit by dribbling out information and evidence. Regardless, my point is simple; more often than not, workplace investigations are ultimately more complex than they first appear. The employer's investment is tied directly to that complexity.

Tip: The amount of effort and investment put into a workplace investigation will be proportional to its complexity.

9.2 Establish Milestones and a Budget

Establishing and using milestones and budgets is a fundamental business practice, yet few fact finders do it. Experienced managers and executives will sometimes insist on it. A contract investigator may even suggest it. Unfortunately, in practice, few ever actually do it. Establishing milestones and managing a budget takes time. It tends to be tedious and often appears unnecessary. Decision makers want to see people on the ground, they want to see action, and they want to see results. As such, this essential aspect of planning is ignored. Instead of taking a little time to chart one's course, almost everybody wants to get started. Do yourself a favor and stop. Take the time to commit some milestones to paper. Even if they are only preliminary, take the time to do it. Put some numbers to them and determine the amount of time and money it will take to achieve your goals. The exercise will surprise you in several interesting ways. First, you will realize that you have actually crafted a *project plan*. The project plan serves as a blueprint from which you will work your investigation. If done properly, you will have identified the incremental steps that when sequentially executed will produce a completed investigation. The second thing that will become apparent will be any actions or steps originally overlooked. It will be hard to complete the exercise without exposing gaps in your process. Collectively, your project plan, milestones, and budget provide the springboard from which your investigation springs to life. The time, money, and resources to be allocated to it are now justifiable. The process enables everyone involved to know what is to be expected and the investment anticipated.

The process is no different if an external resource is used. Similarly, the vendor should propose a project plan with corresponding milestones and a budget. A vendor that does not is either naïve or very unsophisticated. The practice leads to misunderstandings and unmet expectations. It frequently leads to wasted time and money. The employer client generally ends up paying more and receiving less. If you have read the preceding chapters, you will easily appreciate this. If you have, you know it will be nearly impossible to achieve one's objectives without stating them in advance. Without planning, no project plan is possible, no budgets can be established, or is it likely any goals will be attained. It is a recipe for disaster.

> *Tip: Do not engage vendors that offer investigative services if they do not first offer a project plan, articulate milestones, and propose a budget. To accept anything less is reckless and may be fiscally irresponsible.*

9.3 Importance of Measuring Results

The measuring of our investigative results is difficult and frequently impossible. Few fact finders like to do it, fewer even attempt it. Typically, at the completion of one's investigation, the last thing the fact finder and his team want to do is spend more time critiquing their effort and measuring the return on that effort. Frequently, the return cannot be immediately measured. In some instances, the result is more subjective than objective. In other situations, there is no perceived return by measuring the results or evaluating its value to the organization. However, in practice, all investigative efforts should always be measured. Without some form of measurement, analysis, or critical review of the investigative process, neither process improvement nor best practices development is possible. It seems strange to me that we apply these fundamental business practices to every other aspect of our operation and business, but rarely are they applied to the process of investigation.

Furthermore, if the individual responsible for the investigation doesn't measure the results, someone else almost always will. Be it one's immediate supervisor when conducting personnel performance reviews, the budget review committee when deciding the proper allocation of corporate resources, or the criminal justice system, someone will almost always measure the results of our investigative endeavors. It makes little sense that the professional fact finder allows others to determine their value. To abdicate this important responsibility to others makes little professional sense. To obtain the most from your investigations, measure your results.

9.3.1 First Collect Information

Workplace investigations are fluid and dynamic and the fact finder must be creative and resourceful. In the final analysis, his effort will be judged. At the very least, some form of cost-benefit analysis will take place. Whether the fact finder, his investigative team, or his employer does it, some form of analysis will likely take place. Anticipating this, the experienced fact finder begins his preparation from the moment he is assigned the investigation. During the preparation and planning phase, the fact finder identifies milestones and benchmarks by which he will measure his results. During the preparation of his proposal, he will have articulated a measurable return on investment (ROI) and justified his strategy. Like the other professionals in his organization, he has taken a business approach to solving his problem.

Process improvement begins with measuring. Keeping accurate records and measuring one's results is essential to any process improvement effort. Workplace investigations are no different. Depending upon one's volume of cases, here are a few things that might be measured:

- Incident or investigation type
- Number of cases in each category
- Number of cases cleared in each category
- Incident location
- Amount of loss
- Number of employees and nonemployees involved
- Man-hours invested to resolve each case

- Total investment per case
- Number of successful prosecutions
- Recoveries made per case
- ROI per case

Another source of information is the people we interview. A cooperative and remorseful interview is a perfect candidate to provide useful information and input about process and process failures. Though it is not necessary to know why a transgressor committed an offense in order to discipline him, the answer might go a long way in preventing a reoccurrence. The best way to find out is to ask. Here are a few suggestions you might consider adding to your oral statement checklist:

- Why was the offense committed and what was it that motivated the subject to commit it?
- What system or process failures occurred that enabled you to commit the offense?
- What could the organization have done to prevent this from occurring?
- What incentive might the organization have offered that would have possibly prevented this event?
- Why were you initially hesitant in telling the truth about what you had done?
- Why did you choose to be honest during this interview?
- Now that this matter is out in the open, what punishment do you think is appropriate?
- How would you suggest this matter be communicated to the rest of the organization?
- What lessons have you learned from this experience?

Now, imagine the possible answers to some of the questions. Were the subject cooperative and remorseful, not only could the answers be enormously valuable, but think for a moment of their usefulness in the event the employee disputes the discipline he receives and litigates the matter. Wow.

9.3.2 Analyze the Data

With sufficient data, we are quickly able to conduct some trend analysis. Not only are we able to see trends relative to the type and volume of our cases, we are granted insight into the real damage being done to the organization. In determining an ROI, we can determine which type of matters cost the organization the most and which ones deserve more or less resources. The data also will provide insight to where process improvement is possible. If, for example, the data reveal a prevalence of inventory problems, more attention can be focused on the problem. If property crimes are prevalent, yet recoveries are low, new emphasis on these matters can be directed. Over time, the fact finder and his organization can drill into the data and determine the root causes of problems and engineer reliable solutions. With confidence, resources can be allocated where they will produce the most benefit. Remarkably, few organizations do this with any consistency.

The fact finder also needs tools in order to facilitate process improvement. Using a database to collect and manage the data is essential. Among the tools available are those we discussed in several prior chapters. Typically, these services are offered as case management applications in the form of a SaaS (software as a service). These cloud solutions are offered via the Internet. One of the largest and most recognizable is SalesForce. As a CRM (customer relationship management) solution, there is none finer. It requires no software, no maintenance, and is very inexpensive. It is always on and always ready. All one needs to use it is access to the Internet. For investigative case management purposes, my firm, Convercent, offers a state-of-the-art cloud solution as well. Today, approximately 35,000 client locations in 150 countries use our solution. The underlying technology is unlike anything available at any price. It is intuitive, easy to use, and robust. Designed and built for the modern fact finder and those he serves, it is the go-to solution for some of the largest organizations in the world, including our federal government. However, other cloud solutions are available as well. Search them out, ask for a demo, test them, and select one.

9.3.3 Put the Information to Use

Another way to put the information to use is *flowcharting*. Flowcharting is a process improvement strategy widely used in industry. As the name suggests, it charts a process from a flow standpoint. Similar to an electrical wire diagram, a flowchart outlines a process in the form of a schematic. The chart guides the user through a process in a step-by-step fashion and illustrates pathways through which certain outcomes are possible. Cawood and Corcoran do this spectacularly in their work, *Violence Assessment and Intervention: The Practitioner's Handbook.*[1] For the purpose of illustrating the proper handling of the incident assessment and resolution process, they provide readers a detailed incident flowchart. Using the tool, threat managers can easily path their way to one of several predetermined outcomes. Because flowcharts can be works-in-progress, they are uniquely suited for dynamic problem management and resolution, and ultimately process improvement. Think of them as roadmaps. Using a map, one can predetermine a route to most any destination. If one route proves too difficult or time consuming, the user can select another route. Unlike a map, however, a flowchart can be modified. New pathways can be created to any destination. The user is not limited to those offered by a static map.

As a starting point, flowchart some of your basic investigative and fact-finding processes. Keep each chart to one page. Start with the receipt of the report and work your way toward resolution. Use *yes* or *no* options as switches at junctures choices can be made. Use a charting software application like Microsoft Visio˚ to make the task easier. After use of the chart, modify it where improvement is possible. Over time you will have created a collection of flowcharts any capable fact finder in your organization can use. The quality of your investigations and theirs will improve. Moreover, you will have memorialized processes, which will enable the production of predictable results time and again. You will have brought the spirit of process improvement to every investigation you and your organization conduct.

9.4 Alternatives

No analysis of process improvement is complete without asking the basic question: Is the investigation under consideration indeed necessary? Remarkably, few fact finders ponder this question. Professional fact finders, by their very nature, perceive the value they offer by engineering investigative solutions to most problems they are tasked to solve. This is unfortunate and frequently unnecessary. By failing to ask this basic question, the fact finder is easily lured into a possibly expensive no-win situation. Undertaking an investigation when one is not necessary is wasteful and risky. It consumes unnecessary resources and exposes the organization to possible liability. It wastes time and delays an otherwise quick solution. It also does very little for the reputation of the fact finder.

Before undertaking any investigation, the fact finder must ask: Is the investigation necessary and is there a suitable alternative? At first blush, alternatives may appear scarce. However, upon closer analysis and some basic preinvestigation, investigation alternatives invariably reveal themselves. These alternatives may not be suitable, some may be reckless, and others may be simply irresponsible. Regardless, the fact finder owes it to himself and his customer to ponder them. Here a few of the more common alternatives I have encountered:

- Eliminate the suspects through reassignment or termination
- Eliminate the temptation by separating duties or physical access
- Reduce the possibility of reoccurrence by changing processes
- Reduce the exposure by improving methods of early problem detection
- Increasing physical security
- Increasing electronic security
- Increasing employee awareness
- Doing nothing and relying on the intervention of some higher power and luck

Depending on the circumstances, each of these may have arguable merit. Combined in some fashion they, in fact, may constitute a viable alternative to undertaking an investigation. The fact pattern of the given circumstances, the employer's objectives, its past practices and policies, and the law will likely influence which action is appropriate. The fact finder must not avoid these alternatives. He should honestly consider them and offer them (if appropriate) to his decision makers. In some instances, a simple cost-benefit analysis will be sufficient. If the estimated cost to investigate a cash shortage of $500 is $5,000, the decision to pursue an alternative to investigation should be easy. Alternatively, if the allegation is widespread sexual harassment, the decision not to investigate may not even be lawful.

The reader will note that the common theme among the aforementioned alternatives is prevention and early detection. This is not only because it is so intuitively obvious, but because there are no other alternatives. Research shows that the incidence and magnitude of workplace conduct is a function of three fundamental elements:

- The quality of people the organization hires
- The environment in which those people are placed
- The quality of supervision managing that environment and those people

When problems at work are examined closer, it is easy to see what is at their core. Quickly, we see people who should have never been hired. We see those same individuals placed in environments with inadequate controls, overseen by untrained and/or incompetent supervisors. If it is the desire of management to control its workplace and prevent employee crime and misconduct, it should not procure more locks, gates, and guards. It should look introspectively. It should look at the core of the organization, its people, and its values. It has been my experience and I suspect yours as well, that most of the offenders that we have investigated had no business enjoying the jobs they did, and should have never been hired in the first place. Stopping the problem at the door makes sense. Continuing to contaminate one's workforce with individuals who intend to hurt them is the definition of irresponsibility. For just a moment consider the last internal investigation you conducted. If the perpetrator, in fact, had not been an employee, would the offense have ever been committed? Would your investigation have been necessary?

It is the responsibility of every employer to foster a safe and productive workplace. Workplace investigations and the investigative interviews that accompany them are essential tools that enable us to make that possible. Good luck and have fun.

Endnote

1. J. S. Cawood and M. H. Corcoran, *Violence Assessment and Intervention: The Practitioner's Handbook*, 2nd ed. (Boca Raton, FL: CRC Press, 2009), 7, 173.

Afterword

Thank you for reading this book. I hope that you have found it informative and useful. To improve upon it in future editions and any works I might undertake at some later date, your thoughts and comments would be appreciated. My preferred method of correspondence is email. My address is gene.ferraro@Convercent.com. If you have constructive input or a criticism, please share it with me. I will respond personally and will answer all reasonable questions, time permitting.

Alternatively, if you would like to learn more about *investigative interviewing*, attend one of my seminars entitled *The Investigative Interview Method, Advanced Course*. For information about it and the other training opportunities offered by me and my firm, visit our website at www.convercent.com. I hope to see you there.

Appendix 1

Glossary of Common Investigative Terms and Terminology

Accomplice: Criminal cohort or conspirator. One who aids and abets others in the commission of a crime or offense.

Action: A lawsuit brought in court.

Actionable: A matter that may be subject to a legal action or intervention.

Addendum: A statement prepared by an interviewer on behalf of himself, not the interviewee. In it, the interviewer should include information not contained in the interviewee's statement (if one has been provided) or elsewhere during the investigative process.

Adjudicate: To legally resolve and bring to formal closure.

Administrative interview: Interviews conducted for the purpose of gathering information, versus *investigatory interviews,* which are conducted for the purpose to obtain *admissions.*

Admissibility: The legal authority permitting the entry of evidence into a legal proceeding.

Admissible: Evidence that may be formally considered in a legal proceeding.

Admission: The simple admission to the commission of an offense, work rule, or policy violation, or violation of the law. Differs from a confession in that it may or may not contain all of the elements of the offense or crime in question. Not to be confused with *confession.* A properly obtained admission is a valuable piece of evidence in most workplace and private sector investigations.

Affirm: To uphold or establish.

Agency: A legal doctrine in which the legal duties and responsibilities of a government actor (i.e., the police) are conferred to its agent (a private fact finder). The result often imparts rights to an individual (subject) not otherwise available.

Answer: Respond to a formal allegation, normally in writing.

Appeal: An application to a higher court to correct or modify a judgment rendered by a lower court.

Arbitration: An informal means of alternate dispute resolution without the use of a judge or jury. An arbitrator presides over the proceedings and at its conclusion renders a decision in favor of one party or the other.

Arrest: The taking of a person into custody in a manner provided by law for the purpose of detention in order to answer a criminal charge or civil demand.

Attorney client privilege: A legal doctrine that protects certain communications between a client and his or her attorney and keeps those communications confidential.

Attorney work product: Evidence that a party to a lawsuit does not have to reveal during the discovery process because it represents the thought process and strategy of the opposing attorney preparing for trial.

At-will employment: A policy (public or private) that allows an employer to terminate one's employment for any lawful reason or no reason at all. Such policies also permit the employee to quit with or without at-will.

Beyond a reasonable doubt: The standard of proof necessary to obtain a conviction in a criminal proceeding.

Case file: The tool used by fact finders to organize and maintain their records, documents, and reports during an investigation.

Chain of custody: A record detailing those who handled or possessed a piece of evidence. Synonymous with chain of evidence.

Chain of evidence: *See* chain of custody.

Circumstantial evidence: Indirect evidence that in and of itself does not prove a material fact. Often gathered and used cumulatively to prove a fact.

Coercion: To compel by force or deception.

Commercial fraud: Any type of fraud committed against a business or organization.

Compensatory damages: Damages awarded to a plaintiff that are intended to compensate for a loss or other hardship.

Confession: A comprehensive admission to the commission of an offense or violation of the law that contains all of the elements of the offense or crime in question. Not to be confused with *admission*.

Corporate investigations: Investigations performed at the direction of the organization, for the organization. Usually involves the investigation of crimes and offenses committed against the organization. Differs from workplace investigations in that the subject of the investigation may not be an employee or former employee of the organization.

Covert surveillance: Surveillance that is intentionally covert or undetected.

Credibility: The reliability or trustworthiness of an individual.

Custodian of record: The person or entity responsible for record retention and preservation.

Decision maker: The member of the investigative team responsible for making decisions regarding discipline and corrective action.

Defendant: The accused. The party whom the plaintiff opposes.

Direct evidence: Evidence that proves a material fact.

Discovery: The legal process of obtaining information and/or evidence from a legal opponent.

Disparate treatment: Unfair or unequal treatment of an individual or group.

Double-hearsay evidence: Testimony from a person who has third-hand knowledge.

Due process: The collection of rights principally arising from the Bill of Rights that provide criminal suspects protections against abuses by the government.

Electronic surveillance: Any form of surveillance that uses electronic technology and does not require constant human monitoring.

Embezzlement: The unlawful appropriation of property or assets of another of which one has been entrusted.

Entrapment: Actions that might induce an otherwise honest citizen to commit a crime that without the inducement would not have committed. Entrapment is a criminal defense and is not crime. In order to use entrapment as a defense, the accused must first admit he committed the offense.

Evidence: Evidence is any type of proof that, when presented, is materially capable of proving or disproving a contention or fact. In order to be used or admissible, the evidence must be material to the matter in question.

Fact finder: A person engaged in the systematic collection, analysis, and preservation of information and/or facts related to the matter in question. The fact finder is often a member of an investigative team and typically works under the direction of a project manager.

Fact pattern: The collection of known facts associated with or directly related to the matter in question.

False imprisonment: The criminal or civil offense of improper arrest or detainment without confinement, of a person without proper warrant or authority for that purpose by force, intimidation, or coercion.

Fidelity insurance: Commercial insurance coverage against employee theft and dishonesty.

Fraud: Theft by deceit and deception.

Good faith investigation: A fair and impartial investigation conducted by an employer on its behalf. When used to make a *reasonable conclusion,* it becomes the standard of proof needed to justify employee discipline.

Hearsay evidence: Testimony from a person who has secondhand knowledge.

Immunity: Protection against prosecution. Typically granted in order to obtain some form of cooperation.

Impeach: To render one's testimony useless or diminish their credibility.

Inadmissible: Evidence that cannot be formally considered in a legal proceeding.

Intent: A state of mind that, if proved, demonstrates the intention to commit a criminal act.

Interrogation: A highly structured and formal interview intended to yield a confession.

Interrogator: One who conducts interrogations.

Interview: A conversational exchange for the purpose of collecting information.

Interviewer: One who conducts interviews.

Investigative interview: A highly structured interview intended to obtain an admission.

Judgment: A legal finding of responsibility.

Jurisdiction: An area or subject over which a party has authority.

Kickback: Money or something of value improperly provided to obtain something else of value.

Malfeasance: Intentional conduct or behavior contrary to the interests of others. Employee theft or substance would be considered employee malfeasance.

Miranda rights and warning: Legal rights imparted on those taken into custody when suspect of having committed a crime.

Motive: The reason for having committed a crime or offense.

Operative: An undercover investigator.

Physical surveillance: Any form of surveillance that uses people. May be augmented with technology, but requires constant human monitoring.

Plaintiff: The party that brings a legal action.

Preemployment screening: A form of investigation used to verify the identity, personal history, and credentials of an employment applicant.

Privacy, the right to privacy: The expectation of freedom from the unwanted intrusion of others into one's home, papers, or affairs.

Private investigations: Investigations performed in the private sector typically for private citizens involving nonworkplace issues.

Private sector: The realm under the management, supervision, and authority of nongovernment entities. May include public and privately owned companies, nonprofit organizations, and other private institutions. Those not employed by the government are in the public sector. Those suspected of a workplace offense may be the subject of a *private sector* investigation conducted by their employer or agents, and, if determined responsible, punished by their employer.

Privilege: A legal protection that permits the lawful withholding of information or evidence from an opponent during the course of litigation. May be used in both criminal and civil cases.

Pro bono: A term generally used to describe professional work undertaken voluntarily and without payment as a public service. It is common in the legal profession and is increasingly seen in marketing, technology, and strategy consulting firms.

Process of Investigation: A highly structured and sometimes scientific approach to investigation. Sufficiently structured to provide uniformity and consistency yet, fluid and flexible enough to accommodate most any situation or fact pattern.

Project manager: The functional manager leading or directing the investigative process and the investigative team under his supervision. The project manager is typically the point of contact through whom those outside the investigative team communicate.

Public policy: Unwritten expectations relative to one's behavior and conduct.

Public sector: The realm under the management, supervision, and authority of the government. Those in public law enforcement are employed in the public sector. Those charged with committing a crime or accused of violating the law may be subject to the rule of law and tried in the *public sector*.

Punitive damages: Damages awarded that are intended to punish the defendant and serve as a deterrent to prevent others from engaging in similar behavior.

Restitution: The act of making another party whole. Most often, restitution involves the payment of money.

Return on investment: The return enjoyed on any particular investment. The return may be monetary or otherwise.

ROI: *See* Return on investment.

Spoliation: Intentional destruction of evidence.

Standard of proof: The quality and quantity of proof necessary to make a lawful finding of responsibility.

Subject: The individual who is the subject of the investigation or matter in question. Not to be confused with *suspect* as used in the public sector. The subject may or may not be a suspect.

Subrogation: The pursuit of another party one deems ultimately responsible.

Surveillance: The observing or monitoring of people, places, or things.

Trier-of-fact: Any person or body charged with the duty of adjudication.

Undercover investigation: A method of investigation that entails the surreptitious placement of an investigator into an unsuspecting workforce for purpose of information gathering. These are typically complicated investigations and should only be attempted after other means of information gathering have been ruled out. Referred to as UC in the trade.

Upjohn warning: A written warning (typically in letter form) given to an employee at the onset of an investigative interview to ensure that the employee knows that the privileged relationship (should one exist) is between the attorney conducting the interview and the organization and not the employee. *Upjohn Co. v. United States*, 449 U.S. 383 (1981).

Verification and analysis: That phase of investigation during which the fact finder interviews those he thinks are most involved in the matter in question.

Workplace investigations: Any investigation taking place in or involving the workplace. May be conducted by those either in the private or public sector. Typically involving the investigation of employee misconduct, workplace policy violations, or work rule violations. The matter under investigation may or may not be a violation of the law. Not to be confused with *private investigations.*

Appendix 2

Investigations Checklist

This tool is to be used only as a guide. No two workplace investigations are identical; therefore, a single checklist is not suitable for every type of investigation.

- Is the matter work-related and has the organization a duty to investigate?
- If allegations have been made, are they credible?
- Are there any immediate safety implications that must be addressed?
- To who else should the matter be reported?
- Is there a need to report the matter to anyone outside the organization?
- Have reasonable objectives been identified?
- Have milestones and timelines been established?
- Is a budget necessary and has one been decided?

Things to accomplish:

- Identify investigative team members and assign responsibilities.
- Create a case file.
- Perform preinvestigation investigation.
- Identify cast and document cast of characters and potential witnesses.
- Gather and secure any physical evidence.
- Secure personnel files.
- Address PR and the rumor mill.
- Update management and keep those with a need to know properly informed.
- Think *safety*.

Appendix 3

Interview Guidelines

The following tips will help you obtain better, more useful statements:

1. Always use black ballpoint pens.
2. Spell out the full names of all parties involved; do not use just first names.
3. Print your Employee Information Sheets in black ballpoint pen. Make all corrections in red ballpoint.
4. Always print your name under your signature.
5. All statements should state the city, county, and state in which they are taken.
6. Always indicate the last time an event occurred and whether or not it occurred on or off organization property.
7. Check off each item on the written checklist as you accomplish it. Cross out (x) those items that do not apply. Also, complete the heading entirely.
8. Always let the interviewee write his own statement. If he cannot, do it for him, but be sure to state in it that you have done so and why.
9. Write all addendums on statement paper.
10. If the use of drugs or alcohol took place off organization property, but the employee returned to work, indicate in the statement whether or not the employee was impaired at the time he was at work.
11. Sign all written statements and have them witnessed.
12. Treat every interviewee with respect and dignity.

Appendix 4

Interview Guidelines for Management

Introduction of the Subject by Client

> "_____, this is _____ (he or she) and his team recently assisted us to look into (whatever the problem is). They have completed that effort and today he would like to share with you some of what (he or she) and his team learned during that effort. We expect and appreciate your cooperation._"

During the Interview:

> The interviewer will periodically provide updates. Interviews range in length from 30 minutes to over 3 hours. Both the interview supervisor and the interviewers will work to ensure that all interviews are brief as possible. Interviewees will be permitted to take breaks during the interview. However, the interviewee shall not be returned to work without first notifying a decision maker.

During the Oral Portion of the Interview:

> The management representative will participate on tape three times. They include:

> 1. When asked to identify yourself, provide your name, position, and the name of your employer.
> 2. When asked if you have any questions, answer accordingly.
> 3. When asked if you or the organization has made any decisions regarding the subject or discipline, indicate that the organization has made no decisions and will not be doing so until the completion of the investigation. Also indicate that the subject is being sent home (with or without pay) pending any further decision by management.

Appendix 5

Employee Information Sheet

Subject		Date
Interviewer		Witness

Name	#	Information

Appendix 6

Written Statement Checklist

Subject:	Written Start:
Interviewer:	Break Start/Finish:
Witness:	Break Start/Finish:
Witness:	Written Finish:
Witness:	Date:

Check each item as covered with interviewee. Substitute "n/a" for those items that do not apply. If interviewee is unable or unwilling to write a statement, ask if he will allow you to write it for him, which he will sign when completed.

- Complete opening paragraph according to guidelines.
- Document misconduct of subject or other desired information.
- Detail when, where, and the last time event occurred.
- Document known or observed misconduct of others.
- Document motive for subject's actions.
- Document motive for subject's cooperation.
- Document that subject realizes that he has violated organization policy and/ or the law.
- Document that subject understands that because of the above he may be disciplined or discharged (or prosecuted, if applicable).
- Document why the subject has decided to be honest, knowing the possibility of discipline (or prosecution).
- Provide subject the opportunity to add anything in his own words.
- Close statement as a declaration according to guidelines.
- Assure that all present sign the statement.

Appendix 7

Preprinted Statement Form

Statement of	Date:
Regarding:	Phone No.:
Position or Title:	Phone No.:
Interviewer:	Phone No.:
Witness:	Phone No.:
1.	
2.	
3.	
4.	
5.	
6.	
7.	
8.	
9.	
10.	
11.	
12.	
13.	
14.	

15.
16.
17.
18.
19.
20.
21.
22.

Appendix 8

Oral Statement Checklist

Subject:	Oral Start:
Interviewer:	Break Start/Finish:
Witness:	Break Start/Finish:
Witness:	Oral Finish:
Witness:	Date:

Check each item as covered with interviewee. Substitute "n/a" for those items that do not apply. If interviewee is unable or unwilling to provide statement, ask if he will allow you to record it for him and acknowledge it when completed.

- Identify self and state date, time, and place.
- Have everyone else present identify themselves by name, position, and employer.
- Establish that subject understands English and is aware that he is being recorded.
- Establish that subject understands why he is being investigated and/or interviewed.
- Establish that subject is being treated fairly.
- Establish that you are a private investigator and not a police officer.
- Establish that subject is not being imprisoned and that he can leave at any time.
- Establish that subject was not denied use of the telephone, food, drink, or the restroom.
- Establish whether or not the subject requested counsel.
- Establish why the subject did or did not want representation.
- Review the methods of investigation that could have been used and that one or more of them were used to gather information about the subject.
- Review the legal and illegal aspects of electronic investigation.
- Establish that subject agreed to two conditions in order to participate in the interview.

- Establish that you are only an information gatherer, not a decision maker.
- Establish that no threats or promises were made.
- Establish possibility of termination and/or prosecution or other action as appropriate.
- Establish that the subject understands that his cooperation does not guarantee favorable treatment or continued employment.
- Establish why subject has been honest.
- Establish that the subject understands perjury.
- Have the subject identify his signature on his statement and then read the statement.
- Review information provided by subject regarding others.
- Allow client to ask any questions.
- Allow subject to ask any questions or add anything to his statement.
- If interview goes beyond a reasonable length of time, state why.
- Ask subject not to discuss the investigation or interview with others that may be involved.
- Allow client to inform subject of his status.
- Establish that everything the subject has stated during this portion of the interview has been the truth.
- Take statement as an oral declaration, "I _____ declare under the penalty of perjury that the statement that has just been provided by me is true and correct."
- Establish date and time, and that the recorder had not been turned off during the interview (or if it had, why).
- Establish city, county, and state of the interview location, and that this is the end of the tape.
- Recover any organization property in possession of the subject.

Appendix 9

ANY COMPANY
100 Very Marginal Way
Any Town, Any State 92123

POSTINVESTIGATION OBSERVATIONS AND RECOMMENDATIONS

Executive Summary

A five-month internal, undercover investigation revealed an assortment of problems at the Any Town, Any State ice cream plant. These problems included widespread employee substance abuse, unsafe work practices, and reduced productivity. These and the other problems uncovered were the long-term product of:

- inadequate preemployment screening
- poor supervision
- ineffective policies and practices

As in most cases of this type, management's role was significant. However, the following observations and recommendations should not serve as an indictment of that management, but instead augment the continuous improvement process for the good of the organization and the ice cream plant. For the purpose of this report, our observations and our corresponding recommendations have been grouped as follows:

- Personnel Screening
- Supervision and Employee Relations
- Workplace Safety
- Security and Asset Protection

It should be noted that *Business Controls, Inc.* did not conduct an internal audit. Our observations, both objective and subjective, were made during our investigation and the employee interviews that followed it. As such, it is recommended a more detailed examination/audit be conducted at some later date.

Personnel Screening

It is often said that the employees make or break an organization. Consequently, a company's success depends on the quality of its people. No other element more greatly impacts our productivity, competitiveness, and profitability than our people. Effective preemployment screening is the only proven technique to ensure quality people are consistently brought into the organization. In this case, a few of the employees involved in substance abuse and other misconduct should have not been hired.

Recommendations:

- Review current preemployment drug testing protocols. During the course of the undercover investigation, several employees boasted that they were illegal drug users and had beat the drug test. A qualified clinician should examine the collection site and the laboratory conducting the test. Audit periodically to ensure process meets needs and expectations.
- Retain the services of a preemployment screening and background investigation firm. Several of the individuals examined during our investigation had criminal histories, including convictions involving violence and substance abuse. Have each candidate thoroughly screened before an offer of employment is made. The background investigation should include at minimum: a seven-year criminal conviction history (examine both felonies and misdemeanors); a driving record history; and a public filing history (notices of default, civil judgments, tax liens/bankruptcies). Check other states where the applicant lived over the past 7 to 10 years. According to most state highway enforcement agencies, driving histories are the single best place to search for, and identify, a history of substance abuse.
- During the preemployment interview, ask penetrating questions that reveal the applicant's ability to solve problems, resolve conflicts, and communicate ideas.
- Have the current employment application reviewed by counsel to ensure it meets current legal standards and asks nothing unlawful.[1] Ensure the application contains an enforceable release of liability and that it provides the necessary protection for conducting background investigations and drug testing.

■ Provide training to the supervisors, lead persons, and managers involved in the hiring and training process. The training should be designed to augment their interview skills and ensure they are aware of the legal implications of employment interviewing and screening.

Supervision and Employee Relations

The lack of effective and competent supervision contributed significantly to the size and scope of the problem uncovered at the plant. Two foremen were more involved in illegal drugs than managing their employees. As a result, the absence of supervision allowed a substance abuse problem to permeate the hourly ranks and contaminate much of the workforce. Additionally, we learned that it was common knowledge employees regularly smoked marijuana in the company parking lot and inside the plant, and that supervision did nothing to stop it. Also, alcohol containers, partially full or empty, were routinely found in the employee parking lot. In two instances, partially consumed alcoholic beverages were found inside the plant. Employees returning to work with alcohol on their breath was common.

Furthermore, employees were allowed to work at their own pace and produce only that which they wished.[2] Millwrights and mechanics frequently displayed a complete lack of urgency when called for assistance or assigned a repair. Several of them took pride in allowing production to stop while they casually meandered to an assignment. All the while, foremen failed to inspect product and monitor productivity. In one instance, a foreman did not inspect his crew's work until 12 pallets of defective product had been produced. Often, senior employees idled, slept on the job, and neglected to assist or train newer employees. Employee hazing and harassment was commonplace. Often, horseplay led to reckless acts endangering employee safety and product quality. Many of the employees openly criticized authority, while those in supervision openly harassed those who questioned them.

During our interviews, several employees indicated they disliked the company and that safety, productivity, and quality were of no concern. Several interviewees expressed explicit disdain for management and organizational values.

Recommendations:

■ Reassess the qualifications and skills needed for all positions. Take great care when promoting from within. Provide supervisors and managers better training and communicate expectations.

■ Establish performance standards for all levels of the organization including supervision and management. Provide basic training to those employees in need, especially the foremen. Use progressive discipline where necessary. Insist policies and procedures are followed at all times.

■ Hold all employees accountable for their actions (or inactions). Ensure that supervisors and managers are accountable for the actions (or inactions) of their subordinates. Be fair, but be firm. Start from the top, train and inform all the way down. Hold more training and/or safety meetings for all levels.

- Insist that all employees be treated with dignity and respect at all times. Tell employees to report violators and demand an end to hazing and harassing behaviors. Prohibit foul language, horseplay, and roughhousing in the plant.[3]
- Provide alcohol and substance abuse awareness training to all supervisors and managers. Teach the supervisors and managers how to recognize impairment and the at-risk employee. Provide similar training to the hourly employees as well.

Workplace Safety

Workplace safety should constantly be monitored and safety practices reviewed on a regular basis. Safety violations include the failure to lock out while making machine or equipment repairs, failure to wear eye and ear protection, neglecting wet floors, throwing tools, and carelessly operating forklifts and clamp trucks.

- Conduct a safety audit of the manufacturing operation and office areas.
- Recommunicate safety policies and periodically conduct spot inspections.
- Implement mandatory drug testing for all accidents that occur at work. Communicate to the employees that accidents must be reported immediately. Inform supervisors and managers that discipline will result in cases where the policy is not followed.
- Reward safe behavior, punish unsafe behavior.
- Hold supervisors and managers responsible for safe practices of their subordinates.

Security and Asset Protection

Security in the plant was a concern to a number of employees. The plant's location, design, age, and the nature of the business offer significant security challenges. However, there is much that can be done.

Recommendations:

- Better control employee entrances and exits. Monitor visitor traffic in and about the plant.
- Management may want to implement a program for employees to anonymously report company policy/safety violations. The company may want to consider instituting an 800 number to use as the anonymous avenue of communication for such issues or using a professional service like MySafeWorkplace.com.
- Employees should be reminded that incorrect documentation of time is theft and a violation of company policy.[4] This includes overstaying breaks or taking breaks when not authorized. Violators should be warned, then punished if it continues.

Conclusion

While no organization is immune to employee misconduct and dishonesty, management can do a great deal to minimize its exposure, and significantly reduce its risk. That which is outlined above should serve as a start or at least provide some additional insight beyond our formal investigation.

Endnotes

1. It is unlawful to ask the dates of military service or high school graduation.
2. Interestingly, this attitude seemed to exist in the front office as well. The tempo of operations in the office was markedly less than the other locations in which we have worked. There didn't seem to be a sense of urgency anywhere.
3. In two separate instances, an open blade knife and a large wooden mallet were thrown directly at our investigator as he worked.
4. Employees routinely left for lunch without clocking out.

Appendix 10

The Practical Application of Forensic Psychology as an Investigative Tool

In order to fully appreciate forensic psychology as an investigative tool, let's begin with a look into the head of what we shall call, the workplace aggressor.

Avengers and Aggressors

Workplace violence does not occur in a vacuum nor is it spontaneous. The typical workplace aggressor follows a sequence of ever-escalating behavior, called a *progression*. They typically suffer a traumatic, insoluble (or so they believe) experience and project the blame for it on others. Egocentric and often narcissistic, they believe that everyone is against them and that their needs trump those of others. Unable to resolve personal, interpersonal, and work-related conflicts, these individuals sometimes resolve conflict with aggression and violence. What typically unfolds is a progression of ever-increasing inappropriate behavior. Without the help of an experienced clinician or other qualified professional, it is impossible for the typical organization to psychologically assess an emotionally troubled employee and determine his or her potential dangerousness. However, many workplace aggressors share common behaviors and characteristics. They often relate poorly to people, they strongly believe they are victims, and they are obsessed over their perceived lack of control. Invariably, they also have a history of violence, be it of the domestic form, public, or workplace.

Some common risk factors include:

■ Few friends or interests outside work
■ Self-esteem depends heavily on the contribution they make at work
■ Strong sense of injustice to oneself, beliefs, or values
■ A history of personal failures and disappointments
■ Externalizes blame, and habitually projects responsibility for undesired outcomes on others

- Poor people skills, and has difficulty getting along with co-workers and others
- Has a history of substance or alcohol abuse
- History of violence (domestic, public, and at work)

Motivation for Violence

We are a culture steeped in violence. We are bombarded by an entertainment industry that thrives on violent content. Economically, many of us face the threat of a corporate downsizing, restructuring, or layoff. As a result, many are afraid and feel helpless. Some have chosen to accept less personal responsibility while expecting more from others. Much of our society is cynical and angry. In the meantime, the sanctity of the workplace has been challenged like never before. Those who act on these emotions in inappropriate ways fall into several motivational categories:[1]

- Economic: The aggressor believes the target is responsible for the undesirable economic conditions affecting him, his family, or his group.
- Ideological: Ideologically, the aggressor believes that the target is imperiling principles he or his group considers extremely important.
- Personal: The aggressor possesses distorted feelings of rage, hate, revenge, jealousy, or love.
- Psychological: The aggressor is mentally deranged or clinically psychotic—a condition often exacerbated by drug or alcohol abuse.
- Revolutionary: The aggressor obsessively desires to further political beliefs at any cost.
- Mercenary: The aggressor is motivated by opportunity for financial gain. Often he is hired to commit a crime that the avenger does not have the ability or courage to commit himself.

Tip: Contrary to the myth, those who commit workplace violence don't simply snap without warning. Abundant research has shown that aggressors tend to exhibit inappropriate and disruptive behavior prior to committing an act of violence.[2] To the observant, this behavior serves as a warning sign and allows time for intervention.

The visible and incremental escalation of violent behavior, or *ramping up,* may occur over weeks or even years. During this progression, the aggressor becomes increasingly disruptive and dangerous. Unfortunately, experience shows that, once set in motion, rarely does this progression reverse itself or abate without intervention. Even if the individual is terminated, he will often continue to harass and disrupt. In some instances, we have observed that the individual continues the progression at his next place of employment, effectively picking up where he had left off. One of the few things that do change upon moving to another job is the identity of the target.

Intervention

Intervention is the process of interrupting the escalation of inappropriate behavior while helping the subject regain control of his life. To successfully intervene, management must have the will to redefine boundaries and reaffirm its expectations. Upon recognition of inappropriate or disruptive behavior, management must act immediately and put the individual on notice. If a progression is identified early enough, the first warning is usually verbal. Verbal warnings often suffice to cause behavior changes and halt further misconduct. When such warnings are not enough, written warnings should follow. If the progression continues, the aggressor may be referred to the organization's employee assistance program (EAP) or an outside resource for counseling and to help modify his behavior. Managing performance and behavior is called performance-based management. It provides structure to the work environment while at the same time offers the employee choices.

In extreme circumstances, progressive discipline and professional counseling may not be enough. Under these circumstances, termination, temporary restraining orders, hospitalization, or prosecution may be the only solutions available. These intervention strategies require expertise and resources. The deployment of these requires process and a team approach. This group is often called a threat management team. It might include the following areas or disciplines:[3]

- Project management
- Human resources
- Security/executive protection
- Employment/labor law
- Public law enforcement
- Clinical psychology/psychiatry
- Private investigation/fact finder
- Incident/crisis management

Each member of the team has a different but important role. Every member should be familiar with one another and have a firm understanding of the dynamics of workplace violence. As such, they should be carefully selected and have the skill and experience to make difficult decisions quickly. Once the members are identified, the team should meet and determine basic strategies in the event of an emergency. Later, in situations requiring their attention the team should decide preliminary objectives and begin the planning phase. Safety of the intended target should always be considered first. Protection of property, inventory, and equipment is secondary. When the lack of information makes decision making difficult, a comprehensive fact finding effort should be undertaken. One or more team members should be assigned to collect the necessary information. This process may involve discreetly interviewing the target, witnesses, co-workers, supervisors, former employers, or family members.

A professional background investigation of the aggressor also may be appropriate. The typical background investigation includes the detailed research and examination of criminal records, civil indices, driver's history, registration of vehicles and weapon (if possible), all public filings including bankruptcy records, ownership of real estate and, of course, the Internet. Additionally, the aggressor's personnel file (if available) should be reviewed. Treating physicians, law enforcement officials, and other professionals also can be contacted for additional information whenever possible (assuming waivers are in place). As in all employment situations, however, the privacy of all parties should be respected and carefully considered. To ensure that the balance between need and privacy is adequately struck, the team attorney must be consulted during the entire information gathering process.

If the instigator or responsible party is known, it is often necessary that he be placed on administrative leave with pay while the requisite fact finding takes place. In such cases, the employee in question should be interviewed and told that he is not to return to the facility, call the facility, or contact anyone at work, especially the victim, until given permission or instructed to do so. The employee also should be told that a failure to comply with these instructions will be considered insubordination and, in and of itself, such behavior will be punished. The communication might read like this:

> *(Insert subject's name here) as you know, (name of organization) has been built on a reputation of treating all employees with respect and dignity. Unfortunately, it is believed that your behavior has not been consistent with that reputation or our policy regarding workplace conduct. As such, we have no choice but to place you on temporary administrative leave with pay pending a review of our concerns. Allow me to stress this point—you are not fired, but you are now placed on temporary administrative leave with pay.*

Also communicate the following:

> *We expect to complete our review and investigation of this matter in the next several days. We will notify you immediately once we have completed our effort. How might we best reach you? In the meantime, we ask that you remain at home and do not (1) call work, (2) return to work or visit the facility, or (3) contact any employees. However, communications with (counsel, the union) or our EAP is permissible. Thank you. Your cooperation is appreciated.*

Note that the tone is nonaccusatory, yet firm. Already, new boundaries are beginning to be established. Do not engage in a discussion of details or in any way defend your decision. Emphasize that the organization is simply following policy for which there are no options. One might communicate: "Under these circumstances, our policy requires institution of temporary administrative leave with pay. There is no choice in the matter." It is helpful to explain that the action is not personal, but simply a matter of policy. Make sure you obtain any organization property the employee may have (such as keys, badges, computer, access and credit cards) before they leave. Depending on the perceived level of threat and the employee's emotional stability, consider physical security needs. Eliminate the employee's access to the organization's computer system and electronic entry to its buildings.

Upon placement on administrative leave, do not allow the individual to return to his locker, desk, or work area under any circumstances. Any personal property should be obtained for the employee. The employee should not be left alone at any time. Upon providing any necessary personal effects, the individual should be escorted to the front exit and instructed to leave the premises. The individual should be watched until he leaves the property. All building entrances should be secured and the appropriate access control measures should be initiated if not done so already.

Local law enforcement should be notified and a report filed. This is appropriate if the individual has behaved inappropriately and made threats. A protective or restraining order might be considered as well. Also, if appropriate, secure the services of a contract security vendor and notify the appropriate parties at your headquarters and the union, if required.

Dialogue with the workforce is not recommended at this time. Your investigation is still underway and no final action has been taken. It, therefore, would be inappropriate to communicate information regarding the individual in question. However, dispelling rumors and inaccuracies, and resuming normal business operations is in order. A suggested script for this situation is:

> *As many of you know, (insert subject's name here) has been placed on administrative leave. An internal investigation is underway and we are working to bring this matter to a swift conclusion. In the meantime, we are mandating that no one speculates, theorizes, or, in any way, impedes our process. Furthermore, it is unfair to (insert subject's name here) to talk about him/her and what you have heard has taken place. However, (insert subject's name here) has been instructed not to have any contact with you or (this organization). Should he/she contact you or return to the facility, contact _____ immediately. Until this matter is completely resolved, we expect every individual to put this issue aside and focus on his or her work. At an appropriate time and as soon as practicable, we will provide updated information. Thank you.*

Additionally, one should relate that the organization has examined the need for additional security and, for the time being, no further security is necessary (or other appropriate response). Document every action and communication. Script and rehearse everything.

The next step is to interview the targeted individual(s) and witnesses (if any). Obtain statements from those who are willing to provide them. Those statements should include the following:

- The facts surrounding what took place or what was witnessed. If interviewing the target, detail all supporting facts and allegations.
- Identification of any physical or electronic evidence that support the allegations.
- Identification of all witnesses and other possible targets/victims (if known).
- The subject's agreement to testify if necessary.
- The subject's agreement to continue to cooperate with management and participate in the investigation as requested (to produce records and documents or submit to an additional interview).
- The subject's agreement to report any future contact by the aggressor.
- The subject's agreement to keep the matter confidential and not to discuss it or the investigation with others who have no need to know.
- Affirmation that the information provided is true and that any intentional misrepresentations or falsities may result in discipline.
- The opportunity to add anything to their statement they wish.

In some situations, a violence risk assessment or other psychological evaluation needs to be performed. The determination of dangerousness of the aggressor is one of the primary goals of the fact-finding effort. A competent professional (like those described above) with expertise in this area should be utilized for this assessment. If an assessment is to be performed, the individual should not return to work until the results of that evaluation are completed and reviewed.

In most situations, the aggressor should be interviewed before any decision is made regarding his continued employment. A properly conducted investigative interview also allows one to assess the individual and ask questions about his intentions. It is perfectly acceptable to ask if he intends to carry out his threat or if he is capable of it. Employers and their fact finders are often hesitant to ask tough questions. Resultantly, they often do not obtain the information that would most help them or their process. Aggressors often want to talk and discuss their grievances. Sometimes the source of their anger is the belief that no one will listen to them. If given the opportunity, it is appropriate to ask them what outcome they want and how it might be amicably achieved. My team and I have conducted more than 300 such interviews and almost always found the subject to be agreeable to discuss his issues and possible solutions. This opportunity should not be overlooked.

If the aggressor cooperates, also obtain a statement from him. In this statement, ask him to explain what took place and why he behaved the way he did. Similar to all investigative interviews, the interviewer should seek an admission. Inclusive of that admission, the subject should be asked that he acknowledge that his behavior in question was inappropriate and, as a result, discipline up to and including discharge may be appropriate.

If the results of the investigation led the decision makers to decide the individual in question should be terminated, the decision should be communicated to the individual as soon as possible. Circumstances permitting, the individual should be offered the opportunity to resign in lieu of termination. Permitting resignation often allows the subject to leave with his dignity and self-respect intact. Regardless, depending on the circumstances, communication of this decision may be effected via mail or telephone. In some instances, it is appropriate to communicate the decision face-to-face. In that case, the following suggestions are recommended:

- Remember, safety is the first order of business. Take the necessary security precautions and do not leave safety to chance.
- An organizational communicator and witness/notetaker should be designated. The organization's communicator should call the individual and arrange for a meeting off the organization's premises at a designated time. The time and the day of the week will be determined by the nature of the circumstances leading up to the action.
- Prepare a termination notice and a resignation notice with releases.
- If a severance package is to be offered, tie receipt of it to the future behavior of the subject. Plan to indicate that any further inappropriate conduct will result in cancellation of any consideration offered.
- Prepare a final paycheck and any severance package materials.
- If appropriate, contract security should be made available and properly briefed.
- If appropriate, law enforcement should be notified. Call the local watch commander and notify him or her that the organization is planning to discipline a difficult individual, but that you do not expect a problem. Do not go into any further detail. Tell them you will call if assistance is necessary and ask that a patrol car be in the vicinity at the appointed time.
- Upon arrival, the individual should be escorted to a convenient and private area. Once seated, the designated communicator should say in a warm, yet professional tone:

(Insert subject's name here) as you know, our organization has been built on a reputation of treating all employees with respect and dignity. Unfortunately, we have learned that your recent behavior has not been consistent with that reputation, nor has it been in accordance with our policy regarding workplace conduct. As such, and consistent with our policy regarding such behavior, we have no choice but to terminate your employment.

Alternatively, if it is decided to allow the subject to resign, the last portion of the communication might read:

> *As such, and consistent with our policy regarding such behavior, we have no choice but to terminate your employment. However, in lieu of your (pick one: time in service, level of cooperation, historic value to the organization, etc.), we have decided to allow you to resign in lieu of termination.*

There should be no discussion of details or dialogue defending the decision. Stress that the decision is simply a matter of policy. If offering the opportunity to resign in lieu of termination, do so only if the individual also is willing to sign a release. Offer to pay the individual for the balance of the day or through the next business day. Ask that the individual return any remaining property belonging to the organization he/she may possess. If asked, indicate whether or not unemployment benefits will be contested. Indicate that organizational policy will be adhered to relative to the request for references or the verification of employment.

At the completion of the meeting, the now ex-employee should be watched until he leaves the location. If appropriate, law enforcement should be notified and a report made. Again, determine the need for contract security and make the necessary arrangements. Notify the appropriate parties at headquarters. Allow the supervisor of the individual to communicate to his department that the terminated individual is no longer an employee and that he will be replaced immediately (if appropriate). Change locks, security codes, passwords, etc. to ensure that the former employee is unable to gain access to the facility at a later time.

In order to aggressively quash all rumors about the employee and his sudden departure, some dialogue with the workforce is recommended at this time. Final action has been taken and it is appropriate to communicate necessary information to other employees. However, emphasis should be made to quash rumors and encourage the return of normal operations. Here is a suggested script to follow:

> *As many of you know, (insert subject's name here) was recently placed on administrative leave. An internal investigation has been completed and (insert subject's name here) is no longer an employee of our organization. It is imperative that no one speculates, theorizes, or in any way speaks disrespectfully of (insert subject's name here). Furthermore, it is unfair to talk about him and what has taken place. However, (insert subject's name here) has been instructed not to have any contact with you or the organization. Should he contact you or return to the facility, contact (name of appropriate party) immediately. I expect every employee to put this issue aside and focus on his or her own work. Thank you.*

If asked about employee safety, indicate that the organization has examined the need for additional security and, for the time being, no further security is necessary (or other appropriate response). Document every action and every communication. Later, reiterate the organization's policy regarding violence in the workplace and its commitment to maintaining a safe working environment for everyone. Debrief the target and other concerned parties. Ask that they maintain a security mindset and report any unusual or inappropriate behavior or contact by the aggressor immediately.

Debrief the team and determine if any further action is appropriate. Remind team members and employees that they can help protect themselves and their co-workers by exercising the following simple steps:

- Plan ahead and prepare for the unexpected
- Treat co-workers with respect and dignity
- Respect visitors and customers
- Be aware of strangers and of one's surroundings
- Report inappropriate behaviors and activities immediately

Prevention

Though an employer cannot be expected to provide an impenetrable island of safety for its employees, supervisors and managers are expected to do as much as possible to promote safety and prevent workplace violence. Employees can be trained to deescalate tense situations and avoid conflict. Supervisors and managers also can enforce company policies fairly and consistently and allow employee complaints and grievances to be heard. As noted earlier, aggressive behavior is disruptive and dangerous and often is the byproduct of unresolved grievances. Consequently, supervisors and managers must provide employees the opportunity to resolve problems and air grievances. The perfect vehicle is an anonymous incident reporting system or whistleblower hotline. In almost every case of workplace violence in which I have had involvement or studied, someone knew of the intentions of the aggressors. Unfortunately, and all too frequently, those who knew of the impending danger had neither a safe nor convenient way to communicate their information. If your organization does not currently have such a system, use what you have learned in this chapter to make the case for one or seek the professional services of firms like mine at Convercent.com. In summary, organizations concerned about aggression in the workplace should:

- Make a commitment to workplace safety.
- Create practical and sound policies that address workplace violence and aggression.
- Better screen applicants and identify individuals with problems before they are hired.
- Allow all grievances to be heard and resolve workplace problems early.
- Quickly address poor performance and inappropriate workplace behavior.
- Hold supervisors and managers accountable.
- Teach kindness.
- Never hesitate to call for help.

Endnotes

1. E. F. Ferraro, *Investigations in the Workplace*, 2nd ed. (New York: Taylor & Francis Group, 2012), 456.
2. James S. Cawood, *A Plan for Threat Management* (Santa Monica, CA: Protection of Assets Manual, 1994).
3. E. F. Ferraro, *Investigations in the Workplace*, 2nd ed., 459–460.

Annotated Bibliography

ASIS International, *Workplace Violence Prevention and Intervention* (ASIS/ SHRM WVPI.1-2011), 2011.

This Standard provides an overview of policies, processes, and protocols that organizations can adopt to help identify and prevent threatening behavior and violence affecting the workplace, and to better address and resolve threats and violence that have actually occurred. The document describes the personnel within organizations who typically become involved in prevention and intervention efforts; outlines a proactive organizational approach to workplace violence focused on prevention and early intervention; and proposes ways in which an organization can better detect, investigate, manage, and—whenever possible—resolve behavior that has generated concerns for workplace safety from violence. The Standard also describes the implementation of a workplace violence prevention and intervention program, and protocols for effective incident management and resolution.

Black, H. C., *Black's Law Dictionary,* 6th ed., West Publishing Company, St. Paul, MN, 1997.

Provides definitions of basic legal terms and phrases used in various branches of law throughout English and American history. Easy to read and understand and extremely useful to the lawyer and nonlawyer alike.

Cawood, J. S., and M. H. Corcoran, *Violence Assessment and Intervention: The Practitioner's Handbook,* 2nd ed., CRC Press, Boca Raton, FL, 2008.

This book supplies concrete, practical approaches to applying behavioral science to threats of violence in communities, businesses, and schools, and describes how to effectively intervene to preserve the safety of victims. Grounded in the authors' experience in successfully assessing and managing thousands of cases in a variety of contexts and environments, this practical handbook provides a precise methodology for analyzing potential threat situations and taking action before tragedy occurs. The book begins by demonstrating the violence risk assessment process from the point of the initial call and proceeds through the steps that quantify the situation and determine the appropriate response. The next section covers information gathering, victimology, and formulas and tools for risk assessment. Finally, the book explores organizational influences, ethics, security and consultation issues, and laws related to violence assessment.

Collins, James C., *Built to Last*, Harper Business, New York, 2002.

Drawing upon a six-year research project at the Stanford University Graduate School of Business, James C. Collins and Jerry I. Porras took 18 truly exceptional and long-lasting companies and studied each in direct comparison to one of its top competitors. They examined the companies from their very beginnings to the present day—as start-ups, as midsize companies, and as large corporations. Throughout, the authors asked: "What makes the truly exceptional companies different from the comparison companies and what were the common practices these enduringly great companies followed throughout their history?" The book is filled with hundreds of specific examples and organized into a coherent framework of practical concepts that can be applied by managers and entrepreneurs at all levels.

Dempsey, John S., *Introduction to Investigations,* 2nd ed., Cengage Learning, Farmington Hills, MI, 2002.

This is a basic introductory text for college students who are interested in learning who investigators are, what they do, and how they do it. Dempsey has designed a text that gives students a general overview of investigations so they can understand why and how investigations are conducted. This text also introduces students to what types of jobs are available in the investigating industry and what skills are needed to obtain these jobs.

Fay, J. John, *Encyclopedia of Security Management*, Butterworth-Heinemann, Woburn, MA, 1993.

This is a must-have guide for all security professionals, and an essential resource for those who need a reference work to support their continuing education. In keeping with the excellent standard set by the first edition, the second edition is completely updated and emphasizes topics not covered in the first edition, particularly those relating to homeland security, terrorism, threats to national infrastructures (e.g., transportation, energy, and agriculture), risk assessment, disaster mitigation and remediation, and weapons of mass destruction (chemical, biological, radiological, nuclear, and explosives). Fay also maintains a strong focus on security measures required at special sites, such as electric power, nuclear, gas and chemical plants; petroleum production and refining facilities; oil and gas pipelines; water treatment and distribution systems; bulk storage facilities; entertainment venues; apartment complexes and hotels; schools; hospitals; government buildings; and financial centers. The articles included in this edition also address protection of air, marine, rail, trucking, and metropolitan transit systems.

Ferraro, E. F. *Investigations in the Workplace,* 2nd ed., Taylor & Francis, Boca Raton, FL, 2012.

This voluminous work provides both novice and experienced investigators with the most insightful and useful information available on the methods and processes for the proper and safe investigation of workplace crime and misconduct. Gleaned from Ferraro's nearly three decades of experience, the book is designed for easy reading and use—dispelling common myths and presenting new approaches, methods, and strategies. Revised and updated with more methods, techniques, and case studies, this powerful book also includes new diagrams, checklists, and visuals to help readers put the material in context and make their investigations soar. Each chapter begins with Key Learning Points and is supplemented with boxed Tips, Traps, and Common Mistakes. An exhaustive appendix includes a glossary of common investigative terms, sample surveillance and investigative reports, advice on digital evidence, and more.

Ferraro, E. F., *Undercover Investigations in the Workplace*, 1st ed., Butterworth-Heinemann, Woburn, MA, 2000.

As security professionals, lawyers, personnel directors, and corporate executives are confronted by the demands of loss prevention, asset protection, and ever-expanding employee rights, there is a growing demand for more up-to-date information about workplace investigations. This book defines and explores the process of undercover investigations as well as delving into the legal aspects of undercover and the role of an effective litigation avoidance strategy. *Undercover Investigations* makes a rational and authoritative plea for legitimacy of undercover in the workplace. The work is sufficiently detailed as to serve the reader who is contemplating an undercover investigation for the first time, or one who uses them regularly. It contains several modern case studies, statistics checklists, and references making it an authoritative work on the subject of undercover and workplace investigations.

Hall, Edward T., *The Hidden Dimension*, Anchor Books, New York, 1990.

This carefully written work is an examination of various cultural concepts of space and how differences among them affect modern society. Introducing the science of "proxemics," Hall demonstrates how man's use of space can affect personal business relations, cross-cultural exchanges, architecture, city planning, and urban renewal.

Hare, R. D., and P. Babiak, *Snakes in Suits: When Psychopaths Go to Work*, HarperCollins Publishers, Inc., New York, 2006.

Snakes in Suits is a compelling, frightening, and scientifically sound look at exactly how psychopaths work in the corporate environment: what kind of companies attract them, how they negotiate the hiring process, and how they function day by day. The work examines the means of assessing potential targets, controlling influential victims, and abandoning those no longer useful—to business processes, such as hiring, political command and control, and executive succession, all while hiding within the corporate culture. It's a must-read for anyone in the business world, because whatever level you are at, you will learn the subtle warning signs of psychopathic behavior and be able to protect yourself and your company.

Howard, Philip, K., *The Death of Common Sense*, Random House, New York, 1994. This concise and eloquent manifesto shows how the excess of government regulations does not protect Americans, but instead acts as legal quicksand, stifling growth and creating paralyzing over-bureaucratization. Using blood-boiling examples of government regulations run amok, Howard reveals a society in which rules have replaced thinking—allowing law to infiltrate the nooks and crannies of everyday life.

Inbau, F. E., J. E. Reid, J. P. Buckley, and B. C. Jayne, *Criminal Interrogation and Confessions*, 5th ed., Aspen Publishers, Inc. Gaithersburg, MD, 2011. *Criminal Interrogation and Confessions* presents the Reid Technique of interviewing and interrogation and is the standard used in the public sector. This updated fifth edition presents interviewing and interrogation techniques, based on actual criminal cases, which have been used successfully by thousands of criminal investigators. This practical text is built around simple psychological principles and examines interrogation as a nine-step process that is easily understood by the reader.

Khalsa, Mahan, and R. Illig, *Let's Get Real*, Franklin Quest Co., Salt Lake City, UT, 1999. Mahan Khalsa and Randy Illig offer an insightful and easy to comprehend new approach to sales. Salespeople, they argue, do best when they focus 100 percent on helping clients succeed. When customers are successful, both buyer and seller win. When they are not, both lose. It's no longer sufficient to get clients to just buy, a salesperson also must help the client reduce costs, increase revenues, and improve productivity, quality, and customer satisfaction. A great read.

Lewis, Michael, *The New New Thing*, Penguin USA, New York, 2001. As American capitalism undergoes a seismic shift, Michael Lewis, author of the bestselling *Liar's Poker*, sets out on a Silicon Valley safari to find the true representative of the coming economic age. All roads lead to Jim Clark, the man who rewrote the rules of American capitalism as the founder of (so far) three multibillion dollar companies—Silicon Graphics, Netscape, and Healtheon. Lewis' shrewd, often brilliantly funny, narrative provides ahead-of-the-curve observations about the Internet explosion and how the success of Silicon Valley companies is forcing a reassessment of traditional Wall Street business models.

Peck, M. Scott, *The Road Less Traveled*, Touchstone Books, Carmichael, CA, 1998. Perhaps no book in modern times has had a more profound impact on our intellectual and spiritual lives than *The Road Less Traveled*. With sales of more than 7 million copies in the United States and Canada, and translations into more than 23 languages, it has made publishing history, with more than 10 years on the *New York Times* best seller list. Now, with a new Introduction by the author, written especially for this 25th anniversary deluxe trade paperback edition of the all-time national best seller in its field, Peck explains the ideas that shaped this book and that continue to influence an ever-growing audience of readers. Written in a voice that is timeless in its message of understanding, *The Road Less Traveled* continues to help us explore the very nature of loving relationships and leads us toward a new serenity and fullness of life.

Roth, Martin, *The Writer's Complete Crime Reference Book*, Writer's Digest Books, Cincinnati, OH, 1990.

An excellent reference for both the security professional and crime writer. Easy to use, indexed, and with a rich narrative, it provided an excellent resource to anyone studying crime, crime prevention, or simply interested in this fascinating topic.

Sennewald, Charles S., *The Process of Investigation*, 2nd ed., Butterworth-Heinemann, Woburn, MA, 2001.

This book was written to address the needs of the private investigator in the security field, says the author. Continuing in the tradition of its previous editions, this book covers essential topics that are often overlooked in works that concentrate on the public aspects of investigation. Investigative skills, such as surveillance techniques, interviewing and interrogation, evidence, and confessions and written statements, are all discussed and supplemented with updated case studies and examples. Somewhat outdated, this work overlooks many of the nuances of modern workplace investigations.

Stout, Martha, *The Sociopath Next Door*, Three Rivers Press, New York, 2006.

Psychologist Martha Stout reveals that a shocking 4 percent of ordinary people—1 in 25—have an often undetected mental disorder, the chief symptom of which is that that person possesses no conscience. He or she has no ability whatsoever to feel shame, guilt, or remorse. One in 25 everyday Americans, therefore, is secretly a sociopath. They could be your colleague, your neighbor, even family. And they can do literally anything at all and feel absolutely no guilt. It is the ruthless versus the rest of us, and *The Sociopath Next Door* will show you how to recognize and defeat the devil you know.

Toobin, J., *The Run of His Life: The People v. O. J. Simpson*, Random House, New York, 1997.

Called by *The Wall Street Journal* "the pick of the litter" among books on the O. J. Simpson criminal trial, this is the definitive commentary on the most famous trial of this century. Fast paced and breathtaking.

Index

A

abbreviations use, 141
abortion, privacy, 232
accident investigations, 135
accomplice, 305
accused *vs.* suspected wrongdoers, 8
acronym use, 141
actions, 68, 305
ADA, *see* Americans with Disabilities Act
    (ADA)
addressing subjects in reports, 141
administrative interviews, process of
    bulletized summary reports, 138–142
    communication of results, 138–145
    confidentiality, 137–138
    defined, 305
    determining who should be interviewed,
        131–132
    discussion, 135
    documentation, 135–137
    electronic communications, 144–145
    evidence presentation, 147–149
    executives summaries, 142–144
    expert witnesses, 146
    findings of fact, 142
    frequently asked questions, 149–151
    hearsay rule, 146–147
    impeachment, 148–149
    introduction, 133
    key learning points, 129–130
    lay witnesses, 145
    location of interview, 132
    notes, 129
    overview, 25, 130, 145
    preparation, 133–135
    process, 131–138
    purpose of, 129, 130–131
    selection of interviewer, 132
    six phases, 131
    ten commandments, courtroom testimony,
        148
    testifying and preparation for testimony,
        145–149
admissibility, 77–78, 305
admissions, *see also* Confession
    defined, 305
    employee interviews, claims arising from,
        254–255
    false, 89
    investigative interview method, 87, 109–112
    overview, 25–26
    sudden, 150
agent status, 46–47
aggressors, 331–332
Agis v. Howard Johnson Co., 239–240, 269
alcohol rehabilitation programs, privacy, 232
alibi, duty to investigate, 252–253
allegations of discrimination, 253–254, *see also*
    Discrimination
Allis-Chalmers Corp. v. Lueck, 219
Americans with Disabilities Act (ADA), 54
analysis, *see* Verification and analysis
angry nonverbal communication, 179
anonymous tip example, 66
Anthony v. Workers' Compensation Appeal Board,
    272
anxious nonverbal communication, 182
apologies, conditional, 116
appearances
    fact finder, in court, 147
    law enforcement extension, 46–47
    "nothing as it first appears," 61
    of subject, 110
    unfairness and unreasonableness, 46–47
Aranyosi v. Delchamps, Inc., 233

arbitration
  defined, 306
  employee rights and federal law, 221
  example, 16
arrogant nonverbal communication, 179
Ashcroft v. Mt. Sinai Medical Ctr., 230
assault
  employee interviews, claims arising from,
    247–248
  state tort law issues, 227–228
  sympathetic touching, 112, 248
assessment
  investigation checklist, 311
  phase, process of investigation, 27–28
assets, *see* Security and asset protection
at-will employment
  additional cases, 263–266
  defined, 306
  discriminatory discharges, 263
  duty to investigate, 203–204
  good faith and fair dealings, 263
  HIPAA impact, 55–56
  implied contract of employment, 262
  negligent investigation, 243
  public policy, 262
  union and personal employment contracts,
    261
  whistleblower and similar statutes, 262
  wrongful discharge, 261–266
audit, *see* Research and audit method
avengers, 331–332
awareness, litigation avoidance, 276

B

bad decisions, 160–161
Bain the Brain example, 156–157
bank teller example, 243
Bateson, Gregory, 177
battery
  employee interviews, claims arising from,
    247–248
  state tort law issues, 227–228
  sympathetic touching, 112, 248
Beauchamp v. Eckerd's Drugs of Louisiana, Inc.,
    258
Benford's law, 22
bibliography, 299–304
Bill of Rights
  amendments, 197
  ethics, 64–65
Bine v. Owens, 234–235, 273

bipolar disorder example, 265–266
Birdwhistell, Ray, 177–178
black ink, notes, 136, 138
Blailock v. O'Bannon, 247
Blanchard v. Simpson Plainwell Paper Company,
    220
blinds on windows, 92
blue ink, notes, 136
BMW Corporation example, 54–55
Board Certified in Security Management
    (CPP), 38
Bodewig v. K-Mart, Inc., 240
body language
  guilty subjects, 178–182
  interviewers, 153, 183–185
  seating arrangements, 92–94
brainwashing, 53
budget establishment, 291
Built to Last, 53
bulletized summary reports, 138–142
burden of proof, *see also* Standard of proof
  lower, private sector advantages, 49–52
  workers' compensation, 272–273

C

cable company, negligent hiring, 204, 244
Cabreja v. Mount Sinai Medical Center, 270
Caldor court case, 248, 251
California Acrylic Industries v. NLRB, 218
Catanese, Anthony, 160
capital punishment, termination equivalence,
    44
case file
  contents, 74
  defined, 306
  preparation, 96–97
  retention of, 75
CaseMap software, 71
CaseSoft software, 71
cash register tape example, 271
cash stolen verb tense example, 170
Cawood, James, 103, 294
C (corporate) level investigations, 81
chain of custody, *see also* Evidence
  defined, 306
  evidence collection/preservation, 79
  evidence custody form, 81
challenging evidence, 83
Chappelle v. Robinsons-May Inc., et al., 255
charting software, 294
checklists, *see also* Forms

investigations, 311
oral statements, 293, 323–324
Psychopathy Checklist Revised (PC-R), 161
written statements, 319, 321–322
circumstantial evidence, 76, 306
civil procedure, rules of, 36n10
Civil Rights Act, *see* Title VII
civil rights law
discriminatory practices, 223–224
duty to investigate, 222–223
overview, 221–222
claims, employee disciplinary actions
covenant of good faith and fair dealings, 263
defamation, 255–261
discriminatory discharges, 263
emotional distress or outrage, 269–270
implied contract of employment, 262
malicious prosecution, 266–268
off-duty misconduct, 271–272
overview, 255
personal employment contracts, 261
public policy, 262
self-published defamation, 259–261
unemployment claims, 270–271
union contracts, 261
whistleblower and similar statutes, 262
workers' compensation, 272–273
wrongful discharge, 261–266
claims, employee interviews
admissible admissions, 254–255
alibis, 252–253
assault and battery, 247–248
constitutional warnings, 246–247
defamation, 250–251
discrimination allegations, 253–254
duty to investigate, 252–253
economic compulsion, 249
escorting of employees, 251
false imprisonment, 248–250
moral compulsion, 249
overview, 245
precautionary protocols, 249–250
sympathetic touching, 248
classification of report, 142
Clement v. Sheraton-Boston Corporation, 238
closed-end questions, 113
closed nonverbal communication, 180
co-conspirators, giving up, 30
code of ethics, *see* Ethics
Code of Hammurabi, 196
coercion

defined, 306
inappropriate questions, 114
leniency concern, 169
vs. structure and process, 87
cognitive skills, 153, 154–155
collection and preservation, evidence
admissibility and materiality, 77–78
chain of custody, 79
hearsay evidence, 76–77
overview, 76
retention of evidence, 79
spoliation of evidence, 78
collective bargaining agreements
admissibility and materiality, 77
due process, 57n5
duty to investigate, 244
jurisdiction, 219
standard of proof, 127n5
*Combined Insurance Company of America v.
Workers' Compensation Appeal Board,*
272
commissions example, pretext, 263
commitment
honesty, 109–110
management, 9–14, 18
Commonwealth v. Green, 211, 246
communication, privileged, 229–230, 250
communication of results
bulletized summary reports, 138–142
electronic communications, 144–145
evidence collection and management,
80–83
executives summaries, 142–144
findings of fact, 142
overview, 138
"company cop," 40–41
complaining nonverbal communication, 179
Computer Voice Stress Analyzer (CVSA), 176
concerted activities investigation, protected,
217–219
conclusion, investigative interview method,
119–120
conclusions, 329, *see also* Good faith
investigation/reasonable conclusion
conditional apologies, 116
confession, *see also* Admissions
defined, 306
false, 192
overview, 25–26
confidentiality, *see also* Privacy
administrative interview process, 137–138
electronic communications, 144–145

preparatory legal considerations, 209
conscience, sociopaths, 158, 191
Conseco v. Review Board of Indiana Dept. of Employment and Training Services, 271
constitutional considerations
    joint action exceptions, 212–213
    overview, 210
    public function exceptions, 212–213
    search and seizure, 211
    self-incrimination, 210–211
    state constitutional issues, 213–214
constitutional warnings, 246–247
Consumer Reporting Agencies (CRAs), 226–227
consumers, privacy, 287
contemplative nonverbal communication, 179
contracts
    implied, wrongful discharge, 262
    investigator selection, 205–206
    personal employment, wrongful discharge, 261
    shifting of liability risk, 206
    unions, 220–221, 261
    wrongful discharge, 261
convenience store example, 264
conversation examples, *see* Dialogue and script examples
Converscent case management, 4, 71–72, 294, 297
cooperation, refusal, 37, 42–43
copies
    document management, 70
    notes, 136
    vs. originals, 79
Corcoran, Michael H., 103, 294
corporate investigations, 13, 306, *see also* Investigation, process of; Public and private sectors
correction action, 32–33
corroborative evidence, 20, 30
corrupt *vs.* fraudulent data, 22
costs
    cost-benefit analysis, 12, 292, 295–296
    investigations, 13, 289–290
    management, improving results, 289–290
    undercover, 24
Cotran v. Rollins Hudig Hall International, Inc., 36n13, 57n6, 88, 127n4, 202
courtroom
    as destination, 195
    multiple agency and court review, 200–202
    testimony, 147–149
CPP, *see* Board Certified in Security Management (CPP)
CRA, *see* Consumer Reporting Agencies (CRAs)
Cramer v. Consolidated Freightways Inc., 220, 233
creative leadership and rule-breaking, 193n4
credentials of subjects, 97
credibility
    chain of custody, 79
    competence of evidence, 76
    defined, 306
    jury perception, 147
    spoliation, 78
    witnesses, 148–149
credit reporting, 287
Cressey, Donald, 158
crimes of opportunity, 159
criteria-based content analysis (CBCA), 187
criticality, future outlook, 285
cross examination, 148
Crump v. P&C Food Markets, Inc., 231, 256
customer relationship management solutions, 294
customers, 3
CVSA, *see* Computer Voice Stress Analyzer (CVSA)

D

data analysis, 293–294
deadlines, project manager, 10
DeAngelis v. Jamesway Dept. Store, 113
deception detection
    answering questions with a question, 171
    bad decisions, 160–161
    behaviors, 164, 166
    body language of guilty, 178–182
    deception indicators, 169–173
    denials and objections, 165–169
    Employee Polygraph Protection Act, 174–176
    equivocation, 171
    euphemisms, 172
    failure to assign guilt, 189–191
    foolishness, 159
    frequently asked questions, 191–192
    good people, bad things, 156–162
    greed, 159
    guardrails, sensible, 161–162
    guiltlessness and enemy within, 156–157

importance, 159–160
influence of opportunity, 159–160
interviewer body language, 183–185
key learning points, 153
kinesics, 177–186
lack of self-reference, 169–170
liar motivation, 162–165
lie types, 177–178
mistakes, 160–161
narrative balance, lack, 172–173
need, 159
oaths, 171
objections and denials, 165–169
overview, 154–155
prevention, 161–162
rationalization ability, 158
reason to be truthful, 188–189
responses, 168
statement analysis, 186–188
stupidity, 159
technology, 173–188
truthfulness, 155–156, 188–189
verb tense, 170
voice stress analyzer, 176
warning signs, 164
decision makers and decision making
defined, 307
outside counsel, 83
phase, process of investigation, 31–32
removing self, 63, 112
vs. prosecutors, 8
decisions, bad, 160–161
defamation
burdens/standards of proof, 50
emotional distress, 275
escorting of employees, 251
overview, 255–259
precautionary protocols, 250
prevention and education, 273–275
self-published, 259–261
state tort law issues, 229–231
defensive nonverbal communication, 178
deliberate actions, 68–69
Dempsey, John, 147, 148
denials, *see also* Deception detection
intensity profiles, 191–192
overview, 165–169
simple, 178
deserving of treatment, victims, 191
destruction, case files and notes, 75, 112, 136, 138
Devis v. Bank of America, 243

Dewald v. Home Depot, 260–261, 263
dialogue and script examples
administrative interviews, 133
admission, 109, 111
confidentiality, electronic communications, 145
discussion, 113
documentation accuracy, 137
failure to assign guilt, 190–191
handling denials, 167, 169
intervention, motivation for violence, 334–335, 337–338
interview guidelines for management, 315
introductions, 104
lack of narrative balance, 172
oral statements, 324
presentation, 106–108, 133–135
diaries, 71, *see also* Notes
Dietz v. Finlay Fine Jewelry Corp., 235
digital images as evidence, 84–85
dignity
administrative interviews, 138
treating subjects with, 59, 276
diminishing actions, 110
direct evidence, 76, 307
direct examination, 148
directive questions, 113
disabilities, 237, 265–266
disbursement, disciplinary/correction action phase, 32–33
discharge, *see* Wrongful discharge
disciplinary actions, claims from
covenant of good faith and fair dealings, 263
defamation, 255–261
discriminatory discharges, 263
emotional distress or outrage, 269–270
implied contract of employment, 262
malicious prosecution, 266–268
off-duty misconduct, 271–272
overview, 255
personal employment contracts, 261
public policy, 262
self-published defamation, 259–261
unemployment claims, 270–271
union contracts, 261
whistleblower and similar statutes, 262
workers' compensation, 272–273
wrongful discharge, 261–266
disciplinary/corrective actions
hearsay, refusal to consider, 84
motives, 37, 49, 56

phases, process of investigation, 32–33
public *vs.* private sector, 43–44
discrimination
    allegations, 253–254
    BMW example, 54–55
    Civil Rights Act, 221–224
    Dollar General example, 54–55
    duty to investigate, 244
    employee interviews, claims arising from,
        253–254
    evidentiary burdens and standards, 199–200
    jurisdiction, 199
    lower burden of proof, 49, 50
    multiple agency and court review, 201
    practices, civil rights law, 223–224
    searches, 224
    shifting burdens, 50
    wrongful discharge, 263
discussions
    administrative interview process, 135
    investigative interview method, 112–114
distancing self from offense, 165
distractions, human foibles, 160
distress, *see* Emotional distress or outrage
document management
    administrative interview process, 135–137
    organization, 70–71
    overview, 70
    precautionary protocols, 249–250
    preparatory legal considerations, 208–209
    technology, 71–75
Dollar General example, 54–55
double-hearsay evidence, 76, 307
draft reports, 138
dress, professional, 95
drug distribution operation example, 17
drug rehabilitation programs, privacy, 232
due process
    defined, 307
    information gathering and fact finding
        phase, 29
    public *vs.* private sector, 37, 45–47
duty to investigate
    an alibi, 252–253
    civil rights law, 222–223
    implicit and explicit, 244–245
    preparatory legal considerations, 202–205

E

economic compulsion, 249

education, *see* Prevention and education;
        Training
EEOC, *see* Equal Employment Opportunity
        Commission (EEOC)
"Effective Program to Prevent and Detect
        Violations of Law," 227
electronic methods
    communications, 144–145
    investigative interviews, 126
    surveillance, 20, 307
elements, administrative statement, 137
elements, successful investigations
    lawful execution, 18
    management commitment, 9–14, 18
    meaningful objectives, 14–16
    overview, 9
    resources, properly pooled, 17–18
    well-conceived strategy, 16–17
emails, *see* Electronic methods
embezzlement example, pretext, 263
emotional distress or outrage
    claims, employee disciplinary action,
        269–270
    negligent investigation, 242
    prevention and education, 275
    state tort law issues, 220, 239–242
employee handbooks, 263–264
Employee Polygraph Protection Act (EPPA)
    case file retention, 75
    employee rights and federal law, 224–226
    overview, 174–176
employees
    dignity, 59, 138, 276
    empowerment myth, 53
    escorting, 251
    as fact finders/interviewers, 205
    information sheet form, 317
    lunch without clocking out, 329n4
    motives, 37, 49, 56
    postinvestigation observations/
        recommendations, 327–328
    prosecution as objective, 35
    refusal to cooperate, 37, 42–43
    rights and protections, private sector, 55–56
employees, claims arising from disciplinary
        action
    covenant of good faith and fair dealings,
        263
    defamation, 255–261
    discriminatory discharges, 263
    emotional distress or outrage, 269–270
    implied contract of employment, 262

malicious prosecution, 266–268
off-duty misconduct, 271–272
overview, 255
personal employment contracts, 261
public policy, 262
self-published defamation, 259–261
unemployment claims, 270–271
union contracts, 261
whistleblower and similar statutes, 262
workers' compensation, 272–273
wrongful discharge, 261–266
employees, claims arising from interviews
admissible admissions, 254–255
alibis, 252–253
assault and battery, 247–248
constitutional warnings, 246–247
defamation, 250–251
discrimination allegations, 253–254
duty to investigate, 252–253
economic compulsion, 249
escorting of employees, 251
false imprisonment, 248–250
moral compulsion, 249
overview, 245
precautionary protocols, 249–250
sympathetic touching, 248
employees, rights and federal law
arbitration, 221
civil rights law, 221–224
discriminatory practices, 223–224
duty to investigate, 222–223
Employee Polygraph Protection Act,
      224–226
Fair Credit Reporting Act, 226–227
federal preemption and state tort actions,
      219–220
federal sentencing guidelines, 227
federal statutes, 224–227
labor practices, unfair, 214
overview, 214
protected concerted activities investigation,
      217–219
union contract restrictions, 220–221
union representation, 215–216
employers, *see* Organizations
employment, wrongful discharge, 261–262
"employment purposes," FCRA, 226
empowerment myth, 53
entrapment
defined, 307
motive of offender, 48–49
overview, 37, 47–48

preexisting misconduct, 48
envelope with cash example, 165
envy, 159
EPPA, *see* Employee Polygraph Protection Act
      (EPPA)
Equal Employment Opportunity Commission
      (EEOC), 54, 75, 198, 222
equivocation, 171
escalating behavior, 331
ethics, 63–67, 227
euphemisms, 172
evasive nonverbal communication, 178
ever-escalating behavior, 331
evidence, *see also* Chain of custody
admissibility and materiality, 77–78
asking to see, 163–164
chain of custody, 79
challenging, 82–83
circumstantial, 76
collection and preservation, 76–80
communicating results, 80–83
corroborative, 20, 30
custody form, 81
defined, 59, 76, 307
digital images, 84–85
direct, 307
documentation, 70–75
double-hearsay, 76, 307
exaggeration, 110
exculpatory, 64
hearsay, 76–77, 307
images, 84–85
improperly obtained, 47
indirect, 76
innocent people, 163
lower burden of proof, 50
notes as, 84
organization, 70–71
overview, 69–70, 76
preponderance of, 50
presentation, 147–149
recovering physical from interviewee, 125
reporting and communicating results,
      80–83
retention, 79
spoliation, 78
storage, 79
technology, 71–75
tracking form, 80
truthfulness, 68
weighted, 77
evidentiary burdens and standards, 199–200

exaggeration, 178
exclusionary doctrine, constitutional
         considerations, 210
exculpatory evidence, 64
execution, lawful, 18
executive summaries
    communication of results, 142–144
    postinvestigation observations/
         recommendations, 325–326
exhibits in reports, 139
expansion questions, 113
experience
    misconduct and malfeasance, 9
    professional interviewer qualities, 61–62
expert witnesses, 146

F

fabrication, 178
fact finders, *see also* Interviewers; Investigative
         interviewers; Professional
         interviewers
    active listeners, 154
    attitude, 276
    characteristics, 284, 286
    claims arising from employee interviews,
         245
    defined, 307
    discipline, 32
    future trends, 283–288
    impartiality, 59
    objectives define purpose, 14
    overview, 2
    precautionary protocols, 249–250
    process of investigation, 1, 8
    providing recommendations, 84
    vs. investigators, 8
fact finding, *see also* Information gathering and
         fact finding
    legal challenges and litigation avoidance,
         209
    overview, 2
    phases, process of investigation, 28–30
    rights of others, 286
fact pattern, 189, 307
failure to assign guilt, 189–191
Fair Credit Reporting Act (FCRA), 226–227
fair dealings, *see* Good faith and fair dealings
fairness, 67–68
false confessions, 192
false imprisonment and false arrest
    admissible admissions, 254

defined, 307
economic compulsion, 249
fact finder/interviewer misconduct, 206
moral compulsion, 249
overview, 248–249
precautionary protocols, 249–250
state tort law issues, 228
false light invasion of privacy
    emotional distress, 275
    prevention and education, 273–275
falsity, 275
Family and Medical Leave Act (FMLA), 54
FCRA, *see* Fair Credit Reporting Act (FCRA);
         U.S. Fair Credit Reporting Act
         (FCRA)
fear, cause for lying, 165
federal preemption and state tort actions,
         219–220
federal sentencing guidelines, 227
federal statutes
    Employee Polygraph Protection Act,
         224–226
    Fair Credit Reporting Act, 226–227
    federal sentencing guidelines, 227
fetal body language, 180, 187
Fifth Amendment (US Constitution), 210
final questions, 113
findings of fact communication, 142
*First Break all the Rules: What the World's
         Greatest Managers Do Differently,*
         193n4
first impression, 243
first person, reports, 142
fishing expedition example, 131
flexibility, 16–17
flowcharting, 294–295
FMLA, *see* Family and Medical Leave Act
         (FMLA)
food, 264
foolishness, good people, 159
footers in reports, 141
footnotes in reports, 139, 141
forensic analysis, investigation methods, 22–24
forensic psychology application
    avengers and aggressors, 331–332
    intervention, 333–339
    motivation for violence, 332–339
    prevention, 339
forged payroll checks example, 232
forms, *see also* Checklists
    employee information sheet, 317
    preprinted, for statements, 321–322

Foster, D. Glenn, 177
Fourth Amendment (US Constitution), 42,
      210, 237–238, *see also* Search and
      seizure
fraudulent *vs.* corrupt data, 22
French v. Foods, Inc., 264
frequently asked questions
   administrative interviews and
         communicating results, 149–151
   deception detection, objections, and denials,
         191–192
   interviewing, 84–85
   investigative interview method, 121–126
   process of investigation, 34–35
   public and private sector differences, 56–57
Frey v. Unemployment Review Board, 271
Fuller court case, 222, 244
furniture placement, 92
future outlook
   additional proof, 287
   criticality, 285
   higher standards, 287
   key learning points, 283
   overview, 283–385
   privacy, 286–287
   protecting, rights of others, 286
   skills, 285–286
   summary, 288

G

gang example, 62
Garcia v. Aerotherm Corp., 273–274
Garrity court case, 286
Gaumont v. Emery Air Freight Corp., 230
General Motors Corp. v. Piskor, 247
genesis, process of investigation, 2–3
giving up co-conspirators, 30
glossary, 305–310
"good cop/bad cop," 101
good faith and fair dealings, 263
good faith investigation/reasonable conclusion
   court case, 127
   defined, 307
   evidentiary burdens and standards, 202
   information gathering/fact finding, 29
   lower burden of proof, 49
   overview, 57n6
   private sector, 195
good people
   bad decisions and mistakes, 160–161
   foolishness, 159

greed, 159
guardrails, sensible, 161–162
guiltlessness and enemy within, 156–157
   importance, 159–160
   influence of opportunity, 159–160
   need, 159
   prevention, 161–162
   rationalization ability, 158
   stupidity, 159
government abuse and intrusions, *see* Bill of
      Rights
grand jury
   conduct of, 57n1
   lack of availability, 19
   public sector advantages, 42–43
greed, 159
Greenbaum v. Brooks, 206
guarded nonverbal communication, 178
guardrails, sensible, 64, 161–162
guidelines for interviews, *see also* Interviews and
      interviewing
   general, 103, 313
   management, 105, 315
guiltiness, body language, 178–182
guiltlessness and enemy within, 156–157

H

habeas corpus petition, 288n1
Hall, Edward T., 94
Hallcrest Report II, 36n8
Hamdi v. Rumsfeld, 286, 288n1
Hammurabi (King), 196
Hampton v. Norred & Associates, Inc., 248
handbooks, employee, 263–264
Hanley v. Safeway Stores, Inc., 219
harassment, duty to investigate, 244
Hare, Robert D., 161
head movement nonverbal communication, 185
Health Insurance Portability and
      Accountability Act (HIPPA), 55
hearsay, *see also* Evidence
   collection/preservation, 76–77
   defined, 307
   double-hearsay, 76, 307
   refusal to consider, 84
   testifying and testimony preparation,
         146–147
heavy objects, 92
high school graduation, 329n1
Hill v. National Collegiate Athletic Association,
      214

HIPAA, *see* Health Insurance Portability and
    Accountability Act (HIPPA)
historical perspectives, 38–39
hold-harmless agreement, 32–33
holiday interruptions, 10–11
Holliday, George, 288n2
Hollywood Detectives, 2
home, as interview location, 95
honesty, *see* Truthfulness
*Horsehead Resource Development Company v.
    NLRB,* 217–218
hospital janitor example, 270
hotel example, 217–219
Howard, Philip, 55
human foibles, 160–161
Human Resources Department
    as interviewers, 60–61, 62
    as witnesses, 101
humor, 110
Hurlbut v. Unemployment Review Board, 271

I

IBM Corporation, 45
"I don't know" reply, 169
ignorant questions, 114
illegal drugs
    investigation examples, 77, 220
    law enforcement agent, 48
    preexistent misconduct, 48
    public *vs.* private sector, 44
    testing, privacy violation, 214
    videotaping, 233
illiteracy, privacy, 232
illnesses, 10
I2M, *see* Investigative interview method (I2M)
images as evidence, 84–85
impartiality, 59, 63
impatience, 17–18
impeach and impeachment, 148–149, 307
implied contract of employment, 262
importance, good people, 159–160
improperly obtained evidence, 47
inadmissible, 307, *see also* Admissibility
inappropriate questions, 114, 241–242
indirect evidence, 76
industry standards, changing, 4
influence of opportunity, 159–160
information
    bad, human foibles, 160
    collection, measuring results, 292–293
    measuring results, importance, 294–295

"might be useful," 133–134
    retention, 75, 79
information gathering and fact finding, *see also*
    Fact finding
    investigative interviewing, 60
    legal challenges and litigation avoidance,
        209
    phase, process of investigation, 28–30
innocent people
    asking to *see* evidence, 163
    intensity profile of denial, 191–192
innumeracy, 160–161
in personam jurisdiction, 197, *see also*
    Jurisdiction
inside counsel, 82
insubordination, 37, 42–43
integrity, 156, 167
interactivity
    electronic surveillance, 20
    interviews, 26
    physical surveillance, 19
    undercover investigations, 26
internal audit, 20–22
interpreters, language barriers, 102–103
interrogation
    defined, 308
    negative connotations, 25, 57
    process of investigation, 7–8
    vs. investigative interviews, 7–8, 25, 87,
        88–89
intervention, violence, 333–339
interviewees, *see also* Subjects
    fact finder's final report, 150–151
    interviewer's notes, 150
    non-employees, 122–123
    notification of interview, 121
    oral statements, 117–119, 323–324
    recovering physical evidence from, 125
    selection of, 91–92, 131–132
    sudden admission of wrongdoing, 150
    taking notes v. recording, 149
    union representation, 56, 215–216
    written statements, 114, 115–117, 319,
        321–322
interviewers, *see also* Fact finders; Investigators;
    Professional interviewers
    body language, 183–185
    characteristics, 87, 95
    defined, 308
    future trends, 283–288
    handling sudden admission to wrongdoing,
        150

method questioning, 150
misconduct by, 205–206
notes, 150
preparation, 95–96
props, using, 125
qualities, 60–69, 87
seating arrangements, 92–93, 102
selection, 95–96, 132
time management, 95–96
interviews and interviewing, *see also*
       Administrative interviews;
       Investigations
admissibility and materiality, 77–78
admissions, 254–255
alibis, 252–253
assault and battery, 247–248
chain of custody, 79
collection and preservation, 76–80
constitutional warnings, 246–247
defamation, 250–251
defined, 308
deliberate actions, 68–69
discrimination allegations, 253–254
documentation, 70–75
duty to investigate, 252–253
economic compulsion, 249
escorting of employees, 251
ethics, 63–67
evidence, 69–83
experience, 61–62
fairness, 67–68
false imprisonment, 248–250
frequently asked questions, 84–85
guidelines, 103, 105, 313, 315
hearsay evidence, 76–77
impartiality, 63
investigation methods, 25–26
key learning points, 59
moral compulsion, 249
non-employees, 122–123
organization, 70–71
overview, 70, 245
precautionary protocols, 249–250
qualities of professional interviewer, 60–69
reporting and communicating results,
    80–83
retention of evidence, 79
role of interviewer, 60
skills, 61
spoliation of evidence, 78
summary, 83–84
sympathetic touching, 248

technology, 71–75
intimidation, 87, 114
introduction
    administrative interview process, 133
    investigative interview method, 104–105
invasion of privacy
    common law right of privacy, 233–239
    false light, 233–235
    intrusion upon seclusion, 236–239
    overview, 231–232
    publication of a private fact, 235–236
    state statutes, 232–233
investigation, process of
    assessment phase, 27–28
    checklist, 311
    decision makers and decision making, 8,
        31–32
    defined, 1, 309
    disbursement of disciplinary and/or
        corrective action phase, 32–33
    electronic surveillance, 20
    established process, 34
    fact finders, 8
    flexibility, 16–17
    forensic analysis, 22–24
    frequently asked questions, 34–35
    genesis of process, 2–3
    information gathering and fact finding
        phase, 28–30
    interrogation, 7–8
    interviews, 25–26
    investigators, 8
    key learning points, 1
    lawful execution, 18
    management commitment, 9–14, 18
    meaningful objectives, 14–16
    methods of, 19–26
    misconduct *vs.* malfeasance, 9
    overstructured, 16–17
    overview, 1, 3–6, 33–34
    phases of, 26–33
    physical surveillance, 19–20
    preparation and planning phase, 28
    prevention and education phase, 33
    prosecutors, 8
    research and internal audit, 20–22
    resources, properly pooled, 17–18
    subjects, 6–7
    successful, 1, 9–18, 289–290
    summary, 33–34
    suspected wrongdoers, 8
    terminology, 5–9

undercover, 24–25
verification and analysis phase, 30–31
well-conceived strategy, 16–17
Investigations in the Workplace, 34, 193n5
investigative discourse analysis, 187–188
investigative interview method (I2M)
    admission, 109–112
    advantages, 88–89
    conclusion, 119–120
    conducting electronically, 126
    defined, 59, 308
    discussion, 112–114
    frequently asked questions, 121–126
    interrogation differentiation, 7–8, 88–89
    introduction, 104–105
    key learning points, 87
    oral statements, 117–119
    phases, 89–120
    preparation, 90–103
    presentation, 105–109
    summary, 120
    training, 192
    written statements, 115–117
investigative task list, 69
investigative teams, 61
investigators, *see also* Fact finders; Interviewers;
    Professional interviewers
    contract fact finder/interviewers, 205–206
    contractual shifting of liability risk, 206
    effect on welfare of others, 64
    employee fact finder/interviewers, 205
    future trends, 283–288
    misconduct by, 205–206
    misconduct liability, 205–206
    overview, 205
    process of investigation, 8
    vs. fact finders, 8
investment, improving results, 289–290

J

jewelry clerk example, 235
John (King of England), 196
Johnson v. Corporate Special Services, Inc., 236,
    238
Johnson v. K Mart Corporation, 235, 238
Johnson v. United Parcel Services, Inc., 249
joint action exceptions, 212–213
joking around, 110
journal entries, 71, *see also* Notes
jurisdiction
    evidentiary burdens and standards, 199–200

multiple agency and court review, 200–202
origin history of law, 196–197
overview, 196
workplace investigations, 197–199
Justianian Code, 196

K

Kelley v. Stop & Shop Companies, Inc., 207
*Kelly v. West Cash & Carry Building Materials
    Store,* 257–258
key learning points
    administrative interviews and
        communicating results, 129–130
    deception detection, objections, and denials,
        153
    future outlook, 283
    improving results, 289
    interviewing, 59
    investigative interview method, 87
    legal challenges and litigation avoidance,
        195
    process of investigation, 1
    public and private sector differences, 37–38
kickbacks
    defined, 308
    example, 12
    negligent investigation, 242
kinemes, 178
kinesics
    body language of guilty, 178–182
    interviewer body language, 183–185
    lie types, 177–178
    overview, 177
    statement analysis, 186–188
King, Rodney, 287, 288n2
King John (England), 196
K-Mart Corp. v. Trotti, 238–239
knickknacks, 92
knocking on door, 104
Koller v. Pontiac Osteopathic Hospital, et. al.,
    265
Kroger Company v. Warren, 228, 247, 248
Krout and Schneider, Inc., 2, 52

L

Labor Management Relations Act (LMRA),
    214, 219–220
labor practices, unfair, 214
lack of narrative balance, 172–173
lack of self-reference, 169–170

language barriers, 102–103
law
    defined, 195
    future trends, 285
    historical developments, 196–197
    limiting behavior *vs.* punishment, 159
law enforcement
    polygraphs, 173–174
    public *vs.* private sector, 37, 39–41
    terminology, 141
lawful execution, 18
lawyers, 56, 81–83, *see also* Union
Layne v. Builders Plumbing Supply Company,
    Inc., 258
lay witnesses, 129, 145
leading questions, 113
legal challenges and litigation avoidance
    admissible admissions, 254–255
    alibis, 252–253
    arbitration, 221
    assault and battery, 227–228, 247–248
    awareness, 276
    civil rights law, 221–224
    common law right of privacy, 233–239
    confidentiality, 209
    constitutional considerations/warnings,
        210–214, 246–247
    contract fact finders/interviewers, 205–206
    contractual shifting of liability risk, 206
    defamation, 229–231, 250–251, 255–261,
        273–275
    discrimination, 223–224, 253–254, 263
    documentation control, 208–209
    duty to investigate, 202–205, 222–223,
        244–245, 252–253
    economic compulsion, 249
    emotional distress/outrage, 239–242,
        269–270, 275
    employee dignity, 276
    employee disciplinary action, 255–273
    employee fact finders/interviewers, 205
    employee interviews, 245–255
    Employee Polygraph Protection Act,
        224–226
    employee rights and federal law, 214–227
    escorting of employees, 251
    evidentiary burdens and standards, 199–200
    Fair Credit Reporting Act, 226–227
    false imprisonment/arrest, 228, 248–250
    false light, 233–235, 273–275
    federal preemption and state tort actions,
        219–220
    federal sentencing guidelines, 227
    federal statutes, 224–227
    good faith and fair dealings, 263
    history developments, 196–197
    implied contract of employment, 262
    information gathering/fact-finding, 209
    invasion of privacy, 231–239
    investigative objectives, 207
    investigator selection, 205–206
    joint action exceptions, 212–213
    jurisdiction, 196–202
    key learning points, 195
    litigation avoidance, 276
    malicious prosecution, 266–268
    misconduct liability, 205–206
    moral compulsion, 249
    multiple agency and court review, 200–202
    negligent investigation, 242–245
    new tort action, 242–243
    off-duty misconduct, 271–272
    personal employment contracts, 261
    precautionary protocols, 249–250
    preparatory legal considerations, 202–209
    prevention and education, 273–275
    privacy, 233–239, 273–275
    protected concerted activities investigation,
        217–219
    publication of a private fact, 235–236
    public function exceptions, 212–213
    public policy, 262
    risk, contractual shifting, 206
    search and seizure, 211
    self-incrimination, 210–211
    self-published defamation, 259–261
    standards of proof identification, 207–208
    state constitutional issues, 213–214
    state statutes, 232–233
    state tort law issues, 227–242
    sympathetic touching, 248
    unemployment claims, 270–271
    unfair labor practices, 214
    union contracts, 220–221, 261
    union representation, 215–216
    whistleblower and similar statutes, 262
    workers' compensation, 272–273
    wrongful discharge, 261–266
legal duty to investigate, *see* Duty to investigate
Let's Get Real, 53
LexisNexis, 71
liability risk
    contractual shifting of, 206
    employee dignity, 276

fact finder/interviewer misconduct,
 205–206
fact finding concerns, 209
workplace investigations, 5
liar's paradox, 167, 193n8
libel, 250, *see also* Defamation
lies, *see also* Polygraphs
 admission, 109
 learned, 154
 motivation, 162–165
 of omission, 178
 public *vs.* private sector, 43
 risk/benefits, 153, 163
 types, 177–178
life insurance agent example, 47–48
line of questioning, *see* Questions
Lingle v. Norge Div. of Magic Chef, Inc., 219
lint-picker/picking, 180, 183
listening, 154, 163
litigation avoidance
 awareness, 276
 employees treated with dignity, 59, 138, 276
 overview, 276
litigious workforce
 knowledge of law, 196
 private sector trends, 54–55
 process of investigation, 3–4
 silence v. words spoken, 274–275
LMRA, *see* Labor Management Relations Act
 (LMRA)
location of interview, 92–95, 132
lockout example, 217–219
"looking for answers" nonverbal
 communication, 186
Los Angeles County civil lawsuits, 55
loss of face, 165
lower burden of proof, 49–52
lunchbox inspections, 238
lying, *see* Lies
Lyle v. Mercy Hospital Anderson, 226

M

Magna Carta, 196
making promises, 43
malfeasance, 9, 308
malice and malicious prosecution, 266–268,
 275
management
 commitment, 9–14, 18
 interview guidelines, 105, 315
manipulation, 158

materiality, 77–78
Mathieson v. Yellow Book Sales & Distrib. Co.,
 279n84
McLaren v. Microsoft Corp., 239
Mead, Margaret, 177
Mead v. Deloitte & Touche LLP, 264
meaningful objectives, 14–16
measuring data and results
 data analysis, 293–294
 information, 292–293
 overview, 289, 291–292
 research and audit method, 21
 using information, 294–295
Mendez v. M.S. Walker, Inc., 244–245, 252
merchandise theft, 257, 267–268, *see also* Theft
merchants, private, 213
methods, process of investigation
 electronic surveillance, 20
 forensic analysis, 22–24
 interviews, 25–26
 overview, 19
 physical surveillance, 19–20
 research and internal audit, 20–22
 undercover, 24–25
Microsoft, 44–45, 294
milestones, 10, 291
military service, asking about, 329n1
military time (clock), 141
minimization, 110, 178
Miranda v. Arizona
 circumstances required, 57n4
 constitutional warnings, 246
 defined, 308
 employee/employer considerations, 210
 public *vs.* private sector, 45–46
 rights of others, 286
mirroring, 184–185
misconduct
 by fact finders/interviewers, 205–206
 preexisting, 48
 vs. malfeasance, 9
missions, public *vs.* private sector, 39–41
mistakes, good people, 160–161
monologue, *see* Dialogue and script examples;
 Theme
*Montellanico v. Unemployment Compensation
 Board of Review,* 271
moral compulsion, 249
Morris v. Hartford Courant Company, 265
motives
 defined, 308
 discipline action, 37, 49, 56

entrapment, 48–49
intervention, 333–339
overview, 332–333
moving surveillance, 19
multiple agency and court review, 200–202
music example, 54

N

narrative balance, lack, 172–173
narrative reports, 138
National Collegiate Athletic Association, 214
National Institute for Truth Verification, 176
National Labor Relations Act (NLRA), 214
National Labor Relations Board (NLRB)
    jurisdiction, 198, 219
    NLRB v. J. Weingarten, Inc., 99, 127n8, 215, 286
    NLRB v. Unbelievable, Inc., 217
    protected concerted activities, 217
    unfair labor practices, 214
National Steel and Shipbuilding Co. v. NLRB, 218–219
Navarette v. Nike, Inc., 279n84
need, good people, 159
negative connotations, interrogation, 25, 57
negligent hiring, 204–205, 244
negligent investigation
    implicit/explicit duties to investigate, 244–245
    new tort action, 242–243
    prevention and education phase, 33
Nipper v. Variety Wholesalers, 230
NLRA, *see* National Labor Relations Act (NLRA)
NLRB, *see* National Labor Relations Board (NLRB)
NLRB v. J. Weingarten, Inc., 99, 127n8, 215, 286
NLRB v. Unbelievable, Inc., 217
non-employees, interviewing, 122–123
nonpublication, defamation, 229
nonunion workplaces, 100
nonverbal communication, 93–94, 178–179, *see also* Body language
notarized signatures, 136
notes, *see also* Journal entries
    administrative interviews, 129
    black ink, 136, 138
    destruction, 112, 136, 138
    as evidence, 84
    interviewees, 149

shorthand, 138
white paper, 136
"nothing is as it first appears," 61
notification of interviews, 121–122

O

oaths *vs.* facts, 171
objections, 165–169, *see also* Deception detection
objectives
    employee prosecution, 35
    investigative, 207
    successful investigation element, 14–16
    universal, 15–16, 36n9
objects, heavy, 92
obscene phone call example, 264–265
Occupational Health and Safety Administration (OSHA), 55, 75
O'Connell v. Bank of Boston, 243
O'Connor v. Ortega, 237–238
off-duty misconduct, 271–272
offenders, motive of, 48–49
office safe example, 271
Olivas v. DeVino Indus., Inc., 269
Olivas v. DeVivo Indus., Inc., 240
Open Compliance and Ethics Group (OCEG), 64
open-ended questions, 113, 130
opportunity, influence of, 159–160
oral statements, *see also* Statements
    checklist, 323–324
    improving results, 293
    investigative interview method, 117–119
organization, document management, 70–75
organizations
    established investigative process, 34
    investigations policy, 149
    limits to get cooperation, 43
    new-era corporate psychobabble and brainwashing, 149
    prosecution and punishment, 43–44
    retention of case files, 75
    safe and productive workplace, 289, 296
    security management, 38–39
original *vs.* copies of evidence, 79
OSHA, *see* Occupational Health and Safety Administration (OSHA)
outrage, *see* Emotional distress or outrage
outside counsel, 81–83
overinvestigation, 1
overly anxious nonverbal communication, 178

overstructured investigations, 16–17

P

Pacific Telephone and Telegraph v. NLRB, 216
Paolucci v. Robinson Memorial Hospital, 230, 251
paper case file, 73–75
paper distribution facility example, 52
Paradoa v. CNA Ins. Co., 206
Parsippany Hotel Management Co. v. NLRB, 217
passive voice, 169
past recollection recorded exception, 147
past tense, 142, 170
patience, 17–19
patient abuse example, 265
patterns
    facts, 189, 307
    sales and voids example, 225
    searches, 224
paycheck examples, 232, 240, 269
PC-R, *see* Psychopathy Checklist Revised
        (PC-R)
"Peeping Tom" statute, 236–237
people, good
    bad decisions and mistakes, 160–161
    foolishness, 159
    greed, 159
    guardrails, sensible, 161–162
    guiltlessness and enemy within, 156–157
    importance, 159–160
    influence of opportunity, 159–160
    need, 159
    prevention, 161–162
    rationalization ability, 158
    stupidity, 159
People v. Elliott, 246–247
personal employment contracts, 261
personnel screening, 326–327
Petersen, Mark, 165
petty schemes, 159
phases, investigative interview method
    admission, 109–112
    conclusion, 119–120
    discussion, 112–114
    introduction, 104–105
    oral statements, 117–119
    overview, 89–90
    preparation, 90–103
    presentation, 105–109
    written statements, 115–117
phases, process of investigation

assessment, 27–28
decision making, 31–32
disbursement, disciplinary/correction
        action, 32–33
information gathering and fact finding,
        28–30
overview, 2–3, 26–27
preparation and planning, 28
prevention and education, 33
verification and analysis, 30–31
physical paper case file, 73–75
Physical Security Professional (PSP), 38
physical surveillance, 19–20, 308
pickup truck example, 49
pilfering, the needy, 159
Pinkerton National Detection Agency v. Stevens,
        237
planning and preparation, *see also* Preparation;
        Project plan
    objectives of investigation, 14–15
    phase, process of investigation, 28
polygraphs
    case file retention, 75
    Employee Polygraph Protection Act,
        173–176, 224–226
    obscene phone call example, 264–265
poor advice, human foibles, 160
postinvestigation observations/
        recommendations
    conclusion, 329
    employee relations, 327–328
    executive summary, 325–326
    forensic analysis, 24
    personnel screening, 326–327
    security and asset protection, 328
    supervision, 327–328
    workplace safety, 328
Post-it notes, 70
powers of arrest, 41–42
precautionary protocols, 249–250
preexisting misconduct, 48
preparation, *see also* Planning and preparation
    administrative interview process, 133–135
    case file preparation, 96–97
    interviewer selection and preparation,
        95–96
    location of interview, 92–95
    overview, 90–91
    phases, process of investigation, 28
    request for representation, 99–101
    theme and question development, 97–98
    timing, 103

who should be interviewed, 91–92
witnesses, selection and use of, 101–103
preparatory legal considerations
    confidentiality, 209
    contract fact finder/interviewers, 205–206
    contractual shifting of liability risk, 206
    documentation control, 208–209
    employee fact finder/interviewers, 205
    investigative objectives, 207
    investigator selection, 205–206
    legal duty to investigate, 202–205
    misconduct liability, 205–206
    overview, 202, 205
    standards of proof identification, 207–208
preprinted statement form, 321–322
presentation, investigative interview method,
        105–109
present tense, 170
Present v. Avon Products, Inc., 256–257
pretext, 50, 263
prevention and education
    defamation, 273–275
    emotional distress, 275
    false light invasion of privacy, 273–275
    forensic psychology application, 339
    good people, 161–162
    overview, 273
    phase, process of investigation, 33
prima facie discrimination, 50, 199, 263, *see also*
        Discrimination
Principled Compliance, 67, 160
privacy, *see also* Confidentiality; Surveillance
    defined, 308
    electronic surveillance, 20
    false light invasion of, 273–275
    first and foremost consideration, 195
    future outlook, 283, 286–287
    interview location, 92
    intrusion upon seclusion, 238
    public *vs.* private sector, 44
    rape, videotaped, 233
    reasonable expectation, 195
    right to, 308
    tort claims example, 220
    videotaping, 233, 236
private facts, publication of, 235–236
private merchants, 213
private sector
    defined, 308
    due process, 45–47
    entrapment, 47–49
    litigious workforce, 54–55

lower burden of proof, 49–52, 195
motive of offender, 48–49
overview, 45
preexisting misconduct, 48
process of investigation, 7
rights and protection of employees, 55–56
sophistication level, 52
technology usage, 52–54
privileged communication, 229–230, 250, 308
process of administrative interviews
    confidentiality, 137–138
    determining who should be interviewed,
        131–132
    discussion, 135
    documentation, 135–137
    introduction, 133
    location of interview, 132
    overview, 131
    preparation, 133–135
    selection of interviewer, 132
process of investigations
    assessment, 27–28
    decision makers and decision making, 8,
        31–32
    defined, 1, 309
    disciplinary/correction action disbursement,
        32–33
    electronic surveillance, 20
    fact finders, 8
    flexibility, 16–17
    forensic analysis, 22–24
    frequently asked questions, 34–35
    genesis of process, 2–3
    information gathering and fact finding,
        28–30
    interrogation, 7–8
    interviews, 25–26
    investigators, 8
    key learning points, 1
    lawful execution, 18
    management commitment, 9–14
    meaningful objectives, 14–16
    methods of, 19–26
    misconduct *vs.* malfeasance, 9
    overstructured, 16–17
    overview, 3–6
    phases of, 26–33
    physical surveillance, 19–20
    preparation and planning, 28
    prevention and education, 33
    prosecutors, 8
    research and internal audit, 20–22

resources, properly pooled, 17–18
subjects, 6–7
successful, elements of, 9–18
summary, 33–34
suspected wrongdoers, 8
terminology, 5–9
undercover, 24–25
verification and analysis, 30–31
well-conceived strategy, 16–17
professional interviewers, *see also* Fact finders;
        Interviewers; Investigators
deliberate actions, 68–69
ethics, 63–67
experience, 61–62
fairness, 67–68
held to standard, 66
impartiality, 63
overview, 60–61
role of, 60
skills, 61
progression of behavior, 331
projection, 153
project managers, 9–10, 309
project plan, 291, *see also* Planning and
        preparation
promises, making, 43
pronouns, 170
proof
demanding to see, 164
future outlook, 287
lower, private sector advantages, 49–52
standards, 29, 207–208, 309
proofreading reports, 142
properly pooled resources, 17–18
props, 125
prosecution, public *vs.* private sector, 43–44
prosecutors *vs.* decision makers, 8
protected concerted activities investigation,
        217–219
protocols, precautionary, 249–250
proxemics, 93–94, *see also* Body language
pseudo-pride, 171
PSP, *see* Physical Security Professional (PSP)
psychobabble, 53
psycho-linguistic differences, 165
psychology, forensic
avengers and aggressors, 331–332
intervention, 333–339
motivation for violence, 332–339
overview, 22–24
prevention, 339
Psychopathy Checklist Revised (PC-R), 161

public and private sectors
advantages, 41–45
burden of proof, 49–52
defined, 309
due process, 45–47
employee rights and protection, 55–56
entrapment, 47–49
frequently asked questions, 56–57
grand jury and special inquiries, 42–43
historical perspective, 38–39
key learning points, 37–38
litigious workforce, 54–55
missions, 37, 39–41
motives of offenders, 48–49
overview, 41, 45
powers of arrest, 41–42
preexisting misconduct, 48
private sector advantages, 45–52
private sector trends, 52–56
process of investigation, 7
prosecution and punishment, 43–44
public sector advantages, 41–45
resources, 44–45
rights and protection of employees, 55–56
search and seizure, 42
sophistication level, 52
summary, 56
technology usage, 52–54
public function exceptions, 212–213
public policy, 262, 309
public record
future trends, 287
public *vs.* private sector, 44
research and audit method, 21
punishment, 43–44

Q

qualities, professional interviewer
additional, 68–69
deliberate actions, 68
ethics, 63–67
experience, 61–62
fairness, 67–68
impartiality, 63
overview, 87
skills, 61
questions
for additional information, 113–114
admission, 110–111
answering with a question, 171
awareness of for trial, 130

development, 97–98
  failure to answer, 165
  inappropriate, 114, 241–242
  only ask if know answer, 16
  truth-teller, 110, 191

R

railroad ties example, 240, 269
Ramsey, Patsy, 165
rape, videotaped, 236
rationalization, 153, 158, 159
reasonable conclusions, *see* Good faith
              investigation/reasonable conclusion
reckless disregard for truth
  defamation, 231
  emotional distress or outrage, 269, 275
  false statement, 273
recommendations, providing, 33, 84, 123–125
recording interviews, 149, *see also* Surveillance
redacted reports, 140
red pickup truck example, 49
references in reports, 139
refusal to cooperate, 37, 42–43
regional drug distribution operation example,
        17
rehab programs, privacy, 232
rehiring a murderer, negligent hiring, 204–205
Reid Technique interview, 7, 88, 130
relationship-building phase, 10
reports
  bulletized summary, 138–142
  drafts, 138
  evidence collection and management,
        80–83
  spell-checking, 142
  as stand-alone documents, 140
representation, requests for union
  employee rights and federal law, 56, 127n8,
        215–216
  investigative interview method, 99–101
  standards of proof, 208
research and audit method, 20–22
res gestae, see Spontaneous declarations
resignation, 32, 235
resources
  properly pooled, 17–18
  public sector advantages, 44–45
  successful investigation element, 11
respect, *see also* Dignity
  administrative interviews, 130, 138
  treating subjects with, 59

respondeat superior doctrine, 205
results, communication of
  bulletized summary reports, 138–142
  electronic communications, 144–145
  executives summaries, 142–144
  findings of fact, 142
  overview, 138
results, improving
  alternatives, 295–296
  budget establishment, 291
  data analysis, 293–294
  information collection, 292–293
  investment and cost management, 289–290
  key learning points, 289
  measuring, importance of, 289, 291–295
  milestone establishment, 291
  using information, 294–295
retaliatory discharges, *see* Whistleblower and
              similar statutes
retention of information, 75, 79
return on investment (ROI)
  defined, 309
  duty to investigate, 203
  improving results, 292
  management commitment, 12, 14
  prioritization, 293
  process of investigation, 3
reverse stings, 48
rights of others
  electronic surveillance, 20
  future outlook, 286
  respect during interview, 138
right to privacy, *see* Privacy
risks, 34–35, 206
ROI, *see* Return on investment (ROI)
role, professional interviewers, 60
"roll over," co-conspirators, 30
Rolsen v. Lazarus, 251
root causes, 293–294
Rotarian phrase, 65
rule-breaking and creative leadership, 193n4
rules of civil procedure, 36n10
"rumor mill," 274

S

SaaS, *see* software as a service (SaaS)
safe (combination) example, 271
safety
  considerations, 126
  employer responsibility, 289, 296
  planning, 90

postinvestigation observations/
    recommendations, 328
Saine v. Comcast Cablevision of Arkansas, Inc.,
    204, 244
Saldana v. Kelsey-Hayes Company, 237
SalesForce service, 294
Salinas v. Forth Worth Cab and Baggage
    Company, 204, 244
Sapir, Avinoam, 188
satisfizing, 160
scalability, process of investigation, 4
schedule interruptions, 10
Schnelker, Tracy, 2
scientific content analysis (SCAN), 187–188
screws/repackaging example, 21–22
script examples, *see* Dialogue and script
    examples
search and seizure
    burdens/standard of proof, 50
    constitutional considerations, 211
    intrusion upon seclusion, 237
    public *vs.* private sector, 42
search warrants, unavailability, 19
Sears, Roebuck and Co. v. Wholey, 265
seating arrangements, 92–93, 102
seclusion, intrusion upon, 236–269
security and asset protection, 328
security professionals, 38
seizure, *see* Search and seizure
self-incrimination, 210–211
self-published defamation, 259–261
self-reference, lack of, 169–170
seven phases of investigation, *see also*
        Investigative interview method (I²M)
    assessment, 27–28
    decision making, 31–32
    disbursement, disciplinary/correction
        action, 32–33
    information gathering and fact finding,
        28–30
    overview, 2–3, 26–27, 87
    preparation and planning, 28
    prevention and education, 33
    verification and analysis, 30–31
sexual harassment investigations
    confidentiality, 137–138
    duty to investigate, 222–223
    intrusion upon seclusion, 237, 239
    self-published defamation, 260
    structured questions, 135
Shattuck-Owen v. Snowbird Corp., 236
"she said, he said" cases, 91

shifting burdens, 50, 52
shoplifting, 213
shorthand in notes, 138
signatures, 136–137
"silver bullets," 176
Simpson, O.J., 287
Simpson v. Commonwealth, 211, 238
Sisney v. Sha-Tec Foods, Inc., 268
Six Amendment (US Constitution), 210
skills
    future trends, 283, 285–286
    physical surveillance, 19
    professional interviewers, 59, 61
Smith court case, 235, 248–249, 274
Social Security Numbers, 97, 287
sociopaths, 157, 158, 191
software as a service (SaaS), 294
sophistication level, 52
Souder v. Pendleton Detectives, Inc., 236
source identification, 111
Southwest Bell Telephone Co. v. NLRB, 216
Sowards v. Norbar, Inc., 237
special inquiries, 42–43
spell-checking reports, 142
spoliation
    defined, 59, 309
    destroying notes, 112
    evidence collection/preservation, 78
spontaneous declarations, 130, 146
standard of proof, 207–208, 309, *see also*
        Burden of proof
standards and standardization, 73, 287
state constitutional issues, 213–214
statements, *see also* Oral statements; Written
        statements
    analysis, kinesics, 186–188
    preprinted form, 321–322
    validity assessment, 187
    when refused, 129, 136–137
state tort law and actions, *see also* Torts
    assault and battery, 227–228
    common law right of privacy, 233–239
    defamation, 229–231
    emotional distress or outrage, 239–242
    employee rights and federal law, 219–220
    false imprisonment and false arrest, 228
    false light, 233–235
    intrusion upon seclusion, 236–239
    invasion of privacy, 231–239
    overview, 227
    publication of a private fact, 235–236
    state statutes, 232–233

State v. Muegge, 213
Stockley v. A.T.&T. Information Systems, Inc.,
  253–254
Stock v. Wisconsin Electric Power Company, 281
stolen blank checks example, 243
storage of evidence, 79
strategy, well-conceived, 16–17
street gang example, 62
strike example, 217–219
strip search example, 240
stupidity, 159
stupid questions, 114
subjects, *see also* Interviewees
  addressing in reports, 141
  background, 96–97
  conditional apologies, 116
  credentials, 97
  defined, 309
  future trends, 283, 286
  legal protections, 286
  originals *vs.* copies, 79
  overview, 6–7
  physical appearance, 110
  process of investigation, 6–7
  refusal to cooperate, 37, 42–43
  vs. suspects, 7, 309
subpoenas, unavailability, 19
successful investigation elements
  investment and cost management, 289–290
  lawful execution, 18
  management commitment, 9–14, 18
  meaningful objectives, 14–16
  overview, 9
  resources, properly pooled, 17–18
  well-conceived strategy, 16–17
suing, *see* Litigious workforce
Sullivan v. Baptist Memorial Hospital, 259
summaries
  future outlook, 288
  interviewing, 83–84
  investigative interview method, 120
  process of investigation, 33–34
  public and private sector differences, 56
summary reports, bulletized, 138–142
supervision, 53, 327–328
surrendering nonverbal communication, 185
surveillance, *see also* Privacy
  electronic, 20
  moving, 19
  physical, 19–20
  protected concerted activities, 217–219
  workers' compensation, 272

wrongful discharge, 265
suspects, 7–8, 309, *see also* Subjects
suspension of integrity, 156
sympathetic touching, 112, 248
Systemic Planning: Theory and Application,
  193n6
Szot v. Allstate Ins. Co., 274

T

tabs, document management, 70
Tarnef v. State, 246
task list, investigative, 69
taxi driver, negligent hiring, 204, 244
teams, investigative, 61
technology
  body language of guilty, 178–182
  documentation, 71–75
  Employee Polygraph Protection Act,
    174–176
  future trends, 283, 285–286
  interviewer body language, 183–185
  kinesics, 177–186
  lie types, 177–178
  new or unproven, 176
  overview, 173–174
  private sector, 38, 52–54
  statement analysis, 186–188
  voice stress analyzer, 176
"tells," 181–182
templing nonverbal communication, 184
temporary tabs, 70
ten commandments, courtroom testimony, 148
Tenold v. Weyerhaeuser Co., 240–241, 253, 269
termination, capital punishment equivalence,
  44
terminology, process of investigation, 5–9
testifying and testimony preparation
  evidence presentation, 147–149
  expert witnesses, 146
  hearsay rule, 146–147
  impeachment, 148–149
  lay witnesses, 145
  overview, 145
  ten commandments, courtroom testimony,
    148
  testifying, 148
Texas Farm Bureau Mut. Ins. Companies v. Sears,
  242–243
The Case File software, 72–73
The Death of Common Sense, 55
The Four-Way Test, 65

theft
 of funds, 225–226
 merchandise, 257, 267–268
 the needy, 159
 negligent investigation, 243
 paycheck examples, 232, 240, 269
 wood in truck example, 260–261, 263
The Investigative Interview Method, Advanced Course, 297
Theisen v. Covenant Medical Center, Inc., 260, 264–265
theme, 97–98, 133–135
The Millionaire Next Door, 53
The New New Thing, 53
The Road Less Traveled, 53
third person, reports, 142
threats and threatening, 43
TimeMap software, 71
timing
 human foibles, 160
 investigative interview preparation, 103
 timelines in reports, 142
Title VII, Civil Rights Act, 55, 75, 221
torts, *see also* State tort law and actions
 actionable, 197
 negligent investigation, 242–243
touching, 112, 248
training, 192
triers-of-fact, 283–288, 309, *see also* Interviewers
trivializing actions, 110
truck example, 49
truthfulness
 behaviors, 166
 deception detection, 155–156
 defamation, 229, 250
 facts *vs.* oaths, 171
 fairness, 67–68
 honesty earned, 154
 reasons for, 188–189
 reckless disregard, 231
 risk/benefits, 153, 163
 as virtue, 191
truth-teller questions, 110, 191
two-way mirrors, 233

U

Uebelacker v. Cincom Systems, Inc., 251
unconcerned nonverbal communication, 178
undercover investigations
 defined, 309
 examples, 47–48, 220
 methods, 24–25
 overview, 10
 using in organizations, 34
Undercover Investigations in the Workplace, 25, 36n9
unemployment claims
 discipline action, 33
 evidentiary burdens and standards, 200
 hospital janitor example, 270
 off-duty misconduct, 271–272
 overview, 270–271
 standards of proof, 208
unfair labor practices, 214
uninterested nonverbal communication, 181
union contracts
 duty to investigate, 203–204
 employee rights and federal law, 220–221
 wrongful discharge, 261
union employees and representation
 employee rights and federal law, 56, 127n8, 215–216
 investigative interview method, 99–101
 standards of proof, 208
United States v. Antonelli, 210
universal objectives, 15–16, 36n9
Upjohn Co. v. United States, 309
urgency, lack of, 329n2
U.S. Fair Credit Reporting Act (FCRA), 287
USLegal web site, 7

V

vacation leave example, 235
Vaillancourt v. The Gap, Inc., 265–266
Valdez court case, 223, 244
vandalism, 273, 290
vehicle example, 49
vendor fraud investigations, 21
verbal abuse of investigators, 206
verb tense, 170
verification and analysis
 defined, 309
 investigative interviewing, 60
 phase, process of investigation, 30–31
victims
 deserving of treatment, 191
 greediness, 159
 vs. subject's rights, 286

videotaping, 217–219, 233, 236, *see also* Privacy; Surveillance
Violence Assessment and Intervention: The Practitioner's Handbook, 103, 294
violence in workplace, 24, 153, 159, 290
Visio charting software, 294
voice pattern analysis, 264–265
voice stress analyzer, 176

W

Wal-Mart Stores, Inc. v. Binns, 267–268
Wal-Mart Stores, Inc. v. Lee, 234
weapons, thrown at investigator, 329n3
weather interruptions, 10
weighted evidence, 77
well-conceived strategy, 16–17
whistleblower and similar statutes, 262, 265
White Fence street gang example, 62
white paper for notes, 136
who should be interviewed, *see* Interviewees
Williams v. Brigham & Women's Hosp., Inc., 232
Wiltshire v. Citibank, 225
window coverings, 92
wire transfer example, 225
witches, 173
witnesses
    credibility, 148–149
    expert witnesses, 146
    lay witnesses, 145
    selection and use of, 101–103
    testifying and preparation for testimony, 145
wood in truck example, 260–261, 263
Workers' Compensation
    employees, claims from disciplinary action, 272–273

jurisdiction, 198
public policy, 262
violation of FMLA, 54
workforce, litigious, 54–55
working case file, *see* Case file
workplace, *see also* Organizations
    investigations, 5, 310
    safety, 328
    violence, 24, 153, 159, 290
Workplace Violence Prevention and Intervention, 103
work product privilege doctrine, 59, 82–83
Wright v. Montgomery Ward & Co., 249, 267
written statements, *see also* Statements
    checklists, 319, 321–322
    fact finder's final report, 150–151
    investigative interview method, 115–117
    providing after interview, 125–126
wrongful discharge
    additional cases, 263–266
    covenant of good faith and fair dealings, 263
    discriminatory discharges, 263
    implied contract of employment, 262
    overview, 261
    personal employment contracts, 261
    public policy, 262
    union contracts, 261
    whistleblower and similar statutes, 262

Y

yellow paper for notes, 136
Yunker v. Honeywell, Inc., 204

Z

zero sum theory, 55